Purebasic

A Beginners Guide To Computer Programming

Gary Willoughby

PureBasic - A Beginner's Guide To Computer Programming
by Gary Willoughby

PureBasic is a registered trademark of Fantaisie Software. PureBasic and all provided tools and components contained within the PureBasic package are Copyright © 2006 Fantaisie Software.

Fantaisie Software
10, rue de Lausanne
67640 Fegersheim
France
www.purebasic.com

Published 2006, by Aardvark Global Publishing.

Editor
Gary Willoughby

Print History
July 2006 - First Edition

Disclaimer
While every precaution has been taken in the preparation of this book and the programs contained within it, the author and publisher assumes no responsibility whatsoever for errors, omissions, or for damages resulting from the use of the information or programs contained herein. The author or publisher shall not be liable if incidental or consequential damages occur in connection with, or arising from, the furnishings, performance, or use of the programs, associated instructions, and/or claims of productivity gains. All information contained herein is considered accurate at time of publication but because PureBasic is a language in a constant state of refinement and development, some information over time may be rendered out-of-date. For up to date news and information regarding PureBasic please refer to www.purebasic.com.

Trademarks
Trademarked names appear throughout this book. Rather than list the names and entities that own the trademarks or insert a trademark symbol with each mention of the trademarked name, the publisher states that it is using the names for editorial purposes only and to the benefit of the trademark owner, with no intention of infringing on that trademark.

Dedication

Dedicated to my girlfriend, Sara Jane Gostick and her dog 'Stella' for putting up with many lonely nights while I wrote this book and for the encouragement (and chicken dinners) she always gives me.

Acknowledgments

Thanks to Fred and the Purebasic team for the Purebasic language, keep up the good work, it rocks!
Thanks to Paul Dixon for clarifying some of the details regarding binary encoding of floating point numbers.
Thanks to Timo Harter for helping to choose what Purebasic data types would best substitute the Win32 API types, and for demonstrating how to retrieve different strings from memory via the different Win32 API String pointer types.

"With great power there must also come great responsibility!"
--Ben Parker (Spiderman's Uncle)

Code examples contained in this book can be downloaded freely from
www.pb-beginners.co.uk

Printed On-Demand by CafePress.com in the United States of America.
ISBN 1-4276-0428-2 19/7/2006

Table of Contents

Preface

About this Book

This book provides a quick introduction to the PureBasic programming language. PureBasic's popularity has increased significantly in the past few years, being used for many purposes such as rapid software prototyping, creation of commercial applications and games, Internet CGI applications, while some people just use it for small utilities. This book has been written, with the complete novice in mind. We all need to start somewhere and I believe PureBasic is a fantastic first leap into the programming world. With PureBasic becoming more and more widely used, many people are starting out and finding they need the occasional push in the right direction or need an explanation of a certain feature or oddity. This book is to guide novices through their first steps and to give the seasoned programmer a quick overview of the language.

This Book's Scope

Although this book covers the essentials of the PureBasic language, I've kept this book's scope quite narrow to make sure it's not information overload for new users. Sometimes this text will refer to concepts and syntax in a simplistic way to be used as a stepping stone to more advanced texts or as a complement to the existing PureBasic helpfile.

For example I won't talk much about how easy it is to use DirectX or OpenGL directly in PureBasic, otherwise this book would be triple in size and although topics such as pointers, threads and the Win32 API is talked about later in this book, don't expect too many fancy examples as I've only given an overview to such advanced topics.

PureBasic raises the bar to not only what a Basic language should be but also what all languages should be. Clean, uncluttered syntax, small compiled executable files and a fantastically active community of programmers. Hopefully this book will give you a clear understanding of the core features of PureBasic and the design goals and philosophies behind its creation and hopefully make you want to learn more.

Despite this books limited scope, I think you will find this a great first book on PureBasic which will also give you a solid grounding on programming in general if you were to migrate to other languages. You will learn everything you need to start writing useful standalone programs. By the time you've finished this book, you will have learned not only the essentials of the language itself, but also how to apply that knowledge to day-to-day tasks. You will also be better equipped to tackle more advanced topics as they come your way.

This Book's Structure

Much of this book is designed to introduce you to PureBasic as quickly as possible and is organized by presenting the major language features a section at a time. Each chapter is fairly self contained but later chapters, especially the more advanced ones, use ideas introduced earlier. For example, when we get to graphical user interfaces and graphics, I'll assume you now understand procedures and structures.

Part I: The Core Language
This part of the book is a straightforward bottom-up explanation of the major language features, such as types, procedures, structures and so on. Most of the examples given are not really very useful as standalone programs but are there to demonstrate and explain the current topic.

Chapter 1, Getting Started
He we start with a quick introduction to PureBasic and the history behind the language. An overview on how to run a PureBasic program from the IDE and what the debugger is for.

Chapter 2, Data Types
In this chapter I start by listing and explaining all the available built-in data types, such as Strings, number types and constants. Usage guidelines are given for all the built-in data types as well as information on memory usage and where applicable, numerical limits.

Chapter 3, Operators
Here I explain the basic means to actually assign values to variables and explain what operators are needed for calculating data. A full explanation is given for all operators along with diagrams and examples. The 'Debug' command is also introduced here as it is one of the most useful commands in the PureBasic language and its importance should be learned early on.

Chapter 4, Conditional Statements And Loops
In this chapter I explain how PureBasic handles boolean values, the 'If' and 'Select' statements are introduced and loops are explained and demonstrated. Examples and full explanations are given.

Chapter 5, Other Data Structures
This chapter reveals how to create and use other methods for storing and organizing data, such as user defined structures, arrays and linked lists. Full explanations and examples are also given.

Chapter 6, Procedures And Subroutines
Procedures and Subroutines are an essential part of programming in any language as they can be used to execute sections of code (along with variable parameters in the case of procedures) from any part of the running program. This makes programming easier as the entire program can then be broken down into easily manageable sections and this modular code can then be reused time and time again.

Chapter 7, Using Built-In Commands
This chapter demonstrates some of the most widely used built-in commands. It's not a complete reference or guide to every single command of every library but it will give you a good grounding on how and when to use the built-in libraries. An explanation is given on Handles and IDs, both of which are simple to understand but sometimes easily confused.

Chapter 8, Good Programming Style
This chapter gives you a guide on good programming practices for use throughout this book and provides an overview on simple error handling. When programming in any language, errors are always a problem, be it a simple typo or a bug in the language itself. This chapter also deals with ways in which you can be more conscious of not introducing errors and how and why you should test for errors in your program and how to react if one is found.

Part II: Graphical User Interfaces
Nearly every program nowadays has a user interface of some description and here I will show you how to create one. Building on ideas and examples of creating a console application, you will eventually learn how to construct window based applications along with standard controls (gadgets) such as menus, buttons and graphics.

Chapter 9, Creating User Interfaces
Here I show you how you can built your own user interfaces. Starting off by explaining and demonstrating console applications and then moving on to creating native window based interfaces. Events are also described and examples are given on how to react when an event is detected within your interface. The bundled visual form designer is also given an overview here.

Part III: Graphics And Sound
Graphics and sound have an important role in nearly every computer system today. This section deals with playing sounds and ways of displaying graphics on the screen and the manipulation of these graphics, be it in 2D or 3D.

Chapter 10, 2D Graphics
This chapter introduces two dimensional graphics such as lines and shapes and how they are drawn on the screen. It also deals with sprites (images that can be displayed and manipulated) and an explanation of screens and double buffering is also given.

Chapter 11, 3D Graphics
The three dimensional graphics in PureBasic are provided by the OGRE engine. An overview and a few examples are given to demonstrate what is possible with this engine. The OGRE engine is still undergoing development and is still being integrated fully into PureBasic, but some nice things are still possible.

Chapter 12, Sound
This chapter covers how to use sound within PureBasic and covers how to load and play familiar sound formats.

Part IV: Advanced Topics
The last section deals with things which a novice would find very advanced. The topics contained here are not necessary to understand to write fully functioning useful programs but they can achieve some things that ordinary methods cannot. This section is to wet your appetite for knowledge to improve your understanding of PureBasic and programming in general.

Chapter 13, Beyond The Basics
Here the topics covered are advanced memory management using pointers. Compiler directives are explained and a how-to guide is written for DLL creation. There is also a section on the Windows Application Programming Interface.

Part V: Appendices
This is the final section of this book and it ends with appendices that direct the reader to useful pages on the Internet, provides helpful charts and includes a comprehensive glossary of words and terms.

Prerequisites

I hope that you know how to use a computer, there won't be much talk on how to use a mouse or what an icon is, but this book assumes you are a complete novice to computer programming, not only with PureBasic, but in general.

All you will need to start programming today is a little bit of time and a copy of PureBasic, available from www.purebasic.com

I

The Core Language

In this section, we will study the PureBasic language itself. I call this part 'The Core Language', because our focus will be on the essentials of PureBasic programming: its built-in types, statements and expressions. By the time you finish reading this section and studying the examples, you'll be ready to write programs yourself.

The word 'Core' in the title is used on purpose, because this section is not an exhaustive document on every minute detail of PureBasic. While I may skip certain things along the way, the basics you learn here will stand you in very good stead for when the unknown pops up. There is also a mention of the history and development philosophy of PureBasic for those who are interested.

1

Getting Started

This first chapter starts with a brief history of PureBasic and then takes a quick look at how to run PureBasic programs. Its main goal is to get you set up to compile and run PureBasic programs on your own computer, so you can work along with the examples and tutorials given in this book. Along the way we'll study different ways you can compile from within PureBasic - just enough to get you started.

We'll also take a look at the included IDE that comes with the standard installation of PureBasic. It looks a little daunting for new users but after an overview and a little tutorial, things will look less scary

The History Of PureBasic

PureBasic started life in 1995 as a command-set expansion for BlitzBasic after PureBasic's author, Frédéric Laboureur hit many limitations with BlitzBasic while programming an application called 'TheBoss', a powerful application launcher for the Commodore Amiga. The expansion named 'NCS' (NewCommandSet) was entirely coded using 68000 assembly, as all new commands had to be coded in assembly at this time of Blitz's development. Fred's progress was quite slow to begin with as good documentation was hard to find for assembly programming and of course online forums didn't then exist for BlitzBasic plug-in programming.

Development of 'NCS' continued for about a year after which Fred received very positive comments regarding his work, through which he became very familiar with assembly programming and debugging. He was also astonished with the incredible things that could be achieved with an old 68000 processor if everything was programmed correctly.

Around this time, IBM PowerPC based processor cards for the Amiga started to appear and were a very powerful alternative to the Motorola 68000 processor. They were very fast and sold at a relatively cheap cost, even compared to the high-end 68060 processors. With the arrival of these new chips, people wanted a native version of Blitz to support them, as it was an extremely popular language at this time, but everyone knew that all development had been put on hold for the Amiga platform in favor of the Intel x86 based PCs. An opportunity had presented itself for the creation of a new language which would be the logical replacement and enhancement of BlitzBasic, which also would have full support for the 680x0 and PowerPC processors.

Enter PureBasic!

The early design and the first version of PureBasic started in 1998. The main differences between PureBasic and 'normal' compilers then was the inclusion of a 'virtual processor' (which actually used the 680x0 assembly mnemonics) right from the start to allow different kinds of assembly output (or any language) possible without changing the compiler core. After the initial design was finished and programming began, things started to move very fast. Fred fully dedicated all his time to program the compiler and learned a great deal including the C language to be able eventually to produce a fully portable compiler.

The first version of PureBasic was initially released for the Amiga and (even if it was badly bugged) had an integrated and fully cross platform editor, an integrated debugger and a huge internal command-set, you guessed it, taken directly from the former 'NCS' Blitz package.

While refining and bug testing, Fred also studied other programming languages to give him a firm grounding in other areas and to give him the best foundation to make better, more informed decisions about the internal design and how PureBasic should grow and expand in the future.

During the fourth year of Fred's computer science diploma, the Amiga was starting to be considered a dead platform and many of Fred's fellow students asked why wasn't he working on a Windows based version. Fred of course defended himself saying that it would be a piece of cake to port PureBasic to a new system, but he had to prove it!

A Brief Overview of The Assembly Language

Assembly language or simply Assembly, is a human-readable notation for the machine language that a specific computer architecture uses. Machine language, a pattern of bits encoding machine operations, is made readable by replacing the raw values with symbols called mnemonics.

Programming in machine code, by supplying the computer with the numbers of the operations it must perform can be quite a burden, because for every operation the corresponding number must be looked up or remembered. Therefore a set of mnemonics was devised. Each number was represented by an alphabetic code. For example, instead of entering the number corresponding to addition to add two numbers together you can enter 'add'. Assembly is compiled using an Assembler.

A Larger Arena

Fred started to learn Microsoft DirectX and Win32 API programming (see Chapter 13), completely in assembly, an enormous task! During which he found the Intel x86 a nightmare to understand and program coming from a Motorola 680x0 background, because the chip is very different in design. Even the internal storage method of numbers in memory was reversed! After three months in development and after the founding of his new company, Fantaisie Software, a new website was created and PureBasic for Windows was finally released. Usage and testing of PureBasic increased and many supportive and enthusiastic mails were received by Fred further enhancing his dedication to develop the best language possible.

After many years of careful development, a team was formed around Fred to help him with the development and testing of new releases. This team is composed of experienced programmers, web designers and documentation writers, all who share the same vision for the language.

After the massive success of the Windows release the next logical step was to support more operating systems. So Linux and Mac OS were soon to be supported and native versions of PureBasic were released to an ever increasingly impressed public. All versions supporting the native application programming interfaces (APIs) of these particular operating systems, all using the native graphical user interfaces to give them the correct look and feel of the system.

Development was halted for the Commodore Amiga version in 2002 after it became clear to many users that the Amiga itself was losing support to PCs and was eventually becoming accepted (to people other than hardcore enthusiasts) to be a dead platform. The Windows, Linux and Mac OS versions are still being tirelessly developed and supported today!

Version 4 is the latest incarnation of PureBasic which has nearly all been rewritten from scratch. This is to ease future enhancements and further cross platform development. PureBasic v4 also brought huge language improvements, nearly all of which are covered in this book.

The Development Philosophy Of PureBasic

The development philosophy of PureBasic is slightly different from that of other languages in many respects. Here is a list of some of PureBasic's development goals and policies.

After the initial purchase of a PureBasic license, all future updates are free of charge for life.
All Programs compiled using PureBasic can be sold commercially free of any further cost or royalties.
All programs should compile at the minimum file size they can be and contain no bloated code.
All compiled programs should not rely on any runtimes and be completely 'stand-alone' executables.

The above list is a big selling point in itself and contrary to many development philosophies of rival companies. Can you imagine Microsoft giving you free version upgrades of VB.NET for life? Me neither.

PureBasic's development philosophy is one of creating a programming environment that is both fun and functional to use. It's all about giving the users the power to create the programs they need in the simplest way possible. With all past version upgrades there has been included bug fixes, new commands plus brand new IDEs and a Visual Designer, the last two of which are covered in later areas of this book. So not only are bug fixes a feature of future upgrades, there are also additions to the language command-set along with the addition of useful tools and updates to the actual development environment itself.

A First Look At The IDE

PureBasic's Integrated Development Environment consists of a source code editor, a visual form designer and a compiler. The visual form designer will be given an overview later in Chapter 9 (A First Look At The New Visual Designer), so only the source code editor and compiler will be mentioned here. In the PureBasic community the source code editor is usually referred to as the 'IDE', while the visual form designer is usually given the dubious name of the 'VD'. This is mainly due to save typing long names in the forums while asking questions or participating in a discussion, so I'll use that convention here.

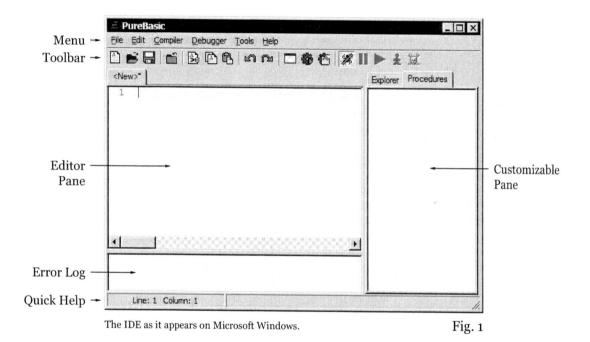

The IDE as it appears on Microsoft Windows.   Fig. 1

The IDE (Fig. 1) is written entirely in PureBasic and is the main tool used to write PureBasic programs, so let's take a tour around the main interface of the editor. At the top is the menu bar giving access to the menu commands, below that is a customizable toolbar which can be configured to hold many different icons each triggering a pre-defined menu command. Underneath the toolbar on the left is the main editor pane, here all PureBasic code is entered. On the right of the editor pane is another user customized pane which can contain a procedure viewer, a variable viewer, a file explorer, etc... Also by default the error log will be shown as a pane attached to the bottom of the editor pane, this can be turned off and on via a menu command (Menu:Debugger->Error Log->Show Error Log). Below the panes there is the status bar which shows information on what row and column is being edited and displays the quick help.

This editor is a 'front-end' to the actual PureBasic compiler. Once code has been entered into the editor pane and the 'Compile/Run' toolbar button has been pressed (Shortcut Key: F5) the code is then passed to the compiler for the creation of an executable. Any plain text editor could be used to write source code for PureBasic but I recommend using the official editor as it has been written from the ground up to only support the PureBasic compiler. Not only that but other editors require some configuration to correctly pass the file to the PureBasic compiler which some users find a little too complicated to begin with.

The IDE Quick Help

As you are entering built-in library commands into the editor pane, the status bar at the bottom of the editor will show you the completed command along with an example of what parameters (if any) are expected. This can be a very handy reference when you are speed coding (maybe after too much coffee) and searching the helpfile is too much hassle. Built-in Library commands are explained further in Chapter 7.

How To Run PureBasic Programs

Right, let's get started to learn how to run programs. Before they are compiled, PureBasic programs are just plain text files (usually containing the suffix '*.pb') that contain the actual PureBasic code. All that needs to be done to compile these text files into an executable program is to pass them to the compiler for processing. There are many ways of doing this such as:

In the IDE:
    Press the 'F5' keyboard shortcut for 'Compile/Run'.
    Press the 'Compile/Run' toolbar button.
    Select the menu command: 'Compiler->Compile/Run'.
    Select the menu command: 'Compiler->Create Executable...'.

Using the command line:
    Enter the command: 'PBCompiler filename' where 'filename' is the name of the text file.

After reading the above list it seems that there is many different ways of achieving the same result, but some of these are slightly different and should be explained more clearly.

The first three IDE methods mentioned above, achieve the same result and any one of these three can be used while actually writing and testing the current program (it doesn't matter which one). The purpose of these three commands is in the name, 'Compile/Run'.

When selected the text file is immediately compiled into a temporary executable file called 'purebasic0.exe' within the '/PureBasic/Compilers' folder and that executable file is then run. This is handy when you need to see immediately how your program runs, without specifying a proper name for the compiled executable. If this temporary program file is still running while another program is compiled and run, then a new temporary file will be created called 'purebasic1.exe', and so on. If, however the first program has ended while using the 'Compile/Run' method, then the compiler re-uses old numbers on the temporary files and keeps on using 'purebasico.exe' as the temporary name. This makes sure that there aren't huge numbers of temporary executable files within the '/PureBasic/Compilers' folder.

The last IDE method, using the 'Compiler->Create Executable...' menu command is for when all development is finished on the current program and you are ready to compile and deploy your executable file. Once this menu command has been selected a dialog box appears asking you to specify a name and location for your final executable program file.

The Windows Command Prompt method is for more advanced users and enables you to manually type in commands to pass the text file to the PureBasic compiler as a parameter. Other parameters can be passed along with the filename to further customize the compilation. These other parameters will be discussed later in Chapter 13 (Advanced Compiler Options).

That is all there is to compile and run your first program. After the commands are entered into the editor pane just hit 'F5' and you're away!

The Debugger

The PureBasic debugger is a tool which controls the execution of the program you're working on. It controls and keeps track of all variables and procedure parameters, etc. as the program is running. It is a second pair of eyes on your code to highlight errors and to avoid potential program crashes such as zero division, illegal array offset access and data overflow errors. It can also be used as a brake to halt the program at any given time to see what actual variable values are. The program execution can be stopped and forwarded step by step to locate any faults or strange behavior. This can be very useful especially if a program falls into an endless loop or you are unsure of what value a particular variable holds at any given time.

The Debugger can be toggled on and off at any time by pressing the 'Enable Debugger' toolbar button or by selecting the menu command (Menu:Debugger->Enable Debugger). Careful when developing a program with the debugger off, you could crash your computer if a problem isn't recognized and is allowed to execute.

A Note On Program Structure

The structure of a PureBasic program is quite easy to understand. The compiler processes the text file from the top to the bottom. It's that easy. Commands written at the top of the file are processed before the ones written below, just as if you were reading the file yourself. If the debugger spots a problem the compilation is stopped and an error is raised. Take this pseudo-code as an example:

```
1 PRINT "THIS LINE IS EXECUTED FIRST"
2 PRINT "THIS LINE IS EXECUTED SECOND"
3 PRINT "THIS LINE IS EXECUTED THIRD"
```

The output of this pseudo-code example would be three lines of text displayed in the order that they were written (1-3). This is exactly how the compiler processes the text file. This is important to understand and remember, because you will run into errors if, for example, you try to gain access to a file that hasn't been opened yet. This all seems pretty straightforward but you may run into this at sometime, especially when you start to use procedures (these will be explained fully in Chapter 6). There is more to a program's structure than this little snippet but this will become apparent as your journey continues and I expand more on using statements and procedures.

Introducing The PureBasic Helpfile

With every PureBasic installation, a complete helpfile is installed alongside. This helpfile is a fantastic reference for the entire PureBasic language but can be a little daunting for new users to refer to because sometimes things are not explained fully. If they were, then it would be a very sizable document and not very printer friendly. As it stands though, it is an invaluable resource for looking up keywords, checking syntax and it integrates nicely with the IDE. In fact, every time I personally create a program using the PureBasic IDE, I like to keep the helpfile open at all times to quickly flick between the two. This simple habit could save hours of valuable time.

IDE Integration

At anytime when you are using the IDE to create your program, you can press the 'F1' key on your keyboard to trigger the launching of the PureBasic helpfile. Also, if you happen to have your cursor within the IDE upon a PureBasic keyword while pressing 'F1', then the helpfile is brought to the front and that keyword will be highlighted within the helpfile, giving you an explanation of that command. This integration between the IDE and helpfile is invaluable once you start to gain speed while programming.

Let's try a small example to show this in action, type this (exactly) into the IDE:

```
OpenConsole()
Print("Press enter to exit")
Input()
End
```

After running this little program it opens a console window, then prints a line of text to it informing the user in order to exit he or she must press 'enter', during which we wait for input. After the enter key is pressed then we then end the program nicely.

If you place the flashing IDE cursor upon any keywords that are used in this program, then press 'F1', the helpfile is brought to the front and flipped to the page that describes that command. For example, place your flashing cursor anywhere within the 'OpenConsole()' keyword and hit 'F1'. You will now see the 'OpenConsole()' help page appear like magic!

If you want to learn more about using the built-in PureBasic helpfile, refer to Chapter 7 (Using The PureBasic Helpfile).

2

Data Types

Now that the introductions are over let's begin this chapter with more substance, namely Data Types. As you may know, in computer programs you manipulate and process data. Data types are the descriptions of the containers of this data. In this chapter I will show you all the available built-in data types and explain fully how and when to use them.

To enable you to get up and running as soon as possible, I have included many of examples and everything is explained using plain speech.

Built-In Data Types

Data types (or sometimes just called 'types') can be thought of as a way of giving stored data a description. The basic idea of typing data is to give some useful meaning to what is ultimately just binary digits. Be it text or numbers, describing this data using types makes it easier to understand, manipulate or retrieve. Data is held within the computers RAM until needed by the program. The amount of RAM needed to hold each data type depends on what type of data type is being used.

Numbers

The first data types to be introduced are the numbers types. Numbers can be used to store anything from a date, a length or even the result from a lengthy calculation. Anything you use numbers for in the real world, you can also use PureBasic's numeric types to store that data.

Numbers come in two flavors in PureBasic, Integers and Floating Point Numbers. Integers are numbers which don't have a decimal point and can either be positive or negative. Here are a few examples of integers:

```
16543      -1951434     100      -1066      0
```

Floating Point Numbers (or 'Floats') on the other hand are numbers which do contain a decimal point and can also be either positive or negative. Here are a few examples of floating point numbers:

```
52.887      -11.0005      1668468.1      -0.000004      0.0
```

PureBasic provides seven numeric data types for you to use in your programming, each one uses a different amount of RAM and all have different numerical limits. The numerical types are described here in Fig.2.

PureBasic's Numeric Types

Type	Suffix	Memory Usage (RAM)	Numerical Limit
Byte	.b	1 byte (8 bits)	-128 to 127
Char (Ascii)	.c	1 byte (8 bits)	0 to 255
Char (Unicode)	.c	2 bytes (16 bits)	0 to 65535
Word	.w	2 bytes (16 bits)	-32768 to 32767
Long	.l	4 bytes (32 bits)	-2147483648 to 2147483647
Quad	.q	8 bytes (64 bits)	-9223372036854775808 to 9223372036854775807
Float	.f	4 bytes (32 bits)	Unlimited*
Double	.d	8 bytes (64 bits)	Unlimited*

* This will be explained fully in Chapter 13 (*A Closer Look At Numeric Data Types*). Fig. 2

Numerical Limits

In Fig.2 you can see that many types have a numerical limit, this is directly linked to the amount of RAM that particular type is allocated. The amount of RAM allocated and the names of the numerical types are more or less the same as the C language. Note in C you will find there are many more types than listed here but PureBasic is about keeping things simple, not bending your head with hundreds of advanced types. For beginners, all you need to remember is the numerical limits of each type and understand that this can't be exceeded. To explain why the memory allocated to each type affects the numerical limit, I'll need to explain how the numbers are stored in RAM using Binary, this you can find in Chapter 13 (A Closer Look At Numeric Data Types).

If a numeric data type is exceeded numerically then that numeric value will wrap around the lower numeric level. For example, if you assigned the value of '129' to a Byte variable, then that value has exceeded the numerical limit for a Byte and will be wrapped to '-127'.

Strings

The last standard PureBasic data type is a String. Strings are such an important and useful datatype that they are implemented in nearly every programming language available.

As their name suggests, Strings are just simply strings of characters. Unlike a number there is a certain way that a String has to be written to ensure it is recognized as such. This way is to use double quotation marks to encapsulate the String. Here are a few examples of this syntax:

```
"abcdefghijklmnopqrstuvwxyz"   "Mary had a little lamb"   "123456789"
```

Notice the last String of these three is a string of numbers. This is recognized as a String rather than a number because of the double quotation marks around it. Strings defined like this are also called literal Strings.

Strings are probably the simplest data type to understand because they are so easy to use. As long as you remember the double quotation marks around the characters then you have a String.

PureBasic's String Types

Type	Suffix	Memory Usage (RAM)	Character Limit
String	.s	4 bytes (32 bits)	Unlimited
String	$	4 bytes (32 bits)	Unlimited
Fixed Length String	.s{length}	4 bytes (32 bits)	User Defined*
Fixed Length String	${length}	4 bytes (32 bits)	User Defined*

* The 'length' parameter defines the string's maximum length.   Fig. 3

Strings can be made up from any character in the ASCII character set, including the control characters (See Appendix B (Helpful Charts) for a full listing of ASCII characters) except the null character as that is used to signify the end of a String. Strings that use the null character to define its end are referred to as 'Zero Terminated Strings'.

Variables And Constants

To store and manipulate data in any program you need to use the correct data type for storage but you also need a way to easily find that data in memory. Variables and Constants provide a simple answer for this problem by assigning a clear descriptive name to a particular piece of data so it can be easily accessed later. Put simply, variables refer to data that can change its value, while constants refer to data that will never ever change.

Variables

Typically, the name of a variable is bound to a particular area and amount of RAM (defined by its data type), and any operations on a variable will manipulate that associated area of memory. Variable names can be named anything you want, but many people like to keep them as descriptive as possible to convey what the actual value is that the variable holds. Variables are the building blocks of any computer program as they hold data that can be manipulated, referred to and ultimately displayed. Variables are essential for the organization and storage of your data.

Okay, let's get playing with PureBasic. Open the PureBasic IDE and let's create a variable of our own. When you want to create a variable the syntax is very simple. You enter a variable name followed by a type suffix to define what type of variable it is to be, followed by an operation you wish to perform on it. This operation is primarily a value definition.

In the following statement, we assign the value of '1' to the name 'NumberOfLinesOfCode', using the equals operator (=) and using a Byte as its data type.

```
NumberOfLinesOfCode.b = 1
```

Look at this statement a little more closely. You will see that the variable name has no spaces, this is very important. No variable ever has spaces! If you need to separate the words in a variable to make it more easy to read you can use underscores like this:

```
Number_Of_Lines_Of_Code.b = 1
```

You can use any name you want for a variable but there are few rules. Variable names must not start with a number and must not contain any operators (see Fig.15 for a complete list of operators). Also no special characters are allowed such as accented characters (ß, ä, ö, ü). The '.b' added to the end of the variable name is a suffix to tell the compiler that this variable is to be a Byte and as such will use the associated amount of memory and impose the associated numerical limit. Fig.2. shows all the suffixes you need to use for the number types, while Fig.3. shows the suffixes necessary for the String types. If a type suffix is not used like this:

```
NumberOfLinesOfCode = 1
```

The variable is declared as a Long as this is the default type of PureBasic. This is important to understand because if you forget the suffix on a variable you will create a Long type variable and possible bugs could occur. PureBasic does provide a way to change the default type by using the 'Define' keyword like this:

```
Define.b
NumberOfLinesOfCode = 1
TodaysDate = 11
```

The 'Define' keyword is given a suffix of its own and every variable after that is declared as that newly designated type. The above two variables for instance are both declared as Bytes because of the '.b' suffix on the end of the 'Define' keyword. If this keyword is not used in a PureBasic program then the default type remains as a Long.

If you want to declare a few variables for later use but don't want to give them a value just yet, you could also use this style syntax:

```
Define.w Day, Month, Year
```

This code switches the default type to a Word and declares three variables, 'Day', 'Month' and 'Year' as Words but because these variables have no value assigned to them, they are given the value of zero (0). Here is an example showing the creation of all variable types using PureBasic code:

```
ByteVariable.b = 123
CharVariable.c = 222
WordVariable.w = 4567
LongVariable.l = 891011
QuadVariable.q = 9223372036854775807
FloatVariable.f = 3.1415927
DoubleVariable.d = 12.53456776674545
StringVariableOne.s = "Test String One"
StringVariableTwo$ = "Test String Two"
StringVariableThree.s{ 6} = "abcdef"
StringVariableFour${ 3} = "abc"
```

You will notice the last four variables are Strings but are all defined by slightly different suffixes. The first two are unlimited length Strings while the last two are defined as fixed length Strings. Each one of these types can be defined by using two suffixes. These two different suffixes are '.s' and '$'. Both of which are identical in every way, it's just that the '$' suffix is an old style, kept to appease Basic purists who like using the old style String suffix. Both can be used in the same program but the two suffixes are not interchangeable. For example, these two variables are different:

```
StringVariable.s = "Test String One"
StringVariable$ = "Test String Two"
```

Even though they have the same name, the different suffixes mean they are different variables all together. Don't believe me? Well this can be tested by using the 'Debug' keyword.

```
StringVariable.s = "Test String One"
StringVariable$ = "Test String Two"
Debug StringVariable.s
Debug StringVariable$
```

In this example the 'Debug' keyword is used to echo the values of the two variables to the Debug Output window. Type this example into the IDE and hit the 'Compile/Run' button (F5). You will see two lines appear in the Debug Output window showing the values of the two variables that we used 'Debug' with. This keyword is probably the most used keyword in the whole of the PureBasic language as it is used to test values and echo other useful text to the Debug Output window during program development. When a final executable is made all the 'Debug' commands are removed from the final program, leaving a small executable size.

The 'Debug' Command

The 'Debug' command is very useful to quickly print useful text into the Debug Output window. Any data type can be used with this command, making it invaluable for quickly printing helpful numbers, memory addresses, returned Strings and/or values of calculations.

Any 'Debug' commands used within your code are ignored and will not be compiled when you disable the debugger or compile your final executable using (*Menu:*Compiler->Create Executable...).

One more thing to note about variables is that they are not case sensitive. Meaning that any capitalization is ignored, which is standard Basic language behavior. Look at this example:

```
TestVariable.s = "Test String One"
testvariable = "Test String Two"
TeStVaRiAbLe = "Test String Three"
Debug tEsTvArIaBlE
```

Here it looks as if I am assigning values to three different variables but in truth I am re-assigning a value to the same variable, it's just that each time I do it, I'm using different a capitalization for the variable name. As you can see, letter case means nothing to a variable as this example outputs the text 'Test String Three'. This example also demonstrates another feature of PureBasic's variables, in that once a variable has been declared using a given data type, that data type remains assigned to that variable throughout the programs life. For example, once a variable has been declared as a String then from then on you can never store an integer or floating point number in that variable. Let me show you a bad example:

```
StringVariable.s = "Test String One"
StringVariable = 100
```

This example will never compile and if you try to, you will get a polite message from the IDE telling you that you cannot write a numeric value into a String variable. This following example will work:

```
StringVariable.s = "Test String One"
StringVariable = "One Hundred"
```

Because the variable 'StringVariable' was originally declared as a String, only Strings can be given as values to that variable from then on. When we change its value to 'One Hundred' it works fine because we change a String for a String. So let's recap on the main variable rules.

1). Variables must not contain spaces.
2). Variable names must not start with a number but can contain them.
3). Variable names must not contain any operators (See Fig.15).
4). Variable names must not contain any special or accented characters (ß, ä, ö, ü).
5). By default if no suffix is given to a variable then its data type is a Long.
6). Once a variable has been declared, its data type can never be changed during runtime.
7). Once a variable is declared you can use it freely without a suffix, the compiler remembers its type.

Constants

Constants are similar to variables in that they provide an easy way to reference data and can be called whatever you want, but that's where the similarity ends. Constants are used when you want to give a particular piece of data a name while knowing that value will never change. Look at this example:

```
#DAYS_IN_THE_YEAR = "365"
```

We know that the number of days in a standard year will never change so we can use a constant to express this. If we tried to change its value like a variable we get an error. The IDE will complain, telling you that a constant with that name has already been declared and halt compilation.

The good thing about constants is that they use no memory, because they are never compiled as such, they are replaced in your code by their initial values before compilation. Look at this example:

```
#DAYS_IN_THE_YEAR = "365"
Debug "There are " + #DAYS_IN_THE_YEAR + " days in the year."
```

Before this example is compiled into your program, it really looks like this to the compiler:

```
Debug "There are 365 days in the year."
```

because the constant is replaced by the value it was assigned, in this case '365', and then compiled.

All constants follow exactly the same naming rules as variables except for the suffixes, constants don't use them regardless of what type of data you assign to a constant, because there is no memory allocation needed. All constants are declared using a prefix rather than a suffix. The prefix is a hash character (#).

Enumerating Constants

If you need a block of constants all of which are assigned numeric values enumerated one after the other, then you can use the 'Enumeration' keyword.

```
Enumeration
  #ZERO
  #ONE
  #TWO
  #THREE
EndEnumeration

Debug #ZERO
Debug #ONE
Debug #TWO
Debug #THREE
```

You will see in the Debug Output window, each constant has a greater value than the one preceding it, starting at '0'. If you want to start the enumeration at a number other than '0', you can use an optional numeric parameter with the 'Enumeration' keyword, like this:

```
Enumeration 10
  #TEN
  #ELEVEN
  #TWELVE
EndEnumeration

Debug #TEN
Debug #ELEVEN
Debug #TWELVE
```

Now you can see the constant '#TEN' has the value of '10' and the rest are incremented from then on. You can even use the 'Step' keyword after the numeric parameter to change the increment value within an enumeration block. Look at this example:

```
Enumeration 10 Step 5
  #TEN
  #FIFTEEN
  #TWENTY
EndEnumeration

Debug #TEN
Debug #FIFTEEN
Debug #TWENTY
```

Now the constants are incremented by '5', starting at '10'.

If you assign a value at any time to a constant within an enumeration block, this sets a new value to be enumerated from. Just like this:

```
Enumeration 5
  #FIVE
  #ONE_HUNDRED = 100
  #ONE_HUNDRED_AND_ONE
  #ONE_HUNDRED_AND_TWO
EndEnumeration

Debug #FIVE
Debug #ONE_HUNDRED
Debug #ONE_HUNDRED_AND_ONE
Debug #ONE_HUNDRED_AND_TWO
```

Here you can see demonstrated, after the line: '#ONE_HUNDRED = 100', all the constants are then enumerated from '100'.

Enumerated constants are used mostly in graphical user interface programing (See Chapter 9) where each window or gadget needs its own ID, enumerated constants are a great way to provide these IDs and enumerated blocks take all the hassle out of assigning incremented values to a lot of constants.

3

Operators

Operators are used to assign values to variables and to manipulate the data that those variables contain. In this chapter I'll introduce you to all operators that PureBasic supports and for each one I'll give you a brief example describing its function and use. There are also many diagrams showing how the more advanced operators manipulate data at a binary level. Operator precedence (or operator priority if you prefer) is also explained and notes on PureBasic's expression evaluation are brought to your attention.

An Introduction To Operators

Operators are a set of functions that can perform arithmetic operations on numerical data, boolean operations on truth values and perform String operations for manipulating strings of text. Some operators are known as Overloaded Operators, meaning that they can be used on more than one type of data and can perform different functions. For example, the equals operator (=) can be used to assign a value to a variable as well as being used as an equality operator to test that two variables or values are equal.

= (Equals)
This is probably the easiest operator to explain even though it can be used in two ways. First, it can be used to assign a value to a variable like this:

```
LongVariable.l = 1
```

Secondly, it can be used to make an equality comparison between two expressions, variables or values, like this:

```
LongVariable.l = 1
If LongVariable = 1
  Debug "Yes, LongVariable does equal 1"
EndIf
```

This is the first time you have seen the 'If' keyword but don't worry. This keyword enables a way in your programs to execute code based on if a certain condition is met. In this case, if 'LongVariable' equals '1' then echo some text to the Debug Output window.

+ *(Plus)*

The plus operator is another commonly used one and is used to concatenate Strings as well as for the addition of numbers. First, here is an example of number addition:

```
NumberOne.l = 50
NumberTwo.l = 25
NumberThree.l = NumberOne + NumberTwo
Debug NumberThree
```

The number echoed to the Debug Output window should be '75' because we've added the value of 'NumberOne' to 'NumberTwo' (50+25) and stored the resulting value (75) in the 'NumberThree' variable, we then echo this value to the Debug Output window. Another way to show this might be:

```
NumberOne.l = 50 + 25
Debug NumberOne
```

You can also use a shortcut when using the plus operator with numbers, if you just need to increment a numeric variable by another value or expression:

```
NumberOne.l = 50
NumberOne + 25
Debug NumberOne
```

Once an initial value is assigned to 'NumberOne' we can use the plus operator to add another value to it, so now the number echoed to the Debug Output window is '75'.

Here is an example of String concatenation using the plus operator:

```
StringOne.s = "Mary had a"
StringTwo.s = " little lamb"
StringThree.s = StringOne + StringTwo
Debug StringThree
```

The word concatenate basically means to chain or join together and that's exactly what we are doing with these two Strings. We concatenate 'StringOne' and 'StringTwo' and store the resulting String in 'StringThree', we then echo this value to the Debug Output window. This is another way:

```
StringOne.s = "Mary had a" + " little lamb"
Debug StringOne
```

You can also use the shortcut when using the plus operator with strings, if you just need to concatenate text onto an existing variable:

```
StringOne.s = "Mary had a"
StringOne + " little lamb"
Debug StringOne
```

This works kind of like the numeric shortcut but instead of adding the value numerically, the second String is joined to the existing String variable.

- (Minus)
The minus operator works the exact reverse of the addition operator, in that it subtracts rather than adds. Unlike the addition operator, the minus operator cannot work with Strings. Here is an example of the minus operator in action:

```
NumberOne.l = 50
NumberTwo.l = 25
NumberThree.l = NumberOne - NumberTwo
Debug NumberThree
```

The text echoed to the Debug Window should be '25' which is 'NumberTwo' subtracted from 'NumberOne'. Again a shortcut can be used if you need to decrement a variable by a specific amount:

```
NumberOne.l = 50
NumberOne - 10
Debug NumberOne
```

Here 'NumberOne' is assigned the value of '50' then 'NumberOne' is decremented by '10' using the minus operator. The new value of 'NumberOne' (40) is then echoed to the Debug Output window.

** (Multiplication)*
The multiplication operator is used to multiply two values together and like the minus operator cannot work with Strings. To demonstrate how this operator is used, here is an example:

```
NumberOne.l = 5
NumberTwo.l = 25
NumberThree.l = NumberOne * NumberTwo
Debug NumberThree
```

The debug output should be '125' because in this example we've multiplied 'NumberOne' by 'NumberTwo' (5*25=125). Again a shortcut can be used to multiply a variable by a specified number.

```
NumberOne.l = 50
NumberOne * 3
Debug NumberOne
```

Here 'NumberOne' is assigned the value of '50' then 'NumberOne' is multiplied by '3' using the multiplication operator. The new value of 'NumberOne' (150) is then echoed to the Debug Output window.

/ (Division)
The division operator is another mathematical operator that works only with numbers and not Strings. You've probably guessed how to use it from reading the other examples but here is an example showing its use anyway:

```
NumberOne.l = 100
NumberTwo.l = 2
NumberThree.l = NumberOne / NumberTwo
Debug NumberThree
```

Here 'NumberOne' is assigned the value of '100' and 'NumberTwo' is assigned the value of '2'. We then divide 'NumberOne' (100) by 'NumberTwo' (2) and store the result (50) in 'NumberThree'. We then echo the value of 'NumberThree' to the Debug Output window. As before a shortcut can be used to divide a variable by a specified number:

```
NumberOne.l = 50
NumberOne / 5
Debug NumberOne
```

Here 'NumberOne' is assigned the value '50' then we use the division operator to divide this value by '5'. Then we echo the result stored in 'NumberOne' (10) to the Debug Output window.

& (Bitwise AND)
The bitwise operators are a group of operators that manipulate numbers at a binary level. If you are a little unfamiliar with binary and how PureBasic stores numbers using binary you can refer to Chapter 13 (A Closer Look At Numeric Data Types) where a full explanation is given. Bitwise operators cannot be used with Floats or Strings.

The bitwise '&' operator tests two values to see if they are both true on a bit by bit basis, if two bits are compared and are both true (1) then the operator returns true (1) otherwise it returns false (0). This applies to all bits within the two numbers that are to be compared. Here is a diagram to try to explain a little better.

The '&' (Bitwise AND) Operator

	False	True	False	False	False	True	False	True	
Binary Value of 77	0	1	0	0	1	1	0	1	&
Binary Value of 117	0	1	1	1	0	1	0	1	
Result value of 69	**0**	**1**	**0**	**0**	**0**	**1**	**0**	**1**	

8 bit number
(1 byte)

Fig. 4

In Fig.4 you can see the two numbers to be evaluated using the '&' operator are '77' and '117'. After the calculation is complete, an end result of '69' is achieved. To explain how this value is achieved you need to look at each column of bits from the top down. If you look at the right most column (which is the column associated with the value of '1' in binary) both bits of the two numbers in this column are set at '1' so the value returned by the '&' operator is '1' (which in PureBasic is true). If we move one column along to the left we can see that both bits of the two numbers are both 'o', so the '&' operator returns 'o' (false). Remember that when using the '&' operator both bits have to be '1' before the operator will return '1' otherwise it will return 'o'.

This operator is applied to all the columns of bits starting from the right to the left and when finished the resulting number is returned. In this case the value returned by this calculation is '69'. Here is an example to translate Fig.4 into code:

```
NumberOne.b = 77
NumberTwo.b = 117
NumberThree.b = NumberOne & NumberTwo
Debug NumberThree
```

In this small example two variables are assigned numbers that are to be evaluated using the '&' operator and the variable 'NumberThree' contains the result of this calculation. The value of 'NumberThree' is then echoed to the Debug Output window, which in this case should be '69'. Just like the other operators the bitwise '&' operator has a shortcut if you just need to '&' a number to a single variable:

```
NumberOne.b = 77
NumberOne & 117
Debug NumberOne
```

Here 'NumberOne' is assigned the value '77' and then in the next line we '&' the value '117' to 'NumberOne'. This value is then echoed to the Debug Output window.

Fig.5 shows the comparison made between two bits and the result given by the '&' operator.

'&' (Bitwise AND) Bit Comparison

Left Hand Side	Right Hand Side	Result
0	0	0
0	1	0
1	0	0
1	1	1

Fig. 5

| (Bitwise OR)
The bitwise '|' operator tests two values to see if one or more is true on a bit by bit basis, if two bits are compared and either one or both are true (1) then the operator returns true (1) otherwise it returns

false (0). This applies to all bits within the two numbers that are to be compared.

The '|' (Bitwise OR) Operator

	False	True	True	True	False	True	True	False
Binary Value of 54	0	0	1	1	0	1	1	0
Binary Value of 102	0	1	1	0	0	1	1	0
Result value of 118	**0**	**1**	**1**	**1**	**0**	**1**	**1**	**0**

———— 8 bit number ————
(1 byte)

Fig. 6

In Fig.6 you can see the two numbers to be evaluated using the '|' operator are '54 and '102'. After the calculation is complete, an end result of '118' is achieved. To explain how this value is achieved you need to look at each column of bits from the top down. If you look at the right most column (which is the column associated with the value of '1' in binary) both bits of the two numbers in this column are set at '0' so the value returned by the '|' operator is '0' (false). If we move one column along to the left we can see that both bits of the two numbers are both '1', so the '|' operator returns '1' (true). If we look at the fifth column from the right you will see that the first number has a bit which is set at '1' and the second number has a bit which is set at '0'. In this case the '|' operator still returns '1' (true) because as long as one or the other bit is true then the operator will return true. The '|' operator will always return true, unless both bits are '0'.

This operator is applied to all the columns of bits in Fig.6 starting from the right to the left and when finished the resulting number is returned. In this case the value returned by this calculation is '118'. Here is an example to translate Fig.6 into code:

```
NumberOne.b = 54
NumberTwo.b = 102
NumberThree.b = NumberOne & NumberTwo
Debug NumberThree
```

In this small example two variables are assigned numbers that are to be evaluated using the '|' operator and the variable 'NumberThree' contains the result of this calculation. The value of 'NumberThree' is then echoed to the Debug Output window, which in this case should be '118'. Just like the other operators the bitwise '|' operator can be used as a shortcut if you just need to '|' a number to a single variable:

```
NumberOne.b = 54
NumberOne | 102
Debug NumberOne
```

Here 'NumberOne' is assigned the value '54' and then in the next line we '|' the value '102' to 'NumberOne'. This value is then echoed to the Debug Output window.

Fig.7 shows the comparison made between two bits and the result given by the '|' operator.

'|' *(Bitwise OR) Bit Comparison*

Left Hand Side	Right Hand Side	Result
0	0	0
0	1	1
1	0	1
1	1	1

Fig. 7

! (Bitwise XOR)
The bitwise '!' operator tests two values to see if one of them is true on a bit by bit basis, if the two bits are compared and either one is true (1) then the operator returns true (1) otherwise it returns false (0). This applies to all bits within the two numbers that are to be compared. Here is a diagram to try to explain a little better:

The '!' (Bitwise XOR) Operator

	False	True	True	False	True	True	False	False
Binary Value of 38	0	0	1	0	0	1	1	0
Binary Value of 74	0	1	0	0	1	0	1	0
Result value of 108	**0**	**1**	**1**	**0**	**1**	**1**	**0**	**0**

———— 8 bit number ————
(1 byte)

Fig. 8

In Fig.8 you can see the two numbers to be evaluated using the '!' operator are '38 and '74'. After the calculation is complete, an end result of '108' is achieved. To explain how this value is achieved you need to look at each column of bits from the top down again. If you look at the right most column (which is the column associated with the value of '1' in binary) both bits of the two numbers in this column are set at '0' so the value returned by the '!' operator is '0' (false). If we move one column along to the left we can see that both bits of the two numbers are both '1', so the '!' operator still returns '0' (false). This is because when two bits are compared the '!' operator will only return '1' (true) if only one bit is set to '1'. If both bits are set to '1' or '0' then the '!' operator will return '0' (false).

This operator is applied to all the columns of bits in Fig.8 starting from the right to the left and when finished the resulting number is returned. In this case the value returned by this calculation is '108'. Here is an example to translate Fig.8 into code:

```
NumberOne.b = 38
NumberTwo.b = 74
NumberThree.b = NumberOne ! NumberTwo
Debug NumberThree
```

In this small example two variables are assigned numbers that are to be evaluated using the '!' operator and the variable 'NumberThree' contains the result of this calculation. The value of 'NumberThree' is then echoed to the Debug Output window, which in this case should be '108'.

Just like the other operators the bitwise '!' operator has a shortcut if you just need to '!' a number to a single variable:

```
NumberOne.b = 38
NumberOne ! 74
Debug NumberOne
```

Here 'NumberOne' is assigned the value '38' and then in the next line we '!' the value '74' to 'NumberOne'. This value is then echoed to the Debug Output window.

Fig.9 shows the comparison made between two bits and the result given by the '!' operator:

'!' (Bitwise XOR) Bit Comparison

Left Hand Side	Right Hand Side	Result
0	0	0
0	1	1
1	0	1
1	1	0

Fig. 9

~ (Bitwise NOT)
The bitwise '~' operator is an easier operator to explain in that it simply returns a number who's bits have been inverted using an input number or expression as a source.

The bitwise '~' operator is known as an Unary operator meaning that it uses one value or expression to return a value. This can be demonstrated with this piece of code:

```
NumberOne.b = 43
NumberTwo.b = ~NumberOne
Debug NumberTwo
```

Here the variable 'NumberOne' is assigned the value of '43' then we create a variable 'NumberTwo' and assign it the value of 'NumberOne' which is inverted at a binary level using the '~' operator. This value (which should be '-44') is then echoed to the Debug Output window.

The '~' (Bitwise NOT) Operator

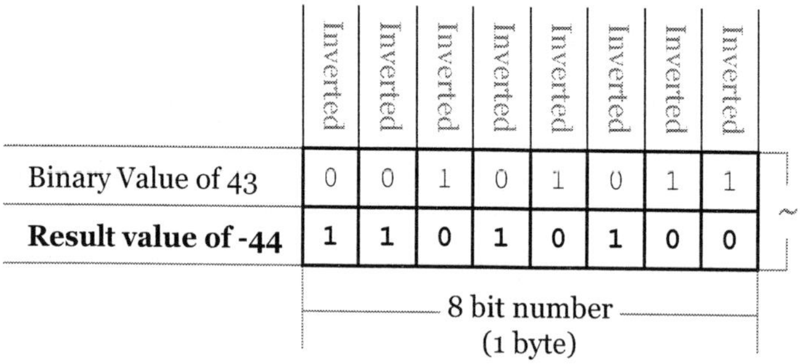

	Inverted	Inverted	Inverted	Inverted	Inverted	Inverted	Inverted	Inverted
Binary Value of 43	0	0	1	0	1	0	1	1
Result value of -44	**1**	**1**	**0**	**1**	**0**	**1**	**0**	**0**

—— 8 bit number ——
(1 byte)

Fig. 10

In Fig.10 you can see the '~' operator simply inverts the bits of the source number then returns that new value. To understand better how numbers are represented in binary within PureBasic, especially negative (signed) numbers, see chapter 13 (A Closer Look At Numeric Data Types).

<< (Bit shift left)
The bit shift operators are similar to the bitwise operators in that they manipulate numbers at a binary level. As their name suggests they shift all bits to the left or right depending on which operator is used. Here is some code demonstrating the use of the '<<' operator:

```
NumberOne.b = 50
NumberTwo.b = NumberOne << 1
Debug NumberTwo
```

In this example we assign 'NumberOne' the value of '50'. Then we create a variable called 'NumberTwo' and assign it the value of 'NumberOne' which has been bit shifted to the left by one place. This resulting value (which should be '100') is then echoed to the Debug Output window. You can understand the function of this operator more clearly looking at Fig.11.

As you can see the resulting value simply has its binary digits (bits) shifted to the left from their original position, in this case by one place. When shifting bits to the left like this, zeros are created and shifted in to fill the gap on the right, while the bits on the left will be shifted 'off the end' of the number (in this case a Byte) and will be lost forever.

The '<<' (Bit Shift Left) Operator

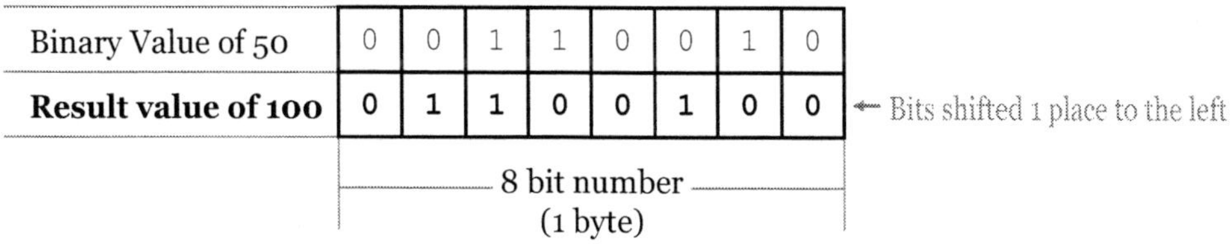

Binary Value of 50	0	0	1	1	0	0	1	0
Result value of 100	0	1	1	0	0	1	0	0

← Bits shifted 1 place to the left

8 bit number
(1 byte)

Fig. 11

>> (Bit shift right)

The '>>' operator is exactly the same as the '<<' operator but works in the opposite direction. Here is some code demonstrating the use of the '>>' operator:

```
NumberOne.b = 50
NumberTwo.b = NumberOne >> 1
Debug NumberTwo
```

In this example we assign 'NumberOne' the value of '50'. Then we create a variable called 'NumberTwo' and assign it the value of 'NumberOne' which has been bit shifted to the right by one place. This resulting value (which should be '25') is then echoed to the Debug Output window. You can understand the function of this operator more clearly in this diagram:

The '>>' (Bit Shift Right) Operator

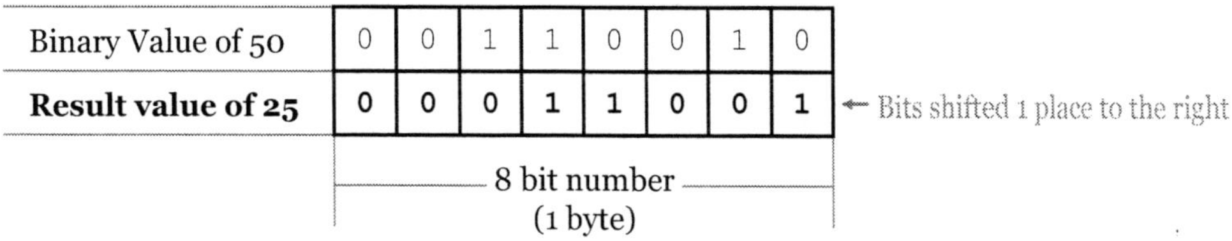

Binary Value of 50	0	0	1	1	0	0	1	0
Result value of 25	0	0	0	1	1	0	0	1

← Bits shifted 1 place to the right

8 bit number
(1 byte)

Fig. 12

As you can see the resulting value simply has its binary digits (bits) shifted to the right from their original position, in this case by one place. When shifting bits to the right like this it is important to understand what bits are used to fill the gap that is created on the left hand side of the binary number. If the number is a positive number, the left most bit (sometimes called the most significant bit) is set to zero. In this case the gap will be filled with bits set to zero. If the source number is a negative (signed) number then the left most bit will be one. In this case the gap will be filled with bits set to one. The bits on the right will be shifted 'off the end' of the number (in this case a Byte) and will be lost forever.

< *(Less than)*

The '<' operator is used in comparisons of two variables or expressions. If the value on the left hand side of this operator is less than the value on the right hand side then this operator will return true (1) otherwise it will return false (0). Here is a code snippet demonstrating its usage:

```
NumberOne.l = 1
NumberTwo.l = 2

If NumberOne < NumberTwo
  Debug "1: NumberOne is less than NumberTwo"
Else
  Debug "2: NumberTwo is less than NumberOne"
EndIf
```

Here in the 'If' statement we test to see if 'NumberOne' is less than 'NumberTwo', which of course it is, so the first debug statement is executed. If we change the value of 'NumberOne' to '3', like this:

```
NumberOne.l = 3
NumberTwo.l = 2

If NumberOne < NumberTwo
  Debug "1: NumberOne is less than NumberTwo"
Else
  Debug "2: NumberTwo is less than NumberOne"
EndIf
```

We now see in the Debug Output window that the second debug statement has been executed because now 'NumberOne' is no longer less than 'NumberTwo'.

> *(More than)*

The '>' operator is used in comparisons of two variables or expressions. If the value on the left hand side of this operator is more than the value on the right hand side then this operator will return true (1) otherwise it will return false (0). Here is a code snippet demonstrating its usage:

```
NumberOne.l = 2
NumberTwo.l = 1

If NumberOne > NumberTwo
  Debug "1: NumberOne is more than NumberTwo"
Else
  Debug "2: NumberTwo is more than NumberOne"
EndIf
```

Here in the 'If' statement we test to see if 'NumberOne' is more than 'NumberTwo', which of course it is, so the first debug statement is executed. If we change the value of 'NumberOne' to '0', like this:

```
NumberOne.l = 0
NumberTwo.l = 1

If NumberOne > NumberTwo
  Debug "1: NumberOne is more than NumberTwo"
Else
  Debug "2: NumberTwo is more than NumberOne"
EndIf
```

We now see in the Debug Output window that the second debug statement has been executed because now 'NumberOne' is no longer more than 'NumberTwo'.

<= *(Less than or equal to)*
The '<=' operator is used in comparisons of two variables or expressions. If the value on the left hand side of this operator is less than or equal to the value on the right hand side then this operator will return true (1) otherwise it will return false (0). Here is a code snippet demonstrating its usage:

```
NumberOne.l = 0
NumberTwo.l = 1

If NumberOne <= NumberTwo
  Debug "1: NumberOne is less than or equal to NumberTwo"
Else
  Debug "2: NumberOne is NOT less than or equal to NumberTwo"
EndIf
```

Here in the 'If' statement we test to see if 'NumberOne' is less than or equal to 'NumberTwo', which of course it is, so the first debug statement is executed. If we change the value of 'NumberOne' to '1' then the 'If' statement will still return true (1) because 'NumberOne' is still less than or equal to 'NumberTwo'.

To demonstrate the second debug statement being executed we have to make sure that the 'If' statement is given a false result from the '<=' operator. This is achieved easily by making sure the value of 'NumberOne' is NOT less than or equal to the value of 'NumberTwo', like this:

```
NumberOne.l = 2
NumberTwo.l = 1

If NumberOne <= NumberTwo
  Debug "1: NumberOne is less than or equal to NumberTwo"
Else
  Debug "2: NumberOne is NOT less than or equal to NumberTwo"
EndIf
```

>= *(More than or equal to)*
The '>=' operator is used in comparisons of two variables or expressions. If the value on the left hand side of this operator is more than or equal to the value on the right hand side then this operator will

return true (1) otherwise it will return false (0). Here is a code snippet demonstrating its usage:

```
NumberOne.l = 2
NumberTwo.l = 1

If NumberOne >= NumberTwo
  Debug "1: NumberOne is more than or equal to NumberTwo"
Else
  Debug "2: NumberOne is NOT more than or equal to NumberTwo"
EndIf
```

Here in the 'If' statement we test to see if 'NumberOne' is more than or equal to 'NumberTwo', which of course it is, so the first debug statement is executed. If we change the value of 'NumberOne' to '1' then the 'If' statement will still return true (1) because 'NumberOne' is still more than or equal to 'NumberTwo'.

To demonstrate the second debug statement being executed we have to make sure that the 'If' statement is given a false result from the '>=' operator. This is achieved easily by making sure the value of 'NumberOne' is NOT more than or equal to the value of 'NumberTwo', like this:

```
NumberOne.l = 0
NumberTwo.l = 1

If NumberOne >= NumberTwo
  Debug "1: NumberOne is more than or equal to NumberTwo"
Else
  Debug "2: NumberOne is NOT more than or equal to NumberTwo"
EndIf
```

<> (Not equal to)

The '<>' operator is used in comparisons of two variables or expressions which works in the exact opposite way of the comparison (not assignment) function of the '=' operator. If the value on the left hand side of this operator is not equal to the value on the right hand side then this operator will return true (1) otherwise it will return false (0). Here is a code snippet demonstrating its usage:

```
NumberOne.l = 0
NumberTwo.l = 1

If NumberOne <> NumberTwo
  Debug "1: NumberOne does not equal NumberTwo"
Else
  Debug "2: NumberOne does equal NumberTwo"
EndIf
```

Here in the 'If' statement we test to see if 'NumberOne' is not equal to 'NumberTwo', which of course it isn't, so the first debug statement is executed. If we change the value of 'NumberOne' to '1', like this:

```
NumberOne.l = 1
NumberTwo.l = 1
```

```
If NumberOne <> NumberTwo
  Debug "1: NumberOne does not equal NumberTwo"
Else
  Debug "2: NumberOne does equal NumberTwo"
EndIf
```

We now see in the Debug Output window that the second debug statement has been executed because 'NumberOne' is now equal to 'NumberTwo' and the '<>' operator returns false.

And (Logical AND)
The logical operators are used to combine the logical true or false results of the comparison operators to provide a more robust solution to comparing values of multiple expressions.

The 'And' operator is used for checking two expressions to make sure both evaluate as true. Look at this piece of code:

```
StringOne.s = "The quick brown fox"
NumberOne.l = 105

If StringOne = "The quick brown fox" And NumberOne = 105
  Debug "1: Both expressions evaluate to true (1)"
Else
  Debug "2: One or both of the expressions evaluate as false (0)"
EndIf
```

We can see here that the 'If' statement is testing to make sure that the String variable, 'StringOne' equals 'The quick brown fox' and that the Long variable 'NumberOne' equals '105'. Because both do so the 'And' operator returns true and the first debug statement is executed. If either of the two expressions on the right and left hand side of the 'And' operator return a false result, the 'And' operator itself returns a false result. This operator is optimized in such a way that if the first of the expressions return a false result then the 'And' operator immediately returns false and doesn't bother to evaluate the next expression. This is handy when you want to write code that runs very quickly.

Not (Logical NOT)
The 'Not' operator is used to perform a logical negation on an expression or a boolean value. In other words anything that evaluates to true on the right hand side of this operator is returned as false and vice versa. See this example:

```
One.l = 1
Two.l = 2

If Not One = 5
  Debug "1: One = 5 is evaluated as true (1)"
Else
  Debug "2: One = 5 is evaluated as false (0)"
EndIf
```

```
If Not Two = 2
  Debug "1: Two = 2 is evaluated as true (1)"
Else
  Debug "2: Two = 2 is evaluated as false (0)"
EndIf
```

We can see here that the first 'If' statement is testing to make sure that the Long variable, 'One' equals '5' which it doesn't and the expression returns false. Because we have the 'Not' operator in front of 'One = 5' this inverts the false return value to a true value. Opposite values are shown in the second 'If' statement. The expression here returns true but because of the 'Not' operator it inverts it to a false value.

Or (Logical OR)
The 'Or' operator is used for checking two expressions to make sure one or the other evaluate as true. Look at this piece of code:

```
StringOne.s = "The quick brown fox"
NumberOne.l = 105

If StringOne = "The quick brown fox" Or NumberOne = 100
  Debug "1: One or more expressions evaluate to true (1)"
Else
  Debug "2: Both of the expressions evaluate as false (0)"
EndIf
```

Here we can see that the 'If' statement is testing to make sure that the String variable, 'StringOne' equals 'The quick brown fox' or that the Long variable 'NumberOne' equals '100'. You will notice that the second expression in the 'If' statement actually returns false because 'NumberOne' does not equal '100'.

Because one of the expressions returns a true result, the 'Or' operator returns true and the first debug statement is executed. The 'Or' operator will only return a false result if both expressions on the right and left hand side return a false result themselves. This operator is also optimized in such a way that if the first expression returns a true result then the 'Or' operator immediately returns true and doesn't bother to evaluate the next expression. This is handy when you want to write code that runs very quickly.

XOr (Logical XOR)
The 'XOr' operator is used for checking two expressions to make sure only one evaluates as true. Look at this piece of code:

```
StringOne.s = "The quick brown fox"
NumberOne.l = 105
If StringOne = "The quick brown fox" XOr NumberOne = 105
  Debug "1: Only one expression is true (1)"
Else
  Debug "2: The expressions are either both true (1) or both false (0)"
EndIf
```

The 'If' statement is testing both expressions using the 'XOr' operator to make sure only one expression is evaluating as true. If both are evaluating as true or false then the 'If' statement itself will return false and execute the second debug statement, which is the case here. If this example was changed to make sure only one expression returned a true value, then the 'If' would return true and execute the first debug statement.

% (Modulo)
The '%' operator divides the number on the left hand side by the number on the right hand side and then returns the remainder of this division. Here is an example:

```
NumberOne.l = 20 % 8
Debug NumberOne
```

Here we divide the number '20' by '8' using the '%' operator. In which there are two '8's in '20', this leaves '4' as a remainder. This remaining number is assigned to the variable 'NumberOne'. We then echo this value to the Debug Output window.

( ) (Brackets)
Brackets are not really an operator in themselves because they never return any result. They are used to determine the execution order of nested expressions. The general rule of thumb is that the expression within brackets is evaluated first. In the case of nested brackets the inner-most set is evaluated first, then the next set and so on until the final set is reached. Here is an example:

```
NumberOne.l = 2 * 5 + 3
Debug NumberOne
```

Here the value of 'NumberOne' is '13' because the order of evaluation is, '2 * 5' then '+ 3', if we add brackets like this:

```
NumberOne.l = 2 * (5 + 3)
Debug NumberOne
```

Then the order of evaluation is changed to '5 + 3' then '* 2' which returns the value of '16' which in turn in assigned to 'NumberOne' and echoed to the Debug Output window.

Operator Precedence

Operator precedence is a term that means the order in which operators are evaluated during compile time. If you look at Fig.13 you can see the order in which operators are evaluated based on their individual priority.

This priority is shown in the left hand column, the lowest number (1) means these operators are evaluated first while the higher the number means that these operators will be evaluated later.

Operator Precedence

Priority*	Operators
1	( )
2	~
3	<< >> % !
4	| &
5	* /
6	+ –
7	> >= < <= = <>
8	And Or Not XOr

* The operators at the top of this list are evaluated first.   Fig. 13

In this example:

```
Debug 3 + 10 * 2
```

the multiplication operator is evaluated first before the addition operator because it has a greater priority even though it appears after the addition operator in this expression. The result echoed to the Debug Output window should be '23'.

To customize the operator precedence, use brackets to encapsulate portions of code to make them execute with a higher priority. For example, if we wanted the addition operator to execute first we would write the expression like this:

```
Debug (3 + 10) * 2
```

Now the value echoed to the Debug Output window would be '26'.

Expression Notes

When PureBasic's compiler evaluates an expression between Integers and Floats, it sometimes changes the data type of the expression's components to evaluate it properly. If the expression contains a Float then each part of the expression is converted to a Float before the expression is evaluated and a result returned. Fig.14 shows examples of how PureBasic evaluates these expressions under certain conditions.

If you find that strange results are being returned from operators or expressions or that the number returned is not of the expected type, it's a good idea to re-check the expression to make sure the compiler is not following these rules.

Expression Evaluation Rules

Expression Example	Evaluation Rule
`a.l = b.l + c.l`	'b' and 'c' both remain as a Long before and during evaluation, a Long is then returned and assigned to 'a'.
`a.l = b.l + c.f`	Because this expression contains a Float, 'b' is converted to Float before the evaluation. 'b' is then added to 'c' and the resulting Float is then converted to a Long and assigned to 'a'.
`a.f = b.l + c.l`	'b' and 'c' both remain as a Long before and during evaluation. The resulting Long returned by the addition operator is then converted to a Float and assigned to 'a'.
`a.l = b.f + c.f`	'b' and 'c' both remain as a Float before and during evaluation. The resulting Float returned by the addition operator is then converted to a Long and assigned to 'a'.

Fig. 14

Operator Quick Reference

Operator	Description
=	Equals. This can be used in two ways. The first is to assign the value of the expression on the RHS to the variable on the LHS. The second way is when the result of the operator is used in an expression to test whether the values of the expression on the LHS and the RHS are the same (if they are the same the equals operator will return true, otherwise it will return false).
+	Plus. Gives a result of the value of the expression on the RHS added to the value of the expression on the LHS. If the result of this operator is not used and there is a variable on the LHS, then the value of the expression on the RHS will be added directly to the variable on the LHS.
-	Minus. Subtracts the value of the expression on the RHS from the value of the expression on the LHS. When there is no expression on the LHS this operator gives the negative value of the value of the expression on the RHS. If the result of this operator is not used and there is a variable on the LHS, then the value of the expression on the RHS will be subtracted directly from the variable on the LHS. (This operator cannot be used with strings).
*	Multiplication. Multiplies the value of the expression on the LHS by the value of the expression on the RHS. If the result of this operator is not used and there is a variable on the LHS, then the value of the variable is directly multiplied by the value of the expression on the RHS. (This operator cannot be used with strings).
/	Division. Divides the value of the expression on the LHS by the value of the expression on the RHS. If the result of this operator is not used and there is a variable on the LHS, then the value of the variable is directly divided by the value of the expression on the RHS. (This operator cannot be used with strings).
&	Bitwise AND. You should be familiar with binary numbers when using this operator. The result of this operator will be the value of the expression on the LHS AND'ed with the value of the expression on the RHS, bit for bit. Additionally, if the result of the operator is not used and there is a variable on the LHS, then the result will be stored directly in that variable. (This operator cannot be used with strings).
|	Bitwise OR. You should be familiar with binary numbers when using this operator. The result of this operator will be the value of the expression on the LHS OR'ed with the value of the expression on the RHS, bit for bit. Additionally, if the result of the operator is not used and there is a variable on the LHS, then the result will be stored directly in that variable. (This operator cannot be used with strings).
!	Bitwise XOR. You should be familiar with binary numbers when using this operator. The result of this operator will be the value of the expression on the LHS XOR'ed with the value of the expression on the RHS, bit for bit. Additionally, if the result of the operator is not used and there is a variable on the LHS, then the result will be stored directly in that variable. (This operator cannot be used with strings).
~	Bitwise NOT. You should be familiar with binary numbers when using this operator. The result of this operator will be the NOT'ed value of the expression on the RHS. i.e. the result will have it's bits inverted compared to the value of the expression. (This operator cannot be used with strings).
<	Less than. This is used to compare the values of the expressions on the LHS and RHS. If the value of the expression on the LHS is less than the value of the expression on the RHS this operator will give a result of true, otherwise the result is false.
>	More than. This is used to compare the values of the expressions on the LHS and RHS. If the value of the expression on the LHS is more than the value of the expression on the RHS this operator will give a result of true, otherwise the result is false.
<=	Less than or equal to. This is used to compare the values of the expressions on the LHS and RHS. If the value of the expression on the LHS is less than or equal to the value of the expression on the RHS this operator will give a result of true, otherwise the result is false.
>=	More than or equal to. This is used to compare the values of the expressions on the LHS and RHS. If the value of the expression on the LHS is more than or equal to the value of the expression on the RHS this operator will give a result of true, otherwise the result is false.
<>	Not equal to. This is used to compare the values of the expressions on the LHS and RHS. If the value of the expression on the LHS is equal to the value of the expression on the RHS this operator will give a result of false, otherwise the result is true.
And	Logical AND. This is used to compare the values of the expressions on the LHS and RHS. If the value of the expressions on the LHS and the RHS are both true then the result is true, otherwise the result is false.
Or	Logical OR. This is used to compare the values of the expressions on the LHS and RHS. If the value of the expression on the LHS or the RHS is true then the result is true, otherwise the result is false.
Not	Logical NOT. This is used to perform logical negation of a boolean value. In other words if an expression returns a true value, using the Not operator can invert this value to a false. Conversely if the expression on the RHS of this operator returns false then Not will return true.
XOr	Logical XOR. This is used to compare the values of the expressions on the LHS and RHS. If only one of the expressions on the LHS or the RHS is evaluated as true then the result is true. If both expressions are either true or both false then the XOr operator returns false.
<<	Arithmetic shift left. Shifts each bit in the value of the expression on the LHS left by the number of places given by the value of the expression on the RHS. Additionally, when the result of this operator is not used and the LHS contains a variable, that variable will have its value shifted by the amount on the RHS. It probably helps if you understand binary numbers when you use this operator, although you can use it as if each position you shift by is multiplying by an extra factor of 2.
>>	Arithmetic shift right. Shifts each bit in the value of the expression on the LHS right by the number of places given by the value of the expression on the RHS. Additionally, when the result of this operator is not used and the LHS contains a variable, that variable will have its value shifted by the amount on the RHS. It probably helps if you understand binary numbers when you use this operator, although you can use it as if each position you shift by is dividing by an extra factor of 2.
%	Modulo. Returns the remainder of the LHS divided by RHS using integer division.
( )	Brackets. You can use sets of brackets to force part of an expression to be evaluated first, or in a certain order. Expressions in brackets are evaluated first before any other part of the current expression. In nested brackets the inner-most set are evaluated first and then each evaluated outwards.

RHS = Right hand side   LHS = Left hand side   Fig. 15

4

Conditional Statements And Loops

In this chapter I'll introduce conditional statements and loops. These are major parts of any program and help define the program flow. I start by explaining what boolean values are and how PureBasic handles them. I then move on to conditional statements such as 'If' and 'Select' which are used to tell the program how to proceed when a particular condition is met. I then finish the chapter with explanations and examples of the different loops that are available for use in PureBasic. As always full explanations are given along with many examples.

Boolean Logic

First let's dig out the history books. George Boole was a mathematician and philosopher who invented a form of algebra now called Boolean algebra. The logic behind this form of algebra has been named Boolean Logic in honor of George Boole. This form has grown to be the basis of all modern computer arithmetic. What is astonishing is that George Boole invented this form roughly seventy years before the creation of the first computer that used it!

In a nutshell, the entire system revolves around two values, True and False. These two values (or states) are tested using logic operations to determine a result. It really is as simple as that. The three most basic logic operations were (and still are) AND, OR and NOT. It was these three operators that formed the basis of Boole's algebra form, and were the only operations necessary to perform comparisons or basic mathematics. (You can see these logical operators implemented in PureBasic and read how to use them in Chapter 3).

PureBasic does not have a boolean data type (as you can see from Fig.2 and Fig.3), unlike some languages such as C++. So in PureBasic to express a true or false value we use numbers. '1' equaling True and '0' equaling False, keep this in mind when testing for a true or false result. If you are using these numeric values to represent true and false, then it would be a good idea to use PureBasic's built-in constants instead, to make your program code easier to read and understand later on.

Here are the two constants:

```
#True
#False
```

'#True' has the value of '1' and '#False' has the value of '0'.

Nearly all commands in PureBasic return a value. Sometimes this is the value of a mathematical function or it may be the status of a window you have just created. These values are returned to be tested if needed and sometimes they are required to make sure certain actions take place. Look at this piece of pseudo-code:

```
if window creation equals True
  then draw graphics and buttons on the window
else
  tell the user there has been a problem
  end the program
```

This is not real compilable code but you get the idea. Here I'm testing to make sure my window has been created. Once I have tested that it has been created then I can draw my stuff on it. If, however, it has not been created, then I end the program after informing the user something went wrong. If I don't test the window creation, I might run the risk of a bad program crash if I try to draw buttons and graphics on something that doesn't exist.

This is a first glimpse of the value of having true and false tests. This also leads us nicely into the next section which explains the 'If' keyword in more detail.

The 'If' Statement

An 'If' keyword is used to construct statements which effect the flow of the program. It affects which path to choose when a certain condition arises or is met. Sometimes when programs are running, you may get unusual input or errors and is nice to be able to direct the flow of the program to handle such things, if and when they occur.

Constructing 'If' Statements
An 'If' statement is used to test for a true value, if it receives this true value, then it immediately executes the piece of code after the first line of the 'If' statement. If it doesn't receive this true value, then it will execute another separate piece of code immediately after the 'Else' keyword further along in the statement. Let's take a look at an example.

```
a.l = 5
If a = 5
  Debug "A true value was found"
Else
  Debug "No true value was found"
EndIf
```

Here the 'If' operator is testing that the variable 'a' equals '5'. It does, and returns a true value, so the first line after the 'If' keyword is executed. If this comparison returned false then the code after the 'Else' keyword would of been executed. To finished the 'If' statement off, you must use the 'EndIf' keyword, as this defines the end of the 'If' statement.

Everything Is True?

As you have read earlier on, and generally in PureBasic, '1'=True and '0'=False. While this is correct, 'If' statements are a special case regarding what they recognized as true. In 'If' statements everything equals true unless the value returned is '0' (zero) and then it equals false (unless you are making specific comparisons). This is handy when using an 'If' statement to test if a variable, command or expression returns any value other than '0'.

The first thing to take notice of when learning about 'If' statements is the expression that directly follows the 'If' keyword. This expression is being tested to see if it evaluates as true. This expression could be a simple variable or a very long expression. The 'Else' keyword is also completely optional and is only used here to present a complete example. We could omit it completely and re-type the above example as this:

```
a.l = 5

If a = 5
  Debug "A true value was found"
EndIf
```

The only drawback with this smaller example is that it doesn't provide any feedback when a false result is encountered. There is no rule to say that you must use the 'Else' keyword within an 'If' statement but sometimes it's nice to provide a way of handling a false result for the sake of completeness.

Let's look at a simple 'If' statement to test to see if a variable has a value.

```
Beads.l = 5

If Beads
  Debug "The variable has a value"
Else
  Debug "The variable does not have a value"
EndIf
```

Here, after the 'If' keyword I have used just one variable as the expression to test. This variable is tested to see if it returns a value, which in this case it does. The value is not '0', so it is considered true (See the info box 'Everything Is True?') and the relevant piece of code is executed. Try changing the value of 'Beads' to '0' and run again to see a false result.

Let's take a look at a more complicated example of an expression inside an 'If' statement. Re-read Chapter 3 if you need to understand fully all the operators used in this expression.

```
Value1.l = 10
Value2.l = 5
Value3.l = 1

If Value1 >= 10 And (Value2 / 5) = Value3
  Debug "The expression evaluates as true"
Else
  Debug "The expression evaluates as false"
EndIf
```

This 'If' statement is testing to see if 'Value1' is greater than or equal to '10' and that 'Value2' divided by '5' is equal to 'Value3'. As you can see the expressions that can be tested can be quite complicated and be very specific about what values you are testing for.

The 'ElseIf' Keyword

Another keyword that can be used within an 'If' statement is the 'ElseIf' keyword. The 'ElseIf' keyword, as its name suggests, is a combination of 'Else' and 'If'. Like 'Else', it extends an 'If' statement to execute a different piece of code if the original 'If' expression evaluates as false. However, unlike the 'Else' keyword, it will execute an alternative piece of code only if the 'ElseIf' conditional expression evaluates as true. Confused? Here's an example:

```
NumberOfBeads.l = 10

If NumberOfBeads < 5
  Debug "The variable has a value below '5'"
ElseIf NumberOfBeads > 5
  Debug "The variable has a value above '5'"
Else
  Debug "The variable has a value of '5'"
EndIf
```

Here we test the value of the 'NumberOfBeads' variable. The first 'If' tests to see if this value is less than '5'. Because this returns false the program then moves onto the 'ElseIf' part. Here the 'ElseIf' line returns true because 'NumberOfBeads' is greater than '5'.

The 'ElseIf' statement is a great way to extend an 'If' to check for multiple values and there is an unlimited number of 'ElseIf' checks you can make within an 'If' statement. The only drawback is that when a large number of these statements are used, things can get a little complicated while deciding the order with which they are typed in. When a great deal of checks are needed sometimes a 'Select' statement is preferred.

Statement Skipping

At anytime during the execution of an 'If' statement, if any part of the statement returns true then the rest of the 'If' statement is skipped and not executed. Because of this behavior some care is needed when designing an 'If' statement.

The last example showed this skipping in action, the 'Else' part is completely skipped because the 'ElseIf' part returns true.

The 'Select' Statement

'Select' statements are a direct complement to 'If's. In that they provide a way of combining several tests of the same variable or expression into a single block of statements. While 'If's are very powerful in what they do, sometimes it's better to use a 'Select' when things are starting to get complicated and a great deal of conditions are needed to be tested for. Let me show you an example of the correct syntax and explain its use.

```
Days.l = 2

Select Days
  Case 0
    Debug "0 Days"
  Case 1
    Debug "1 Day"
  Case 2
    Debug "2 Days"
  Default
    Debug "Over 2 Days"
EndSelect
```

The 'Select' statement starts with the 'Select' keyword, which basically selects an expression or variable to be tested, in this case it is the variable 'Days'. The 'Case' keywords that follow are branches that could potentially be executed should the value of 'Days' be equal to the variable or expression following that particular 'Case' statement. In our example here, if the variable 'Days' has the value '0' then the code immediately following 'Case 0' is executed, if the variable 'Days' has the value '1' then the code immediately following 'Case 1' is executed and so on.

You will notice that in the last place where there would normally be a 'Case' statement, there is another keyword named 'Default'. This is the piece of code that executes if all other 'Case's return false, kind of like the 'Else' within an 'If' statement.

Checking For Multiple Values
'Select' statements can check for lots of different values and can be neatly presented to produce clear concise code. To facilitate this nice and clean approach of testing lots of values, a 'Select' statement can use a few shortcuts when defining the 'Case' statements within. Here is an example:

```
Weight.l = 12

Select Weight
  Case 0
    Debug "No Weight"
  Case 1, 2, 3
    Debug "Light"
```

```
  Case 4 To 15
    Debug "Medium"
  Case 16 To 30
    Debug "Heavy"
  Default
    Debug "Massive"
EndSelect
```

Here you can see shortcuts that can be used to specify a range of cases. Using the 'To' keyword to specify a range or specify several numbers in one 'Case' statement using commas. When specifying ranges using the 'To' keyword, the second number must always be larger than the first. In this example I've used numbers but these can be replaced by expressions or variables for more precise handling of the potential values that the selected variable or expression might have.

Here's another fun example using a 'Select' statement within a console program:

```
If OpenConsole()
  PrintN("1. Official PureBasic Home")
  PrintN("2. Official PureBasic Forums")
  PrintN("3. PureArea.net")
  PrintN("")
  PrintN("Enter a number from 1 To 3 and press Return: ")
  Destination.s = Input()
  Select Destination
    Case "1"
      RunProgram("http://www.purebasic.com")
    Case "2"
      RunProgram("http://forums.purebasic.com")
    Case "3"
      RunProgram("http://www.purearea.net")
  EndSelect
EndIf
End
```

In this example I've used a few new commands that you will not be familiar with but I think this simple program neatly demonstrates one use of the 'Select' statement. These new commands will be explained a little later but I think you can gather what's going on by their descriptive names.

The main thing to notice about this example is that the 'Select' statement is testing the 'Destination' variable. This variable is assigned a String value which is returned from the 'Input()' command after the Return key is pushed. The 'Case' statements are then also defined using Strings to match correctly the variable's value. Any PureBasic type or any type resulting from an expression can be tested using a 'Select' or 'Case' statement.

As a side note, you can also see in this last example that I've used an 'If' statement to test that 'OpenConsole()' returns true and correctly opens a console window.

Loops

To be able continuously to receive and process data you need loops. All programs that use graphical user interfaces employ loops to manage the drawing of the interface and to continuously monitor for input from the user. For example, the PureBasic IDE uses many loops within its code, to monitor for keypresses and mouse clicks, to update displays, etc. Loops are also a great way of processing large amounts of data within arrays or linked lists by iterating through them, one element at a time.

'For' Loops
The first loop I will talk about is probably the most well known and maybe the most used loop of all, it is the 'For' loop. These loops, sometimes called 'For/Next' loops, are a great way of looping through data when you need an incrementing variable available to be used as a counter or as an index for an individual element of a looping array. Here's an example to get things started.

```
For x.l = 1 To 10
  Debug x
Next x
```

In this example we construct a loop using the 'For' keyword. A user defined Long variable must be entered immediately following this keyword, which in this example I've called 'x'. The value assigned to 'x' is the start value of our loop, here I've assigned it the value of '1'. After this variable assignment the 'To' keyword is used to define a range, so I've entered '10' as the upper limit that 'x' should reach during our loop. This completes the beginning of the loop, all we need to do now is specify the end point of the loop. We do this using the line 'Next x'. This last line tells the compiler that after every single step of the loop, move on to the next value of 'x' specified in the range in the first line, then start the loop again.

The code between these two lines is repeated in a loop depending on how many steps there are between the start and end value in the range specified. Once the value of 'x' reaches the upper limit specified after the 'To' keyword, the loop exits and normal program flow is resumed.

You will notice if you run the above example, the Debug Output window shows the different values that 'x' has during the loop. You will see that the loop is repeated ten times as each time the 'x' variable is incremented according to the specified range.

Here's another example of using a loop to easily traverse an array.

```
Dim Names.s(3)

Names(0) = "Gary"
Names(1) = "Sara"
Names(2) = "Stella"
Names(3) = "MiniMunch"

For x.l = 0 To 3
  Debug Names(x)
Next x
```

Because all array values are accessed using indices, and these indices always start from zero, 'For' loops are fantastic for performing operations on all the elements within an array using just a small amount of code. As you can see from the last example, it just takes three lines of code to echo all of the array's element values to the Debug Output window, no matter what size the array. A bigger array just needs a bigger range in the first line of the 'For' loop definition.

'For' loops can also be constructed using expressions too:

```
StartVar.l = 5
StopVar.l = 10

For x = StartVar - 4 To StopVar / 2
  Debug x
Next x
```

and, of course, loops can be nested if you need to process multi-dimensional arrays:

```
Dim Numbers.l(2, 2)

Numbers(0, 0) = 1
Numbers(0, 1) = 2
Numbers(0, 2) = 3
Numbers(1, 0) = 4
Numbers(1, 1) = 5
Numbers(1, 2) = 6
Numbers(2, 0) = 7
Numbers(2, 1) = 8
Numbers(2, 2) = 9

For x = 0 To 2
  For y = 0 To 2
    Debug Numbers(x, y)
  Next y
Next x
```

As long as the counter variables are different names, you can nest as many 'For' loops as you wish. The unique configurability of 'For' loops make them powerful to use and extremely useful for looping code a user defined amount of times.

Until now you've seen how 'For' loops increment the counter variable by '1' on every iteration of the loop but the incremental step can be configured manually using the optional 'Step' keyword. Here is another example:

```
For x.l = 0 To 10 Step 2
  Debug x
Next x
```

You'll notice the 'Step' keyword appears on the first line of the 'For' loop. This keyword can only be used in a 'For' loop and this is the only place in the loop that it can be used. Immediately after the 'Step' keyword you specify the amount that the counter variable should be incremented by on each iteration of the loop. In this case I've used the number '2', this increments the variable 'x' by '2' on every iteration. If you run this example and look at the Debug Output window you will see the values echoed are all multiples of '2'.

'ForEach' Loops

This type of loop is different from all the others in that it only works with linked lists. The syntax is very similar to the 'For' loop except it doesn't need a counter variable setting up. Here is a simple example.

```
NewList Shopping.s()

AddElement(Shopping())
Shopping() = "Bunch of bananas"

AddElement(Shopping())
Shopping() = "Tea bags"

AddElement(Shopping())
Shopping() = "Cheese"

ForEach Shopping()
  Debug Shopping()
Next
```

In this example after the linked list is defined and a few elements added, I use a 'ForEach' loop to echo the list's contents to the Debug Output window. As you can see the syntax is very clear and very simple. The loop starts with the 'ForEach' keyword followed by the linked list name. Then the end of the loop is defined by using the 'Next' keyword. The code that sits between these two lines is the code that's repeated for the length of the linked list. Once the end of the linked list is reached the loop will exit. A 'ForEach' loops works on all type of linked list, even structured linked lists. I will talk more about linked lists a little later on in Chapter 5.

'While' Loops

This particular loop uses an expression to determine wether it should start and how long it should continue. If this expression returns true then the loop will start. After each individual iteration through the loop, the expression is tested again for a true value, if this expression still returns true, the loop continues. If this expression returns false at any time, the loop ends. Look at this example:

```
Monkeys.l = 0

While Monkeys < 10
  Debug Monkeys
  Monkeys + 1
Wend
```

This loop is very simple to construct. It starts with the 'While' keyword, then an expression is used to control the loop, in this case I've used 'Monkeys < 10'. The loop is then completed using the 'Wend' keyword. The initial expression checks to see if the variable 'Monkeys' is below '10', if it is the loop will enter and start. The code within this loop is then repeated until 'Monkeys < 10' returns false. If you look at the output in the Debug Output window you will see that when 'Monkeys' equals '10' the expression returns false (because it is no longer less than '10') and the loop ends.

One thing to keep in mind when using 'While' loops is that if the initial expression returns false then the loop will never be entered and started. This can be demonstrated in this example:

```
Monkeys.l = 20

While Monkeys < 10
  Debug "This code is never executed"
Wend
```

'Repeat' Loops

These types of loops are pretty much the opposite of 'While' loops. 'Repeat' loops begin with the 'Repeat' keyword and end in one of two ways. The first way is using the 'Until' keyword preceding an expression and the second way is using the 'Forever' keyword. I'll fully explain both ways, starting with the 'Until' keyword.

Look at this example:

```
Bananas.l = 0

Repeat
  Debug Bananas
  Bananas + 1
Until Bananas > 10
```

Opposite to 'While' loops, the controlling expression is at the end of the loop and this is evaluated to see if it returns false. If it does, the loop continues, if it returns true, the loop ends. As you can see from the above example, when 'Bananas' value is greater than '10' the loop ends.

Another point to take notice of is that unlike 'While' loops, a 'Repeat' loop always enters and runs at least once before the expression on the end is evaluated. This is demonstrated here:

```
Bananas.l = 20

Repeat
  Debug Bananas
Until Bananas > 10
```

You can see that even thought 'Bananas' is greater than '10' the loop is started and run once before evaluating the expression at the end of the loop. Once this expression is evaluated, 'Bananas' is greater than '10' so the expression returns true and the loop ends.

'Repeat' loops also have an alternative side to them, they can be used with another keyword in order to make fully continuous loops. To construct a continuous loop just use the 'Forever' keyword instead of the 'Until' keyword and an expression, like this:

```
Counter.l = 0

Repeat
  Debug Counter
  Counter + 1
ForEver
```

This is handy if you want to keep a loop going forever or you are not sure what condition is to be met in order to exit it, or you may have multiple conditions that all need to be met in order jump out of the loop. Use the 'Kill Program' menu command (Menu:Debugger->Kill Program) to exit this example.

Manually Stopping Never Ending Loops

Sometimes when you are using loops in your program you may run into the problem of unintended continuous loops. This can cause problems in your programs because these loops can stop everything else from working until they exit. One of the main headaches of unintended continuous loops is that programs containing them are notoriously difficult to quit.

The PureBasic IDE makes this easy for you. If you need to stop the running program manually then just hit the 'Kill Program' button on the IDE toolbar, it's the one that looks like a skull or use the menu command (Menu:Debugger->Kill Program). This not only ends the loop but also quits the whole program straight away.

Controlling Loops Using 'Break' and 'Continue'
At any time all these different types of loop can be controlled by two common keywords. These two keywords are 'Break' and 'Continue'. I'll explain 'Break' first.

If the 'Break' keyword is used anywhere within any type of loop then that loop is immediately exited as soon as this keyword is encountered. In the case of nested loops, there is an optional parameter that can be added to the end of the 'Break' keyword which specifies how many loops to exit out of. Let's have a look at an example of the 'Break' keyword:

```
For x = 1 To 10
  If x = 5
    Break
  EndIf
  Debug x
Next x
```

Here in this 'For' loop I've prematurely broken out of the loop using the 'Break' keyword when 'x' equals '5'. You will notice the loop exits even before '5' is echoed to the Debug Output window. Here is an example of breaking out of nested loops using the optional level parameter of the 'Break' keyword:

```
For x.1 = 1 To 10
  Counter = 0
  Repeat
    If x = 5
      Break 2
    EndIf
    Counter + 1
  Until Counter > 1
  Debug x
Next
```

Here, once 'x' equals '5' then both loops are exited by using the command 'Break 2'.

Next up is the 'Continue' keyword. This enables you at anytime to jump out of the current iteration and continue to the next one inside the current loop. This is more simple than it sounds:

```
For x.1 = 1 To 10
  If x = 5
    Continue
  EndIf
  Debug x
Next
```

Here you can see that when 'x' equals '5' (on the fifth iteration) the 'Continue' keyword is used. This jumps out of the loop and continues from the top at the beginning of the sixth iteration where 'x' now equals '6'. Because of this jump and continuation of the loop, you will notice in the Debug Output window that '5' was never echoed because on that iteration it jumped out of the loop before the 'Debug x' line was executed.

Loops can be used for a variety of things in computer programming, mainly to reduce tedious code and to iterate quickly through vast amounts of data. Hopefully, you should now have an insight to how they can be used.

5

Other Data Structures

In this chapter I'll explain how to create and use other methods for storing and organizing data, such as user defined structures, arrays and linked lists. Data structures such as these are essential for programing applications and games as they allow for easier and faster access to multiple values of related and non-related data. As always, full explanations and multiple examples are given.

Structures

Earlier in Chapter 2, I introduced to you the built-in types, Byte, Character, Word, Long, Quad, Float, Double and String. Using the 'Structure' keyword you are able to define your own structured type and then assign that type to a variable. Creating your own structured variable is handy if you need to group lots of common variable names under one structure name. Confused? Then let's look at an example of a structure that contains several fields:

```
Structure PERSONALDETAILS
  FirstName.s
  LastName.s
  Home.s
EndStructure

Me.PERSONALDETAILS

Me\FirstName = "Gary"
Me\LastName = "Willoughby"
Me\Home = "A House"

Debug "First Name: " + Me\FirstName
Debug "Last Name: " + Me\LastName
Debug "Home: " + Me\Home
```

Here the structure 'PERSONALDETAILS' is created using the 'Structure' keyword. After that the components of the structure are then defined in exactly the same way as defining normal variables. The 'EndStructure' keyword is used to define the end of the new structure. After the structure is declared it is immediately ready for use. We assign this structured type in exactly the same way as we assign any type to a variable, like this:

```
Me.PERSONALDETAILS
```

Here the variable name is 'Me' and its type is 'PERSONALDETAILS'. To assign values to the individual variables (sometimes called fields) within the new 'Me' structured variable, we use the '\' character. If you look at the larger example, the '\' character is also used to retrieve data from the individual fields too, like this:

```
Father.PERSONALDETAILS
Father\FirstName = "Peter"
Debug Father\FirstName
```

Here in this little example, we create a new structured variable called 'Father' with a user defined structured type of 'PERSONALDETAILS'. We assign the value of 'Peter' to the 'FirstName' field within 'Father'. We then echo this value to the Debug Output window.

It might not of hit you yet but structures are incredibly useful things. In applications they can help to define anything from personal records to window coordinates, in games they can be used to help define bullets, spaceships along with all associated values.

Memory Considerations
The size in memory of a structured variable depends on the field variables used within the initial structure definition. In the 'PERSONALDETAILS' structure there are defined three field variables of the String type, each having a size of 4 Bytes (see Fig.3 earlier in Chapter 2 for sizes of String types). So the newly declared variable 'Me' takes up 12 Bytes (3 x 4 Bytes) in memory. We can test this by echoing the output returned by the 'SizeOf()' command.

```
Structure PERSONALDETAILS
  FirstName.s
  LastName.s
  Home.s
EndStructure
Debug SizeOf(PERSONALDETAILS)
```

Here 'SizeOf()' returns the value of '12' which is how many Bytes this structure uses in memory.

The 'SizeOf()' Command

This command returns the size of any structure or defined variable in Bytes. It does not work with arrays, linked lists or interfaces. This command is invaluable for Windows programming as some Win32 API functions need the size of a particular structure or variable as a parameter. Read more about the Windows Application Programming Interface (Win32 API) later in Chapter 13.

Inheriting Fields From Another Structure

Structures can also inherit fields from another structure by using the optional 'Extends' keyword.

```
Structure PERSONALDETAILS
  FirstName.s
  LastName.s
  Home.s
EndStructure

Structure FULLDETAILS Extends PERSONALDETAILS
  Address.s
  Country.s
  ZipCode.s
EndStructure

User.FULLDETAILS

User\FirstName = "John"
User\LastName = "Smith"
User\Home = "A House"
User\Address = "A Street"
User\Country = "UK"
User\ZipCode = "12345"

Debug "Users First Name: " + User\FirstName
Debug "Users Last Name: " + User\LastName
Debug "Users Home: " + User\Home
Debug "Users Address: " + User\Address
Debug "Users Country: " + User\Country
Debug "Users Zip Code: " + User\ZipCode
```

In this example the 'FULLDETAILS' structure is extending the 'PERSONALDETAILS' structure during its creation, inheriting all the fields from the 'PERSONALDETAILS' structure. These fields then appear first in our new structure. We assign this newly created structured type to the variable 'User', then proceed to assign values to all its fields. These are then tested by echoing their values to the Debug Output window.

Structure Unions

Structure unions are a way of conserving memory by forcing groups of variables within a structure to share the same memory address. This is maybe a little too advance to introduce this to you now but I've included it here for completeness. You may want to read Chapter 13 (Pointers) to understand better how unions work. Here is a simple example:

```
Structure UNIONSTRUCTURE
  StructureUnion
    One.l
    Two.l
    Three.l
  EndStructureUnion
EndStructure
```

```
Debug SizeOf(UNIONSTRUCTURE)

UnionVariable.UNIONSTRUCTURE

UnionVariable\One = 123
Debug UnionVariable\One

UnionVariable\Three = 456
Debug UnionVariable\One
```

When we declared the 'UNIONSTRUCTURE' we have used the 'StructureUnion' and 'EndStructureUnion' keywords to encapsulate the variables we want to use the same memory area. When we run this small program, the first debug statement echoes '4' (Bytes) to the Debug Output window. This is because there are three variables inside this structure, that all share the same place in memory so only the size of one Long variable is returned.

Further on in the program we assign the 'UnionVariable' the type of 'UNIONSTRUCTURE' and assign the value of '123' to 'UnionVariable\One', then it's echoed. We then assign a completely new value of '456' to 'UnionVariable\Three' but because this field shares the same place in memory as the other fields, we can access this value using any other field name, in this case we again echo the value of 'UnionVariable\One' to the Debug Output window and it predictably displays the shared value of 'UnionVariable\Three'.

Structures can also contain what are known as Static Arrays but I'll need to explain Arrays before we can apply that knowledge to structures. Arrays and Static Arrays are explained fully in the next section.

Arrays

In PureBasic, An Array can hold a user defined amount of variables of the same data type. Individual variables within the array are accessed by an index using a consecutive range of integers (whole numbers). Arrays can also be defined to contain structured variables instead of the standard PureBasic variable types. This section will teach you all you need to know about arrays in PureBasic.

The 'Dim' Keyword
Arrays in PureBasic are created by using the 'Dim' keyword, like this example:

```
Dim LongArray.l(2)
```

Let me explain this line of code a little more clearly, first we use the 'Dim' keyword to tell the compiler we are about to define an array. Then we give this new array a name, In this case, I've imaginatively called it 'LongArray'. After the name, we then assign the array type in a similar way as variable types via a type suffix. Here I've used the '.l' suffix to define that this is an array whose type is Long. After the type is defined then we have to define how many indices this array is to hold. We use brackets to define the last index number. In the above example we've used a '2' to define the last index, so this actually gives our new array three indices, this is because array indices always start at zero. Once this array has been created, each index contains a Long variable.

This simple array is sometimes referred to as a One Dimensional array because it requires only one index to assign and return all values within it. In this more complete example we define an array and assign values to its indices:

```
Dim LongArray.l(2)

LongArray(0) = 10
LongArray(1) = 25
LongArray(2) = 30

Debug LongArray(0) + LongArray(1)
Debug LongArray(1) * LongArray(2)
Debug LongArray(2) - LongArray(0)
```

After the values are assigned, we then echoed some tests to the Debug Output window using the values stored in the array indices. For example, the first return value to be echoed is from '10 + 25', which are the values stored in indices '0' and '1'. The results of '25 * 30' and '30 - 10' are then echoed too. Array indices can also be expressed using variables or expressions.

```
LastIndex.l = 2
FirstIndex.l = 0
Dim StringArray.s(LastIndex)

StringArray(FirstIndex) = "One is one and all alone"
StringArray(FirstIndex + 1) = "Two, two, the lily-white boys"
StringArray(FirstIndex + 2) = "Three, three, the rivals"

Debug StringArray(FirstIndex)
Debug StringArray(FirstIndex + 1)
Debug StringArray(FirstIndex + 2)
```

Here we've defined an array with three indices each containing a String variable (note the '.s' suffix attached to the array name while using the 'Dim' command). We used the variable 'LastIndex' to assign the last index of the new array. Then we used the variable 'FirstIndex' to assign a String to the first index of the array and in later assignments we use an expression using the addition operator. This same technique (using an expression as an index) is used to return results from the different array indices to the Debug Output window. See Fig.16 for a graphical representation of the above array.

One Dimension String Array

Index	Value
0	One is one and all alone
1	Two, two, the lily-white boys
2	Three, three, the rivals

Fig. 16

Because arrays are neatly ordered into indices, this makes it possible to iterate through them using loops very quickly. Just to wet your appetite, here is an example of an array with a thousand indices having each index assigned a value using a 'For' loop and then each index's value is echoed to the Debug Output window using a second 'For' loop.

```
Dim TestArray.l(999)

For x = 0 To 999
  TestArray(x) = x
Next x

For x = 0 To 999
  Debug TestArray(x)
Next x
```

Run it and take a look at the Debug Output window. As you can see, with arrays it's very fast to set and get even a thousand values.

Multi-dimensional Arrays
The best way of describing multi-dimensional arrays are in terms of tables holding columns and rows. To create multi-dimensional arrays simply specify the number of columns and rows you want the array to have. In the following example, we will create an array called 'Animals' which contains three indices, each of which contain a further three indices.

```
Dim Animals.s(2, 2)
Animals(0, 0) = "Sheep"
Animals(0, 1) = "4 Legs"
Animals(0, 2) = "Baaa"

Animals(1, 0) = "Cat"
Animals(1, 1) = "4 Legs"
Animals(1, 2) = "Meow"

Animals(2, 0) = "Parrot"
Animals(2, 1) = "2 Legs"
Animals(2, 2) = "Screech"

Debug Animals(0, 0) + " has " + Animals(0, 1) + " And says " + Animals(0, 2)
Debug Animals(1, 0) + " has " + Animals(1, 1) + " And says " + Animals(1, 2)
Debug Animals(2, 0) + " has " + Animals(2, 1) + " And says " + Animals(2, 2)
```

After defining the array, we then assign values to its indices. Because the 'Animals' array has two indices from which data is assigned and retrieved it is known as a Two Dimensional array. Two dimensional arrays can easily be understood by representing them in a two dimensional table consisting of rows and columns. Fig.17 shows the 'Animals' array in a similar way that Fig.16 shows a one dimensional array. It shows the rows and columns that can be accessed using two indices required by a two dimensional array.

Two Dimension String Array

Index	0	1	2
0	Sheep	4 Legs	Baaa
1	Cat	4 Legs	Meow
2	Parrot	2 Legs	Screech

Fig. 17

Using Fig.17 as a reference we can see now how easily it is to assign and retrieve values of the various indices. For example, if I want to echo the value of row index '1' and column index '2' to the Debug Output window, we type:

```
Debug Animals(1, 2)
```

This should echo the text 'Meow'. If you wanted to replace an entire row then we can do so like this:

```
Animals(0, 0) = "Tripod"
Animals(0, 1) = "3 Legs"
Animals(0, 2) = "Oo-la"
```

This replaces the Strings 'Sheep', '4 Legs' and 'Baaa' with 'Tripod', '3 Legs' and 'Oo-la' inside row index '0' within the 'Animals' array. Fig.17 now looks like Fig.18, notice the modified first row.

Two Dimension String Array (modified)

Index	0	1	2
0	Tripod	3 Legs	Oo-la
1	Cat	4 Legs	Meow
2	Parrot	2 Legs	Screech

Fig. 18

Another way to explain Multi-dimensional arrays are that they are arrays within arrays. Just think that in each array index is contained another array and you get the idea of multi-dimensional arrays. The number of arrays that are contained within each index of the first dimension is dependent on how the array was first defined.

In this following example, I show how to define one, two, three, four and five dimensional arrays:

```
Dim Animals.s(5)
Dim Animals.s(5, 4)
Dim Animals.s(2, 5, 3)
Dim Animals.s(1, 5, 4, 5)
Dim Animals.s(2, 3, 6, 2, 3)
```

After two dimensions, things start to get a little hard on your head, but if you keep in mind, the array within an array explanation, you should be able to work things out. Even though the maximum number of dimensions that can be assigned to an array is two hundred and fifty five (255), using arrays over two or three dimensions is unusual in everyday programming practices.

Structured Type Arrays

Until now we have seen how to define different arrays using only the standard PureBasic types but we can also 'Dim' an array using a structure. Let's look at a simple example using a one dimensional array:

```
Structure FISH
  Kind.s
  Weight.s
  Color.s
EndStructure

Dim FishInTank.FISH(2)

FishInTank(0)\Kind = "Clown Fish"
FishInTank(0)\Weight = "4 oz."
FishInTank(0)\Color = "Red, White and Black"

FishInTank(1)\Kind = "Box Fish"
FishInTank(1)\Weight = "1 oz."
FishInTank(1)\Color = "Yellow"

FishInTank(2)\Kind = "Sea Horse"
FishInTank(2)\Weight = "2 oz."
FishInTank(2)\Color = "Green"

Debug FishInTank(0)\Kind+" "+FishInTank(0)\Weight+" "+FishInTank(0)\Color
Debug FishInTank(1)\Kind+" "+FishInTank(1)\Weight+" "+FishInTank(1)\Color
Debug FishInTank(2)\Kind+" "+FishInTank(2)\Weight+" "+FishInTank(2)\Color
```

Here after we define the 'FISH' structure we define the array using the 'Dim' keyword and use 'FISH' as the array's type in exactly the same way as we used the '.s' (String) as the 'Animals' array type. I've also used '2' as the last index for this array. To assign values to the fields of each of the array's indices it's incredibly simple. We just amalgamate the syntax of assignment to arrays and structures like this:

```
FishInTank(0)\Kind = "Clown Fish"
```

Let's break this down into easily understandable chunks. First is the name of the array, in this case it is 'FishInTank'. Then comes the current index contained within brackets in this case, index 'o'. Next we use the '\' character to access the field called 'Kind' within the 'FISH' structure which has been assigned to the 'FishInTank' array. We then use the '=' operator to assign a String value to that field. Simple! To retrieve the value we have just assigned, we just use exactly the same syntax but without the assignment part, like this:

```
Debug FishInTank(0)\Kind
```

If we need to assign or retrieve a value from another index we do it like an array:

```
Debug FishInTank(0)\Kind
Debug FishInTank(1)\Kind
Debug FishInTank(2)\Kind
```

This would list the 'Kind' fields of all the indices of the 'FishInTank' array. To assign or retrieve any of the other fields we just use their names:

```
Debug FishInTank(1)\Kind
Debug FishInTank(1)\Weight
Debug FishInTank(1)\Color
```

Here we echo all the different fields to the Debug Output window of index '1'. To make things more understandable refer to Fig.19 for a graphical representation of the 'FishInTank' array.

One Dimension Structured Type Array

Index	'FISH' Structure		
0	*Kind:* Clown Fish	*Weight:* 4 oz.	*Colour:* Red, White and Black
1	*Kind:* Box Fish	*Weight:* 1 oz.	*Colour:* Yellow
2	*Kind:* Sea Horse	*Weight:* 2 oz.	*Colour:* Green

Fig. 19

As with the standard type arrays you can also specify multi-dimensional arrays using a structure as the array type. This gives you access to the unique fields of a structure within every index available inside multi-dimensional arrays. To define a multi-dimensional structured type array we do it in exactly the same way as one dimension structured type array but we just add more dimensions.

Here is an example of how to define a two dimensional structured type array:

```
Structure FISH
  Kind.s
  Weight.s
  Color.s
EndStructure

Dim FishInTank.FISH(2, 2)
...
```

I'll not type anymore code out regarding this two dimensional array because it will be far too long. Instead refer to Fig.20 for a fictional two dimensional structured type array.

Two Dimension Structured Type Array

Index	0	1	2
0	Kind: Clown Fish Weight: 4 oz. Colour: Red, White and Black	Kind: Box Fish Weight: 1 oz. Colour: Yellow	Kind: Sea Horse Weight: 2 oz. Colour: Green
1	Kind: Parrot Fish Weight: 5 oz. Colour: Red	Kind: Angel Fish Weight: 4 oz. Colour: Orange	Kind: Shrimp Weight: 1 oz. Colour: Pink
2	Kind: Gold Fish Weight: 2 oz. Colour: Orange	Kind: Lion Fish Weight: 8 oz. Colour: Black and White	Kind: Shark Weight: 1 lb. Colour: Grey

Fig. 20

To retrieve a value from this kind of array we need to supply two indices and a field name such as this:

```
Debug FishInTank(1, 1)\Kind
```

which would echo the text 'Angel Fish' to the Debug Output window. If we wanted to change this or other values we use the same method to access this area in the array:

```
FishInTank(1, 1)\Kind = "Devil Fish"
FishInTank(1, 1)\Weight = "6 oz."
FishInTank(1, 1)\Color = "Dark Red"
```

This would change all fields of the 'FISH' structure located in the middle area in the array located at indices '1, 1'. This is shown in Fig.21.

As you can see these types of arrays are extremely handy if a little complex (especially when you start going beyond three dimensions), but to know how they work will give you an advantage later on in your programming.

Two Dimension Structured Type Array (Modified)

Index	0	1	2
0	*Kind:* Clown Fish *Weight:* 4 oz. *Colour:* Red, White and Black	*Kind:* Box Fish *Weight:* 1 oz. *Colour:* Yellow	*Kind:* Sea Horse *Weight:* 2 oz. *Colour:* Green
1	*Kind:* Parrot Fish *Weight:* 5 oz. *Colour:* Red	*Kind:* Devil Fish *Weight:* 6 oz. *Colour:* Dark Red	*Kind:* Shrimp *Weight:* 1 oz. *Colour:* Pink
2	*Kind:* Gold Fish *Weight:* 2 oz. *Colour:* Orange	*Kind:* Lion Fish *Weight:* 8 oz. *Colour:* Black and White	*Kind:* Shark *Weight:* 1 lb. *Colour:* Grey

Fig. 21

You will probably only use one dimensional structured type arrays in your programs for now but to know how multi-dimensional structured type arrays work will give you a good understanding of more advanced code.

Redefining Arrays Once Created

Standard arrays in PureBasic are not completely static, meaning they can be redefined in two different ways. The first way is to use the 'Dim' command again which redefines the array but in the process destroys all previous data assigned to it. The second way is to use the 'ReDim' command which redefines the array but keeps previous data intact. Here are examples showing both these behaviors. First let's look at redefining an array with the 'Dim' command:

```
Dim Dogs.s(2)

Dogs(0) = "Jack Russell"
Dogs(1) = "Alaskan Husky"
Dogs(2) = "Border Collie"

Debug Dogs(0)
Debug Dogs(1)
Debug Dogs(2)

Dim Dogs.s(2)

Debug Dogs(0)
Debug Dogs(1)
Debug Dogs(2)
```

Here after the initial array creation and assignment of data I've used the 'Dim' command again to redefine the array with the same amount of indices as before. After the second definition, you will notice that the 'Debug' commands return nothing from the newly defined array. This is because all data has been destroyed during the redefinition. This data destruction can have a good use though. For example, if I needed to free up the memory used by an array, I could just redefine it with zero (0) as the maximum index which would free all memory associated with it. When redefining arrays like this you must always redefine them using the same type or an error will be raised.

Here is an example of how to keep the data intact while redefining an array using the 'ReDim' command:

```
Dim Dogs.s(2)

Dogs(0) = "Jack Russell"
Dogs(1) = "Alaskan Husky"
Dogs(2) = "Border Collie"

For x.l = 0 To 2
  Debug Dogs(x)
Next x

Debug ""

ReDim Dogs.s(4)

Dogs(3) = "Yorkshire Terrier"
Dogs(4) = "Greyhound"

For x.l = 0 To 4
  Debug Dogs(x)
Next x
```

Here I've used the 'ReDim' command to redefine the array but this time as well as redefining it, I've given it two extra indices. The extra two indices ('3' and '4') are assigned data and then the whole array has its data echoed to the Debug Output window. Notice that the data from the initial creation is not lost. You must be aware though, if I used the 'ReDim' command to redefine an array with fewer indices than it previously had then of course the data within the discarded indices are lost. Also if you are redefining a multi-dimensional array using the 'ReDim' command then only the last dimension can be resized. This is standard behavior for a Basic command such as this.

Rules For Using Arrays
Even though arrays are very flexible they have a few rules to take into account when using them. These rules should be observed when using arrays in your programs.

1). If an array is re-defined using the 'Dim' command, its previous data is lost.
2). If an array is re-defined using the 'ReDim' command, its previous data is kept.
3). Arrays can only be made up of one type of variable (a structured or a standard variable type).
4). Arrays can be Global, Protected, Static and Shared. See Chapter 6 (Program Scope).
5). The size of an array is only limited by the current machine's installed RAM.
6). Multi-dimensional arrays can have 255 dimensions.
7). Arrays can be dynamically defined, using a variable or an expression to define dimension size.
8). When defining dimension size, you define the last index number (all indices start at '0').
9). Dimensions can be of different sizes in multi-dimensional arrays.

Static Arrays Within Structures

Static arrays within structures are a little bit different from the normal arrays that have been previously described. Static arrays in their very nature are static and therefore cannot be modified once they have been defined. These types of arrays also only exist within structures.

Static arrays also have a different set of rules to take into account when using them:

1). Once a static array is defined its internal structure cannot be modified.
2). Static arrays (like structures) cannot be redefined.
3). They can only be made up of one type of variable (a structured or a standard variable type).
4). The size of an array is only limited by the current machine's installed RAM.
5). Static arrays can only have one dimension.
6). They can be dynamically defined, using a variable or an expression to define dimension size.
7). When defining dimension size, you define the amount of indices it is to contain, not the last index.
8). Static arrays can only be accessed through the structure variable within which they are defined.

So now that I've given you the main rules, let me give you an example of how they are used:

```
Structure FAMILY
  Father.s
  Mother.s
  Children.s[ 2]
  Surname.s
EndStructure

Family.FAMILY

Family\Father = "Peter"
Family\Mother = "Sarah"
Family\Children[ 0] = "John"
Family\Children[ 1] = "Jane"
Family\Surname = "Smith"

Debug "Family Members:"
Debug Family\Father + " " + Family\Surname
Debug Family\Mother + " " + Family\Surname
Debug Family\Children[ 0] + " " + Family\Surname
Debug Family\Children[ 1] + " " + Family\Surname
```

Here in this example, the 'FAMILY' structure has a field called 'Children' which is a static String array. When we defined this array, we used the number '2'. This defines this static array will hold two indices. This behavior is completely different to standard arrays, with which you define the last index on creation. In our new static array we now have two indices, '0' and '1', further on in the example I assign values to all the fields in the 'Family' structured variable, including the two indices in the 'Children' static array. You will notice that static arrays have a slightly different syntax for assigning and retrieving data, they use square brackets instead of the usual curved ones.

Assigning data to a static String array (using square brackets):

```
Family\Children[0] = "John"
```

Assigning data to a standard Long array (using curved brackets):

```
LongArray(0) = 10
```

You will also notice that you do not need to use a keyword such as 'Dim' when you define a static array. You just add square brackets to the end of a field within a structure. Within the square brackets you define how many indices you wish to give to this newly created static array. In the 'FAMILY' structure above, we use the String type to create a static array but you can use any PureBasic built-in type or even use another structure!

Let's look at another simple example:

```
Structure EMPLOYEES
  EmployeeName.s
  EmployeeClockNumber.l
  EmployeeAddress.s
  EmployeeContactNumbers.l[2]
EndStructure

Dim Company.EMPLOYEES(9)

Company(0)\EmployeeName = "Bruce Dickinson"
Company(0)\EmployeeClockNumber = 666
Company(0)\EmployeeAddress = "22 Acacia Avenue"
Company(0)\EmployeeContactNumbers[0] = 0776032666
Company(0)\EmployeeContactNumbers[1] = 0205467746

Company(1)\EmployeeName = "Adrian Smith"
Company(1)\EmployeeClockNumber = 1158
...
```

Here I create a user defined structure called 'EMPLOYEES' to describe a small company employee record and then create a standard array to contain ten of these records (remember that in a standard array you define the last index and these indices start at '0'). Inside the 'EMPLOYEES' structure I've used a Long static array to store two contact phone numbers. I've then started to define the individual employee records starting with 'Company(0)\...' and then onto 'Company(1)\...', etc. I don't actually complete this example due to not wanting to waffle on, but you can see where I'm going with it and how everything works.

Linked Lists

Linked Lists are similar to arrays in that they are able to refer to lots of data using one name. They are however different to arrays in that they don't use an index to assign and retrieve data.

These lists are like a book where you can flip through the data from start to finish or just turn to a page within and read the data from there. Linked lists are also totally dynamic, meaning that they can grow or shrink depending on how much data you need them to hold. When increasing the size of a linked list you won't harm or change any of the other data held within it and you can safely add elements to the list in any position necessary.

Linked lists are a great way of storing and organizing data of an unknown length and can be sorted in several ways. There is also a built-in 'Linked List' library which provides functions to perform element additions, deletions and element swapping. Inside the built-in 'Sort' library there are also two functions that are used purely for sorting linked lists, I shall mention these later. A general overview and an introduction to PureBasic's built-in commands is given later in Chapter 7.

The 'NewList' Keyword

Linked Lists in PureBasic are created by using the 'NewList' keyword as in this example:

```
NewList Fruit.s()
```

Defining a linked list is very similar to defining an array using the 'Dim' command. First we use the 'NewList' keyword to tell the compiler we are about to define a linked list. Next, we define a name for the new list, in this case we've called it 'Fruit'. After a name has been given we then define its type, which again in this case is the String type. Brackets are then used to finish the list definition. You will notice in this small example that there are no indices defined within the brackets. This is because linked lists don't need them, they are dynamic and will grow as you add elements. Let's look at how we add elements to our new list, here is a more complete example:

```
NewList Fruit.s()

AddElement(Fruit())
Fruit() = "Banana"

AddElement(Fruit())
Fruit() = "Apple"
```

Because linked lists don't have any indices it may at first seem a little strange using them because you might not know where in the list you are. In the above example, I've added two new elements to the 'Fruit()' list. To do this I used the 'AddElement()' function of the built-in Linked List library. When you add a new element using this function, not only does it automatically define a new element but it also makes the linked list name point to that newly created, empty element. So we just use its name to assign a piece of data to the list, notice we still use the brackets:

```
Fruit() = "Banana"
```

When we add another element using the 'AddElement()' function then exactly the same process takes place. First the new element is created, then the linked list name again points to the newly created empty element. So then we add data to the new element in exactly the same way:

```
Fruit() = "Apple"
```

A Note About Using The Word 'Point'

In this introduction and explanation of Linked Lists I've used the word 'point' a lot. When I'm using it here it must not be confused with the computer science term 'point' or 'pointers'. The computer science term means to point to a particular area in memory or in the case of a 'pointer', a variable that holds a memory address. When I use it here, especially when I say the Linked List name points to the current element, I use it in a descriptive sense and not literally pointing to the area in memory that this element uses. For a further explanation of pointers (in the computer science sense) refer to Chapter 13 (Pointers).

You would think that this is wrong because we are assigning the text 'Apple' to the same name as we assigned the text 'Banana'. Because we added a new element, the linked list name 'Fruit()' will point to the new element within the list. We can also check how many elements are in our list at any time using the built-in 'CountList()' function, like this:

```
Debug CountList(Fruit())
```

If we executed the above code then the number of elements contained within the 'Fruit()' list will be echoed to the Debug Output window. In this case it would be '2'.

Let's add a few more elements to this list and then echo all of the element values to the Debug Output window. Here is a full example again:

```
NewList Fruit.s()

AddElement(Fruit())
Fruit() = "Banana"

AddElement(Fruit())
Fruit() = "Apple"

AddElement(Fruit())
Fruit() = "Pear"

AddElement(Fruit())
Fruit() = "Orange"

ForEach Fruit()
  Debug Fruit()
Next
```

In this larger example, we create a new linked list called 'Fruits()' and within it we create four elements and assign them individual values. We then loop through this list using a 'ForEach' loop and echo all of the element's values to the Debug Output window. The 'ForEach' keyword is used to define a loop which is only used for linked lists.

Fig.22 gives a brief overview of the linked list commands available in the built-in 'Linked List' library. This diagram is not a complete reference but is included here as a brief guide to see which command to use when the need arises. The more advanced commands can be found in the PureBasic helpfile.

The Built-in Linked List Library

Function	Description
`AddElement(List())`	Adds an element to the linked list.
`ClearList(List())`	Clears the list of all elements.
`CountList(List())`	Counts the elements inside a list.
`DeleteElement(List())`	Deletes the current element within the list
`FirstElement(List())`	Go to the first element in the list.
`InsertElement(List())`	Insert another element in the list before the current element, or at the start of the list if the list is empty.
`LastElement(List())`	Go to the last element in the list.
`ListIndex(List())`	Return the current element's position within the list. (Element positions start at '0').
`NextElement(List())`	Go to the next element within the list.
`PreviousElement(List())`	Go to the previous element within the list.
`ResetList(List())`	Reset the list's position to '0' and make the first element the current element.
`SelectElement(List(), Position)`	Make the current element the one specified by the '*Position*' parameter.

Fig. 22

Structured Linked Lists

Now that I have explained standard linked lists, let's move onto structured linked lists. These are very similar to structured type arrays in that they are defined with a structure instead of a built-in variable type. You can then effectively have a dynamically resizing linked list masquerading as a structured type array that grows and shrinks depending on what information you have to store. Let's take a look at a previous example but this time re-code it to use a structured linked list.

```
Structure FISH
  Kind.s
  Weight.s
  Color.s
EndStructure

NewList FishInTank.FISH()
```

```
AddElement(FishInTank())
FishInTank()\Kind = "Clown Fish"
FishInTank()\Weight = "4 oz."
FishInTank()\Color = "Red, White and Black"

AddElement(FishInTank())
FishInTank()\Kind = "Box Fish"
FishInTank()\Weight = "1 oz."
FishInTank()\Color = "Yellow"

AddElement(FishInTank())
FishInTank()\Kind = "Sea Horse"
FishInTank()\Weight = "2 oz."
FishInTank()\Color = "Green"

ForEach FishInTank()
  Debug FishInTank()\Kind+" "+FishInTank()\Weight+" "+FishInTank()\Color
Next
```

You can see from this example that after you create a list it is then very similar to a structured type array to assign and retrieve data. The main difference here though is that array style indices are not used. Remember that when you use the 'AddElement(FishInTank())' command you create a new element using the structure from the initial definition. This command then moves the current position of the list to this newly created element. It is then safe to assign data to the new structured element like this:

```
FishInTank()\Kind = "Clown Fish"
FishInTank()\Weight = "4 oz."
FishInTank()\Color = "Red, White and Black"
```

Because the name 'FishInTank()' now points to your new element there is no need to use an index. To access the fields inside this structured element you again use the '\' character. At the end of the example another 'ForEach' loop is used to quickly and efficiently echo the data to the Debug Output window.

Pros And Cons Of Linked Lists?
Linked lists are great for storing data when you don't know how much of it there is. For example, in the past I've written a program to track household expenses, and used a structured linked list to hold the details of these expenses. Using a linked list rather than an array made it easier to add, delete and sort the data.

While writing this program I thought that I must make this program flexible to handle new expenses when they occur and to be able to delete old ones, just in-case I buy a new car and/or pay off a loan, etc. This is handled very nicely by linked lists. When I need to add an entry I use the 'AddElement()' function and when I need to delete an entry I use the 'DeleteElement()' function. After the adding and deleting is done within the list, I then transfer all this data into a nice Graphical User Interface (GUI) for the user to see and interact with. I will give talk more extensively about GUIs in Chapter 9.

Linked lists are more flexible than arrays in that they can grow and shrink in size more easily but arrays will always use less RAM to store the same amount of data than linked lists. This is because arrays are continuous areas of memory which only use the standard amount of RAM per type for each index. Linked lists are different in the way that each element uses roughly three times the amount of RAM for its particular type. This is because linked lists are not in the same continuous piece of memory and need to store information on where to find the other elements within RAM. This is something to keep in mind when dealing with huge amounts of data as your memory requirements could be triple if you use linked lists.

Sorting Arrays And Linked Lists

Arrays and linked lists are great for storing all sorts of data and these data structures can easily be traversed to quickly retrieve that data. Sometimes though you may need to reorganize the data contained within an array or linked list, so it is sorted alphabetically or numerically. Here are a few examples of how to use the commands of the 'Sort' library (Helpfile:Reference Manual->General Libraries->Sort) to sort arrays and linked lists.

Sorting A Standard Array
Sorting a standard array is extremely simple. First of all you need an array pre-filled with values then use the 'SortArray()' command to sort it. Here is the syntax example:

```
SortArray(Array(), Options [ , Start, End] )
```

The first parameter is the array to be sorted, notice the curved brackets after the array name, these are required to correctly pass an array as a parameter. The second parameter is an option, to specify how you would like the array to be sorted. Here are the options for the second parameter:

'0' : Sort the array in ascending order being case sensitive.
'1' : Sort the array in descending order being case sensitive.
'2' : Sort the array in ascending order without being case sensitive ('A' is the same as 'a').
'3' : Sort the array in descending order without being case sensitive ('A' is the same as 'a').

The square brackets around the last two parameters indicate that these are optional and don't need to be specified when using this command. These last two parameters are used to specify an array position range to perform the sort within.

Using the above information, we can sort a full array in ascending order and being case sensitive, using the command like this:

```
Dim Fruit.s(3)

Fruit(0)  =  "Banana"
Fruit(1)  =  "Apple"
Fruit(2)  =  "Pear"
Fruit(3)  =  "Orange"
SortArray(Fruit(), 0)
```

```
For x.l = 0 To 3
  Debug Fruit(x)
Next x
```

Sorting A Structured Array

This is slightly more complicated as it uses a slightly more complicated sort command; 'SortStructuredArray()'. Here is the syntax example:

```
SortStructuredArray(Array(), Options, Offset, Type [, Start, End] )
```

The first parameter is the array name complete with brackets. The second is the sort options, these are exactly the same as the 'SortArray()' command. The third parameter is an offset (a position within the originating structure) of the field you would like to sort by. This is retrieved using the 'OffsetOf()' command. The 'OffsetOf()' command returns the number of Bytes that a particular variable field is offset, from the beginning of a structure. The forth parameter defines what type of variable is found at the previously passed offset. You can use built-in constants for the forth parameter to describe what type of variable you are sorting by, these are:

'#PB_Sort_Byte'   : The field in the structure to sort by, is a Byte (.b)
'#PB_Sort_Character'   : The field in the structure to sort by, is a Character (.c)
'#PB_Sort_Word'   : The field in the structure to sort by, is a Word (.w)
'#PB_Sort_Long'   : The field in the structure to sort by, is a Long (.l)
'#PB_Sort_Quad'   : The field in the structure to sort by, is a Quad (.q)
'#PB_Sort_Float'   : The field in the structure to sort by, is a Float (.f)
'#PB_Sort_Double'   : The field in the structure to sort by, is a Double (.d)
'#PB_Sort_String'   : The field in the structure to sort by, is a String (.s or $)

The last two parameters in this command are optional and don't need to be specified when using this command. These are used to specify an array position range to perform the sort within. Using the above information, we can sort a full structured array in ascending order and sorting by the 'Range' field, like this:

```
Structure WEAPON
  Name.s
  Range.l
EndStructure

Dim Weapons.WEAPON(2)

Weapons(0)\Name = "Phased Plasma Rifle"
Weapons(0)\Range = 40

Weapons(1)\Name = "SVD-Dragunov Sniper Rifle"
Weapons(1)\Range = 3800

Weapons(2)\Name = "HK-MP5 Sub-Machine Gun"
Weapons(2)\Range = 300
```

```
SortStructuredArray(Weapons(), 0, OffsetOf(WEAPON\Range), #PB_Sort_Long)

For x.l = 0 To 2
  Debug Weapons(x)\Name + " : " + Str(Weapons(x)\Range)
Next x
```

In this example, I've chosen the 'Range' field to sort the structured array by, so in the sort command I've defined this using the offset 'OffsetOf(WEAPON\Range)' and telling the sort command it is a Long type variable field by using the '#PB_Sort_Long' constant.

Sorting A Standard Linked List

Sorting a standard linked list is extremely simple. First of all you need a linked list pre-filled with values then use the 'SortList()' command to sort it. Here is the syntax example:

```
SortList(ListName(), Options [, Start, End])
```

The first parameter is the linked list to be sorted, notice the curved brackets after the list's name, these are required to correctly pass the linked list as a parameter. The second is the sort options, these are exactly the same as the 'SortArray()' command. The last two parameters are used to specify a linked list position range to perform the sort within.

Using the above information, we can sort a full linked list in ascending order and being case sensitive, using the sort command like this:

```
NewList Fruit.s()

AddElement(Fruit())
Fruit() = "Banana"

AddElement(Fruit())
Fruit() = "Apple"

AddElement(Fruit())
Fruit() = "Orange"

SortList(Fruit(), 0)

ForEach Fruit()
  Debug Fruit()
Next
```

Sorting A Structured Linked List

Sorting a structured linked list is slightly more complicated as it uses a slightly more complicated sort command; 'SortStructuredList()'. Here is this command's syntax example:

```
SortStructuredList(List(), Options, Offset, Type [, Start, End])
```

The first parameter is the linked list name complete with brackets. The second is the sort options, which are exactly the same as the 'SortArray()' command. The third parameter is an offset (a position within the originating structure) of the field you would like to sort by. This is retrieved using the 'OffsetOf()' command. The forth parameter defines what type of variable is found at the previously passed offset. You can use built-in constants for the forth parameter to describe what type of variable you are sorting by, these are exactly the same as the 'SortStructuredArray()' command. The last two parameters are used to specify a linked list position range to perform the sort within.

Using the above information, we can sort a full structured linked list in ascending order and being case sensitive, using the sort command like this:

```
Structure GIRL
  Name.s
  Weight.s
EndStructure

NewList Girls.GIRL()

AddElement(Girls())
Girls()\Name = "Mia"
Girls()\Weight = "8.5 Stone"

AddElement(Girls())
Girls()\Name = "Big Rosie"
Girls()\Weight = "19 stone"

AddElement(Girls())
Girls()\Name = "Sara"
Girls()\Weight = "10 Stone"

SortStructuredList(Girls(), 0, OffsetOf(GIRL\Name), #PB_Sort_String)

ForEach Girls()
  Debug Girls()\Name + " : " + Girls()\Weight
Next
```

In this example, I've chosen the 'Name' field to sort this structured linked list by, so in the sort command I've defined this using the offset 'OffsetOf(GIRL\Name)' and telling the commands it's a String by using the '#PB_Sort_String' constant.

Sorting Made Easy
All the previous sorting examples can be used in the same way to sort all numeric fields as well as Strings, it's just a case of choosing the right sorting option when using the different sort commands. Sorting arrays and linked lists, wether created using a structure or not is just a case of using the right options and offsets. Try some examples yourself to practice sorting using these commands.

6

Procedures And Subroutines

In this chapter I'll talk about Procedures and Subroutines. Procedures are an essential part of any programming language and provide a way of neatly structuring code and enabling code re-use. PureBasic is considered a structured programming language and procedures provide the means to create the structure of a program. I will also mention subroutines in this chapter but these are not a major feature in many programming languages. Because they play a part in PureBasic they are mentioned here for the sake of completeness.

Why Use Procedures Or Subroutines?

In theory, I guess you never need to use procedures or subroutines. You could just write a very big piece of code, but this would get very confusing, very quickly and I think you would repeat yourself many times within this jumbled code. Procedures and subroutines provide ways of calling separate pieces of code at any time during your main code. These separate pieces of code can be written to do anything. For example, you could call a procedure to play a sound or update a display or even call one that contains a fully functional program.

Using procedures and subroutines are good ways of keeping your code neat and tidy and providing it with a clear structure. Well structured code is always better for reading later on, especially if you revisit your code for tweaking, or you are working in a team and many people are likely to work on the same file.

Subroutines

Subroutines are not used very often in PureBasic and some consider them poor coding style but sometimes they can be useful if you want to quickly call some code. Subroutines provide a way of jumping to another piece of code further down in your source code and then returning to the point of the jump after executing it. In order to jump to a separate piece of code using this method you need to specify a point to jump to. This jump destination in your code is specified using a subroutine label.

To specify a subroutine label in your code you can use any name you like but you must adhere to the same naming guidelines as set out for variables, except that instead of using a suffix to define a label, you use a colon, like this:

```
Label:
```

This subroutine label can be jumped to at any point in your code by using this command:

```
Gosub Label
```

Notice in the 'Gosub' command that we don't use a colon when we specify what subroutine label to jump to. After the destination label, you enter normal PureBasic code that you wish this subroutine to execute. After this code you must then specify that you want to jump back to the main code by using this command:

```
Return
```

Here is a brief example demonstrating the use of a subroutine:

```
a.l = 10

Debug a
Gosub Calculation
Debug a
End

Calculation:
  a = a * 5 + 5
Return
```

In this example, we give the variable 'a' the value of '10' and echo it to the Debug Output window. We then use the 'Gosub' keyword to jump to the 'Calculation' label. You can tell it's a label by the colon after its name and you will probably notice that the IDE colors labels differently too. After we have jumped to this label a small calculation is performed on the 'a' variable and we return to the main code using the 'Return' keyword. When returning to the main code, we return to the next line just after the original 'Gosub' command. In this case we return to the 'Debug a' line, which echoes the value of 'a' to the Debug Output window again. This value has now changed according to the calculation performed in the subroutine.

A Note Regarding The Position Of Subroutines In Your Code

One important thing I need to point out here is that if you include subroutines to be used in your program, they must always be after an 'End' keyword. The 'End' keyword not only immediately terminates a program when it's executed but also defines the end point of a program during compilation. All subroutines must appear after this point or your program could function incorrectly.

Jumping From A Subroutine

This is generally considered very bad coding practice but as I'm talking about subroutines, I may as well follow the style of the rest of this book and describe them in their entirety, as well as mentioning the correct syntax to be able to do it.

Because all subroutines must contain a 'Return' keyword to jump back into your main code, a subroutine must be prematurely returned in order to leave it correctly if you need to jump out at any time. This is achieved by using the 'FakeReturn' and 'Goto' keywords. Here's an example:

```
a.l = 10

Debug a
Gosub Calculation
Debug a
End

RunAgain:
a.l = 20
Debug a
Gosub Calculation
Debug a
End

Calculation:
  If a = 10
    FakeReturn
    Goto RunAgain
  Else
    a = a * 5 + 5
  EndIf
Return
```

As you can see from this small example, things have started to get complicated and the code jumps around all over the place, as I said before this is bad coding style and makes very ugly code.

This example is pretty straightforward if you follow it carefully. You can see the in the 'Calculation' subroutine, that when we need to jump out using the 'Goto' command we have to use 'FakeReturn' before it. We jump to another label (subroutine) called 'RunAgain' which references another almost self-contained program complete with another 'End' keyword, which really is not ideal.

I hope these examples give you an overview of subroutines and how to jump around programs, but I do hope you don't abuse these practices and don't adopt them as a regular way of coding. I feel you can structure code a lot better using procedures.

Procedure Basics

The term 'Structured Programming' is a term that clearly defines PureBasic and the ethos behind its creation. PureBasic can be described as a 'Procedural' and 'Structured' programming language. The architecture behind structured programming is provided by Procedures. They are quite literally the structure in structured programming.

Procedures (sometimes called 'Functions' in other languages) are the most important piece of functionality that PureBasic provides. In their most basic form they are just a holder for a piece of code that can be called (run) at any time in your program, very similar to subroutines. They can be called as many times as you like just like subroutines and they can hold any PureBasic code you like. Unlike subroutines however, procedures can be given multiple starting parameters and they can even return one value of any built-in type.

Let's start with a simple procedure example.

```
Procedure NurseryRhyme()
  Debug "Mary had a little lamb, its fleece was white as snow."
  Debug "And everywhere that Mary went, that lamb was sure to go."
EndProcedure

NurseryRhyme()
```

In order to use a procedure in your code you have to define it first. Here I've defined a procedure called 'NurseryRhyme' using the 'Procedure' keyword. Code is then entered after this line which the procedure is to contain. The end of the procedure is then defined using the 'EndProcedure' keyword. We can call this piece of code contained within this procedure at any time by just using its name, like this:

```
NurseryRhyme()
```

Before we move on, I need to point out a few things in this example that need further explanation. First, you may of noticed that there are a mysterious set of brackets after the procedure name. These are used to hold any parameters that need to be passed to the procedure. Even if you are not passing any parameters, like in this example, you still need to include the brackets. Also, when you call the procedure, you always need to include the brackets as part of the procedure call, parameters or no parameters. I will explain passing of parameters to a procedure later on in this chapter.

One more thing to point out is that the procedure name, e.g. 'NurseryRhyme()' must not contain any spaces and should adhere to the same naming guidelines as set out for variables.

If you run the above example, you should see in the Debug Output window the nursery rhyme as coded in the 'NurseryRhyme()' procedure. If you want to repeat this procedure code at any time in this small example, just call it over and over again using its name.

```
Procedure NurseryRhyme()
  Debug "Mary had a little lamb, its fleece was white as snow."
  Debug "And everywhere that Mary went, that lamb was sure to go."
EndProcedure

For x.l = 1 To 5
  NurseryRhyme()
Next x
```

Procedures can be called from anywhere in programs, as in the above example, where I've called the 'NurseryRhyme()' procedure from a loop. Procedures can also be called from other procedures too.

```
Procedure NurseryRhyme2()
  Debug "And everywhere that Mary went, that lamb was sure to go."
EndProcedure

Procedure NurseryRhyme1()
  Debug "Mary had a little lamb, its fleece was white as snow."
  NurseryRhyme2()
EndProcedure

NurseryRhyme1()
```

Here, you can see that 'NurseryRhyme1()' contains a call to 'NurseryRhyme2()'.

A Note Regarding The Position Of Procedures In Your Code
The above example neatly demonstrates why the position of procedures in your code matters. You will notice that I've coded 'NurseryRhyme2()' first, above 'NurseryRhyme1()'. This was intentional and was necessary because of the fact that you must always define a procedure before calling it. Because 'NurseryRhyme1()' calls 'NurseryRhyme2()', the latter had to be defined first. The PureBasic compiler is known as a 'One Pass' compiler, which reads the source code from the top to the bottom. It will raise an error if it encounters a procedure call and no procedure has yet been defined. This simple example also demonstrates why procedures are defined at the top of most source codes.

As with most things in life though there is an exception to this rule. You can use the 'Declare' keyword to alter the position of procedure definitions in your code. The 'Declare' keyword doesn't define a procedure, it merely lets the compiler know what procedures it will be asked to call. This allows any procedures to be defined later on in the source code. Here's an example:

```
Declare NurseryRhyme1()
Declare NurseryRhyme2()

NurseryRhyme1()

Procedure NurseryRhyme1()
  Debug "Mary had a little lamb, its fleece was white as snow."
  NurseryRhyme2()
EndProcedure
```

```
Procedure NurseryRhyme2()
  Debug "And everywhere that Mary went, that lamb was sure to go."
EndProcedure
```

When using the 'Declare' keyword, you just define the first line of the procedure, identically as you would when using the 'Procedure' keyword. You are then free to call this procedure at any time after this declaration. Because this is purely a declaration and not a definition, you must also define the procedure as normal somewhere else in your code. The procedure can be defined anywhere now, even at the end of your source code, instead of the top.

If you look at the above example, you can see I've used two declarations using the 'Declare' keyword. After that I'm then free to call the 'NurseryRhyme1()' procedure. The actual procedure definitions are at the end of the code.

Program Scope

When using procedures it is also very important to understand the different scopes that a program can contain. This term refers to what scope any given variable, array or linked list is available to be used in. Let me start explaining this using a simple example using a variable.

```
a.l = 10

Procedure DisplayValue()
  Debug a
EndProcedure

DisplayValue()
```

Here I've defined a Long type variable called 'a' and assigned to it the numeric value of '10'. I've also defined a procedure called 'DisplayValue()' and in this procedure I've written one line of code to echo the value of 'a'. The last line of this example calls the procedure. Now, if you run this example you would expect that the value of 'a' (which is '10') to be echoed to the Debug Output window but this is not the case. You will notice that the value of '0' is echoed instead. This is due to program scope.

Let me break down this example even more and explain exactly what is happening. The first thing to remember when using variables in PureBasic is that they are by default Local in scope. This means that in the above example when the first variable definition is made 'a.l = 10' this variable is local to the scope in which it is defined, in this case, local to the main source code. Unless this variable is made Global then no procedure will be able to see it or use it.

In the 'DisplayValue()' procedure we echo the value of 'a', but this variable 'a' is not the same as the one outside the procedure. They have the same name but are not the same variable. The one inside the procedure is local to the procedure so neither variable is accessible to one another.

This can get very confusing especially if both local variables share the same name as in this little example, but I think I've neatly demonstrated local scope well.

As I said before, if the original variable was made to be a global variable, then all procedures can see it and use it, let me demonstrate how this is done.

```
Global a.l = 10

Procedure DisplayValue()
  Debug a
EndProcedure

DisplayValue()
```

Here you will notice the only change I've made is that I've used the 'Global' keyword before the variable definition. This now defines the 'a' variable as global and all procedures can now see and use this variable. In the Debug Output window you will now see the correct value of '10' echoed.

Conversely, if we define variables within a procedure they too are considered local to that procedure. Take a look at this:

```
Procedure DisplayValue()
  a.l = 10
EndProcedure

DisplayValue()

Debug a
```

As expected the last line 'Debug a' echoes the value '0' to the Debug Output window. If we want to see and use the 'a' variable outside the defining procedure, we need to make it global. Like this:

```
Procedure DisplayValue()
  Global a.l = 10
EndProcedure

DisplayValue()

Debug a
```

Reading through these last few examples you may be thinking why not make all variables global? This might make sense to some people but when programs reach a larger scale, things can get muddled and confusing if all variables are global. You may also find that you'll start to run out of useful variable names. Using different scopes within your program also enables you to use temporary variable names within procedures for calculations or loops, safe in the knowledge that they won't effect any variables outside. Some programmers strive to use as little global variables as possible as this makes debugging a program much less effort. Suspect values and variables can be narrowed down more quickly to a particular scope if less global variables are used.

When using arrays and linked lists with procedures, they too can have different scopes within your program exactly like variables. Up until PureBasic v4, all arrays and linked lists were global by default ensuring they all could always be manipulated by procedures. With the arrival of PureBasic v4, arrays and linked lists can be local, global, protected and static in exactly the same way as variables. They even use the same scope keywords.

In the next section I've listed all of the scope keywords and given a full explanation for each one along with plenty of examples to demonstrate their usage for variables, arrays and linked lists.

The 'Global' Keyword

Global Variables
I've already given an example of the 'Global' keyword while explaining program scope but here it is again to make this list complete.

```
Global a.l = 10

Procedure DisplayValue()
  Debug a
EndProcedure

DisplayValue()
```

The 'Global' keyword is used before a variable definition to make that variable's scope global. Once a variable has been defined as global then that variable can be seen and modified within all procedures that your source code may contain. The syntax is very simple as you can see from the above example.

Global Arrays

```
Global Dim Numbers.l(1)

Procedure ChangeValues()
  Numbers(0) = 3
  Numbers(1) = 4
EndProcedure

ChangeValues()

Debug Numbers(0)
Debug Numbers(1)
```

In this example, similar to global variables, I've used the 'Global' keyword in front of the array definition so I'm able to access it within the procedure. Without the 'Global' keyword in front of the array, the procedure would not be able to see or use it.

Global Linked Lists

```
Global Newlist Numbers.l()

AddElement(Numbers())
Numbers() = 1

Procedure ChangeValue()
  SelectElement(Numbers(), 1)
  Numbers() = 100
EndProcedure

ChangeValue()

SelectElement(Numbers(), 1)
Debug Numbers()
```

In this example, similar to arrays I've used the 'Global' keyword in front of the linked list definition so I'm able to access it within the procedure. Without the 'Global' keyword in front of the linked list, the procedure would not be able to see or use it.

The 'Protected' Keyword

Protected Variables

The 'Protected' keyword forces a variable to be local in a procedure even if the same variable has been declared as global in the main source code. This is very useful for defining temporary variable names inside procedures or just to make sure procedure variables never interfere with any global variables in the main code.

```
Global a.l = 10

Procedure ChangeValue()
  Protected a.l = 20
EndProcedure

ChangeValue()

Debug a
```

You can see that even though the protected variable inside the procedure has the same name as the global variable, they are considered separate variables in two different scopes. If you run the above example the result echoed to the Debug Output window will be '10' because even though we call the 'ChangeValue()' procedure the protected variable doesn't alter the global one. This keyword is essential for writing generic procedures that you intend to use in variety of different source codes so as not to interfere with anything in the main code.

Protected Arrays

```
Global Dim Numbers.l(1)

Procedure ChangeValues()
  Protected Dim Numbers.l(1)
  Numbers(0) = 3
  Numbers(1) = 4
EndProcedure

ChangeValues()

Debug Numbers(0)
Debug Numbers(1)
```

In this example we use the 'Protected' keyword in exactly the same way as the protected variable example. If you run this above example, the results echoed to the Debug Output window will be '0' because even though we call the 'ChangeValues()' procedure, the protected array doesn't alter the global one at all. This keyword is great for protecting arrays within procedures so they never interfere with the main code even if they have the same name as global arrays.

Protected Linked Lists

```
Global Newlist Numbers.l()
AddElement(Numbers())
Numbers() = 1

Procedure ChangeValue()
  Protected Newlist Numbers.l()
  AddElement(Numbers())
  Numbers() = 100
EndProcedure

ChangeValue()
SelectElement(Numbers(), 1)
Debug Numbers()
```

Again, If you run the above example, the result echoed to the Debug Output window will be '1' because even though we call the 'ChangeValue()' procedure, the protected linked list doesn't alter the global one. This keyword is great for protecting linked lists within procedures so they never interfere with the main code even if they have the same name as global linked lists.

The 'Shared' Keyword

Shared Variables
Sometimes in your code you may need to access a variable from inside a procedure that hasn't been defined as global. This is when the 'Shared' keyword is used. Here's an example:

```
a.l = 10

Procedure ChangeValue()
  Shared a
  a = 50
EndProcedure

ChangeValue()
Debug a
```

Here, even though 'a' is originally not defined as global, you can still access it from within a procedure by using the 'Shared' keyword. When the above example is run, the 'ChangeValue()' procedure changes the value of 'a' even thought it isn't a global variable.

Shared Arrays

```
Dim Numbers.l(1)

Procedure ChangeValues()
  Shared Numbers()
  Numbers(0) = 3
  Numbers(1) = 4
EndProcedure

ChangeValues()

Debug Numbers(0)
Debug Numbers(1)
```

In this example, even though the 'Numbers()' array is not defined as global, I can still access it from inside the 'ChangeValues()' procedure by using the 'Shared' keyword. When specifying what array you want to share, you just need to specify the array name along with brackets on the end, like this: 'Numbers()', there's no need for the type suffix, indices or dimensions to be specified.

Shared Linked Lists

```
Newlist Numbers.l()

Procedure ChangeValue()
  Shared Numbers()
  AddElement(Numbers())
  Numbers() = 100
EndProcedure

ChangeValue()

SelectElement(Numbers(), 1)
Debug Numbers()
```

In this example even though the 'Numbers()' linked list is not defined as global, I can still access it from the 'ChangeValue()' procedure using the 'Shared' keyword, very similar to the shared array example. When specifying what linked list to share, you just need to specify the linked list name with brackets on the end, like this 'Numbers()', there's no need for the type suffix to be specified.

The 'Static' Keyword

Static Variables

Every time a procedure exits, all variable values defined within it are lost. If you would like a procedure to remember a variable's value after each call, then you need to use the 'Static' keyword. See this example:

```
Procedure ChangeValue()
  Static a.l
  a + 1
  Debug a
EndProcedure

For x.l = 1 To 5
  ChangeValue()
Next x
```

Here in the 'ChangeValue()' procedure I've set the 'a' variable to be static by using the 'Static' keyword. After this I increase the value of 'a' by '1' and then echo that value to the Debug Output window. I then call this procedure five times using a standard 'For' loop. If you look at the echoed values they are all different and incremented by '1'. This is because the value of 'a' is remembered between procedure calls.

Static Arrays

You can also keep array values intact between procedure calls by using the 'Static' keyword.

```
Procedure ChangeValue()
  Static Dim Numbers.l(1)
  Numbers(0) + 1
  Numbers(1) + 1
  Debug Numbers(0)
  Debug Numbers(1)
EndProcedure

For x.l = 1 To 5
  ChangeValue()
Next x
```

In the above example, I've used the 'Static' keyword to preserve the array's values between procedure calls in exactly the same as static variables. If you look at the echoed values they are all different and incremented by '1'. This is because the static array's values have all been preserved between the calls.

Static Linked Lists

```
Procedure ChangeValue()
  Static NewList Numbers.l()
  If CountList(Numbers()) = 0
    AddElement(Numbers())
  EndIf
  SelectElement(Numbers(), 1)
  Numbers() + 1
  Debug Numbers()
EndProcedure

For x.l = 1 To 5
  ChangeValue()
Next x
```

In this example I use the 'Static' keyword to preserve a linked list's values between procedure calls in exactly the same as static arrays. If you look at the echoed values they are all different and incremented by '1'.

Because this linked list is static and I only wanted to add one element for the purpose of this example, I've used an 'If' statement in the procedure to test the amount of elements within the list. If the list has no elements then I add one, otherwise I just change the value of the existing element within the static linked list. If I didn't do things like this, I would keep adding elements with each procedure call which is not what I wanted.

Passing Variables To Procedures

As I mentioned before, one of the most useful abilities procedures possess is that they can accept initial starting parameters. These parameters can be variables of any built-in type, arrays or even linked lists. Parameters are used as a way of passing values from the main program into any procedure for processing. Procedures can then be defined and used over and over again throughout the program with different starting values. This is how you define a procedure to accept parameters;

```
Procedure AddTogether(a.l, b.l)
  Debug a + b
EndProcedure

AddTogether(10, 5)
AddTogether(7, 7)
AddTogether(50, 50)
```

All parameters that are to be passed to a procedure should be inside the brackets and if multiple parameters are needed then they should be separated by commas. When parameters are included in the definition like this, they all must have their type defined too. Here, I've defined two parameters, 'a' and 'b', both of which are Long type variables.

Once a procedure is defined like this, you have to remember to include the values you wish to pass as parameters when calling it, like this:

```
AddTogether(10, 5)
```

After this particular call, the value '10' is passed into the 'a' variable and the value '5' is passed into the 'b' variable. The procedure then adds these variables together and displays the result in the Debug Output window. This applies to all of the other calls too, the first parameter value in the call is passed into 'a' and the second into 'b'.

Here's another example using Strings:

```
Procedure JoinString(a.s, b.s)
  Debug a + b
EndProcedure

JoinString("Mary had a little lamb, ", "its fleece was white as snow.")
JoinString("And everywhere that Mary went, ", "that lamb was sure to go.")
JoinString("..", "..")
```

Here we're using the secondary role of the '+' operator, using it for String concatenation instead of addition. I've basically modified the 'AddTogether(a.l, b.l)' procedure and replaced the Long type parameters with String types and renamed it to 'JoinString(a.s, b.s)'. I can now call this procedure from anywhere in my program passing Strings to match the defined parameters.

Another point to remember regarding procedures is that their parameters don't have to be all of the same type, you can mix and match as much as you like.

```
Procedure LotsOfTypes(a.b, b.w, c.l, d.f, e.s)
  Debug "Byte: " + Str(a)
  Debug "Word: " + Str(b)
  Debug "Long: " + Str(c)
  Debug "Float: " + StrF(d)
  Debug "String: " + e
EndProcedure

LotsOfTypes(104, 21674, 97987897, 3.141590, "Mary had a little lamb")
```

Here I've used a few different variable types as parameters in my 'LotsOfTypes()' procedure to demonstrate that parameters don't all have to be of the same type. The values that are passed in the procedure call are assigned to the defined procedure parameters 'a', 'b', 'c', 'd' and 'e' respectively. You will also notice that all values passed must match their respective parameter types or else a syntax error will occur.

You've also probably noticed I've used two built-in functions that you may not be familiar with. These two functions, 'Str()' and 'StrF()' will be explained in more detail in Chapter 7 (Examples Of Common Commands), but to explain simply, they convert numeric types into Strings.

Strictly Passing Values To Procedures

When calling a procedure you must make sure that any defined parameters are called using the correct types or you will raise a syntax error when compiling. For example, if a procedure is defined as this:

```
AddTogether(a.l, b.l)
```

then only Long variables must be passed as parameters. If String type variables are defined as parameters then you must call the procedure using Strings as values for these parameters. Procedures using arrays and linked lists as parameters must also be called correctly and all parameters must be in the correct order and using the correct type. I know this seems obvious but I think it's worth pointing out.

Even from these simple examples the power of procedures should start to become apparent. Not only are they a great timesaver in respect of typing code but they allow programmers to extend the functionality of PureBasic and then have freedom to use this functionality in any source code from then on. This allows for great code reusability, especially if you've written some really helpful generic procedures.

Optional Variable Parameters
A new feature in PureBasic v4 was the inclusion of optional procedure parameters. These are very easy to explain and demonstrate and are extremely useful.

Basically you can set an initial value for any parameter in case it isn't used on the procedure call. Here's an example:

```
Procedure DisplayParameters(a.l, b.l, c.l = 3)
  Debug a
  Debug b
  Debug c
EndProcedure

DisplayParameters(1, 2)
```

If you look at the procedure definition in the above example you will see that the last parameter has been defined differently to the others and has been given the initial value of '3'. If the last parameter is not specified within a procedure call then it will have this default value. When I call the procedure in the above example using 'DisplayParameters(1, 2)', missing out the last parameter, then you can see this default value recognized and used in the echoed output within the Debug Output window.

Any number of parameters can be optional and defined in this way. You must understand however that all optional parameters must always appear to the right of standard non-optional parameters. This is because all values passed during a procedure call are assigned left to right to parameters and optional ones can't be skipped.

Passing Arrays To Procedures.

As an accompaniment to variables, you can also pass arrays and linked lists to procedures as parameters. Their usage is simplicity itself and very easy to demonstrate.

To pass an array as a parameter you must first define an array using the standard 'Dim' keyword. Here is a simple one dimensional String array defined with four indices (remember that the indices start at 'o') I've called it 'Countries':

```
Dim Countries.s(3)

Countries(0) = "England"
Countries(1) = "Northern Ireland"
Countries(2) = "Scotland"
Countries(3) = "Wales"
```

Once this array has been defined, let's then define a procedure to pass it to:

```
Procedure EchoArray(MyArray.s(1))
  For x.l = 0 To 3
    Debug MyArray(x)
  Next x
EndProcedure
```

To define a procedure to accept an array as a parameter you must do so in a very strict way. For starters, you define an array parameter within the same procedure brackets as any other standard parameter. The actual array parameter itself is composed of three parts.

First a name is used to act as the array name within the procedure. Then a suffix of the expected array type is added to this name and brackets are added to the end. These brackets usually contain a number which expresses an array index. But here, this number should be the number of dimensions contained within the array that is to be passed. In the above example I've used a one dimensional array, so the full array parameter looks like this:

```
MyArray.s(1)
```

Showing an array parameter name, the array type suffix and then between the brackets, the number of dimensions defined in the expected array.

You will notice that I've used 'MyArray' as the array parameter name, this is not essential and you can call your parameters whatever you like. You must however, always adhere to the same naming guidelines as set out for variables, i.e. no spaces, no keyword names, etc.

Inside this procedure you are now able to use the 'MyArray()' as any other normal array, getting and setting values to and from it using standard indices. In the above example, I've used a simple 'For' loop to iterate through this array and echo its values to the Debug Output window. You can however, be as creative as you like, in finding ways to process arrays.

Once the procedure has been correctly defined you can call it, passing the 'Countries' array like this:

```
EchoArray(Countries())
```

Notice when we pass our 'Countries()' array we only use its name with brackets on the end, almost like a procedure call itself. No types, indices or dimensions are necessary when actually passing an array in a procedure call.

If you run this example, you should see the four countries of the United Kingdom echoed to the Debug Output window.

Passing Multi-dimensional arrays

You can also pass multi-dimensional arrays as parameters as demonstrated in this example:

```
Dim Countries.s(3, 1)

Countries(0,0) = "England"
Countries(0,1) = "57,000,000"

Countries(1, 0) = "Northern Ireland"
Countries(1,1) = "2,000,000"

Countries(2, 0) = "Scotland"
Countries(2,1) = "5,200,000"

Countries(3, 0) = "Wales"
Countries(3,1) = "3,100,000"

Procedure EchoArray(MyArray.s(2))
  For x.l = 0 To 3
    Debug MyArray(x,0) + "  -  " + "Population: " + MyArray(x,1)
  Next x
EndProcedure

EchoArray(Countries())
```

Even though this is a two dimensional array we still use the same rules as before when defining a procedure to handle this array as a parameter. You will notice that in this array parameter definition we use '2' within the brackets to specify that the expected array will be a two dimensional array, like this:

```
MyArray.s(2)
```

Even thought this parameter is defined for a two dimensional array we still call the procedure, passing the array as before, with no types, indices or dimensions:

```
EchoArray(Countries())
```

Passing Structured type arrays

Structured type arrays can also be passed to a procedure very easily. You do it exactly as illustrated on the previous page, you just need change the array parameter type to match the structure used in the array definition. Look at this example:

```
Structure COUNTRY
  Name.s
  Population.s
EndStructure

Dim Countries.COUNTRY(3)

Countries(0)\Name = "England"
Countries(0)\Population = "57,000,000"

Countries(1)\Name = "Northern Ireland"
Countries(1)\Population = "2,000,000"

Countries(2)\Name = "Scotland"
Countries(2)\Population = "5,200,000"

Countries(3)\Name = "Wales"
Countries(3)\Population = "3,100,000"

Procedure EchoArray(MyArray.COUNTRY(1))
  For x.l = 0 To 3
    Debug MyArray(x)\Name + "  -  " + "Population: " + MyArray(x)\Population
  Next x
EndProcedure

EchoArray(Countries())
```

Here I've used a structured array, defined using the 'COUNTRY' structure. In order for this type of array to be passed to a procedure, you have to make sure you define the array parameter to use the same structure that was used when defining the expected array, in this case it was the 'COUNTRY' structure. You can see this parameter for yourself in the above procedure definition:

```
MyArray.COUNTRY(1)
```

This shows the parameter name, the structured array type suffix and then the dimensions in the passed array. If all of this is coded correctly as above, then a one dimensional, 'COUNTRY' structured array will pass into this procedure just fine.

Passing Linked Lists To Procedures

Sometimes while programming using PureBasic you may want to pass a linked list to a procedure. This is very similar to passing an array. First, take a look at this example:

```
NewList Numbers.l()

AddElement(Numbers())
Numbers() = 25

AddElement(Numbers())
Numbers() = 50

AddElement(Numbers())
Numbers() = 75

Procedure EchoList(MyList.l())
  ForEach MyList()
    Debug MyList()
  Next
EndProcedure

EchoList(Numbers())
```

Here, I've created a standard linked list called 'Numbers' which will contain Long type elements. After adding three elements to this list, I've defined the 'EchoList()' procedure that this linked list will be passed into. The linked list parameter is coded very similarly to an array parameter, in that it starts with the parameter name, followed by the list type suffix and finally a set of brackets. Linked lists don't use indices like arrays, so you don't need to type a number inside the brackets. Once this is all done, you can then call the procedure, passing the linked list just like an array, without any type, etc. Like this:

```
EchoList(Numbers())
```

Of course inside the 'EchoList()' procedure the 'MyList()' linked list now contains all of the information that the passed linked list had and can be used in exactly the same as any other standard linked list. You can see inside the 'EchoList()' procedure, I've used a standard 'ForEach' loop to quickly iterate through the linked list and echo its values to the Debug Output window.

Passing Structured linked lists

Structured linked lists can also be passed easily as procedure parameters. Again, similar to passing structured arrays into procedures, you must remember to define the structure in the procedure parameter to be the same as the structure used to define the linked list that is expected to be passed.

```
Structure FLAGS
  Country.s
  Flag.s
EndStructure

NewList Info.FLAGS()

AddElement(Info())
Info()\Country = "Great Britain"
```

```
Info()\Flag = "Union Jack"

AddElement(Info())
Info()\Country = "USA"
Info()\Flag = "Stars And Stripes"

AddElement(Info())
Info()\Country = "France"
Info()\Flag = "Tricolore"

Procedure EchoList(MyList.FLAGS())
  ForEach MyList()
    Debug MyList()\Country + "'s flag is the " + MyList()\Flag
  Next
EndProcedure

EchoList(Info())
```

Notice from the above example, the linked list parameter looks like this:

```
MyList.FLAGS()
```

I've made sure that the linked list parameter now includes the 'FLAGS' type in order for the structured linked list to be passed correctly.

Arrays And Linked Lists Are Passed By Reference

Unlike variables, arrays and linked lists are passed by reference. This means that values aren't actually passed from arrays and linked lists into the procedures and 'copied' into the parameters. Instead an internal memory pointer is passed to the procedure and this is used to manipulate the array or linked list.

This is all done internally so you wouldn't really notice anything different from using variables. The only thing you need to consider is that when you pass an array or linked list into a procedure, the parameter name used will not be a separate local array or linked list. Whatever name you give to the array or linked list parameter inside the procedure, you are still manipulating the original passed array or linked list.

For example, if you pass an array called 'Dogs()' into a procedure as a parameter, this parameter could have a different name and be called 'Cats()' for instance. Then inside the procedure you could assign the 'Cats()' array different values. When the procedure exits you will notice that the 'Dogs()' array has been modified in the same way as the 'Cats()' array. This is because the 'Cats()' parameter will be just a reference to the original passed 'Dogs()' array.

This is only true for arrays and linked lists, variables on the other hand are passed by value, meaning that an actual value is copied into the variable parameter. So, if you alter a variable parameter in a procedure, it will not alter the original variable that was passed to it.

Returning A Value From Procedures

Another great feature of procedures is that they can return a value. This value can be of any of PureBasic's built-in types. Returning a value from a procedure is a great way to be able to calculate or manipulate data within a procedure and then return something useful. This could be a calculation result, an error code or even a descriptive String of what the procedure has just done or achieved. See Fig.2 and Fig.3 for a list of types that can be returned by procedures.

The syntax for returning a value from a procedure is simplicity itself. First you need to define what type is to be returned from the procedure, this is done by slightly extending the procedure definition. Look at this example:

```
Procedure.l AddTogether(a.l, b.l)
  ProcedureReturn a + b
EndProcedure

Debug AddTogether(7, 5)
```

The above procedure definition has been given a new type suffix on the end of the 'Procedure' keyword. This is where you define the type to be returned by this procedure. The above definition has been given the '.l' suffix, meaning that this procedure will return a Long type value. To actually make the procedure return a value we need to use the 'ProcedureReturn' keyword. The value or expression following this keyword is the one that is returned. In this case the resulting value evaluated from 'a + b' is returned.

You can also see demonstrated, that when we call the above procedure using 'AddTogether(7, 5)', a value is returned directly from this call, and itself can be used in an expression or statement. In this case I've used it as an expression for a 'Debug' statement. The value '12' is returned from the procedure call and directly echoed to the Debug Output window using the 'Debug' keyword.

If we want a procedure to return a String we just switch the return type to '.s'. As shown here:

```
Procedure.s JoinString(a.s, b.s)
  ProcedureReturn a + b
EndProcedure

Debug JoinString("Red ", "Lorry")
Debug JoinString("Yellow ", "Lorry")
```

Notice the return type is specified in the 'Procedure.s' keyword. This now specifies that this procedure will return a String. In this new example, I pass two Strings into the procedure, which are then concatenated and returned from the line 'ProcedureReturn a + b'. I call this procedure three times using it with the 'Debug' keyword again to echo the returned values to the Debug Output window and to demonstrate the returned values.

Procedures that return values can be used anywhere where expressions are. For example, they could be used in another procedure call, like this:

```
Procedure.l AddTogether(a.l, b.l)
  ProcedureReturn a + b
EndProcedure

Debug AddTogether(AddTogether(2, 3), AddTogether(4, 1))
```

Here I've used the 'AddTogether(a.l, b.l)' procedure to return values added together from two separate calls to the same procedure. First the 'AddTogether(2, 3)' is called and this returns '5' then 'AddTogether(4, 1)' is called and this returns '5' too. Both of these procedure calls are being used as parameters within another procedure call. This final call adds together both of the returned values and returns that value to be echoed to the Debug Output window.

Parameters Do Not Affect Return Types
One thing to remember when using procedure return types is that they don't have to be the same as defined parameter types. For example:

```
Procedure.s DisplayValue(a.l, b.s)
  ProcedureReturn Str(a) + b
EndProcedure

x = 5
While x >= 0
  Debug DisplayValue(x, " green bottles hanging on the wall.")
  x - 1
Wend
```

Even though I've used a Long type and a String type parameter in the 'DisplayValue(a.l, b.s)' procedure, it can still return a String as defined by the type suffix on the 'Procedure.s' keyword. Return types and parameter types can mixed as much as you like.

Return types are very strict though, just as much as variable types. If you have defined a procedure to return a String and you wish to return a Long type value from it, you must convert that value into the correct return type (String) before returning it, otherwise you will get a syntax error. You can see this in action in the above example. I've used the built-in 'Str()' command to convert 'a' to a String before concatenating and returning it correctly.

Limitations Of Returning Results
While using procedures to return results there are however two limitations. First, procedures can only return one result per call. Meaning that you cannot return two or more values in one procedure call. Second, you cannot return arrays, linked lists or any user defined type from procedures. You can only return built-in PureBasic types. It is however, possible to get around these limitations, by returning a pointer. See Chapter 13 (Pointers) for an explanation of this technique.

7

Using Built-in Commands

Programming languages are nothing without built-in libraries of useful commands, so PureBasic has available over eight hundred built-in commands to be used within your programs. These range from String manipulation, to mathematics, to file handling and even graphics commands. They cover almost any programming task imaginable and if nothing exists that meets your needs you also have the option of creating your own procedures.

In this chapter I will introduce and explain the most commonly used built-in commands that PureBasic has to offer. While this list is not complete by any means, this introduction should serve to explain fully some of the most common commands you will come across in general programming.

This chapter starts with a description on how to read the command syntax in the PureBasic helpfile and then moves on to the actual command descriptions and explanations. I finish this chapter with a section on how to handle files, such as loading, writing to and reading from, and then saving, all using the PureBasic built-in commands.

Using The PureBasic Helpfile

Here we will take a proper look at the PureBasic helpfile and I explain how the pages are organized, how to read them and more importantly, how to use the built-in commands that are described there.

When you view a command page in the PureBasic helpfile you are confronted with a standard layout, this goes similar to:

    Syntax
    Description
    An Example
    Supported Operating Systems

The latter three sections of each helpfile page are mostly self explanatory so let's concentrate for a minute on the syntax section. The syntax portion at the top of each helpfile page is an example of how the command is actually typed into the IDE and what parameters are expected to be passed to it. For example, let's look at the 'SaveImage()' command in the helpfile. This is how to navigate to the correct page: (Helpfile:Reference Manual->General Libraries->Image->SaveImage). On this page at the very top, under the syntax heading, this syntax example appears:

```
SaveImage(#Image, FileName$ [ , ImagePlugin [ , Flags]])
```

The first thing on this line is the actual command name, in this case 'SaveImage', after that is a pair of brackets and if this certain command can accept parameters they will be shown within these brackets. In the 'SaveImage()' syntax example it is shown that this command can accept four parameters and so all four are within the brackets. You will also notice that the last two parameters are shown within square brackets too. This is to signify that these last two parameters are optional and don't have to be used when you need to call the 'SaveImage()' command. If we keep this in mind, the 'SaveImage()' command can be properly used like these three examples:

```
SaveImage(1, "Image.bmp")
SaveImage(1, "Image.jpg", #PB_ImagePlugin_JPEG)
SaveImage(1, "Image.jpg", #PB_ImagePlugin_JPEG, 10)
```

The first example will save an image called 'Image.bmp' in the default 24bit Bitmap format. The second example will save the image as JPEG format and use the standard compression value. The third example will save the image as JPEG format and use the maximum compression value of ten ('10'). Simple!

What Are Those Square Brackets Within The Syntax Examples?

The square brackets shown in syntax examples are never used when using these commands. They are only included in the examples to show what parameters (if any) are optional, when using these commands. Square brackets are only ever used in actual code when you are using Static Arrays. For more information about static arrays see Chapter 5 (Arrays).

The first thing you may realize while using built-in commands is that they look and act exactly like normal procedure calls. All built-in commands are simply calling pre-written procedures that are defined as part of the PureBasic package. The trick to using them correctly is that when you call a built-in command, you must pass it the correct parameters as defined in that command's syntax example, otherwise a syntax error will be triggered by the compiler.

The structure of the above syntax example is emulated throughout the entire helpfile, so if you understand how to read this one, you will understand how to read all syntax examples for all the other built-in commands.

PB Numbers And OS Identifiers

When using built-in commands it is important to understand the role of PureBasic's object numbering system and that of operating system identifiers, as these are used directly when controlling what happens in your program. Both are nothing more than numbers but both are used to identify objects within programs. For example, to identify parts of a graphical user interface or different images you have to identify them by a number. Knowing how and when to use them is essential, not only to PureBasic but programming in general.

The PureBasic helpfile is invaluable for the information it contains but it can get a little confusing when first trying to understand PureBasic's object numbering system and operating system identifiers. This is because sometimes the helpfile refers to both being identifiers. Let me explain exactly what they are so you can understand the helpfile better.

PB Numbers Explained
PureBasic works on a number system to identify each object that you create in your program. A PureBasic object, among others, can be a window, a gadget or even an image. These numbers, we'll call them PB numbers, are then used by your program to refer to these objects later when you want to perform some action on them.

Many PureBasic commands need either one or two PB numbers passed to them as parameters to function correctly. These are shown in the PureBasic helpfile within the syntax example of any given command. If a command needs a PB number, these are usually shown as a constant, beginning with a hash (#) and ending with the name of the library that the command resides in, e.g. '#Image' is used for an image number, '#Window' is used for a window number, etc.

Here is an example of a built-in command from the 'Image' library that makes use of a PB number: (Helpfile:Reference Manual->General Libraries->Image->CreateImage).

```
CreateImage(#Image, Width, Height)
```

As you can see this command expects a PB number to be passed to it as the first parameter, shown by '#Image'. Although this is shown as a constant in the syntax example, it doesn't necessarily mean that a constant must be passed to the command, it just means that constants are usually used. In fact, any integer can be used as a PB number for an object, as long as it is unique amongst others if many of the same objects are used. This number refers to this newly created object from then on throughout your program.

The Same Kind Of Objects Can't Share PB Numbers
PureBasic numbers provide a great way to refer to anything that PureBasic creates on an individual basis. Because of this you can't have two of the same object sharing the same PB number. If you create an image with a number of '1' then later in your program you create another image with the number of '1', PureBasic automatically destroys the first and frees the memory it was using before creating the second. This makes sure no two objects from the same library share the same PB number. This feature is also very handy if you want to replace objects at any time.

PureBasic numbers can be shared across libraries though. For example, you can create a window using '1' as its PB number and then create a button gadget on it using '1' as its PB number too. These two numbers don't conflict with one another because they refer to objects from two different libraries.

When using different commands to create objects, things can get confusing when trying to keep track of all the numbers that must be used. To avoid this problem, many PureBasic programmers (including me) use constants for these PB numbers. These constants are usually defined in an enumeration block to keep the numbers sequential. Here's an example:

```
Enumeration
  #IMAGE_DOG
  #IMAGE_CAT
  #IMAGE_BIRD
EndEnumeration
CreateImage(#IMAGE_DOG, 100, 100)
CreateImage(#IMAGE_CAT, 250, 300)
CreateImage(#IMAGE_BIRD, 450, 115)
```

After the constants have been defined, I can use these to create the above images (or any other object) and not worry about their values conflicting. Throughout the program I can also use these constants to refer to the images by name. For example, now I can refer to the first image by using the '#IMAGE_DOG' constant. This method of using constants for PureBasic's numbers guarantees clearly organized and readable code.

Dynamic PB Numbers
As an alternative to using enumeration blocks to handle PB numbers for newly created objects, you can use a special constant for them all. This constant is:

```
#PB_Any
```

This constant can be used wherever a PB number is expected in an object creation command. The value of this constant is the next PB number that is available for use. So for example, the first time it is used its value may be '1', then the second time it is used its value may be '2'. This behavior is great for building dynamic programs, where you may or may not know how many objects you will be creating.

The only thing to keep in mind while using '#PB_Any' as a PB number, is that in order for you to refer to this object later, you have to know what value '#PB_Any' had during the object's creation. This is made simple by PureBasic, because you use this special constant as a parameter within a command, that command returns the PB number of this newly created object. Here is an example of using a dynamic PB number in the 'CreateImage' command:

```
ImageDog.l = CreateImage(#PB_Any, 100, 100)
```

Here the 'CreateImage()' command now returns the PB number of the newly created image because we have used the '#PB_Any' constant as the PB number parameter. This works in exactly the same way for all object creation commands.

PB numbers are unique to PureBasic and enable a quick and easy way of referring to different objects within your program. To view them in real working examples, see Chapter 9.

Operating System Indentifiers

Some objects you create using PureBasic's built-in commands are also assigned numbers from the operating system. These numbers are how the actual operating system keeps track of such things as windows, fonts and images, etc. The PureBasic helpfile calls these, OS Identifiers or just IDs. While programming in PureBasic you will notice that some commands return OS identifiers while others may need them as parameters.

Here are a few commands that return an OS identifier of the object defined by the PB number parameter:

```
WindowOSId.l = WindowID(#Window)
GadgetOSId.l = GadgetID(#Gadget)
ImageOSId.l = ImageID(#Image)
```

I've listed three here but there are a few more. Command names that end with '...ID()' usually return OS Identifiers. As mentioned before, here is an example of a command that uses an OS Identifier as a parameter:

```
CreateGadgetList(WindowOSId)
```

This command is used to create a gadget list within a window and uses an operating system identifier to define where the list is created. An OS identifier is used in this command instead of a PB number for maximum compatibility, just in case the window has been created by the operating system's native API. If you wanted to use this command to create a gadget list on a window created by using PureBasic's number system, then we could do something like this:

```
CreateGadgetList(WindowID(#Window))
```

Notice we are using the 'WindowID()' command as a parameter which returns the OS identifier of a PB numbered window.

Every operating system has a native application programming interface or API for short. This is a built-in command-set for all programming languages to use, to control the operating system and draw an interface for it. OS identifiers are used to keep track of, and access all objects that the operating system contains. All OS identifiers are unique for every program and they exist for all objects, even for those not written in PureBasic. For an operating system to track thousands of items, the numbers used can be quite large, so don't be surprised to see OS identifiers that are over eight digits in length.

OS identifiers do not have to be used to create full working PureBasic programs but it's good for beginners to understand what they are even though they probably won't use them. OS identifiers play a major part when using the API of any operating system, especially the Windows API, which I cover a little more in Chapter 13.

Examples Of Common Commands

In this section I'm going to demonstrate some of the most commonly used commands in PureBasic. These commands are usually found in most PureBasic programs and because of this, learning their syntax and purpose is very advantageous. All these commands exist in different libraries and are not necessarily related, they are just very useful for general programming tasks. Here they are presented below in alphabetical order, complete with their helpfile location and examples on usage.

Asc()

(Helpfile:Reference Manual->General Libraries->String->Asc)

Syntax Example:

```
ASCIIValue.l = Asc(Character.s)
```

This command returns the associated character's ASCII value retrieved from a standard ASCII chart. In the standard ASCII character set, numbers from '0' to '255' are used to represent characters and computer control codes. The parameter passed to this command is a String that's one character long, with which this command retrieves its associated ASCII value.

```
Text.s = "This is a test"

For x.l = 1 To Len(Text)
  Debug Mid(Text, x, 1) + "  :  " + Str(Asc(Mid(Text, x, 1)))
Next x
```

The above example uses a 'For' loop and the built-in 'Mid()' command to break up the text contained in the 'Text' variable into separate letters. While the loop is running each letter is passed to the 'Asc()' command and their associated ASCII value is retrieved. These values along with the associated letters are echoed to the Debug Output window. I've used some new commands in this example, but don't panic, these are explained a little later in this section. See Appendix B (Helpful Charts) for a full ASCII chart, showing all characters and associated numbers from '0' to '255'.

Chr()

(Helpfile:Reference Manual->General Libraries->String->Chr)

Syntax Example:

```
Character.s = Chr(ASCIIValue.l)
```

This command returns a one character String, retrieved from a standard ASCII chart. The returned string is the associated ASCII character of the value passed as a parameter. In the standard ASCII character set, numbers from '33' to '126' are actual printable characters that you can find on a standard English keyboard.

The parameter passed to this command: 'ASCIIValue.l', is the number with which you retrieve the associated character.

```
Text.s = Chr(84) + Chr(104) + Chr(105) + Chr(115) + Chr(32)
Text.s + Chr(105) + Chr(115) + Chr(32)
Text.s + Chr(97) + Chr(32)
Text.s + Chr(116) + Chr(101) + Chr(115) + Chr(116)
Debug Text
```

The above example constructs the String 'This is a test' by concatenating the results from multiple 'Chr()' commands. For example, the first command 'Chr(84)' returns the 'T' character, the rest are then concatenated to the 'Text' variable. See Appendix B (Helpful Charts) for a full ASCII chart, showing all characters and associated numbers from '0' to '255'.

Delay()

(Helpfile:Reference Manual->General Libraries->Misc->Delay)

Syntax Example:

```
Delay(Milliseconds)
```

This command pauses all program activity for the amount of time specified in the 'Milliseconds' parameter. The time is measured in milliseconds (which is a thousandth of a second).

```
Debug "Start..."
Delay(5000)
Debug "This is executed 5 seconds later"
```

When the above example is run, the second 'Debug' statement is executed five seconds after the first one because I've used the value of '5000' milliseconds (5 seconds) in the 'Delay()' command.

ElapsedMilliseconds()

(Helpfile:Reference Manual->General Libraries->Misc->ElapsedMilliseconds)

Syntax Example:

```
Result.l = ElapsedMilliseconds()
```

This command returns the number of milliseconds that have elapsed since your computer was turned on.

```
Debug "Start..."
StartTime.l = ElapsedMilliseconds()
Delay(5000)
Debug "Delayed for "+Str(ElapsedMilliseconds() - StartTime)+" milliseconds."
```

This command is great for performing any kind of timing operation in your program. For example, if you want to measure any elapsed number of milliseconds, you first record the start time in a Long variable using this command. Then when you want this timer to stop, you record the time again using 'ElapsedMilliseconds()'. To get the result, subtract the end time from the start time and this leaves you with the number of milliseconds that have elapsed between each command. This is all demonstrated in the above example. When you use this command for the first time you may be shocked at the large numbers returned by it. You have to remember that it's recording the milliseconds elapsed from system switch on. Don't panic at the big numbers, just remember that it is providing a good point in time as a reference and you can use the above method to calculate elapsed time from any point.

FindString()

(Helpfile:Reference Manual->General Libraries->String->FindString)

Syntax Example:

```
Position.l = FindString(String.s, StringToFind.s, StartPosition.l)
```

This command tries to find the 'StringToFind' parameter within the 'String' parameter, starting from the position indicated by the 'StartPosition' parameter. If it finds this String it immediately returns the position of the first occurrence. These positions referred to are character counts from the beginning of the 'String.s' parameter, starting at '1'.

```
String.s = "I like to go fishing and catch lots of fish"
StringToFind.s = "fish"

FirstOccurrence.l = FindString(String, StringToFind, 1)
SecondOccurrence.l = FindString(String, StringToFind, FirstOccurrence + 1)
Debug "Index of the first occurrence: " + Str(FirstOccurrence)
Debug "Index of the second occurrence: " + Str(SecondOccurrence)
```

This example shows how to find a String within another String. The first 'FindString()' command tries to find the String 'fish' starting from a position of '1', which it does successfully and assigns the position '14' to the 'FirstOccurrence' variable. The second 'FindString()' command tries to find the same String but from a position of 'FirstOccurrence + 1' to make sure we avoid the first occurrence being found again. This returns the position as being '40' which is assigned to the 'SecondOccurrence' variable. Both are then echoed to the Debug Output window.

Len()

(Helpfile:Reference Manual->General Libraries->String->Len)

Syntax Example:

```
Length.l = Len(String.s)
```

This command returns the length in characters of the 'String' parameter.

```
Alphabet.s = "abcdefghijklmnopqrstuvwxyz"
LengthOfString.l = Len(Alphabet)

Debug LengthOfString
```

This example is very simple because the 'Len()' command is very simple itself. The alphabet is assigned to a String variable called 'Alphabet'. This variable is then passed to the 'Len()' command which returns '26' (this is how many characters the 'Alphabet' variable contains). This value is assigned to the 'LengthOfString' variable which is then echoed to the Debug Output window.

MessageRequester()

(Helpfile:Reference Manual->General Libraries->Requester->MessageRequester)

Syntax Example:

```
Result.l = MessageRequester(Title.s, Text.s [, Flags])

;Possible Flags:
#PB_MessageRequester_Ok
#PB_MessageRequester_YesNo
#PB_MessageRequester_YesNoCancel

;Possible Return Values:
#PB_MessageRequester_Yes
#PB_MessageRequester_No
#PB_MessageRequester_Cancel
```

This command is used to create a small window that can display any information in your program. It can be used within any type of program, not just programs with a graphical user interface. The first parameter in this command is the String displayed in the titlebar of the window. The second parameter is the actual message string displayed in the window itself. The third and last parameter are available for optional flags. By using different flags for the last parameter, you can alter the style of the requester window to include different buttons. Your program is halted until one of these buttons has been pressed. To find out which one, you can test the return value, like this:

```
Title.s = "Information"
Message.s = "This is the default style message requester"
MessageRequester(Title, Message, #PB_MessageRequester_Ok)

Message.s = "In this style you can choose 'Yes' or 'No'."
Result.l = MessageRequester(Title, Message, #PB_MessageRequester_YesNo)

If Result = #PB_MessageRequester_Yes
  Debug "You pressed 'Yes'"
Else
  Debug "You pressed 'No'"
EndIf
```

```
Message.s = "In this style you can choose 'Yes' or 'No' or 'Cancel'."
Result.l = MessageRequester(Title, Message, #PB_MessageRequester_YesNoCancel)

Select Result
  Case #PB_MessageRequester_Yes
    Debug "You pressed 'Yes'"
  Case #PB_MessageRequester_No
    Debug "You pressed 'No'"
  Case #PB_MessageRequester_Cancel
    Debug "You pressed 'Cancel'"
EndSelect
```

This example shows all the different ways that the 'MessageRequester' command can be used. It also shows you how to use the return value constants to determine which button was pressed. Using constants like this takes all the worry out of remembering numeric values. You don't need to know what values are assigned to these constants internally, we are just interested if they are equal (or not) to the return value of the command.

Mid()

(Helpfile:Reference Manual->General Libraries->String->Mid)

Syntax Example:

```
Result.s = Mid(String.s, StartPosition.l, Length.l)
```

This command returns a cropped String which is extracted from another. The starting String is passed as the 'String' parameter. The extracted String can then be taken from any position within the starting String, defined by the 'StartPosition' parameter. The length of the new String to be extracted is defined in the 'Length' parameter. Here's an example:

```
StartingString.s = "Hickory Dickory Dock"
ExtractedString.s = Mid(StartingString, 17, 4)
Debug ExtractedString
```

Here I extract the String 'Dock' by specifying the start position as '17', then I extract '4' characters. Like the 'FindString()' command, the position within the starting string is measured in characters.

Random()

(Helpfile:Reference Manual->General Libraries->Misc->Random)

Syntax Example:

```
Result.l = Random(Maximum.l)
```

This command is simple to demonstrate because all it does is return a random integer between (and including) '0' and the value defined in the 'Maximum' parameter.

```
Debug Random(100)
```

In the above example, the 'Random()' command will return a random value between '0' and '100'.

Str(), StrF(), StrQ(), StrD()

(Helpfile:Reference Manual->General Libraries->String->Str)

Syntax Examples:

```
Result.s = Str(Value.b)
Result.s = Str(Value.w)
Result.s = Str(Value.l)
Result.s = StrF(Value.f [ , DecimalPlaces.l] )
Result.s = StrQ(Value.q)
Result.s = StrD(Value.d [ , DecimalPlaces.l] )
```

These four commands are essentially the same. Their main use is to turn numeric values into Strings. There are four different commands here to handle four different types of numeric values, 'Str()' to handle Byte, Word and Long types, 'StrF()' to handle Floats, 'StrQ()' to handle Quads and 'StrD()' to handle Doubles. You must use the right type of 'Str()' function to convert any particular numeric value to a String. In the case of 'StrF()' and 'StrD()' you will notice that there is also an optional parameter called 'DecimalPlaces'. If this parameter is used, it defines how many decimal places the value should be cropped to before converting it to a String.

```
Debug "Long converted to a String: " + Str(2147483647)
Debug "Float converted to a String: " +StrF(12.05643564333454646, 7)
Debug "Quad converted to a String: " +StrQ(9223372036854775807)
Debug "Double converted to a String: " +StrD(12.05643564333454646, 14)
```

The above example shows how to convert four different kinds of numeric values into Strings. In each case I've concatenated a literal String to the converted one to form complete sentences, I then echo these to the Debug Output window. One important thing to take note of is that if you omit the 'DecimalPlaces' parameter in the Float or Double type commands, then they will both default to six decimal places and you may lose a lot of precision.

Val(), ValF(), ValQ(), ValD()

(Helpfile:Reference Manual->General Libraries->String->Val)

Syntax Examples:

```
Result.l = Val(String.s)
Result.f = ValF(String.s)
Result.q = ValQ(String.s)
Result.d = ValD(String.s)
```

These four commands are essentially the same as one another and the complete opposite of the 'Str()' commands. The difference is that these commands take a String as a parameter and return a numeric value depending on which flavor of 'Val()' is used. For example, 'Val()' returns a Long, 'ValF()' returns a Float, 'ValQ()' returns a Quad and 'ValD()' returns a Double. Here's a simple example:

```
LongTypeVar.l = Val("2147483647")
FloatTypeVar.f = ValF("12.05643564333454646")
QuadTypeVar.q = ValQ("9223372036854775807")
DoubleTypeVar.d = ValD("12.05643564333454646")

Debug LongTypeVar
Debug FloatTypeVar
Debug QuadTypeVar
Debug DoubleTypeVar
```

In this example I've used all four different types of the 'Val()' command to convert four Strings into their respective numeric types. You must note however, if you are converting numbers from within Strings that are numerically larger than the resulting type can hold, then some clipping will occur. For example, if you look at the 'ValF("12.05643564333454646")' line in the example above, this number is far too large or precise for a normal Float type to hold, so when it's converted by the 'ValF()' command it's clipped to fit the destination type.

Handling Files

Using files is a natural way for any program to store and retrieve data. PureBasic provides full support to read and write files, and can read from, and write to, any number of files at the same time. All the file manipulation commands are stored in the same File library, located here in the PureBasic helpfile:

(Helpfile:Reference Manual->General Libraries->File)

Not all the file commands will explained fully within this section, but I will give you a good grounding on reading and writing files so that the remainder of the commands will become easy to understand, when you use them.

Writing To A File
Let's get started with an example on how to write some data to a file, here we'll write a few Strings to a simple text file.

```
#FILE_RHYME = 1

Dim Rhyme.s(3)

Rhyme(0) = "Baa baa black sheep, have you any wool?"
Rhyme(1) = "Yes sir, yes sir, three bags full!"
Rhyme(2) = "One for the master, one for the dame,"
Rhyme(3) = "And one for the little boy who lives down the lane."
```

```
If CreateFile(#FILE_RHYME, "Baa baa.txt")
  For x.1 = 0 To 3
    WriteStringN(#FILE_RHYME, Rhyme(x))
  Next x
  CloseFile(#FILE_RHYME)
EndIf
```

To begin with I've used the constant '#FILE_RHYME' to be used as the PB number for our new file object and I've defined a String array to hold my nursery rhyme. After the Strings have been added to the 'Rhyme()' array, we then move on to writing our file. If I wanted to open and write to an existing file, I could use the 'OpenFile()' command, but in the above example, I want to create and write to a new file, so I use the 'CreateFile()' command instead.

The 'CreateFile()' command takes two parameters, the first is the PB number that this new file object will be associated with, and the second is the actual file name that this file will be named once created. I've also used the 'CreateFile()' command within an 'If' statement to test that the command returns true. If it does, then the file has been created successfully and I can carry on with my program. It's always a good idea to test file creation, as things could go very wrong if you try to write to an invalid file.

To actually write a String to the file, I've used the 'WriteStringN()' command. This takes two parameters, the first is the PB number associated with the file object I want to write to, the second is the actual String I wish to write. I'm using a loop to iterate through the array to write all its contents to the file, thus writing the whole nursery rhyme. The 'WriteStringN()' command used in this example is an extended version of the 'WriteString()' command. In fact the only difference is the 'N' before the brackets. This 'N' denotes that a 'new line' character is written after the String during the command's execution. Because I want a new line to start after every String I write to this file, I use the 'WriteStringN()' command, otherwise it would all be on the same line.

Once I have written all Strings to the file and the loop exits, I close the file using the 'CloseFile()' command. This only takes one parameter which is the PB number of the file object you wish to close.

Different Ways Of Creating Or Opening Files

When using PureBasic's file commands to read or write to files, you must choose the right command depending on how you wish to use that file. The below list describes commands that enable any read or write to be catered for.

'ReadFile()' will open the defined file for reading and prevents any writing to it.
'OpenFile()' will open the defined file for reading or writing and will create it if it doesn't exist.
'CreateFile()' creates an empty file for writing to. If the file already exists, it replaces it with a blank one.

Each one works in exactly the same way and all share the same two parameters. The first parameter is the PB number to be associated to the file object and the second parameter is the actual file name on disk.

This file containing the nursery rhyme should now be somewhere on your hard drive. If you create a file using a relative file name such as 'Baa baa.txt', then the newly created file will be in the same directory as your source code file. If you need a file to be created somewhere more specific you must specify an absolute path which should include the drive name, any directories and the file name, something similar this:

```
...
If CreateFile(#FILE_RHYME, "C:\My Directory\Baa baa.txt")
...
```

When using this method though, you must always make sure that all directories specified in the path do exist before you write the file, else the file creation will fail.

The 'CloseFile()' Command Is Very Important

When you have finished reading and especially writing to files you must close the file correctly using the 'CloseFile()' command. This command not only closes the selected file but frees it up again to be opened by another program if needed. Another important role that the 'CloseFile()' command plays is that it completely writes to the file any data that has been left in the file buffer. PureBasic uses a buffer system to increase performance of file access, so if you are open a file in another editor and some data you expected to be there is missing you must check that you've closed the file properly using 'CloseFile()'. This command ensures any data remaining in the file buffer is written to disk.

The file buffers are completely transparent to the regular user, so you won't have to worry about them too much, you just need to close each file when you have finished with it to avoid any errors.

How Do I Write Other Built-in Type Values?

Writing the other built-in types to a file is just as easy as writing Strings. Now that you understand how the 'WriteString()' command works the others are simple to grasp. Here are syntax examples for writing the other built-in types:

```
WriteByte(#File, Value.b)
WriteChar(#File, Value.c)
WriteWord(#File, Value.w)
WriteLong(#File, Value.l)
WriteQuad(#File, Value.q)
WriteFloat(#File, Value.f)
WriteDouble(#File, Value.d)
```

These can be used to write any built-in type value to a file and all commands can be used as many times as you like. These values, along with Strings can be mixed and matched in a single file over and over again if needed. To make things even more simple, these commands are all used in the same manner as the 'WriteString()' command, the first parameter is the file object to write to and the second is the actual value to write.

Reading From A File

Reading from files is just as simple as writing to them. PureBasic makes it extremely simple with powerful file reading commands. If you look at the next example, I read Strings from a file called 'Report.txt', and place them into a linked list called 'FileContents'. The contents of this linked list are then echoed to the Debug Output window, purely to show the String data within. You don't have to echo this data though, you can go on to manipulate the Strings in any way you see fit during your program.

```
#FILE_REPORT = 1

NewList FileContents.s()

If ReadFile(#FILE_REPORT, "Report.txt")
  While Eof(#FILE_REPORT) = #False
    AddElement(FileContents())
    FileContents() = ReadString(#FILE_REPORT)
  Wend
  CloseFile(#FILE_REPORT)
EndIf

ForEach FileContents()
  Debug FileContents()
Next
```

At the beginning of the code I've used a constant which is to be used as the PB number of the opened file. Then I create a linked list called 'FileContents' to hold the Strings we're going to read. You don't have to use a linked list to hold these Strings, I find it just makes things a little more organized if done like this. I've used a linked list here because they are easy to use and can grow with new items, unlike arrays who's size is pre-defined.

I open the file using the 'ReadFile()' command, this opens it with read-only permission and prevents any writing to the file while it is open. Like the 'CreateFile()' command, the first parameter is a PB number that this newly opened file will be associated with, while the second is the name of the file to be read. As before, I've use this command within an 'If' statement to make sure the command returns true. If it does then I can be sure this file has been opened correctly and I'm able to access it properly.

Once the file is open, I need to read the information inside it. I've used a 'While' loop here, so I don't have to type out repeated commands to read the Strings within. The loop is constructed using the 'Eof()' command, 'Eof' stands for 'End of file' and this command will return true if you have reached the end of an opened file. In the loop I check to see if this is returning false on each iteration, if it is I know I'm not at the end the file and I can continue reading from it. The 'Eof()' command takes one parameter, which is the PB number of the file you want to test.

While the file is open, I use the 'ReadString()' command to read one String at a time from it. The String returned by this command starts at the beginning of the current line and ends when a new line is encountered, this also moves the file access pointer forward one line. Each time I read a String from the file, I create a new element within the 'FileContents' linked list and assign the String to it. I continue to do this until the 'Eof()' command returns true causing the loop to exit.

Once the loop is broken, I then correctly close the open file with the 'CloseFile()' command. Closing the file is important and should be done as soon as you've finished with it. A simple 'ForEach' loop is then used to echo the read data to the Debug Output window.

How Do I Read Other Built-in Type Values?

While the last example dealt with Strings, you can also read other types values just as easy. PureBasic provides specific commands for each of the built-in types to read them correctly.

```
ReadByte(#File)
ReadChar(#File)
ReadWord(#File)
ReadLong(#File)
ReadQuad(#File)
ReadFloat(#File)
ReadDouble(#File)
```

To keep things simple all these commands share the same parameter with the 'ReadString()' command. This parameter is the PB number of the open file object to read from. The only difference between these commands and 'ReadString()' is that these will only read a single value from the file which will contain that type's associated number of Bytes. Unlike 'ReadString()' they won't keep reading until another line is encountered. For example, if I wanted to read a Long type value from a file, I would use 'ReadLong()' which would read '4' Bytes and return the value contained within these Bytes as a Long. This would also move the file access pointer forward '4' Bytes within the file, ready for the next read command.

The File Access Pointer

Within each opened file there exists an invisible file access pointer. This imaginary position is where you will read from or write to in an open file. When using the 'ReadFile()', 'OpenFile()' or 'CreateFile()' commands the access pointer starts at the beginning of the file ready for the next operation. Once you start reading or writing, the file access pointer starts moving. If you are writing to the file then the access pointer will progress through it, moving to just after the value last written, ready for the next. If you are reading from a file then the access pointer will move after each read operation to the end of the last value read until the end of the file is encountered, and the 'Eof()' command returns true.

Locating The File Access Pointer?

At any time while reading or writing to a file you can retrieve the location of the file access pointer by using the 'Loc()' command. 'Loc()' stands for 'Location'. The return value is measured in Bytes.

(Helpfile:Reference Manual->General Libraries->File->Loc)

Syntax Example:

```
Position.q = Loc(#File)
```

This command will return the position of the file access pointer (in Bytes) within the file object specified in the PB number parameter. The position is returned as a Quad value to support large files.

Moving The File Access Pointer?
The file access pointer can be moved at any time by using the 'FileSeek()' command.

(Helpfile:Reference Manual->General Libraries->File->FileSeek)

Syntax Example:

```
FileSeek(#File, NewPosition.q)
```

This command takes two parameters, the first is the PB number of the file object to be modified and the second is the new position (in Bytes) of the file access pointer. This allows you to read from any position, within in any file at any time. The 'NewPosition' parameter type is a Quad for large file support.

Finding Out The Current File Size?
To find out the size of the currently used file, you use the 'Lof()' command. 'Lof()' stands for 'Length of file'.

(Helpfile:Reference Manual->General Libraries->File->Lof)

Syntax Example:

```
Length.q = Lof(#File)
```

This command will return the size of the file object specified in the PB number parameter in Bytes. The length is returned as a Quad type, to support large files.

Loc, Lof And FileSeek Example
In this next snippet I'm going to demonstrate the use of 'Loc()', 'Lof()' and 'FileSeek()' to provide you with a relevant example of these commands. In the code below I'm reading a MP3 music file to discover if it has an ID3(v1) tag embedded inside it. These tags usually contain information such as the artist name, song name and genre, etc.

After reading the specifications of MP3 ID3 tags on the Internet, I discovered that the tag information is always added to the end of a regular MP3 file and this tag is always '128' Bytes long. The specification mentions that the first '3' Bytes of this tag are the characters 'TAG', so this is what I will check for.

Here's the code:

```
#FILE_MP3 = 1

MP3File.s = "Test.mp3"
```

```
If ReadFile(#FILE_MP3, MP3File)
  FileSeek(#FILE_MP3, Lof(#FILE_MP3) - 128)
  For x.l = 1 To 3
    Text.s + Chr(ReadByte(#FILE_MP3))
  Next x
  CloseFile(#FILE_MP3)
  If Text = "TAG"
    Debug "'" + MP3File + "' has an ID3v1 tag embedded within it."
  Else
    Debug "'" + MP3File + "' does not have an ID3v1 tag embedded within it."
  EndIf
EndIf
```

After opening the file using 'ReadFile()', I move the file access pointer to the correct place by finding out the length of the file, then back tracking '128' Bytes. Like this:

```
FileSeek(#FILE_MP3, Lof(#FILE_MP3) - 128)
```

After this command has finished the file access pointer is now in the correct place. So I use a loop to perform a 'ReadByte()' operation three times and I pass each Byte to the 'Chr()' command to return a character. These characters are then concatenated to form a String variable called 'Text'. Once the loop has ended and the is file closed I check the value of 'Text'. If the String contained within 'Text' is equal to 'TAG' then an ID3(v1) tag is present in the MP3 file.

Read The Helpfile

This has been the warcry of many good programmers for years, especially on Internet forums. To truly understand something you have to study it, and to study something properly you have to read everything about it. There really is no getting around the fact that people who read more about a subject are usually better at understanding it. This is especially true with programming languages.

The best piece of advice I can give to you to start learning PureBasic is to read the PureBasic helpfile from front to back and read every page about every command. This sounds extremely boring but believe me it will substantially increase your understanding of PureBasic and give you an excellent insight to just what is possible using this great language.

Sometimes the only thing that distinguishes a good programmer from a truly great one is the amount of reading and study of relevant information that has taken place.

Hopefully this chapter will give you enough insight to be able read the helpfile and understand how to use most built-in commands purely from their helpfile syntax examples.

8

Good Programming Style

Until now I've concentrated on explaining core essentials of PureBasic programming. Its built-in types, statements and expressions, etc. I think it's now time that I mention something about the style of how a program should be written.

In this chapter, I'm going to talk about something that all programmers should recognize and use and that's good programming style. Learning to program can be great fun but that fun can soon erode away when you are confronted with (and trying to understand) poorly written code, especially if you are the author. Writing neatly formatted code not only makes it look more professional, but it actually helps you to read and understand it better.

In the following paragraphs I'm going to describe ways in which you can format your code for maximum readability. This is not necessarily the right or wrong way to do so, just the way I usually work. Hopefully after reading further you will settle into your own style and stick to it.

Later in this chapter, I go on to show you tips and tricks to help you avoid errors in your code and give you examples on how to handle them when they do happen. I've also included some guidance on how to use the PureBasic debugger to track down where problems may be occurring in your code.

Why Bother Formatting Code Neatly?

This question is sometimes asked by beginners and should be addressed. One answer would be, if I were to write this book without headings, subheadings, paragraphs or capitalization and flow the text into one big block, would it be as easy to read as it is now?

Formatting code neatly has absolutely nothing to do with program compilation and it doesn't alter the function or execution of the compiled program either, it's purely done to make code easily readable. So why bother? Well I can guarantee that in the future you will work on source code that you will revisit time and time again. Sometimes because you might not finish what you are doing in one day or you might revise an old program to include new functionality. Each time, you will have to re-read your code and understand what it does. If you have ugly, unorganized code then I guarantee you will have difficulty in reading it and carrying on with your project.

If a bug appears in your program and the program code is not very well organized you will also have a harder time trying to track down where the error is in your code. A program that is perfectly clear to understand today may not be clear tomorrow. If it takes you a while to figure it out, how long would it take someone else to figure it out?

Working in teams is another good reason for writing well formatted code. If you are working on a project within a team and amending other people's code, as well as writing new stuff, it is essential that the whole team uses the same formatting standard. This is so all team members can quickly and easily understand any programmer's code and carry on with the project effectively.

The Value Of Comments

The very first thing to talk about when mentioning good programming style is the use of Comments. Until now, comments have not been used in any examples. I thought, I would wait until this chapter for a chance to describe them properly as I regard comments as one of the most important aspects of writing good code.

To put simply, comments are just lines of text included within your program that are used to describe or document what you are doing with your code. They are never compiled into the final executable or have any other bearing on the program. You can use as many as you like as they will never interfere with program performance.

Comments are a way to provide a more detailed explanation of what you are writing as well as provide an overview on how different parts of your program are meant to work and how they interact with the rest of the code. Here's a brief example:

```
;The procedure Pi() is called to return the value of Pi.
;This calculation is only accurate to six decimal places.

Procedure.f Pi()
  ProcedureReturn 4 * (4 * ATan(1/5) - ATan(1/239))
EndProcedure

CircleDiameter.l = 150

Debug "A circle which has a diameter of " + Str(CircleDiameter) + "mm"
Debug "has a circumference of " + StrF(CircleDiameter * Pi()) + "mm."
```

Here I've used comments within this example to describe the function of the 'Pi()' procedure and more importantly explain its limitation of only being accurate to six decimal places.

Creation of comments is simple because all comments start with a semi-colon (';') and that's it:

```
;This is a comment
```

Comments can appear absolutely anywhere within your source code even on the same line as another command, like this:

```
Procedure.l AddTogether(a.l, b.l) ;Add two numbers and return the result
  ProcedureReturn a + b
EndProcedure
```

You have to remember is the semi-colon at the beginning, this defines where the comment starts. The comment will then be as long as the current line and when a new line is encountered the comment ends. If you want a comment to continue onto a new line then you have to start that new line with another semi colon.

To properly comment code, make every comment significant and fight the temptation of just repeating your code with the comment. Comments shouldn't be too lengthy but long enough to explain what you need to. The general rule of thumb while writing comments is to imagine that you are clarifying the more complicated parts of your code to another person. In six month's time when you revisit your code, you will be glad comments are there to help you understand your work.

Comments can be used for:

1). Adding license or copyright information.
2). Explaining why a particular approach has been used.
3). Adding notices of where code could be improved.
4). Clarifying the functions of complicated procedures.
5). Clarifying procedure internals by drawing graphs or formulae using ASCII art.

My Coding Format

The general layout of my code and the way I structure certain bits and bobs is based on the standard code format of several programming languages. This entire book has been written in this style, which I personally feel is an easy to read and learn format. Here, I'm going to explain why, and show you how I write code, to give you a head start in writing neat and readable programs. Hopefully you will find this style helpful and continue to use it.

Variables, Arrays, Linked Lists And Procedures

I usually name these with clear, accurate, pronounceable and descriptive names based on 'CamelHump' notation. This notation is easy to understand, you capitalize the first letter of the name and then capitalize any other words that follow. The capital letters act as a separator for these words as no spaces can be used. This capitalization format makes these words look as if they have humps running along them, hence the name 'CamelHump' notation. This how is how I prefer to format all variables, arrays and linked lists as I find this makes them easier to read.

Example:

```
NumberOfDays.l = 365
Dim MonthsOfTheYear.s(11)
NewList Days.s()
```

Constants
I format constants using the standard C and Windows API style, which is all uppercase. If I need to distinguish separate words within them, I use underscores.

Example:

```
#SPEED_OF_LIGHT = 299792458 ; Meters per second
```

Structures
I use the same standard for structures as I do for constants, I use all uppercase names. This again is the standard format of C and the Windows API. Also, like constants, if I need to distinguish separate words then I use underscores. Notice, the following structure name is all uppercase.

Example:

```
Structure USER_SERVICE
  ServiceType.s
  ServiceCode.l
EndStructure
```

Indentation
Indents provide a way to structure code and make it easy to see the beginning and end of procedures, loops and conditional statements. Indents are very often used to give purely visual aids to reading code. Here are examples of good indentation:

```
; Returns a String containing a floating point number that's been rounded up.
; 'Number' = Number to round up and return as a String.
; 'DecimalPlaces' = Number of decimal places to round up to.

Procedure.s StrFRound(Number.f, DecimalPlaces.l)
  Protected R.f
  Protected T.f
  If DecimalPlaces < 0
    DecimalPlaces = 0
  EndIf
  R.f = 0.5 * Pow(10, -1 * DecimalPlaces)
  T.f = Pow(10, DecimalPlaces)
  ProcedureReturn StrF(Int((Number + R) * T) / T, DecimalPlaces)
EndProcedure

Debug StrFRound(3.1415927, 4)
```

In this example, you can see, I've indented the code using tabs. This clearly defines code between the beginning and ending keywords of a code block such as a procedure or an 'If' statement. I also indent code this way for loops, procedures, 'If' and 'Select' statements and 'Enumeration' blocks. Indentation is especially helpful in nested statements, like this:

```
For x = 0 To 2
  For y = 0 To 2
    z.l = 0
    While z =< 10
      Debug x * y + z
      z + 1
    Wend
  Next y
Next x
```

Here, you can see the start and end keywords of each loop statement clearly and see all the code contained within. Only one tab to the right is used per code block so the code contained within a particular block isn't too far away from the beginning and end keywords, which could also make code harder to read.

If you look at the line: 'For y = 0 To 2' you can easily track down in the code and find the line: 'Next y'. This is the beginning and end of an 'If' statement. By looking at this we know that all code indented to the right, is inside this block. This will become more useful the larger your programs get.

Multiple Commands On The Same Line
I sometimes write multiple commands on the same line to make some source code smaller. This is easily done using the colon (':') character. The colon character when used, tells the compiler that a new line has started and treats the next command as if it appears on its own separate line. Look at this:

```
Dim Birds.s(3)
Birds(0)="Sparrow" : Birds(1)="Wren" : Birds(2)="Cuckoo" : Birds(3)="Owl"
```

Some programmers frown on this kind of formatting as it can impede readability. I feel sometimes it can help, while it's not over used.

Breaking Source Code Up
When I'm writing a program and it's starting to get big, I tend to break it up into many separate source code files. These files are standard PureBasic files but have either the '*.pb' or '*.pbi' extension. '*.pb' files are standard PureBasic code files while '*.pbi' files are PureBasic Include files. These two types of file are exactly the same and both are associated with the IDE for opening correctly. The '*.pbi' extension however is purely cosmetic to be able to identify quickly included files from the main program file when grouped together in a folder.

In these separate files I hold different parts of the main program and then include them all into the main source code file by using the 'IncludeFile' or 'XIncludeFile' keyword.

For example, if I am defining a lot of procedures I might create a separate source file called 'Procedures.pbi' where all my procedures will be defined. Then at the top of my main source code file I will include the procedures code like this:

```
IncludeFile "Procedures.pbi"
```

This has the effect of taking all lines of code from the "Procedures.pbi" file and pasting them into my main source code starting from this line. Wherever the 'IncludeFile' command appears, this is where the code from the included file will be added into your main code. This is done before compilation so all the compiler sees is one big file to compile.

If you add an 'IncludeFile' line many times within your main code using the same file name, you will get duplicate pieces of code inserted into your main code file. If, however you want to avoid this you must use the 'XIncludeFile' keyword. This is used in the same way as above:

```
XIncludeFile "Procedures.pbi"
```

The 'XIncludeFile' line will include the code from the 'Procedures.pbi' file, only if this line has not been used before. I seldom use the 'IncludeFile' command as you only usually need one of each include file including in any given program. I prefer to use 'XIncludeFile' for everything, as it cuts down on errors occurring.

Correctly Ending A Program

To end a program properly you should always use the 'End' keyword. This closes everything correctly within your program and frees any memory used by it. An optional exit code can also be used with the 'End' keyword if needed. The syntax for use is simple, just use this keyword where you would like your program to end. Multiple 'End' statements can also appear in any one program if you need to potentially end your program in more than one place in your code.

Without exit code:

```
End ; Immediately ends the program and frees all memory used by it.
```

With exit code:

```
End 1 ; Immediately ends the program, frees all memory and returns 1.
```

Golden Rules For Writing Easily Readable Code

Here is a list of golden rules I follow while writing a program. I stick to these rules even when writing very small programs. If you follow this list you too will write good, clean, understandable code. Using a standard way of working gives your code clear and concise structure to anyone reading it and will make your code look and feel more professional.

1). Give all variables, procedures, arrays, etc. clear, accurate, pronounceable, descriptive names.
2). Group logically connected variables or data into arrays or structures.
3). Procedures should perform one function and perform it well.
4). Use indentation to show code structure.
5). Use parentheses (brackets) in expressions to avoid any evaluation confusion.
6). Use blank lines to separate different procedures and other blocks of code.
7). Try not to use the 'Goto' or 'Gosub' keyword.
8). Use comments to help people (or you) understand your code more clearly.
9). Try not to document bad code with comments, re-write the code properly.
10). When working in a team, agree a formatting style before starting, then stick to it.

How To Minimize And Handle Errors

In this chapter I'm going to talk about methods that will help you catch errors in your code. Even the most experienced and dedicated programmer can make mistakes or forget to handle common ones or maybe even overlook them altogether. Here I reveal good working practices along with some valuable tips and tricks, enabling you to be more vigilant in your programming, minimizing the chance of any problems occurring.

Use An Error Handler Procedure

If your using PureBasic for large projects you might find that you'll be making many tests to confirm a true value. This is because a great deal of commands return a value. This value is nearly always an integer and always above '0' if things have gone right. Some programmers use 'If' statements to test commands for a true value before proceeding, because if you remember from Chapter 4, everything above '0' is considered a true value in PureBasic.

While some people use 'If' statements to check things have gone right before proceeding, I find this approach is only useful for small programs as it can lead to a lot of confusing nested 'If' statements when used for larger ones. What I tend to do is use a procedure as an error handler instead of an 'If' statement. This not only makes your source code much more easy to read but you can pass user defined messages to this procedure to inform users of where exactly in your program things have gone wrong and with what command. To see both sides, here is an example of using an 'If' statement to test a command:

```
#TEXTFILE = 1

If ReadFile(#TEXTFILE, "TextFile.txt")
  Debug ReadString(#TEXTFILE)
  CloseFile(#TEXTFILE)
Else
  MessageRequester("Error", "Could not open the file: 'TextFile.txt'.")
EndIf
```

Here I test to make sure I can read the file 'TextFile.txt' if I can then I read a String from it. While this method is fine for small programs, I prefer this way for bigger projects:

```
#TEXTFILE = 1

Procedure HandleError(Result.l, Text.s)
  If Result = 0
    MessageRequester("Error", Text, #PB_MessageRequester_Ok)
    End
  EndIf
EndProcedure

HandleError(ReadFile(#TEXTFILE,"TextFile.txt"),"Couldn't open: 'TextFile.txt'.")
Debug ReadString(#TEXTFILE)
CloseFile(#TEXTFILE)
```

Here I've used a procedure called 'HandleError()' to take care of testing return values of any commands passed to it. The first parameter called 'Result', is where the return value from a command is passed. If a command is passed like this to a procedure, that command will always be executed before the procedure is called. This is to make sure any return values are passed correctly. The second parameter 'Text.s', is the String you wish to be displayed if the passed command returns '0'. Let's break this down a little more.

When I pass this command to the 'HandleError()' procedure:

```
ReadFile(#TEXTFILE, "TextFile.txt")
```

If the file 'TextFile.txt' does not exist on your hard drive or something else goes wrong, the 'ReadFile()' command will return '0'. This value of '0' is then passed to the first parameter of the error handling procedure. Inside the procedure this parameter is tested to see if its value is equal to '0', if it is then the error message passed in the second parameter will be displayed using a message requester and the program will end. This is handy to give clear and concise error messages for every command that raises an error.

If the command passed to the error handling procedure returns a value above '0', then this command is considered to have been successful and the error handling procedure takes no action.

The procedure demonstrated in the above example may look like overkill for such a small example but this kind of thing is not what it would mainly be used for. Using an error handling procedure really becomes useful in larger programs, where many commands need to be tested one after another. Once the procedure is defined you can use it to test as many commands as you like and each can be tested on one line, unlike an 'If' statement. Look at this example of testing multiple commands:

```
HandleError(InitEngine3D(), "InitEngine3D() failed to initialized!")
HandleError(InitSprite(), "InitSprite() failed to initialized!")
HandleError(InitKeyboard(), "InitKeyboard() failed to initialized!")
HandleError(OpenScreen(1024, 768, 32, "Game"), "A screen could not be opened!")
```

Can you image using 'If' statements to test all these commands? It would be a nested 'If' nightmare, and this isn't even a full program yet! Using error handling procedures makes your code look neater, cleaner and more readable.

Working like this, you will find mistakes are easier to spot and unexpected problems are more simple to handle. The only problem with this approach is that 'HandleError' appears at the start of every line, which some people find intrusive.

Use The 'EnableExplicit' Command

This command is a godsend for some people and a hindrance to others and that's why it is completely optional to use. This command enables explicit variable definition within the whole of your program. So what does this mean? Well, in Chapter 2, I explained that if you didn't specify a type suffix for a variable, then that variable's type will default to the current default type, which is normally a Long. If the 'Define' keyword has been used to define another default type then any un-typed variables will use that instead. The 'EnableExplicit' command stops this behavior and requires after use that all new variables have their scope and type strictly defined. Let me show you how this command could prove useful.

Say for example, I have a procedure which needs to be passed a variable of some crucial value and then the result of this procedure needs to be used, I could write it like this:

```
WeeklyAmount.l = 1024

Procedure CalculateYearlyAmount(Value.l)
  YearlyAmount.l = Value * 52
  ProcedureReturn YearlyAmount
EndProcedure

Debug CalculateYearlyAmount(WeaklyAmount)
```

Now, this looks okay and if you quickly scan through this example you don't see any problems. If you run it however, the 'CalculateYearlyAmount()' procedure returns '0'. This is obviously not right as we are supposed to be passing it the 'WeeklyAmount' variable which has a value of '1024'. If you look closely at the procedure call you can see that I actually pass a variable called 'WeaklyAmount'. Notice that this variable is spelt incorrectly and so it's treated as a new variable. When passing variables like this, if they haven't been defined before then PureBasic creates a new variable automatically and passes that. Variables that haven't had their type or value defined during creation are always assigned the default type, and given a null value. This new variable named 'WeaklyAmount' in the above example, therefore has a value of '0'.

Automatically defining variables that have been typed like this is considered by some programmers to be careless and very error prone. This default behavior can be turned off and the compiler told to be more strict about variable definition by using the 'EnableExplicit' command. If we used this command in the above example we would get a few messages informing us that some variables need to be more strictly defined. This means that all variables used after the 'EnableExplicit' command must be defined using any one of the variable definition keywords. These are 'Define', 'Global', 'Protected', 'Static' and 'Shared', as explained in Chapters 2 and 6.

If we go through the above example, strictly defining all variables and then re-launching the program, the compiler would bring our attention to the last line and would show a message informing us that the variable 'WeaklyAmount' needs to be defined more strictly too. This would be a bit strange as it should already be done earlier in the program. On further investigation it would then be noticed that this variable is spelt wrong and needs correcting. Here's what the above example would look like using the 'EnableExplicit' command and all variables defined in a more explicit way.

```
EnableExplicit

Define WeeklyAmount.l = 1024

Procedure CalculateYearlyAmount(Value.l)
  Protected YearlyAmount.l = Value * 52
  ProcedureReturn YearlyAmount
EndProcedure

Debug CalculateYearlyAmount(WeeklyAmount)
```

Hopefully using this command should prevent many more variable based spelling mistakes because every time a spelling mistake is encountered the compiler will treat it as a separate variable name and you will be asked to clarify this variable's scope and definition. Giving you chance to correct the variable, thus restoring any values that may be lost through these errors.

At anytime if you want to revert to default PureBasic behavior, you can switch off the 'EnableExplicit' command's influence by using the 'DisableExplicit' command.

Defining Variables Using The 'Define' Command

The 'Define' command can be used in two ways. First it sets the default type for un-typed variables, as shown in Chapter 2. In this way the 'Define' keyword is used with a type suffix which defines the new default type, like this:

```
Define.s
MyString = "Hello"
```

Secondly, the 'Define' command can be used to define variables after an 'EnableExplicit' command has been used. If the 'EnableExplicit' command has been used, all variables from then on in your program have to be strictly defined. In this case, the 'Define' command may be used like this:

```
EnableExplicit
Define MyVar.b = 10
```

Notice that when used in this way you don't have to use the type suffix on the end of the 'Define' keyword because we define the variable type using the variable's own type suffix instead.

Introducing The PureBasic Debugger

PureBasic provides a full featured debugger that helps find errors and bugs within your code. This debugger is invaluable as it gives you the ability to control program flow and take a look at the values of variables, arrays and linked lists at any time during the running of your program. It also provides advanced functions for assembly programmers to examine and modify CPU registers or view values stored in associated memory addresses. It's also possible to view the CPU usage of your program using the built-in CPU monitor.

If you run your program and the debugger encounters an error, the program will halt and the line where the error occurred will be marked in the IDE (using red) and the error will be displayed in the IDE Error Log and IDE status bar. When an error is caught like this, you can use the program control functions or end the running program. To end the running program use the 'Kill Program' menu item (Menu:Debugger->Kill Program) or its associated toolbar button. If the debugger is disabled, no errors will be caught and could lead to a program crash.

While writing a program in the IDE, the debugger is enabled by default. This you can see at a glance by looking at the debugger toggle button located in the IDE's toolbar, see Fig.23. If this button is shown as pressed down then the debugger is enabled, if it is shown as being up, the debugger is disabled. This button is also a shortcut to the 'Use Debugger' menu item, (Menu:Debugger->Use Debugger) which is also a toggle. The debugger can also be enabled in the compiler options for your program too, (Menu:Compiler->Compiler Options...->Compiler Options->Enable Debugger). All these different ways of toggling the status of the debugger are linked. If one is used, the others mirror its status.

The Windows PureBasic package comes with three different kinds of debugger to be used. These can all be used to debug your program but some don't have the same functionality. The first is the built-in debugger which is the most feature rich among the different ones and is used by default because it's integrated directly into the IDE. The PureBasic IDE running on some operating systems doesn't support this built-in version so a stand-alone debugger is also supplied with the installation. This stand-alone version has almost the same feature set as the built-in debugger but because it's separate from the IDE, some of the efficiency of direct access from the IDE is lost. The third debugger runs in a console only. This version's primary use is for non-graphical environments such as text based Linux operating systems or remotely developed applications working with clients using the SSH protocol. The available debuggers can be selected as default in the IDE preferences, (Menu:File->Preferences->Debugger).

Even though the debugger is a great tool to use to track down problems, all this debugging functionality however comes at a price. You will find that programs running while the debugger is enabled will be a great deal slower than running them with it disabled. This shouldn't pose any problems though, because the vast majority of final executables are compiled without the debugger for maximum speed and compactness. This must be kept in mind if you are developing speed critical programs or need to time certain bits of code, etc.

If you need to use the debugger to debug your code but in some sections you could do with it being disabled, you can use the built-in debugger commands, 'DisableDebugger' and 'EnableDebugger'. These are pretty self explanatory to use, the 'DisableDebugger' command disabled the debugger from then on in your code and the 'EnableDebugger' command re-enables it. If you disable the debugger you will also notice that this disables any 'Debug' commands. This is because 'Debug' commands are also part of the debugger and they are not compiled if the debugger is disabled.

Using The Debugger

The debugger functions can be used at any time while your program is running, these can be accessed from the debugger menu as well as using the associated toolbar buttons. The Error Log (Menu:Debugger->Error Log) and the CPU monitor (Menu:Debugger->CPU Monitor) are always accessible too. While you are using the debugger, all source code files that are connected to your running program are immediately switched to read-only until the program has ended. This makes sure that the currently used code is not modified in any way, to provide a simple version control on your code.

To give you an overview of the debugger I'm going to start by explaining the program control functions it provides. These controls let you stop the program at any given time and examine any variable, array or linked list value. It also allows you to step through your program a line at a time to examine exactly how your program executes. The state of any program while using the debugger will be shown in the IDE status bar and in the Error Log. The debugger's program control toolbar buttons are shown in Fig.23, these are also mirrored by commands in the 'Debugger' menu.

The Debugger Toolbar Buttons

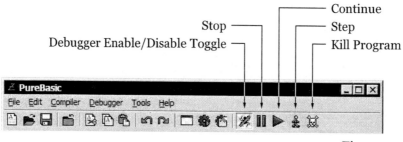

Fig. 23

To halt your program at any time and use the debugger controls, you can either use the 'CallDebugger' keyword in your code, use 'Stop' from the debugger menu (Menu:Debugger->Stop) or press the 'Stop' toolbar button while your program is running. You can also use Breakpoints to halt the program's execution. To use a breakpoint within the IDE, put the cursor on the line where you would like the program to halt and switch control to the debugger. Then choose the 'Breakpoint' menu command (Menu:Debugger->Breakpoint) to add a breakpoint. You will notice that a small circle appears in the line numbering gutter of the IDE. This is a visual indication to show where breakpoints are defined. When this program is next run, it will halt on that line where the breakpoint is defined and then the debugger program control functions will be available. You are then able to examine any data values or step through your program to analyze your code more closely. Here is a short description of the program control functions:

'Stop'
This halts the program and displays the current line.

'Continue'
This continues the program execution until another halt command is met.

'Step'
This executes one line of source code and then stops the execution again.

'Kill Program'
This forces the program to end, and closes all associated debugger windows.

Here is a brief example of halting program execution using the 'CallDebugger' command:

```
CallDebugger
For x.l = 1 To 10
  Debug x
Next x
End
```

Once the above program has been halted using the 'CallDebugger' command. You can step through it, a line at a time using the 'Step' toolbar button. Click it ten times and you will see the value of 'x' echoed to the Debug Output window, incremented by one each time this button is pressed. While a program is halted in this way you can view any variable, array or linked list value by opening the Variable Viewer (Menu:Debugger->Variable Viewer). This small overview should be enough for you to learn the basics of the debugger. For more advanced information of what it is capable of, see the PureBasic Helpfile.

The 'OnError' Library
The built-in 'OnError' library enables you to perform error checking in your final executable when the debugger is not available. Normally you would use the debugger during development to help catch errors, but when you compile your final executable for distribution, you disable the debugger in order to compile the smallest and fastest executable possible. The speed gain for disabling the debugger is about six times than with it enabled. Using the 'OnError' library it is easy to implement advanced error checking and handling into a final executable and still have the full speed of PureBasic available.

There are many very advanced commands that can be used from this library but these are beyond the scope of this book, so I'll just focus on the more commonly used and easily understood ones. First, I'll show you how to effectively catch and describe an error without using the debugger. Take a look at the following example:

```
;Set the error handler
OnErrorGoto(?ErrorHandler)

;Trigger a classic 'divide by zero' error.
Null.l = 0
TestVariable.l = 100 / Null
```

```
;Handle any system error that occurs
ErrorHandler:
Text.s = "Error count:" + #TAB$ + #TAB$ + Str(GetErrorCounter()) + #CRLF$
Text.s + "Error ID number:" + #TAB$ + #TAB$ + Str(GetErrorNumber()) + #CRLF$
Text.s + "Error description:" + #TAB$ + #TAB$ + GetErrorDescription() + #CRLF$
Text.s + "Error occurred on line:" + #TAB$ + Str(GetErrorLineNR()) + #CRLF$
Text.s + "Error occurred in module:" + #TAB$ + GetErrorModuleName() + #CRLF$
MessageRequester("ERROR", Text)
End
```

Here, I use the 'OnErrorGoto()' command to specify where to jump to if an error is encountered. The parameter of this command is a label destination of where to jump. If you look closely at the label that I have passed as a parameter, you will notice I have appended a question mark to the beginning of the label name. This is because the 'OnErrorGoto()' command actually needs a pointer of the label passing instead of just a label. Using a question mark like this returns the label's memory address. A pointer is a variable which contains a memory address of where something is stored, see Chapter 13 (Pointers) for a more complete explanation. Like the 'Goto' and 'Gosub' command we also omit the colon on the end of the label when we pass the label name to this command.

After the label has been specified using the 'OnErrorGoto()' command, then other 'OnError' library commands help us to understand what went wrong and where. In the above example I've used these commands:

'GetErrorCounter()'
This command returns the number of errors that have occurred in your program since it was started.

'GetErrorNumber()'
This command returns the unique error number of the last error that occurred.

'GetErrorDescription()'
This command returns a String fully describing the error that has occurred.

'GetErrorLineNR()'
This command returns the line number of where the error has occurred in your source code, either in the main source file or in any included files. For this command to work properly you must switch on the 'Enable OnError Lines Support' compiler option before compiling your program.

'GetErrorModuleName()'
This command returns a String telling you in which source code file the error occurred in. This is very useful if you are using a lot of included source code files. For this command to work properly you must switch on the 'Enable OnError Lines Support' compiler option before compiling your program.

The last two commands listed here require that you switch on the 'Enable OnError Lines Support' compiler option before compiling your program. This is located in the compiler options within the IDE, (Menu:Compiler->Compiler Options...->Compiler Options->Enable OnError Lines Support).

To actually demonstrate the 'OnError' commands catching and handling an error, I've created a reproducible error in the code. This error is a simple 'divide by zero' error and is coded like this:

```
;Trigger a classic 'divide by zero' error.
Null.l = 0
TestVariable.l = 100 / Null
```

If the debugger is enabled then it would catch this easily but if we disabled it this error is missed. We can use the 'OnError' library to catch this error without the need for the debugger. To run the example and see it working properly, you need to first disable the debugger and enable the 'Enable OnError Lines Support' compiler option. Now when you compile the program, it should now catch the 'divide by zero' error and give you some detailed feedback, all without the help of the debugger. Fig.24 shows this example in action and shows the information collected by the other 'OnError' commands.

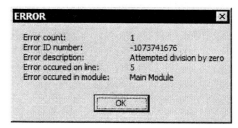

Fig. 24

In the last example, I used the 'OnErrorGoto()' command to specify a label to jump to if an error occurs. This command, however does not let you return from that label and continue with the program, even if you use the 'Return' keyword. This is where the 'OnErrorGosub()' command comes in handy. Using this command you can specify a label or a procedure as the error handler and this command does let you return from these with the appropriate keyword. Here's an example of using a procedure:

```
;Handle any system error that occurs
Procedure ErrorHandler()
  Text.s = "Error count:" + #TAB$ + Str(GetErrorCounter()) + #CRLF$
  Text.s + "Error ID number:" + #TAB$ + Str(GetErrorNumber()) + #CRLF$
  Text.s + "Error description:" + #TAB$ + GetErrorDescription() + #CRLF$
  Text.s + "Occurred on line:" + #TAB$ + Str(GetErrorLineNR()) + #CRLF$
  Text.s + "Occurred in module:" + #TAB$ + GetErrorModuleName() + #CRLF$+#CRLF$
  Text.s + "Would you like to continue execution of the program? "
  ReturnValue.l = MessageRequester("ERROR", Text, #PB_MessageRequester_YesNo)
  If ReturnValue = #PB_MessageRequester_No
    End
  EndIf
EndProcedure

;Set the error handler
```

```
OnErrorGosub(@ErrorHandler())

;Trigger a classic 'divide by zero' error.
Null.l = 0
TestVariable.l = 100 / Null

;If the program reaches here then the program was resumed
MessageRequester("STATUS", "The program was allowed to continue running.")
End
```

Here I demonstrate how to resume the program execution after an error, something which you can't do using the 'OnErrorGoto()' command. There is however one problem with this approach and that is if you choose to continue with the program execution, the error that occurred, may make this program unstable and crash. That's why, if you give your program the ability to resume after an error, depending on how serious the error was, you should inform the user what has happened and encourage them to restart the program. Resuming program execution should ideally be used if you think your user may lose work after a program crash. Resuming gives them a chance to save what they was doing in your program (if it has this functionality) before they restart it.

'OnErrorGoto' And 'OnErrorGosub'

These two commands are very similar in that they let you specify a place to jump to if an error occurs so you can handle and describe the error. The main difference between these two commands is wether or not the error handler lets you return back to the normal program flow.

The 'OnErrorGoto()' command lets you specify a label that you can jump to when an error occurs but you can't return from it. Meaning that once an error is handled the program must quit immediately.

The 'OnErrorGosub()' command lets you specify a label or a procedure to use as an error handler, giving you the ability to return from these with the appropriate keyword. This means you have the option of resuming normal program execution after an error has been handled.

Say for example, you have written a text editor and Bob is using it to write a letter. If after an hour of writing an unexplained error occurs and the program throws up an error message, Bob doesn't want to have wasted that last hour and lose his letter due to an error. In this case, Bob can be informed of what has happened and be given the choice to resume the program execution to save his letter to a file before restarting the program. An email address could even be displayed in the error message for Bob to contact and explain what went wrong in order for the program writer to correct it.

Raising And Catching User Defined Errors
So far I've shown you a way of catching and documenting system errors that can occur in your program and this way will catch almost any serious system error you may encounter. Sometimes however you may want to raise your own error for the sake of customization. If this is the case you can use the 'SetErrorNumber()' command to create and fire an error of your own.

The 'SetErrorNumber()' command needs one parameter in order to work properly and this parameter is a Long type number that identifies this error. I usually use constants to define custom error numbers then I can refer to these by name, like this:

```
#ERROR_READFILE = 1
#ERROR_WRITEFILE = 2
#FILE_TEXT = 1

;Set the error handler
OnErrorGoto(?ErrorHandler)

If ReadFile(#FILE_TEXT, "Report.txt") = #False
  ;If the file read fails then fire an error
  SetErrorNumber(#ERROR_READFILE)
EndIf
End


;Handle any custom error that occurs
ErrorHandler:
Text.s = "Error count:" + #TAB$ + #TAB$ + Str(GetErrorCounter()) + #CRLF$
Text.s + "Error ID number:" + #TAB$ + #TAB$ + Str(GetErrorNumber()) + #CRLF$
Select GetErrorNumber()
  Case #ERROR_READFILE
    Description.s = "The file could not be read."
  Case #ERROR_WRITEFILE
    Description.s = "The file could not be written."
EndSelect
Text.s + "Error description:" + #TAB$ + #TAB$ + Description + #CRLF$
Text.s + "Error occurred on line:" + #TAB$ + Str(GetErrorLineNR()) + #CRLF$
Text.s + "Error occurred in module:" + #TAB$ + GetErrorModuleName() + #CRLF$
MessageRequester("ERROR", Text)
End
```

In the above example if the file 'Report.txt' cannot be read using the 'ReadFile()' command, I raise a custom error using the 'SetErrorNumber()' command. This error is identified by the constant '#ERROR_READFILE' which has a value of '1'. Once an error has been triggered in this way the error handler label or procedure is called. In the error handler you can check to see what error number has been raised by using the 'GetErrorNumber()' command. Depending on what the result is of this command you can then tailor the error description to your hearts content. Here I'm testing the 'GetErrorNumber()' command with a 'Select' statement and using different description Strings depending on its value. The pop-up error message then displays this description.

As you can see from these examples, using the 'OnError' library gives you advanced error checking but using a very simple syntax.

Graphical User Interfaces

In this next section I'm going to talk about Graphical User Interfaces and how they are created in PureBasic. Nearly all modern operating systems have a built-in graphical user interface available, allowing the user to interact fluidly with programs that choose to use it. The operating system exposes the user interface to programs through an Application Programming Interface (or API) through which a program can tell the operating system how draw its user interface. This sounds extremely complicated but is simply and elegantly handled within PureBasic using the 'Window', 'Menu' and 'Gadget' libraries.

PureBasic creates these graphical interfaces for your programs using the native application programming interface of the system they've been compiled for. In other words, when you code an interface for a program and compile it on a particular system, that program will have the correct look and feel of the operating system it has been compiled for. This is essential for all professional application development.

This section begins with explaining and demonstrating programs that use a console as their user interface, which is arguably the simplest user interface of all. Later, I move on to explain how to create programs with native user interfaces and how to add menus and graphics. In the last section I give you and overview of the PureBasic Visual Form Designer. Using this tool you can design an interface visually as if you were painting it upon a program.

After reading this section you should have a firm grasp on how to create graphical user interfaces for your programs and understand how to handle interaction from the user.

9

Creating User Interfaces

In this chapter I'll explain how to create graphical user interfaces for your programs. PureBasic makes this task very easy by distilling complex application programming interfaces into simple, easy to learn commands. I explain fully how to code the graphical interface, complete with menus and sometimes with graphics. I also cover how to handle events from your program's interface, such as, when the user presses a button or selects a menu item. Hopefully after reading this chapter you will be well equipped to create user interfaces for any program you decide to develop.

Console Programs

To begin with, we shouldn't run before we can walk, so first I'll introduce to you what is known as a Console Program. Console programs, as the name suggests, are programs that use a console as their user interface. A console is a text based interface that can accept typed input and display output using text characters. On some operating systems the console can display simple graphics by substituting some of the ASCII character set for graphical symbols instead of characters.

Console interfaces are usually used in programs where a fully blown user interface is not needed. These types of programs are usually command line tools that are run from other consoles or things like CGI programs that run in the background on web servers, etc. Basically, a console is used to display basic output information from the program and to accept basic text input from the user. Commands that create and work with a console interface are grouped inside the 'Console' library (Helpfile:Reference Manual->General Libraries->Console). This library offers PureBasic programmers various commands to print text, accept user input, clear the console and even change its colors. Here is an example of how to create a console program in PureBasic:

```
If OpenConsole()
  Print("This is a test console program, press return to exit...")
  Input()
  CloseConsole()
EndIf
End
```

In this example I've used the 'OpenConsole()' and 'CloseConsole()' commands to open and close the actual console window, these are self explanatory. The second command I've used is the 'Print()' command which accepts one String parameter that is printed to the console interface. This command is almost identical to the other console library command 'PrintN()'. The 'PrintN()' will also print a line of text but it will append an end-of-line character on the end to move to a new line after the text has been printed. This is very similar behavior to the file writing commands 'WriteString()' and 'WriteStringN()' as mentioned in Chapter 7 (Handling Files).

The last command used in the above example is 'Input()'. This command halts the program's execution until the Return key is pressed on the keyboard. This command then returns any characters (as a String) that were entered into the console before the Return key was finally pressed. Because in my example, I'm not dealing with any return value from this command, it's used here purely to keep the console open so people can read the text I've printed to it. If this command was omitted, then the console would almost immediately close as soon as it had opened. Using 'Input()' like this, can provide a simple way to keep the console open while we read what is printed there, as long as we inform the user that to continue the program execution he or she must press Return.

Reading User Input
Sometimes in your console programs you may want to read user input, this could be a simple number or a String of text. Although it is pretty straightforward to gather any user input you must always remember that the 'Input()' command only returns Strings. This next piece of code shows this, while introducing some new console commands:

```
If OpenConsole()

  EnableGraphicalConsole(#True)

  Repeat

    ConsoleColor(10, 0)
    PrintN("TIMES TABLES GENERATOR")
    PrintN("")
    ConsoleColor(7, 0)
    PrintN("Please enter a number, then press Return...")
    PrintN("")

    Number.q = ValQ(Input())
    If Number = 0
      ClearConsole()
      Continue
    Else
      Break
    EndIf

  ForEver
  PrintN("")
```

```
   For x.1 = 1 To 10
     PrintN(Str(x) + " x " + StrQ(Number) + " = " + StrQ(x * Number))
   Next x
   PrintN("")

   Print("Press Return to exit...")
   Input()
   CloseConsole()
 EndIf
 End
```

This example looks rather complicated but it's not really if you read it a line at a time. The first new command I've used here is the 'EnableGraphicalConsole()' command. This enables or disables the graphical capabilities of the console program by passing either the '#True' or '#False' constants as a parameter. Because we later use 'ClearConsole()' which only works with a graphical console, we set 'EnableGraphicalConsole()' to true.

Differences Between Graphical And Non Graphical Console Modes

Using the 'EnableGraphicalConsole()' command you can switch between text mode and graphical mode of the current console. Here are the differences for each mode:

Text Mode (Default):
ASCII control characters work correctly (ASCII range '0' to '31').
Output redirection using Pipes works correctly (Essential for CGI programs).
Long Strings of printed text wrap onto a new line if they reach the end of the console window.
You can read and write data to the console that is not necessarily text based.

Graphical Mode (Changed using 'EnableGraphicalConsole(#True)'):
Text characters outside the ACSII range '33' to '126' are displayed as small simple graphics.
Long Strings of printed text are truncated if they reach the end of the console window.
'ClearConsole()' clears the entire console of any output.
'ConsoleLocate()' Moves the cursor to be able to print text in any position in the console window.

This list contains some advanced topics you might not be familiar with right now but I have included this list here to be used a future reference when you are more comfortable with these things.

I've also changed the console text color in some places by using the 'ConsoleColor()' command. The first parameter is the text color and the second is the text background color. The parameters are numbers that range from '0' to '15' which represent different color presets, see the helpfile to see what color is associated with each number (Helpfile:Reference Manual->General Libraries->Console->ConsoleColor).

Also in this example I've used a loop to handle verifying user input, this is used as a way of almost re-running the program if the user entered an incorrect value. I want a number to be entered so I use the 'ValQ()' command to change the String returned from the 'Input()' command into a Quad. This returned value is then tested, if it is equal to '0' then the user must have typed a non-numeric String or the number '0'. If this is the case I clear the console of all output by using the 'ClearConsole()' command and force the loop to continue from the beginning, totally redrawing the original text and requesting user input again. If the user input is a number above '0' then I 'Break' from the loop and continue with the rest of the program which draws the times table for that number.

Reading User Input In Realtime

The last example showcased the 'Input()' command which is fine if you need to enter a String or such but its only limitation is that you have to press the Return key in order for the input to be passed to the program. What if you wanted to get user input in realtime to detect immediately when a key was pressed in order to trigger an action? Well, this can be achieved by using the 'Inkey()' and 'RawKey()' commands. Look at this next piece of code for an example on the usage of both:

```
Procedure DisplayTitle()
  ConsoleColor(10, 0)
  PrintN("KEY CODE FINDER")
  PrintN("")
  ConsoleColor(7, 0)
EndProcedure

Procedure DisplayEscapeText()
  PrintN("")
  ConsoleColor(8, 0)
  PrintN("Press another key or press Escape to exit")
  ConsoleColor(7, 0)
EndProcedure

If OpenConsole()

  EnableGraphicalConsole(#True)
  DisplayTitle()
  PrintN("Press a key...")
  Repeat
    KeyPressed.s = Inkey()
    RawKeyCode.l = RawKey()

    If KeyPressed <> ""

      ClearConsole()
      DisplayTitle()
      PrintN("Key Pressed: " + KeyPressed)
      PrintN("Key Code: " + Str(RawKeyCode))
      DisplayEscapeText()

    ElseIf RawKeyCode
```

```
        ClearConsole()
        DisplayTitle()
        PrintN("Key Pressed: " + "Non-ASCII")
        PrintN("Key Code: " + Str(RawKeyCode))
        DisplayEscapeText()

    Else

      Delay(1)

    EndIf

  Until KeyPressed = #ESC$
  CloseConsole()
EndIf
End
```

This example is similar to the one before in that we are opening a console and switching it to graphical mode then printing some text to it. The main difference is the 'Repeat' loop is continuously calling two commands to determine which key, if any, has been pressed. These two commands are 'Inkey()' and 'RawKey()'.

The first command, 'Inkey()' returns a one character String of the key held down when this command was called. So if I held down the 'D' key on the keyboard while this command is called, then 'Inkey()' would return the String 'd'. Although this command is simple to understand you must remember that the keys on a standard keyboard are usually printed in uppercase, while the 'Inkey()' command returns them as lowercase unless the Shift key is held down at the same time. If a non-ASCII key is held down while this command is called then 'Inkey()' will return an empty String until an ASCII key is held down.

The second command for gathering information on what key has been pressed is a companion to the 'Inkey()' command, its name is 'RawKey()'. This command, as the name suggests, returns a numeric raw key code of the key being held down while this command is called. In the above example, you can see how to use both commands to extract information about which key is being held down during the loop. This is a great way to read user input in realtime and react accordingly when a particular key is being pressed.

Delaying Things A Little

You may notice that in the above example I've also used a 'Delay()' command to tell the program to delay itself for '1' millisecond. While this looks a little strange and unnecessary, the 'Delay()' command is there for a reason. Because you will be using a multitasking operating system to run your programs, it's good programming practice not to monopolize CPU time if you can help it. Using the 'Delay()' command gives other programs a chance to use the CPU while your program is delayed. Even a delay of '1' millisecond allows the operating system to free up the CPU long enough to let other programs have a chance to run. This command is especially useful when using loops to perform the same action over and over again. If a 'Delay()' command is not used within such a loop then your program will take up all the CPU's resources until it has quit, leaving no processing power available for other programs to run. This can sometimes make these other programs appear to 'freeze' and not respond as normal.

Compiling A True Console Program

Running the console program examples in the IDE will build programs that look and act like real console programs but won't be console programs in the true sense until you compile them using the 'Console' executable format.

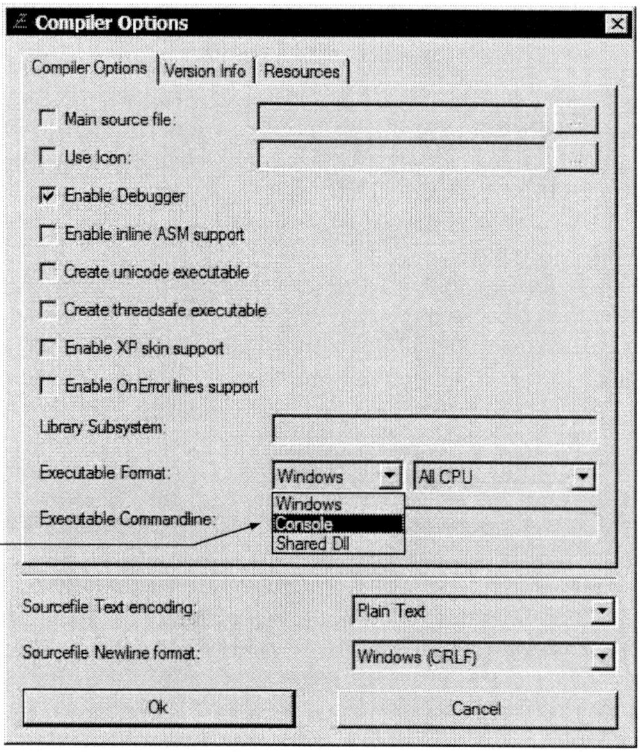

The executable format is selected here

The 'Compiler Options' dialog box
as it appears on Microsoft Windows.

Fig. 25

Fig.25 shows a diagram of where the executable format option is in the 'Compiler Options' dialog box (Menu:Compiler->Compiler Options...). Once this is selected, click 'Ok' and compile your program using 'Create Executable...' (Menu:Compiler->Create Executable...) to compile your final executable. The PureBasic compiler will now build a true console program.

The main difference between these executable formats is that the IDE defaults to compile all programs using the native operating system's executable format. These programs when run either by double clicking or evoking them from a command line interface will always open a new console window before proceeding. Using the 'Console' executable format you can explicitly declare that this program should be compiled as a true console program, meaning that the program will run as normal if double clicked but when it's run from a command line interface it doesn't open a new console window, it acts correctly as a tool within the currently opened command line interface.

And that's all there is to programming interfaces in console programs really. They are not supposed to be used for complicated interfaces (although in the past, games have been written using the graphical console mode). These interfaces are really used nowadays for displaying simple output from command line tools.

Creating Native User Interfaces

In this next section I'm going to show you how to create user interfaces that have the same native look and feel as all the programs currently running on your operating system. These are called 'Native' interfaces because PureBasic uses the underlying operating system's API to draw the interface components. For an example of such an interface, look at the PureBasic IDE, this has been completely written from scratch using PureBasic which in turn uses the operating system's API.

All this talk of the operating system's API may dishearten you, making you think that this all sounds very complicated, but don't panic. The good news is that you don't have to know anything about 'what goes on under the hood' because PureBasic handles this automatically and hides any complicated issues from you. Just using PureBasic's built-in libraries you can build powerful applications that rival any other programming language. On average PureBasic programs prove to be faster and compile to a smaller executable size than many industrial strength languages. This has been proved many times through small competitions created by members of PureBasic's official online forums.

So, let's get going and create our first native user interface with PureBasic.

Hello World
As is customary in the programming world, the first example of any programming language's interface commands is usually a 'Hello World' program. This consists of a simple window that says hello to the user and provide a way of closing the program. Start a new file in the IDE and type this in:

```
#WINDOW_MAIN = 1

#FLAGS = #PB_Window_SystemMenu | #PB_Window_ScreenCentered
If OpenWindow(#WINDOW_MAIN, 0, 0, 300, 200, "Hello World", #FLAGS)
  Repeat
    Event.l = WaitWindowEvent()
  Until Event = #PB_Event_CloseWindow
EndIf
End
```

If you run this piece of code you will see a window similar to Fig.26 overleaf. To close this window click the close button in the top right hand corner. Even though this example only consists of a blank window and a close button in the title bar, this is the start of all native user interfaces in PureBasic.

In the above example, I use the 'OpenWindow()' command to actually open the window and define what features it should have. If you open the helpfile and refer to the 'OpenWindow()' command (Helpfile:Reference Manual->General Libraries->Window->OpenWindow) then look at the syntax example, you can see I've used the '#PB_Window_SystemMenu' and '#PB_Window_ScreenCentered'

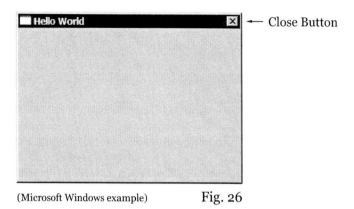

(Microsoft Windows example)   Fig. 26

window flags to define that this window should have a functioning system menu, complete with close button and be centered on the screen when it's opened. When using multiple flags like this, you join them together using the bitwise 'OR' operator as shown in the code above. This operator combines the value of any flags used at the binary level (for a more complete explanation see Chapter 3).

After the 'OpenWindow()' command is used I've then used a 'Repeat' loop to act as the Main Loop to process any events that this window may encounter.

Why Are The Window Position Parameters Set At '0'?

When opening a window using the 'OpenWindow()' command the second and third parameters of this command determine the coordinates where this window will be drawn on screen. However, if you use the '#PB_Window_ScreenCentered' or '#PB_Window_WindowCentered' flags in the same command call the position parameters are ignored. This is because PureBasic is over-riding these position parameters to center the window on the screen or over another window. If this is the case you can safely use '0' for both the position parameters or use the '#PB_Ignore' constant to explicitly show in your source code that these two parameters are been ignored because of the flags passed.

The Main Loop

The main loop in a program is what keeps the program 'alive'. It allows the program to continually keep running while redrawing the interface (if it's moved around the desktop) and handle any events that the interface may generate. Thankfully PureBasic handles all redrawing of the interface automatically so we only need to use a main loop to keep the program running and to process other events.

In my little 'Hello World' program I've used a 'Repeat' loop as my main loop, this gives me the ability to keep the loop going forever until a particular condition is met, in this case, until I have encountered an event of '#PB_Event_CloseWindow' type, which is the event triggered when you click the close button. Once this event is received, the loop then exits thus ending the program.

Understanding Events

Every program you write using any programming language will use roughly the same way of handling events. This involves detecting an event during the main loop then directing the program to run another piece of code depending on what the event was. So what kinds of events are there? Well, an event can be triggered by many actions within your programs, an event might be triggered by clicking on a gadget, pressing a button on the keyboard, selecting an item from a menu or just by moving or closing the program. The trick is knowing what event has happened so you can deal with it properly. To do this we use the 'WaitWindowEvent()' and 'WindowEvent()' commands.

What Is A Gadget?

In PureBasic a gadget is a graphical user interface object that provides some sort of interactivity for your program. Microsoft Windows calls these 'Controls' and some Linux distributions calls these 'Widgets'. Gadgets are buttons, tick boxes, sliders, input fields, tabs, frames, progress bars, etc. All the different interactive components that make up an interface, PureBasic calls gadgets.

These two commands are almost identical because they both return an event identifier in the form of a Long type number when an event occurs. The difference between these two is that the 'WaitWindowEvent()' command halts your program until an event is detected, then returns the event identifier and lets the program continue normally until it's called again. (This is great for use in graphical user interfaces as it allows the program to use as little of the CPU as possible, only utilizing it when an event actually occurs.) The 'WindowEvent()' command however, does not halt the program at all, it just tests to see if there are any events to return. If there is, this command will return its identifier. This command is very seldom used in user interfaces as it can make them very CPU 'hungry', hogging the processing power of the computer on which they run. The 'WindowEvent()' command is often used when you need to keep the main loop running at all cost, for example, if you are displaying a dynamic graphic in your program that needs to be continually redrawn, etc. If this is the case and you must use the 'WindowEvent()' command, good programming style dictates that you try to use the 'Delay(1)' trick with it (as explained in the console program section) to make sure your program is CPU friendly. If no events are detected use 'Delay(1)' to let other programs get a chance to use the CPU.

In the 'Hello World' program I've used a 'WaitWindowEvent()' command during the 'Repeat' loop to halt the program until an event is triggered. Once an event is triggered the 'WaitWindowEvent()' command returns its identifier which is stored in a Long type variable called 'Event'. The loop is then coded to exit if 'Event' equals the value of '#PB_Event_CloseWindow', which is a built-in constant that contains the identifier of a 'close window' event from the interface. If these two are equal then a 'close window' event must of occurred so the loop exits and the program is ended.

Events Happen All The Time
Even though no other events are handled in this small example, it doesn't mean that they aren't occurring. If we take the same 'Hello World' program and add another line containing a 'Debug' command it will now display identifiers of events in the Debug Output window during runtime.

Run the following piece of code, then move and click in and around the window. You will see many events occurring.

```
#WINDOW_MAIN = 1

#FLAGS = #PB_Window_SystemMenu | #PB_Window_ScreenCentered
If OpenWindow(#WINDOW_MAIN, 0, 0, 300, 200, "Hello World", #FLAGS)
  Repeat
    Event.l = WaitWindowEvent()
    Debug Event
  Until Event = #PB_Event_CloseWindow
EndIf
End
```

This is the 'WaitWindowEvent()' command returning identifiers for all triggered events, even if they are not handled by your program. This is completely normal and won't noticeably slow your program down in the slightest.

Adding Gadgets

So far we've seen a simple window created which displayed 'Hello World' in the title bar, although this is a nice introduction to user interfaces it really doesn't show any form of interaction with the user other than being able to close the window. In this next section I'll show you how you can add gadgets to your program's window to increase functionality and interactivity.

In this next piece of code I've added two buttons and demonstrated how to detect events from them.

```
Enumeration
  #WIN_MAIN
  #BUTTON_INTERACT
  #BUTTON_CLOSE
EndEnumeration

Global Quit.b = #False
#FLAGS = #PB_Window_SystemMenu | #PB_Window_ScreenCentered

If OpenWindow(#WIN_MAIN, 0, 0, 300, 200, "Interaction", #FLAGS)
  If CreateGadgetList(WindowID(#WIN_MAIN))

    ButtonGadget(#BUTTON_INTERACT, 10, 170, 100, 20, "Click me")
    ButtonGadget(#BUTTON_CLOSE, 190, 170, 100, 20, "Close window")
    Repeat

      Event.l = WaitWindowEvent()
      Select Event
        Case #PB_Event_Gadget
          Select EventGadget()
```

```
        Case #BUTTON_INTERACT
          Debug "The button was pressed."
        Case #BUTTON_CLOSE
          Quit = #True
      EndSelect
    EndSelect

  Until Event = #PB_Event_CloseWindow Or Quit = #True

  EndIf
 EndIf
 End
```

If you read through this code it should be pretty straightforward for you to understand, so I'll just run through some of the key areas that will be new to you. Fig.27 shows you what this window looks like.

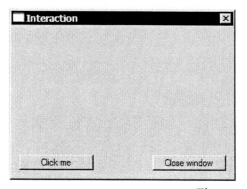

(Microsoft Windows example)   Fig. 27

In this example after the main window has been created I've used the 'CreateGadgetList()' command. This is needed to tell your window that you would like to draw gadgets on it. This command only takes one parameter which is the OS identifier of the main interface window so I use the 'WindowID()' command to retrieve it, like this:

```
...
CreateGadgetList(WindowID(#WIN_MAIN))
...
```

OS identifiers were discussed in detail in Chapter 7 (PB Numbers And OS Identifiers).

After we create a gadget list within the main window we can draw gadgets upon it. I've created two buttons using the 'ButtonGadget()' command. If you open the helpfile and refer to the 'ButtonGadget()' page (Helpfile:Reference Manual->General Libraries->Gadget->ButtonGadget) you will be able see in the syntax example exactly what parameters are expected by this command.

Using the position parameters in the 'ButtonGadget()' command, I've placed the buttons along the bottom edge of the window.

To highlight another key area, if you look at the main loop, after an event identifier has been returned from the 'WaitWindowEvent()' command and assigned to the 'Event' variable, I've used a 'Select' statement to test its value, like this:

```
. . .
Select Event
  Case #PB_Event_Gadget
    . . .
EndSelect
. . .
```

You will notice that the first 'Case' statement tests for a value of '#PB_Event_Gadget'. This is a special global event value, used to test an identifier to determine if it's from a gadget, in other words, if 'Event' is equal to '#PB_Event_Gadget' then 'Event' must hold an event identifier from a gadget.

Once we know that an event comes from a gadget we then have to distinguish what gadget it is from. We do this using the 'EventGadget()' command which returns the PB number of the originating gadget. So in this example I test the return value of 'EventGadget()' by using another 'Select'.

```
. . .
Select EventGadget()
  Case #BUTTON_INTERACT
    Debug "The button was pressed."
  Case #BUTTON_CLOSE
    Quit = #True
EndSelect
. . .
```

Here, I have two 'Case' statements, one testing for '#BUTTON_INTERACT' and one testing for '#BUTTON_CLOSE'. If the return value from 'EventGadget()' equals '#BUTTON_INTERACT' then the 'Click me' button has been pressed. This we know because this gadget's PB number has been returned from 'EventGadget()'. Then I type some code that I want executing when this button is pressed on the next line after the 'Case' statement.

The same theory applies to the next 'Case' statement too. If the return value equals '#BUTTON_CLOSE' then the 'Close window' button has been pressed. If so, I assign a true value to the 'Quit' variable which makes the main loop exit and eventually ends the program.

This is why using a constant 'Enumeration' block is so incredibly helpful. After defining numeric constants for all gadgets at the start of the source code, I can then refer to each of them by a constant name instead of a number, which makes the source code infinitely more clear and readable.

Accepting Text Input

Let's expand the last example a bit more and add a String gadget so we can enter some text that the program can use. String gadgets are very handy as they provide a simple way of allowing your program to accept strings of text. This next example is to show you how you can retrieve the value of the String gadget, i.e. retrieve the text, and use it in your program. Let's create one that is the full width of the window. Fig.28 overleaf, shows what this compiled program should look like, here's the code:

```
Enumeration
  #WIN_MAIN
  #TEXT_INPUT
  #STRING_INPUT
  #BUTTON_INTERACT
  #BUTTON_CLOSE
EndEnumeration

Global Quit.b = #False
#FLAGS = #PB_Window_SystemMenu | #PB_Window_ScreenCentered

If OpenWindow(#WIN_MAIN, 0, 0, 300, 200, "Interaction", #FLAGS)
  If CreateGadgetList(WindowID(#WIN_MAIN))

    TextGadget(#TEXT_INPUT, 10, 10, 280, 20, "Enter text here:")
    StringGadget(#STRING_INPUT, 10, 30, 280, 20, "")
    ButtonGadget(#BUTTON_INTERACT, 10, 170, 120, 20, "Echo text")
    ButtonGadget(#BUTTON_CLOSE, 190, 170, 100, 20, "Close window")
    SetActiveGadget(#STRING_INPUT)
    Repeat

      Event.l = WaitWindowEvent()
      Select Event
        Case #PB_Event_Gadget
          Select EventGadget()
            Case #BUTTON_INTERACT
              Debug GetGadgetText(#STRING_INPUT)
            Case #BUTTON_CLOSE
              Quit = #True
          EndSelect
      EndSelect

    Until Event = #PB_Event_CloseWindow Or Quit = #True

  EndIf
EndIf
End
```

In this updated version I've added a couple more constants to the 'Enumeration' block so I can add a few more gadgets easily. The first new gadget I've added is a text gadget which literally displays a non-editable text string on the window, I use one to display the String: 'Enter text here:'. The second new gadget I've used is a String gadget which creates an input field upon the window which allows you to enter your own text.

If you open the PureBasic helpfile on the 'StringGadget()' page (Helpfile:Reference Manual->General Libraries->Gadget->StringGadget) you can see the parameters that this gadget can accept. I've used the position and size parameters to align a String gadget to the top of the window, just below the text gadget. For the 'Content$' parameter I've passed a blank String, which is expressed through two sets of double quotation marks with nothing between. This is still a String but a String that has no content. I've done this because the 'Content$' parameter sets an initial text value for the String gadget and I want the String gadget to start off with none entered.

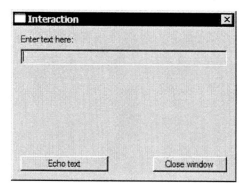

(Microsoft Windows example)   Fig. 28

Once this program is running you will notice that the text cursor is immediately flashing in the String gadget. This is not the default behavior, normally you would have to click on the gadget to give it focus for the cursor to appear there. In my program I have set that gadget to be the active one on startup by using the 'SetActiveGadget()' command. This command takes one PB number as a parameter of the gadget you want to give focus to, making it the currently active gadget. I've done this in this little example to help the user and to save him or her a mouse click.

To test the interactivity of this program, enter some text in the String gadget once the program is running and then press the 'Echo text' button. You will now see that text echoed to the Debug Output window. This is because I've changed the '#BUTTON_INTERACT' 'Case' statement to alter what happens once the 'Echo text' button is pressed. This line of code has been altered to now read 'Debug GetGadgetText(#STRING_INPUT)'.

The 'GetGadgetText()' command takes one parameter which is the PB number of the gadget you want to retrieve text from, here I use it to retrieve text from the String gadget. This command can be used with many gadgets in PureBasic but with a String gadget it simply returns the text as a String which I then immediately echo using a 'Debug' command.

Displaying Text

Let's expand this program even further and instead of echoing the text from the String gadget to the Debug Output window, let's add a gadget to display the text actually inside our program. In this next example I've added a list view gadget to display the input text in a list of non-editable Strings.

A list view gadget is a great way to display lists of Strings because each String has its own line within the gadget.

PureBasic offers a lot of commands to work with list view gadgets, ranging from adding and removing to counting and sorting of items contained within this type of gadget. In the following small example I've only used the 'AddGadgetItem()' command to add new Strings to mine. Fig.29 overleaf, shows the new program running, here is the code:

```
Enumeration
  #WIN_MAIN
  #TEXT_INPUT
  #STRING_INPUT
  #LIST_INPUT
  #BUTTON_INTERACT
  #BUTTON_CLOSE
EndEnumeration

Global Quit.b = #False
#FLAGS = #PB_Window_SystemMenu | #PB_Window_ScreenCentered

If OpenWindow(#WIN_MAIN, 0, 0, 300, 200, "Interaction", #FLAGS)
  If CreateGadgetList(WindowID(#WIN_MAIN))

    TextGadget(#TEXT_INPUT, 10, 10, 280, 20, "Enter text here:")
    StringGadget(#STRING_INPUT, 10, 30, 280, 20, "")
    ListViewGadget(#LIST_INPUT, 10, 60, 280, 100)
    ButtonGadget(#BUTTON_INTERACT, 10, 170, 120, 20, "Enter text")
    ButtonGadget(#BUTTON_CLOSE, 190, 170, 100, 20, "Close window")
    SetActiveGadget(#STRING_INPUT)
    Repeat

      Event.l = WaitWindowEvent()
      Select Event
        Case #PB_Event_Gadget
          Select EventGadget()
            Case #BUTTON_INTERACT
              AddGadgetItem(#LIST_INPUT, -1, GetGadgetText(#STRING_INPUT))
              SetGadgetText(#STRING_INPUT, "")
              SetActiveGadget(#STRING_INPUT)
            Case #BUTTON_CLOSE
              Quit = #True
          EndSelect
      EndSelect

    Until Event = #PB_Event_CloseWindow Or Quit = #True

  EndIf
EndIf
End
```

This example is very similar to the last one, in fact the only real difference is the inclusion of the list view gadget. Reading the PureBasic helpfile on the 'ListViewGadget()' page (Helpfile:Reference Manual->General Libraries->Gadget->ListViewGadget) will give you a good overview of this gadget and what you can achieve using it. Reading the syntax example contained here also lets you know exactly what parameters this gadget accepts. I've used the position and size parameters to put the list view gadget in the middle of the main window, above the buttons but under the String gadget.

(Microsoft Windows example)   Fig. 29

Once this program is running, enter some text into the String gadget and press the 'Enter text' button. This will take the text from the String gadget and add it to the list view gadget. Once this is done the program clears the String gadget to be ready for more input.

This is all achieved because once again, I have changed the '#BUTTON_INTERACT' 'Case' statement to alter what happens once the renamed 'Enter text' button is pressed. Here are the three new lines I have added to the '#BUTTON_INTERACT' 'Case' statement:

```
...
Case #BUTTON_INTERACT
  AddGadgetItem(#LIST_INPUT, -1, GetGadgetText(#STRING_INPUT))
  SetGadgetText(#STRING_INPUT, "")
  SetActiveGadget(#STRING_INPUT)
...
```

The first line after the 'Case' statement adds an item to the list view gadget. If you open the page in the helpfile on 'AddGadgetItem()' (Helpfile:Reference Manual->General Libraries->Gadget->AddGadgetItem) you will see the parameters that this command accepts. The first parameter is the PB number of the gadget you would like to add an item to, in our case it is '#LIST_INPUT' which is a constant that holds our gadget's number. The second parameter is what position in the list (of existing or non existing values) you would like this new entry to be added, remembering that indices start at '0'. In the above example, I want this text to be added to the end of the list regardless of what that index that may be, so I specify this parameter as '-1'. This tells the command not to bother with inserting it at a particular index, just add it to the end of the current list no matter how big it may be.

The third parameter is the actual String you want to add to the gadget. I've used the 'GetGadgetText()' command here to return the current value of the String gadget; '#STRING_INPUT' and to pass it as a parameter. 'AddGadgetItem()' takes more parameters than I've used here but the others are optional and therefore not necessary so I haven't used them.

The second line of code after the 'Case' statement uses the 'SetGadgetText()' command to set the String gadget's value to nothing by using a blank String. This is because, once text has been entered into the list view gadget, I want to clear the String gadget ready for a new String to be entered.

The last line uses the 'SetActiveGadget()' command again to give the '#STRING_INPUT' String gadget focus so the text cursor appears there ready for more input saving a mouse click or two from the user.

What Have We Learned So Far?
Hopefully the last few examples have been a good introduction to native graphical user interfaces and provide a good starting point for further learning. In this book I can't give you examples of every interface you are likely wanting to build, all I can do is give you the basic building blocks of an interface and let you build upon them.

The beginnings of every native interface in PureBasic is the same. First you must open a window using the 'OpenWindow()' command. Secondly, if you want to place gadgets upon this window you must create a gadget list using the 'CreateGadgetList()' command and Third, you must have a main loop to keep the program running and handle any events that may occur. All events that do occur are returned from a 'WaitWindowEvent()' or 'WindowEvent()' command within the main loop.

Read The Gadget Section In The Helpfile
If you have understood what has been written so far you are on your way to fully grasping how to build native interfaces in PureBasic. Once you have understood the basics, the rest is learning about what gadgets are available and learning how to use them. This can be achieved by reading through the PureBasic helpfile in the 'Gadget' section (Helpfile:Reference Manual->General Libraries->Gadget). I recommend reading this section from front to back to understand what is available for you to use and to understand what commands work with each gadget.

Take for example, the 'SetGadgetText()' command, this can be used with many different gadgets. If you look at the 'SetGadgetText()' page in the helpfile (Helpfile:Reference Manual->General Libraries->Gadget->SetGadgetText) it lists all the gadgets that this command works with along with any special instructions for use with a particular gadget.

To cover all gadgets and the commands that work with them would take far too long here and probably be another book in itself. So I think it's perhaps a better idea to familiarize yourself with the 'Gadget' section in the helpfile.

Meanwhile, if you need a quick reference of what gadgets are available for use with PureBasic, then have a look at Appendix B (Helpful Charts) for a full list of all gadgets and a brief description of each one.

Adding A Menu

Adding a native menu to an interface is very easy in PureBasic and very similar to adding gadgets. When menu items are selected they trigger events just like gadgets and these events are handled in the main loop alongside gadget events.

All menu items are defined with their own PB number like gadgets and these are used later to distinguish which menu item has triggered an event. Here is a small example:

```
Enumeration
  #WINDOW_MAIN
  #MENU_MAIN
  #MENU_QUIT
  #MENU_ABOUT
EndEnumeration

Global Quit.b = #False
#FLAGS = #PB_Window_SystemMenu | #PB_Window_ScreenCentered

If OpenWindow(#WINDOW_MAIN, 0, 0, 300, 200, "Menu Example", #FLAGS)
  If CreateMenu(#MENU_MAIN, WindowID(#WINDOW_MAIN))

    MenuTitle("File")
      MenuItem(#MENU_QUIT, "Quit")
    MenuTitle("Help")
      MenuItem(#MENU_ABOUT, "About...")
    Repeat

      Event.l = WaitWindowEvent()
      Select Event
        Case #PB_Event_Menu
          Select EventMenu()
            Case #MENU_QUIT
              Quit = #True
            Case #MENU_ABOUT
              MessageRequester("About", "This is where you describe your program.")
          EndSelect
      EndSelect

    Until Event = #PB_Event_CloseWindow Or Quit = #True

  EndIf
EndIf
End
```

This small example shows a native menu added to an empty window. There are two menu titles and each title contains one menu item. If you look at the above example, you can see how to create such a menu.

First, you need to open a window, which I guess is common sense but we need one here because the menu will be attached to this window. Once the window has been created, we create the menu framework by using the 'CreateMenu()' command. This command takes two parameters, the first is the PB number of this menu object and the second is the OS identifier of the window it is to be attached to. This is very similar to the 'CreateGadgetList()' command's syntax and I've also used the 'WindowID()' command here to provide the OS identifier of the main window.

After the menu framework has been created successfully then you can populate it with the actual menu titles and items themselves. To do this, I begin with using a 'MenuTitle()' command. This command creates a menu title that is displayed at the top of the window (or in the case of Mac OS X, at the top of the screen). This command takes one String parameter which is the name of the title.

Once a menu title has been defined any menu items created from then on in your program will appear beneath this title. Menu items are created by using the 'MenuItem()' command. This command takes two parameters, the first is the PB number that this item will be associated with, and the second is the String that you would like to display in the menu for this item.

In my example, I've defined one menu item under the 'File' menu title called 'Quit' then I've used the 'MenuTitle()' command again to create another menu title called 'Help'. Once another menu title is created like this, then again, all subsequent menu items are created beneath this new title, just like the newly created 'About...' menu item.

Detecting Menu Events

Once the menu has been created, including all menu titles and items, we then detect events being triggered by them in the main loop. Almost exactly like detecting event from gadgets we use a global event value called '#PB_Event_Menu'.

If the event returned from the 'WaitWindowEvent()' command is equal to '#PB_Event_Menu', then this event is from a menu item. I've used this command in a 'Select' statement like this:

```
...
Select Event
  Case #PB_Event_Menu
    Select EventMenu()
      Case #MENU_QUIT
        Quit = #True
      Case #MENU_ABOUT
        MessageRequester("About", "This is where you describe your program.")
    EndSelect
EndSelect
...
```

To determine exactly which menu item triggered this event we have to use the 'EventMenu()' command. This command returns the PB number of the menu item that triggered the event. I've used this command in another 'Select' statement to handle multiple cases of events, so I can elegantly handle events from any menu item. In this 'Select' statement, if the value returned by the 'EventMenu()' command equals '#MENU_QUIT' then the 'Quit' menu item has been selected and I assign a true value to the 'Quit' variable which makes the main loop exit, thus ending the program. If the value returned by the 'EventMenu()' command equals '#MENU_ABOUT' then the 'About...' menu item has been selected and I display a message requester displaying information about my program.

Sub Menu Items

So far I have demonstrated how to create standard menus but you can also create what is known as sub menus. These are menus which branch out from a parent menu into another connected child menu. Providing a tree-like menu structure kind of like the 'Start' menu on Microsoft Windows. All menu items inside these new child menus trigger events in exactly the same way as any other menu item and can be caught in the same way in the main loop. Here's an example:

```
Enumeration
  #WINDOW_MAIN
  #MENU_MAIN
  #MENU_CHILD
  #MENU_QUIT
  #MENU_ABOUT
EndEnumeration

Global Quit.b = #False
#FLAGS = #PB_Window_SystemMenu | #PB_Window_ScreenCentered

If OpenWindow(#WINDOW_MAIN, 0, 0, 300, 200, "Menu Example", #FLAGS)
  If CreateMenu(#MENU_MAIN, WindowID(#WINDOW_MAIN))
    MenuTitle("File")
      OpenSubMenu("Parent Menu Item")
       MenuItem(#MENU_CHILD, "Sub Menu Item")
      CloseSubMenu()
      MenuBar()
      MenuItem(#MENU_QUIT, "Quit")
    MenuTitle("Help")
      MenuItem(#MENU_ABOUT, "About...")
    Repeat
      Event.l = WaitWindowEvent()
      Select Event
        Case #PB_Event_Menu
          Select EventMenu()
            Case #MENU_CHILD
              Debug "Sub menu item selected."
            Case #MENU_QUIT
              Quit = #True
            Case #MENU_ABOUT
              MessageRequester("About", "This is where you describe your program.")
          EndSelect
      EndSelect
    Until Event = #PB_Event_CloseWindow Or Quit = #True
  EndIf
EndIf
End
```

A sub menu is created by using the 'OpenSubMenu()' command after a 'MenuTitle()' command. This is so the sub menu is related to a menu title just like any other menu item. The 'OpenSubMenu()' command takes one parameter which is the String that is displayed in the menu in front of the sub menu arrow. Once a 'OpenSubMenu()' command is used then all subsequently used 'MenuItem()' commands will place new menu items within the sub menu. To close this sub menu to be able to add more items to the main menu, you have to call the 'CloseSubMenu()' command. This switches menu item creation back to the parent menu.

New menu items that are added to sub menus trigger events that can be caught in the main loop in the same way as any other menu item. If you look at the 'EventMenu()' 'Select' statement, you can see I've added a new value to be handled; '#MENU_CHILD'. If the return value from 'EventMenu()' equals the value of '#MENU_CHILD' then the child menu item must of been selected, so I echo some text to the Debug Output window to show this.

Separating Menu Items
If you take a closer look at the above example I've added another new command too. This command draws a nice graphical separator bar in the menu which is useful to separate certain menu items. This new command is the 'MenuBar()' command. It takes no parameters and is used wherever you would like to place a separator in the current menu. Usually one is placed to separate the 'Quit' menu item from the rest of the menu items in the 'File' menu, so that's what I have done in this example.

Combining Gadgets And Menus In The Same Program
Including menus and gadgets in the same program is easy. First, you open a window and create a menu. Then you create a gadget list and draw your gadgets, it's that simple. Here's a code example:

```
Enumeration
  #WINDOW_MAIN
  #MENU_MAIN
  #MENU_QUIT
  #MENU_ABOUT
  #TEXT_INPUT
  #STRING_INPUT
  #LIST_INPUT
  #BUTTON_INTERACT
  #BUTTON_CLOSE
EndEnumeration

Global Quit.b = #False
#FLAGS = #PB_Window_SystemMenu | #PB_Window_ScreenCentered

If OpenWindow(#WINDOW_MAIN, 0, 0, 300, 222, "Interaction", #FLAGS)
  If CreateMenu(#MENU_MAIN, WindowID(#WINDOW_MAIN))
    MenuTitle("File")
      MenuItem(#MENU_QUIT, "Quit")
    MenuTitle("Help")
      MenuItem(#MENU_ABOUT, "About...")
    If CreateGadgetList(WindowID(#WINDOW_MAIN))
      TextGadget(#TEXT_INPUT, 10, 10, 280, 20, "Enter text here:")
      StringGadget(#STRING_INPUT, 10, 30, 280, 20, "")
```

```
      ListViewGadget(#LIST_INPUT, 10, 60, 280, 100)
      ButtonGadget(#BUTTON_INTERACT, 10, 170, 120, 20, "Enter text")
      ButtonGadget(#BUTTON_CLOSE, 190, 170, 100, 20, "Close window")
      SetActiveGadget(#STRING_INPUT)
      Repeat
        Event.l = WaitWindowEvent()
        Select Event
          Case #PB_Event_Menu
            Select EventMenu()
              Case #MENU_QUIT
                Quit = #True
              Case #MENU_ABOUT
                MessageRequester("About", "This is your program description.")
            EndSelect
          Case #PB_Event_Gadget
            Select EventGadget()
              Case #BUTTON_INTERACT
                AddGadgetItem(#LIST_INPUT, -1, GetGadgetText(#STRING_INPUT))
                SetGadgetText(#STRING_INPUT, "")
                SetActiveGadget(#STRING_INPUT)
              Case #BUTTON_CLOSE
                Quit = #True
            EndSelect
        EndSelect
      Until Event = #PB_Event_CloseWindow Or Quit = #True
    EndIf
  EndIf
EndIf
End
```

To handle events from either menu items or gadgets you can use the different global event constants. In the above example, I've used both in the same 'Select' statement which tests the 'Event' variable, like this:

```
...
Select Event
  Case #PB_Event_Menu
    Select EventMenu()
      ...
      ;Menu events are handled here
      ...
    EndSelect
  ...
  Case #PB_Event_Gadget
    Select EventGadget()
      ...
      ;Gadget events are handled here
      ...
    EndSelect
EndSelect
...
```

If an event is triggered from a menu item then it is handled in the '#PB_Event_Menu' 'Case' statement and the exact menu item can be determined by using the 'EventMenu()' command. If an event is triggered from a gadget then it is handled in the '#PB_Event_Gadget' 'Case' statement and the exact gadget can be determined by using the 'EventGadget()' command. This allows you to handle all menu and gadget events from one nested 'Select' statement, as shown in the snippet on the previous page.

Why Can't I Put Icons In Menus?

You will probably notice in Fig.30 that there are icons in the PureBasic IDE's menus but there are no native commands included in PureBasic for putting icons in menus. PureBasic is a cross-platform programming language and PureBasic code, once written, should compile for any supported platform. Therefore, all supported commands must achieve the same desired effect on each platform. Icons in menus were regarded as being too difficult to support in a cross-platform way so they were omitted, from the final PureBasic command set. The icons included in the PureBasic IDE were coded using each platform's native API (Such as the WinAPI in the case of Microsoft Windows). To learn more about what a native API is and learn more about the WinAPI, see Chapter 13.

Menu Keyboard Shortcuts

Most pieces of software nowadays have some form of keyboard shortcuts available for selecting menu items. These shortcuts are just key combinations that you can press on the keyboard to trigger menu items so you don't physically have to select them from the menu. PureBasic can insert these into you program with ease.

To demonstrate this we need to create a window with a menu. In this menu we define our menu items but this time we'll define them with Accelerators. An accelerator is a computer term for the String on

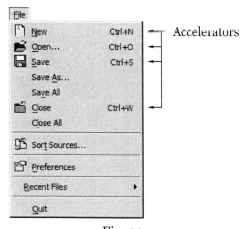

Fig. 30

the end of a menu item describing what shortcut you need to press in order to trigger it, Fig.30 shows the accelerators defined in the PureBasic IDE's file menu. Looking at this you can see that if you want to create a new document in the PureBasic IDE you can press 'Ctrl+N' which is the 'Control' key and the 'N' key at the same time on the keyboard, etc.

You will also notice in Fig.30, that the accelerators are aligned to the right hand side of the menu. This is to make sure they are clearly marked and to keep the menu itself uncluttered.

In this next piece of code I'm going to extend the previous menu example and add accelerators and keyboard shortcuts, run it and try them for yourself.

```
Enumeration
  #WIN_MAIN
  #MENU_MAIN
  #M_QUIT
  #M_ABOUT
EndEnumeration

Global Quit.b = #False
#FLAGS = #PB_Window_SystemMenu | #PB_Window_ScreenCentered

If OpenWindow(#WIN_MAIN, 0, 0, 300, 200, "Menu Example", #FLAGS)
  If CreateMenu(#MENU_MAIN, WindowID(#WIN_MAIN))

    MenuTitle("File")
      MenuItem(#M_QUIT, "Quit" + #TAB$ + "Ctrl+Q")
    MenuTitle("Help")
      MenuItem(#M_ABOUT, "About..." + #TAB$ + "Ctrl+A")

    AddKeyboardShortcut(#WIN_MAIN,#PB_Shortcut_Control|#PB_Shortcut_Q,#M_QUIT)
    AddKeyboardShortcut(#WIN_MAIN,#PB_Shortcut_Control|#PB_Shortcut_A,#M_ABOUT)

    Repeat

      Event.l = WaitWindowEvent()
      Select Event
        Case #PB_Event_Menu
          Select EventMenu()
            Case #M_QUIT
              Quit = #True
            Case #M_ABOUT
              MessageRequester("About", "This is where you describe your program.")
          EndSelect
      EndSelect

    Until Event = #PB_Event_CloseWindow Or Quit = #True

  EndIf
EndIf
End
```

If you run the example, you will see that besides the menu items there are now accelerators. These are defined by using a tab character within the menu item String, like this:

```
. . .
MenuItem(#M_QUIT, "Quit" + #TAB$ + "Ctrl+Q")
. . .
```

This command still takes two parameters, but the second String parameter is being made up of three parts. The first part is the menu item String, which in this case is 'Quit'. Then we concatenate a tab character to the end using the built-in '#TAB$' String constant. This constant has the ASCII value of '9' in String form. Then we concatenate a further String which is the menu accelerator; 'Ctrl+Q'.

A tab is used here instead of a space so that the accelerators are always aligned to the right of the menu regardless of the lengths of the menu item Strings.

Once the accelerators have been entered alongside the menu items then that's the visual part done, the accelerators are after all just for the user to refer to visually. To add the shortcut functionality of the accelerators we must use the 'AddKeyboardShortcut()' command. I've used these commands in my code like this:

```
. . .
AddKeyboardShortcut(#WIN_MAIN,#PB_Shortcut_Control|#PB_Shortcut_Q,#M_QUIT)
AddKeyboardShortcut(#WIN_MAIN,#PB_Shortcut_Control|#PB_Shortcut_A,#M_ABOUT)
. . .
```

This command takes three parameters, the first is the PB number of the window that this shortcut is associated with, in this case it's '#WIN_MAIN'. The second parameter is a value that represents the actual keyboard shortcut. This value is made up of built-in constants that represent different key combinations on the keyboard. On the first line in the above snippet, I've combined the constants '#PB_Shortcut_Control' and '#PB_Shortcut_Q' to specify that I want the shortcut to be 'Control+Q' on the keyboard. These constants are combined in the usual way by using the bitwise 'Or' operator ('|'). All shortcut constants available for use to create all other key combinations are listed in the PureBasic helpfile on the 'AddKeyboardShortcut()' page (Helpfile:Reference Manual->General Libraries->Window->AddKeyboardShortcut). The third parameter is the menu item's PB number that you wish to associate this shortcut to. On the first line in the above snippet, I've used '#M_QUIT' which is the same PB number I used to create the 'Quit' menu item earlier on. This means that once this shortcut is pressed on the keyboard it will trigger an event with the same value as if the 'Quit' menu item was selected.

On the next line of the snippet I've repeated this command but with different parameters to provide a keyboard shortcut for the 'About' menu item.

These events triggered from keyboard shortcuts are handled in exactly the same way as if they were triggered from selecting a menu item and there is absolutely no difference in the main loop as you can see from the shortcut example.

Keyboard Shortcuts Without A Menu
Using the same keyboard shortcut commands you can create keyboard shortcuts without having a menu to base them on. All you have to do, is use the 'AddKeyboardShortcut()' command to create a shortcut associated to your window and instead of mirroring a menu item's PB number in the third parameter, just use a unique value. You then test for this value as a menu event in the main loop even though there is no menu. Here's an example:

```
#WIN_MAIN = 1
#SC_EVENT = 2

#FLAGS = #PB_Window_SystemMenu | #PB_Window_ScreenCentered

If OpenWindow(#WIN_MAIN, 0, 0, 300, 200, "Hello World", #FLAGS)
  AddKeyboardShortcut(#WIN_MAIN,#PB_Shortcut_Control|#PB_Shortcut_Z, #SC_EVENT)
  Repeat
    Event.l = WaitWindowEvent()
    Select Event
      Case #PB_Event_Menu
        Select EventMenu()
          Case #SC_EVENT
            Debug "The shortcut was pressed"
        EndSelect
    EndSelect
  Until Event = #PB_Event_CloseWindow
EndIf
End
```

While the above example is running, press 'Control+Z' on your keyboard and you should see the text 'The shortcut was pressed' echoed to the Debug Output window. This example works because the 'AddKeyboardShortcut()' command triggers a menu event that is handled correctly in the main loop even though there is no physical menu attached to the window. This is a handy trick to know if you ever want to add keyboard shortcuts to your programs even though you don't want a menu.

Including Graphics In Your Program

Sometimes in your programs you might like to include certain images and PureBasic makes this very easy. In this next section I'll show you how to add images to your interfaces in one of two ways. First, you can load them from an external source, for example, the image may be in the same directory as your program. Second you can embed the image directly into your program so you only have one executable file. Both ways achieve the same thing but it depends how you want to handle the image file itself. Both these methods require an image gadget to be placed on your window to display the image. This is placed upon your window in the same way as any other gadget and conforms to the same rules.

Loading Images Into Your Program
This method of loading images for use in your interface is reliant on external images. Unlike embedding images, this method requires you to distribute any images used along with your executable file. Here is an example:

```
Enumeration
  #WIN_MAIN
  #IMAGE_FILE
  #IMAGE_DISPLAY
  #BUTTON_CLOSE
EndEnumeration

Global Quit.b = #False
#FLAGS = #PB_Window_SystemMenu | #PB_Window_ScreenCentered

If OpenWindow(#WIN_MAIN, 0, 0, 300, 200, "Image Example", #FLAGS)
  If CreateGadgetList(WindowID(#WIN_MAIN))
    If LoadImage(#IMAGE_FILE, "image.bmp")

      ImageGadget(#IMAGE_DISPLAY, 10, 10, 280, 150, ImageID(#IMAGE_FILE))
      ButtonGadget(#BUTTON_CLOSE, 100, 170, 100, 20, "Close window")
      Repeat

        Event.l = WaitWindowEvent()
        Select Event
          Case #PB_Event_Gadget
            Select EventGadget()
              Case #BUTTON_CLOSE
                Quit = #True
            EndSelect
        EndSelect

      Until Event = #PB_Event_CloseWindow Or Quit = #True

    EndIf
  EndIf
EndIf
End
```

For this example to work properly, you will need a '280' by '150' pixel image and save it in Bitmap format inside the same directory as the source code or final compiled executable. Once this is in place the program (once run) will look something like Fig.31 overleaf.

In this example, I've used the 'LoadImage()' command to load the image from a place on the hard drive into memory ready for displaying in the program, like this:

```
...
LoadImage(#IMAGE_FILE, "image.bmp")
...
```

If you look at the 'LoadImage()' command in the PureBasic helpfile (Helpfile:Reference Manual->General Libraries->Image->LoadImage) you can see this command takes three parameters, the first is the PB number that will be associated with this loaded image and the second is the place on the hard drive where this image will be loaded from. If no file path information is included in the second parameter the file location is assumed to be relative to the program itself. I've not used the third optional parameter in this example. As usual I've tested the return value of this command with an 'If' statement to make sure it has loaded correctly before continuing with the rest of the program.

Once the image has been loaded correctly you can then display it in your interface using an image gadget. If you look at the image gadget example, after I've created a gadget list, I've used the 'ImageGadget' command, like this:

```
...
ImageGadget(#IMAGE_DISPLAY, 10, 10, 280, 150, ImageID(#IMAGE_FILE))
...
```

'ImageGadget()' is a simple command to understand, the first parameter is the PB number that is associated to this gadget, not the loaded image. The next four parameters deal with the position and size of this gadget, similar to other gadgets. The fifth parameter is where we specify what image this gadget will display, so this parameter must be an OS identifier of a previously loaded image. Because we have loaded a suitable image already we can use the 'ImageID()' command to retrieve its OS identifier. In the above code I've used the 'ImageID()' command to retrieve the OS identifier of the '#IMAGE_FILE' image which was loaded previously using the 'LoadImage()' command.

(Microsoft Windows example)   Fig. 31

This way of loading images to display them in an image gadget is a simple way of doing things, but you must remember that when including images in your interfaces like this, you must always distribute the images used along with your final executable file. Because your program will always look for the external images to load, even when it's compiled. If you want to embed your images within your program completely, read on.

Embedding Images In Your Program
The previous method of loading images is fine but sometimes you need to create a completely stand-alone executable file with all used images completely embedded so it doesn't rely on any other external media. This method uses what is known as a data section where you can embed binary files for the executable to use when needed. Here is an example:

```
Enumeration
  #WIN_MAIN
  #IMAGE_MEMORY
  #IMAGE_DISPLAY
  #BUTTON_CLOSE
EndEnumeration

Global Quit.b = #False

#FLAGS = #PB_Window_SystemMenu | #PB_Window_ScreenCentered

If OpenWindow(#WIN_MAIN, 0, 0, 300, 200, "Image Example", #FLAGS)
  If CreateGadgetList(WindowID(#WIN_MAIN))
    If CatchImage(#IMAGE_MEMORY, ?Image)
      ImageGadget(#IMAGE_DISPLAY, 10, 10, 280, 150, ImageID(#IMAGE_MEMORY))
      ButtonGadget(#BUTTON_CLOSE, 100, 170, 100, 20, "Close window")
      Repeat
        Event.l = WaitWindowEvent()
        Select Event
          Case #PB_Event_Gadget
            Select EventGadget()
              Case #BUTTON_CLOSE
                Quit = #True
            EndSelect
        EndSelect
      Until Event = #PB_Event_CloseWindow Or Quit = #True
    EndIf
  EndIf
EndIf
End

DataSection
  Image:
    IncludeBinary "image.bmp"
EndDataSection
```

This example is very similar to the previous one, except this one is embedding the image into a data section when compiled. Once this program is run, the image is read from the data section instead of being read from the hard drive. If you look at the example you can see the data section at the bottom of the source code, it looks like this:

```
  ...
DataSection
  Image:
    IncludeBinary "image.bmp"
EndDataSection
```

The commands 'DataSection' and 'EndDataSection' are the start and finish of the section. You are then able to embed binary files within it using the 'IncludeBinary' command. This command doesn't use any brackets, it just uses a String after it to define a file to embed.

In this case I've embedded the file called 'image.bmp'. You will also notice that I've used a label before the 'IncludeBinary' command, very similar to a subroutine definition. This label enables your program to find the start of this image in memory once loaded with this program. Once an image has been embedded like this then we can easily use it in our main code.

In the main code, we no longer use the 'LoadImage()' command to load the image into memory. Once it's placed within a data section, it's already loaded once the program is running. So we use the 'CatchImage()' command to retrieve the image from the data section, like this:

```
...
CatchImage(#IMAGE_MEMORY, ?Image)
...
```

If you look at the 'CatchImage()' command in the PureBasic helpfile (Helpfile:Reference Manual->General Libraries->Image->CatchImage) you can see this command takes three parameters, the first is the PB number that will be associated with this image. The second parameter is the memory address where this image resides. If you remember, I've used a label in the data section to show this so I need to get the memory address of this label. I do this using a question mark in front of the label when I use it as a parameter. This question mark is a special one character function that returns the memory address of any label. This is explained in more detail later in Chapter 13 (Pointers). I've not used the third parameter in this example because it is optional.

Displaying an image loaded with the 'CatchImage()' command is exactly the same as using the 'LoadImage()' command. Again, we use an image gadget and populate its parameters in the same way as before:

```
...
ImageGadget(#IMAGE_DISPLAY, 10, 10, 280, 150, ImageID(#IMAGE_MEMORY))
...
```

Once you run this example it should look like Fig.31 again. This is because it is the same program, but now it no longer needs the external 'image.bmp' file.

What Image Formats Can Be Used?
In the last few examples I've loaded and embedded images which are in Bitmap (*.bmp) format but you are not limited to this one single format.

As standard, PureBasic can load and display Bitmap (*.bmp) and Icon (*.ico) format files but sometimes these can be restrictive. If you need to use other formats you can use optional decoder commands to give further functionality to PureBasic's image loading commands. These other decoders are extremely simple to use, you just use the decoder command at the start of your source code and from then on in your program all the image loading commands have full support of the image format decoder used. You can find more information on the decoders in the PureBasic helpfile (Helpfile:Reference Manual->General Libraries->ImagePlugin).

Here are the other decoder commands:

'UseJPEGImageDecoder()'
This decoder adds support for the Jpeg image (*.jpg/*.jpeg) file format.

'UsePNGImageDecoder()'
This decoder adds support for the Png image (*.png) file format.

'UseTIFFImageDecoder()'
This decoder adds support for the TIFF image (*.tif/*.tiff) file format.

'UseTGAImageDecoder()'
This decoder adds support for the Targa image (*.tga) file format.

As stated before, using these decoder commands is simplicity itself. Let's take the last image embedding example and add Jpeg support to it so we can embed a Jpeg file instead of a Bitmap file:

```
UseJPEGImageDecoder()

Enumeration
  #WIN_MAIN
  #IMAGE_MEMORY
  #IMAGE_DISPLAY
  #BUTTON_CLOSE
EndEnumeration

Global Quit.b = #False
#FLAGS = #PB_Window_SystemMenu | #PB_Window_ScreenCentered

If OpenWindow(#WIN_MAIN, 0, 0, 300, 200, "Image Example", #FLAGS)
  If CreateGadgetList(WindowID(#WIN_MAIN))
    If CatchImage(#IMAGE_MEMORY, ?Image)

      ImageGadget(#IMAGE_DISPLAY, 10, 10, 280, 150, ImageID(#IMAGE_MEMORY))
      ButtonGadget(#BUTTON_CLOSE, 100, 170, 100, 20, "Close window")
      Repeat

        Event.l = WaitWindowEvent()
        Select Event
          Case #PB_Event_Gadget
            Select EventGadget()
              Case #BUTTON_CLOSE
                Quit = #True
            EndSelect
        EndSelect

      Until Event = #PB_Event_CloseWindow Or Quit = #True
```

```
    EndIf
   EndIf
 EndIf
 End

 DataSection
   Image:
     IncludeBinary "image.jpg"
 EndDataSection
```

In this example the only difference I've made to the source code to make it able to support Jpeg files is I've added the 'UseJPEGImageDecoder()' command as the first line in the code and then changed the image in the data section to a Jpeg format one. This program now embeds a Jpeg image instead of a Bitmap.

All other decoders are used in the same way, just add the decoder command at the top of your source code to add support for these further file formats.

A First Look At The New Visual Designer

Included with PureBasic is a powerful Visual Designer to enable you to build interfaces visually and dynamically. This means in plain speak, that you can literally draw your gadgets upon a window to create your interface and all the underlying PureBasic code is generated for you automatically and in realtime.

Using a tool like this can save you considerable time when designing interfaces, adjusting the look and feel of an interface while seeing immediate results. You should also be able to load the code back in again at a later date if you need to add something or provide further functionality in your program. There is currently one limitation regarding loading existing sources, code not written by the visual designer might not be loaded correctly if you open it for re-editing. This is because the visual designer generates code in a certain way and if a hand written file deviates from this format the designer might have a hard time reading it in. The visual designer, like other tools provided, is written entirely from the ground up using PureBasic and is colorfully referred to as the 'VD' by the PureBasic community.

Why Haven't You Mentioned This Earlier?
I thought it was very important for you to learn how things work in PureBasic regarding gadgets, menus and events, to give you a more solid grounding of the code generated by the VD. So I thought I would mention it last within this chapter.

The Main Window
When you start the visual designer up it will look something like Fig.32. The main window is a multiple document interface containing all the tools you will need to design your interface. The visual designer consists of a menu at the top and a toolbar beneath. To the left of the screen there is a long tool panel containing the Gadget Tool Box and the Properties panel. In the center will be the current interface being designed and below that, the automatically generated code.

Using The Visual Designer

If you look at Fig.32 you will see the interface that is in progress indicated by an arrow to the right. This window is easy to spot because it is covered in tiny dots. These dots are a 'snap grid' that allow placed gadgets to snap to a set grid to make aligning them much quicker and easier. These dots do not appear on the finished program.

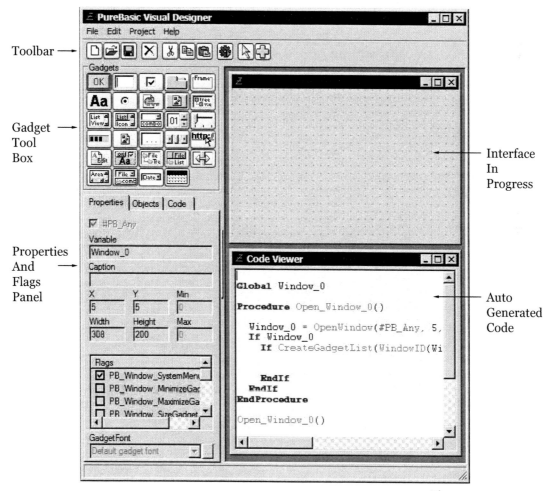

Fig. 32

Once the interface's window has been resized to the desired dimensions you can then start placing gadgets on it. To do this, pick a tool from the Gadget Tool Box and draw on the interface using that tool. You will now be drawing a dynamically resizing gadget of the selected tool type directly on the window. Once you have drawn the gadget, you will see that it is surrounded by big blue dots. These are handles allowing you to resize and move the gadget after it has been drawn. While you are adding gadgets to your interface you will notice that the PureBasic code is automatically generated in the Code Viewer near the bottom of the screen.

Once all gadgets are placed and you have finished designing your user interface you can save your project by clicking the disk button in the Toolbar. This allows you to save the automatically generated code to a standard PureBasic file so you can open, edit and compile it as normal in the PureBasic IDE.

Pro's and Con's Of The Visual Designer
While the visual designer is a great tool to quickly and easily throw together user interfaces the format of the code generated cannot be changed. Therefore, you have to accept the way the program has been coded and if tweaks are needed by hand in the IDE then you have to conform to this format. This is not really a problem if you are experienced with PureBasic but for the novice user, the exported code can be quite complicated and advanced.

The real plus point about using the visual designer is speed. You can throw together a useful user interface in seconds and see how it looks and then just as easily move and resize the gadgets until you get it just right. This cannot be overstated. The amount of time you could save designing a user interface using the VD is staggering, simply because you are negating the need to compile the program to see how it looks.

Some people like visual designers and some don't, it's as simple as that. Some say that it's best to handle all the code yourself so you truly know what's going on 'under the hood' while others argue that in today's competitive world you need a fast solution to designing interfaces. The argument will rage on I'm sure but it's up to you what you feel like using. The tools are there it's up to you if you want to use them.

Learning More About The Visual Designer
The PureBasic Visual Designer comes complete with an extensive helpfile which covers all the workings of the VD in a similar style to the IDE helpfile. To view it press 'F1' within the visual designer and the helpfile will load. I recommend reading through this helpfile fully at least once.

The new version of the visual designer which is (shown in Fig.32) being currently developed, can be read about, and downloaded from the PureBasic visual designer website. There is an Internet link given for this in Appendix A (Useful Internet Links).

III

Graphics And Sound

Programs that use graphics and sound are a prerequisite now in this world of computer games and interactive applications. When programming such cool stuff you need a computer language that will provide you with the necessary tools to realize your ideas. PureBasic offers simple, powerful and fully featured commands that can create professional quality games, demo's, screensavers and other interactive programs. In this section I will show you the basics of using graphics and sound within your PureBasic programs.

First I'll explain the 2D drawing commands that allow you to draw simple shapes, lines and text and then demonstrate how to save these images. Then I'll move on to show you how to open full size graphical screens to be able to draw graphics onto. Also I will introduce you to sprites and how to use them to create nice graphical effects.

After that, we'll move onto 3D graphics where I will introduce you to PureBasic's adopted 3D engine and show you the basics of using 3D graphics in PureBasic. This engine is called OGRE and is a third party professional quality engine capable of producing stunning graphics and effects.

The last chapter in this section deals with sound. The topics covered, are how to load and play sounds, with an emphasis on wav's, tracker modules, mp3's and CD audio.

The chapters contained in this section are not complete guides on how to achieve every graphical effect or how to write games, I'll leave that to other texts. These chapters are here to introduce you to the libraries of commands that make these things possible and to provide a starting point so you can experiment and have some fun. Hopefully this section will give you a taste of what is possible graphically using PureBasic and inspire you to create a cool demo or game.

10

2D Graphics

In this chapter, I am going to explain how to draw 2D graphics using PureBasic. The term '2D graphics' encompasses quite a large subject and many drawing operations fall beneath this descriptive umbrella. When I refer to 2D graphics in this book, I mean simple, two dimensional graphics that can be drawn onto graphical user interfaces, screens, images in RAM or even to a printer. These graphical types can also contain different complexities, from a single pixel right up to a full color image. All 2D graphics are two dimensional as you would guess from their name, unlike 3D graphics, which display 3D models that have a third 'depth' dimension.

Using 2D graphics, it's possible to achieve some very impressive visuals and as a result, many games, screensavers and demo's have been created using PureBasic. Hopefully you will be able to copy, learn from and adapt the examples in this chapter to create cool graphics in your own programs.

2D Drawing Commands

PureBasic contains commands that allow you to draw primitive shapes and colors in your programs. These simple 2D drawing commands are all contained in the '2D Drawing' library (Helpfile:Reference Manual->General Libraries->2DDrawing). These commands are useful for drawing simple shapes and text in different colors and there is even a couple of commands to draw using a previously created or loaded image.

What Can I Draw Onto?
The built-in 2D drawing commands can be used to draw onto various outputs such as, a graphical user interface window, a PureBasic screen, a sprite, a newly created image in memory, a 3D model texture or straight to a printer. These six methods pretty much cover anything you might need to draw onto, and each one is as easy to use as any other. Using these different output methods is a trivial matter in PureBasic because you only need to specify once where you would like the drawing output to go, and then use the drawing commands to draw to it. To simplify things even further, all the output methods share the same drawing command syntax.

Drawing On A Window

In this first example, I'll show you how to draw 2D graphics directly onto a window. You probably will never do this in a real world application but it's a simple exercise for you to understand and learn the syntax from. Look at this piece of code:

```
#WINDOW_MAIN = 1

#FLAGS = #PB_Window_SystemMenu | #PB_Window_ScreenCentered
If OpenWindow(#WINDOW_MAIN, 0, 0, 200, 240, "Window Drawing", #FLAGS)

  If StartDrawing(WindowOutput(#WINDOW_MAIN))
     Box(15, 15, 75, 75, RGB(255, 0, 0))
     Circle(140, 125, 45, RGB(35, 158, 70))
     ;The next 2D drawing commands draw a triangle
     LineXY(62, 140, 112, 220, RGB(0, 0, 255))
     LineXY(112, 220, 12, 220, RGB(0, 0, 255))
     LineXY(12, 220, 62, 140, RGB(0, 0, 255))
     FillArea(62, 180, RGB(0, 0, 255), RGB(0, 0, 255))
   StopDrawing()
  EndIf

  Repeat
    Event.l = WaitWindowEvent()
  Until Event = #PB_Event_CloseWindow
EndIf
End
```

If you run the above example, you will see a window similar to Fig.33 opened, and a red square, a green circle and a blue triangle drawn upon it. These shapes are drawn directly onto the window itself and no gadgets have been used. For you to fully understand the code above, I need to further explain the drawing command syntax.

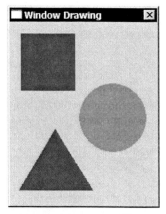

(Microsoft Windows   Fig. 33
example)

First, you will see I've used a new command called 'StartDrawing()'. This command tells PureBasic that I wish to start drawing using the 2D graphics commands and specifies what the drawing commands should draw on. If you look at the 'StartDrawing()' command's helpfile page (Helpfile:Reference Manual->General Libraries->2DDrawing->StartDrawing) you will see that this command can take six other commands as its parameter to specify the drawing output method. These are:

'WindowOutput()'
Use this to draw onto PureBasic user interface windows. This output method requires a PB number as a parameter to specify what window to draw onto.

'ScreenOutput()'
Use this to draw directly onto a PureBasic screen.

'SpriteOutput()'
Use this to draw onto a PureBasic sprite. This output method requires a PB number as a parameter to specify what sprite to draw onto.

'ImageOutput()'
Use this to draw onto a loaded or newly created image in memory. This output method requires a PB number as a parameter to specify what image to draw onto.

'PrinterOutput()'
Use this to draw directly to a printer.

'TextureOutput()'
Use this to draw onto a 3D model's texture. This output method requires a PB number as a parameter to specify what texture to draw onto.

In my example I've specified that I want to start drawing onto a window, like this:

```
...
StartDrawing(WindowOutput(#WINDOW MAIN))
...
```

Once I have set up the drawing output like this, I am free to use any of the 2D drawing commands to draw to it. In other words, everything drawn by the 2D drawing commands will now be drawn onto the window as specified in the parameter of the 'WindowOutput' command. Once you have used a 'StartDrawing()' command you must always use a 'StopDrawing()' command to finish off the drawing operations. This tells the PureBasic compiler, I now wish to stop using 2D drawing commands and I want to continue as normal with the rest of my program. This is essential because it may cause bugs in your program if you do not tell the compiler that you have stopped drawing.

Inside the drawing block, I've used four 2D drawing commands to actually draw the shapes onto the window. These are 'Box()', 'Circle()', 'LineXY()' and 'FillArea()'. All these 2D drawing commands are explained in detail through links on the '2D Drawing' helpfile page (Helpfile:Reference Manual-

>General Libraries->2DDrawing). Nearly all the 2D commands share similar parameters. There is usually parameters for 'x' and 'y' position and sometimes different size parameters and then usually the last parameter is the color that you would like this shape to be. If we take the 'Box()' command for example, the first two parameters are the position of the box on the output. The third and fourth parameters are the width and height of the box and the fifth parameter is its color.

Working With Colors

The colors in PureBasic are specified using a single 24 bit color value. This value is a large number that represents different combinations of red, green, and blue. To get a 24 bit value of a color we need to use the 'RGB()' command. This command takes three parameters which specify the values of red, green and blue individually. Each one of these parameters has a value range of '0' to '255'. Using these, it's possible for the 'RGB()' command to return over 16.7 million colors as individual 24 bit values. Here's how I used it in the window drawing example shown in Fig.33:

```
. . .
Box(15, 15, 75, 75, RGB(255, 0, 0))
. . .
```

Here, I've used the 'RGB()' command inline as a parameter of the 'Box()' command. If you look closely, you can see that I have specified a maximum value for the red parameter and the lowest value of '0' for the green and blue parameters. This means that the 'RGB()' command will return a 24 bit value that describes a full red which is not mixed with any green or blue. The same is true for the triangle:

```
. . .
LineXY(62, 140, 112, 220, RGB(0, 0, 255))
LineXY(112, 220, 12, 220, RGB(0, 0, 255))
LineXY(12, 220, 62, 140, RGB(0, 0, 255))
FillArea(62, 180, RGB(0, 0, 255), RGB(0, 0, 255))
. . .
```

These four lines make up the blue triangle drawn on the window in Fig.33. The first three are 'LineXY()' commands that draw the three sides to the triangle. The last command is a 'FillArea()' command that picks a point in the center of the triangle and fills it with the same color as the sides. You can see the color is the same throughout all these four drawing commands. The first and second parameters of the 'RGB()' command representing red and green are at '0' while the third parameter representing blue is at '255'. This means that the 'RGB()' command here will return a 24 bit value that describes a full blue which is not mixed with any red or green. The green circle in Fig.33 is a little bit different because I use all three colors to achieve the desired color, like this:

```
. . .
Circle(140, 125, 45, RGB(35, 158, 70))
. . .
```

Here I've used a mix of red, green and blue values to give a nice grass green instead of a full bright green. Using colors like this, makes things simple in PureBasic and very easy to understand for beginners. Using the 'RGB()' command you can return almost any color that the human eye can distinguish.

While the 'RGB()' command can take red, green and blue values and return a combined 24 bit value, there may be a time when you want to extract the red, green and blue component values from a single 24 bit color value. If this is the case, you can do so using the 'Red()', 'Green()' and 'Blue()' commands. Look at this example:

```
ColorValue.l = RGB(35, 158, 70)

Debug "The 24 bit color value is made up of: "
Debug "Red: " + Str(Red(ColorValue))
Debug "Green: " + Str(Green(ColorValue))
Debug "Blue: " + Str(Blue(ColorValue))
```

Each one of the 'Red()', 'Green()' and 'Blue()' commands takes one 24 bit color value as a parameter then returns the corresponding color component value. On the first line in the above example, I compose the 24 bit color value using (amongst the others) a red parameter value of '35'. If I wanted to retrieve the red component value from this 24 bit color value at a later stage, I could pass this value to the 'Red()' command which returns the red component value used to compose it, in this case '35'. The other color commands work in exactly the same way.

Why Drawing On Windows Is Not Preferred

Drawing on windows although possible is not necessarily the right way of displaying graphics drawn with the 2D drawing commands. This is mostly because of the way different operating systems handle the refreshing of the window display. For example, on Microsoft Windows, if you draw graphics directly onto a window and then move another window across it, the graphics will be wiped off the original window. This is because of the internal event handling that takes place within Microsoft Windows. It determines wether or not to redraw window contents automatically and sometimes makes the decision not to. You can force the redraw of graphics after a window has passed in front of another but this is advanced stuff and requires the use of API knowledge of the particular operating system you are dealing with. A more elegant way of displaying drawn graphics, would be to create a new image in memory, draw stuff on it, then display this image using an image gadget on your window. Using an image gadget makes sure that the window automatically takes care of any refreshing that may be needed to keep the image visible.

Drawing Onto An Image

Working with new images in PureBasic is easy, as there is a whole library written purely for creating and manipulating these images. In this next example, I'm going to try to emulate the last program but with a difference. I'm going to create a new image using the 'CreateImage()' command, draw the colored shapes onto it then display the finished result in an image gadget. This should then avoid any window refresh issues and behave how we think it should. You can read more about the image commands contained in PureBasic by looking at the 'Image' library page in the helpfile (Helpfile:Reference Manual->General Libraries->Image). Here's our example:

```
Enumeration
  #WINDOW_MAIN
  #IMAGE_GADGET
  #IMAGE_MAIN
EndEnumeration
```

```
If CreateImage(#IMAGE_MAIN, 180, 220)
  If StartDrawing(ImageOutput(#IMAGE_MAIN))
     ;Because a new image has a Black background, draw a white one instead:
     Box(0, 0, 180, 220, RGB(255, 255, 255))
     ;Now, continue drawing the shapes:
     Box(5, 5, 75, 75, RGB(255, 0, 0))
     Circle(130, 115, 45, RGB(35, 158, 70))
     LineXY(52, 130, 102, 210, RGB(0, 0, 255))
     LineXY(102, 210, 2, 210, RGB(0, 0, 255))
     LineXY(2, 210, 52, 130, RGB(0, 0, 255))
     FillArea(52, 170, RGB(0, 0, 255), RGB(0, 0, 255))
  StopDrawing()
  EndIf
EndIf

#FLAGS = #PB_Window_SystemMenu | #PB_Window_ScreenCentered

If OpenWindow(#WINDOW_MAIN, 0, 0, 200, 240, "Drawing On A New Image", #FLAGS)
  If CreateGadgetList(WindowID(#WINDOW_MAIN))
    ImageGadget(#IMAGE_GADGET, 10, 10, 180, 220, ImageID(#IMAGE_MAIN))
    Repeat
      Event.l = WaitWindowEvent()
    Until Event = #PB_Event_CloseWindow
  EndIf
EndIf
End
```

The main bulk of this code should be self explanatory because the only difference in this code from the last example is that we are now creating a new image using the 'CreateImage()' command and drawing on it instead of a window. The 'CreateImage()' command takes four parameters, the first is the PB number associated with this new image. The second and third are the width and height (in pixels) of the new image and the fourth parameter is the new image's bit depth, which is optional. If the fourth parameter is not used, like in my example, then it uses the same bit depth as your desktop.

After a new image has been created, I tell the program that I want to draw on it by using this line:

```
...
StartDrawing(ImageOutput(#IMAGE_MAIN))
...
```

Here, using the 'StartDrawing()' command with the 'ImageOutput()' method I've specified that all drawing commands should now draw on this image who's PB number is '#IMAGE_MAIN'.

This way of specifying an image to draw onto is not limited to a newly created image. You can just as freely load an image into your program and draw on that too. As long as an image has a PB number associated to it, then you can set the drawing output to draw on it.

Once the image has been created and the drawing output set, I am then free to draw on the image. Because all newly created images in PureBasic start with a black background, the first drawing operation I must make is to color the background with white. I do this using the 'Box()' command which draws a white box as big as the new image itself, covering all the black. After this, I draw the square, circle and triangle shapes as before. When I have finished all necessary drawing operations, I call the ever important 'StopDrawing()' command.

To display this image correctly and avoid the previous refresh problems of drawing directly onto a window, I use an image gadget. This lets the operating system take care of refreshing the gadget's display if other windows pass over it, etc.

What Is The Bit Depth Of An Image?

Each pixel on a computer display or in a digital image is described by binary numbers, as you would expect on a computer. The greater, the number of bits (or binary digits) used to describe a single pixel allows that pixel to express a broader range of colors. The number of bits describing a single pixel in any given digital image or a computer display is called its bit depth. Common bit depths are 1 bit, 8 bit, 16 bit, 24 bit, and 32 bit.

1 bit images can only describe black and white (2 color) images since the one single bit that describes each pixel can either have a value of '1' or '0'.

32 bit pixels on the other hand are capable of displaying more colors than the human eye can see, so this format is regularly used in images for digital film, digital photos, realistic computer games, etc. Modern computers nowadays tend to only use 32 bits per pixel.

Changing The Drawing Mode

In this next example, I'll show you how to change the drawing mode of certain commands including text. Using the 'DrawingMode()' command you can switch to outline mode for shape commands, draw text with a transparent background or even mix (XOr) the output from a drawing command with the background. Here's the drawing mode example:

```
Enumeration
  #WINDOW_MAIN
  #IMAGE_GADGET
  #IMAGE_MAIN
  #FONT_MAIN
EndEnumeration

Global ImageWidth = 401
Global ImageHeight = 201
Global XPos.l, YPos.l, Width.l, Height.l, Red.l, Green.l, Blue.l
Global Text.s = "PureBasic - 2D Drawing Example"
```

```
Procedure.l MyRandom(Maximum.l)
  Repeat
    Number.l = Random(Maximum)
  Until (Number % 10) = 0
  ProcedureReturn Number
EndProcedure

If CreateImage(#IMAGE_MAIN, ImageWidth, ImageHeight)
  If StartDrawing(ImageOutput(#IMAGE_MAIN))
    For x.l = 0 To 1500
      XPos.l = MyRandom(ImageWidth) + 1
      YPos.l = MyRandom(ImageHeight) + 1
      Width.l = (MyRandom(100) - 1) + 10
      Height.l = (MyRandom(100) - 1) + 10
      Red.l = Random(255)
      Green.l = Random(255)
      Blue.l = Random(255)
      Box(XPos, YPos, Width, Height, RGB(Red, Green, Blue))
      DrawingMode(#PB_2DDrawing_Outlined)
      Box(XPos - 1, YPos - 1, Width + 2, Height + 2, RGB(0, 0, 0))
      DrawingMode(#PB_2DDrawing_Default)
    Next x
    LineXY(ImageWidth - 1, 0, ImageWidth - 1, ImageHeight, RGB(0, 0, 0))
    LineXY(0, ImageHeight - 1, ImageWidth, ImageHeight - 1, RGB(0, 0, 0))
    Box(10, 10, 230, 30, RGB(90, 105, 134))
    DrawingMode(#PB_2DDrawing_Outlined)
    Box(10, 10, 231, 31, RGB(0, 0, 0))
    DrawingMode(#PB_2DDrawing_Transparent)
    DrawText(21, 18, Text, RGB(0, 0, 0))
    DrawText(19, 18, Text, RGB(0, 0, 0))
    DrawText(21, 16, Text, RGB(0, 0, 0))
    DrawText(19, 16, Text, RGB(0, 0, 0))
    DrawText(20, 17, Text, RGB(255, 255, 255))
  StopDrawing()
  EndIf
EndIf

#FLAGS = #PB_Window_SystemMenu | #PB_Window_ScreenCentered
If OpenWindow(#WINDOW_MAIN,0,0,ImageWidth+20,ImageHeight+20,"Abstract",#FLAGS)
  If CreateGadgetList(WindowID(#WINDOW_MAIN))
    ImageGadget(#IMAGE_GADGET,10,10,ImageWidth,ImageHeight,ImageID(#IMAGE_MAIN))
  EndIf
  Repeat
    Event.l = WaitWindowEvent()
  Until Event = #PB_Event_CloseWindow
EndIf
End
```

This example is basically an extended version of the last one in which I create a new image, albeit a slightly bigger one, and draw random boxes all over it. With each box I draw, I switch the drawing mode to outline and draw a black outline with the same dimensions over the top. This makes the boxes really stand out. Not only does each box have a random color but each one has a black outline too. To switch modes while drawing you use the 'DrawingMode()' command along with one of several different constants that is used as a parameter. Here are these constants and what they achieve:

'#PB_2DDrawing_Default'
This is the default mode, text is displayed with a solid background color and graphic shapes are filled.

'#PB_2DDrawing_Outlined'
This mode enables outline mode for the shape commands such as 'Box()', 'Circle()' and 'Ellipse()'.

'#PB_2DDrawing_Transparent'
This sets the text background to transparent so only the 'DrawText()' front color parameter is used.

'#PB_2DDrawing_XOr'
This mode enables the XOr mode, this means all graphics are XOR'ed with the current background.

Using this command is very easy. When you want to change drawing modes within a 'StartDrawing()' command block, all you do is call this command with the constant of your choice as a parameter and the mode is instantly changed. These constants can also be combined using the bitwise 'Or' operator. Take a look through the code, you can see I've switched modes quite often.

Once you run this example you will see a window very similar to Fig.34 showing colorful boxes complete with black outlines and white text in the top left hand corner.

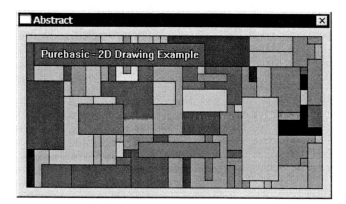

(Microsoft Windows example)   Fig. 34

I used the '#PB_2DDrawing_Transparent' drawing mode when I drew the text on the image, so the text has a transparent background instead of a solid color. To actually draw the text, I used the 'DrawText()' command. This takes five parameters, the 'x' and 'y' position on the output, the String to draw and the front and back color values. Because I've used a transparent background, the fifth parameter is ignored.

The text outline was achieved by drawing four lots of black text at different offsets then drawing the white text on top. I've done this like this because the '#PB_2DDrawing_Outlined' drawing mode does not yet support text.

Drawing Text

Drawing text onto an output is achieved using the 'DrawText()' command (Helpfile:Reference Manual->General Libraries->2DDrawing->DrawText). If you look at the last example, you can see I've used this command a few times. The first and second parameter is the 'x' and 'y' location of the drawn text on the output. The third parameter is the actual string of text to draw. The fourth and fifth parameter are the front and back colors of the text. The front color means the actual text color and the back color means the background color. If the last two optional parameters are not used the color information is taken from the default values, which can be changed using the commands, 'FrontColor()' and 'BackColor()'. These color parameters are 24 bit color values, composed easily using the 'RGB()' command.

Drawing Using An Image

In the last couple of examples, I've demonstrated how to draw simple shapes and lines using the built-in 2D drawing commands but sometimes these can be a bit limiting. In this next example, I'll show you how you can take an external image and draw it onto another newly created image, in any position you like.

```
Enumeration
  #WINDOW_MAIN
  #IMAGE_GADGET
  #IMAGE_SMALL
  #IMAGE_MAIN
  #FONT_MAIN
EndEnumeration

Global ImageWidth = 400
Global ImageHeight = 200
Global XPos.l, YPos.l, LoadedImageWidth.l, LoadedImageHeight.l

Global File.s
Global RequesterText.s = "Choose an image"
Global DefaultFile.s = ""
Global Pattern.s = "Bitmap (*.bmp)|*.bmp|Icon (*.ico)|*.ico"
File = OpenFileRequester(RequesterText, DefaultFile, Pattern, 0)

If File
  LoadImage(#IMAGE_SMALL, File)
  LoadedImageWidth = ImageWidth(#IMAGE_SMALL)
  LoadedImageHeight = ImageHeight(#IMAGE_SMALL)
  If CreateImage(#IMAGE_MAIN, ImageWidth,ImageHeight)
    If StartDrawing(ImageOutput(#IMAGE_MAIN))
      Box(0, 0,ImageWidth, ImageHeight, RGB(255, 255, 255))
      For x.l = 1 To 1000
        XPos = Random(ImageWidth) - (ImageWidth(#IMAGE_SMALL) / 2)
        YPos = Random(ImageHeight) - (ImageHeight(#IMAGE_SMALL) / 2)
```

```
        DrawImage(ImageID(#IMAGE_SMALL), XPos, YPos)
      Next x
      DrawingMode(#PB_2DDrawing_Outlined)
      Box(0, 0, ImageWidth, ImageHeight, RGB(0, 0, 0))
      StopDrawing()
    EndIf
  EndIf
  #TEXT = "Drawing Using Images"
  #FLAGS = #PB_Window_SystemMenu | #PB_Window_ScreenCentered
  If OpenWindow(#WINDOW_MAIN,0,0,ImageWidth+20,ImageHeight+20,#TEXT,#FLAGS)
    If CreateGadgetList(WindowID(#WINDOW_MAIN))
      ImageGadget(#IMAGE_GADGET,10,10,ImageWidth,ImageHeight,ImageID(#IMAGE_MAIN))
    EndIf
    Repeat
      Event.l = WaitWindowEvent()
    Until Event = #PB_Event_CloseWindow
  EndIf
  End
EndIf
```

In the above code, I allow the user to open an image, either in Bitmap or Icon format using the 'OpenFileRequester()' command. Once this requester correctly returns an image file name, I load that file using the 'LoadImage()' command, very similar to the image gadget example in Chapter 9. Once this file is loaded, I can create a new image to draw onto, and use the 'DrawImage()' command to draw the loaded image many times. The resulting image is displayed on a window using an image gadget. If you look at Fig.35 you can see what it looks like after I have loaded a sphere shaped icon which is then randomly drawn all over the new image and then displayed.

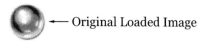 ← Original Loaded Image

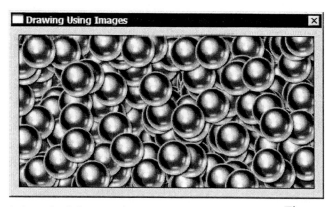

(Microsoft Windows example)   Fig. 35

If you want to draw a loaded image onto a newly created image, you use the 'DrawImage()' command. This command takes five parameters and is very easy to understand. The first is the OS identifier of the image you would like to use to draw with and this can be retrieved by using the 'ImageID()' command. The second and third parameters are the horizontal and vertical position of the drawn image in pixels. The fourth and fifth parameters are optional and I haven't used them here but these are the width and height in pixels of the drawn image. You use these if you need to resize the image dynamically before you draw it. In my example, I've randomized most of the parameters to randomly fill the new image with a thousand copies of the loaded image.

Also, I think this is the first time you have seen the 'OpenFileRequester()' command so I will explain that a little more clearly too, so there is no confusion. This command opens an operating system standard file requester for users to easily select a file. Once a file has been selected the 'OpenFileRequester()' command returns its name as a String. This can be demonstrated by this little stand-alone snippet of code:

```
Global File.s
Global RequesterText.s = "Choose an image"
Global DefaultFile.s = ""
Global Pattern.s = "Bitmap (*.bmp)|*.bmp|Icon (*.ico)|*.ico"
File = OpenFileRequester(RequesterText, DefaultFile, Pattern, 0)
Debug File
```

If you look at the 'OpenFileRequester()' page in the helpfile (Helpfile:Reference Manual->General Libraries->Requester->OpenFileRequester) this command takes four parameters. The first is a String which is the text displayed in the titlebar of the requester when it opens. The second is a String parameter of a file name that this requester may be looking for. If this parameter is specified, this file name is already entered in the selection box once the requesters opens. The third parameter is a file pattern to allow the programmer to determine what files should and shouldn't be displayed for selection in the requester. The fourth parameter is what file type from the file pattern is first selected once the requester opens. In this snippet, 'Bitmap' is first selected because the file pattern index starts at '0'.

The file pattern looks quite complicated but is very simple once you understand it. The file types are broken down into chunks within the pattern String, divided by pipe characters '|' identical to the bitwise Or operator. These chunks work in pairs to be able to specify a String describing a file extension and then the file extension itself. For example, in the above snippet, the pattern looks like this:

```
"Bitmap (*.bmp)|*.bmp|Icon (*.ico)|*.ico"
```

If we break this into chunks using the pipe characters as separators we can see more clearly what is being specified:

```
Bitmap (*.bmp)      *.bmp      Icon (*.ico)      *.ico
```

The first chunk is a String to display in the 'Files of type' selection box within the requester, and once this is selected, it uses the next chunk to tell the requester what type of files to display inside the main window, in this case all '.bmp' files. Remember, the asterisk used here is a String wildcard character to signify any name. The third chunk is another String to display in the 'Files of type' selection box and when this is selected, the requester will display the files with the extension as specified in the fourth chunk, and so on. If you need to specify many extensions for one particular file type you can use the semi colon to specify more extensions within a chunk, like this:

```
"JPEG|*.jpg;*.jpeg"
```

This will now display any files with the extensions of '.jpg' or '.jpeg' when the 'JPEG' String is selected in the requester. You must remember, that if you want to load more types of images other than Bitmaps or Icons, you will have to use another image decoder as explained in Chapter 9 (Including Graphics In Your Program).

Drawing Images With Alpha Channels

Sometimes you may need to draw an image which contains an alpha channel to preserve a drop shadow or maybe parts of the image should be transparent. In Fig.35 I used an icon to draw all over the newly created image, and as standard PureBasic preserves any alpha channel information found inside that icon. But what happens if you need to draw a Png or Tiff format image and preserve its alpha channel? This is where the 'DrawAlphaImage()' command is used. This command will preserve any alpha channel found in image formats that support them, such as 32 bit Png or Tiff files.

The 'DrawAlphaImage()' command is used in exactly the same way as the 'DrawImage()' command, the only difference being that the 'DrawAlphaImage()' command only has three parameters and therefore doesn't allow dynamic resizing of the image while drawing. Here is an example of how the command could be used:

```
...
DrawAlphaImage(ImageID(#IMAGE_PNG), XPos, YPos)
...
```

The above line would display a Png format image and preserve its alpha channel, blending it nicely over any background. One thing to always remember though, is that when loading images other than a Bitmap or Icon format, you have to use the appropriate decoder command to add that functionality to your program, as explained in Chapter 9.

Saving Images

Once you have created an image in your program, you may want to save it to disk. PureBasic makes this task simple by providing the 'SaveImage()' command (Helpfile:Reference Manual->General Libraries->Image->SaveImage). This command will save any image in your PureBasic program that has a PB number. The 'SaveImage()' command takes four parameters. The first is the PB number of the image you want to save. The second is the file name that you want to save your image as. The third parameter is optional and defines what image format this image should be saved as. The fourth parameter is for specifying an optional value to be used with whatever file format is chosen.

If we wanted to save the image created from the last example, we could add this line of code onto the end of the example code. Once the program finishes it would save our image:

```
...
SaveImage(#IMAGE_MAIN, "Image.bmp")
...
```

By default, PureBasic will save a Bitmap format image file when you use this command without the last two optional parameters. So the filename will need to have the correct extension (*.bmp) when saved.

Saving Images In Other Formats
You can save images in other graphical formats by specifying this as a third parameter. This can be one of these three built-in constants:

'#PB_ImagePlugin_BMP'
Save the image in Bitmap format. This is the default setting and doesn't really need specifying.

'#PB_ImagePlugin_JPEG'
Save the image in Jpeg format. (To work properly, the 'UseJPEGImageEncoder()' command must be called before this command is used).

'#PB_ImagePlugin_PNG'
Save the image in Png format. (To work properly, the 'UsePNGImageEncoder()' command must be called before this command is used).

When saving an image using either '#PB_ImagePlugin_JPEG' or '#PB_ImagePlugin_PNG' you must put the appropriate encoder command at the top of your source code before using the 'SaveImage()' command to make sure it knows how to encode that given format. The encoders only need to be called once to add the required functionality throughout your program. Here are they are:

' UseJPEGImageEncoder()'
This encoder adds support for the Jpeg image (*.jpg/*.jpeg) file format.

' UsePNGImageEncoder()'
This encoder adds support for the Png image (*.png) file format.

When using the ' UseJPEGImageEncoder()' to add Jpeg support, you can optionally use the fourth parameter of the 'SaveImage()' command to specify the compression value of the saved image. This is the only image type that currently supports this fourth parameter.

Here are a few examples of using the 'SaveImage()' command:

```
SaveImage(#IMAGE_MAIN, "Image.bmp")
```

This first example will save an image called 'Image.bmp' in the default 24bit Bitmap format. Notice that no encoder is needed because PureBasic supports Bitmap format images as standard.

```
UseJPEGImageEncoder()
...
SaveImage(#IMAGE_MAIN, "Image.jpg", #PB_ImagePlugin_JPEG)
```

The second example will save an image called 'Image.jpg' in JPEG format using a default compression value of '7' because we haven't specified one ourselves.

```
UseJPEGImageEncoder()
...
SaveImage(#IMAGE_MAIN, "Image.jpg", #PB_ImagePlugin_JPEG, 10)
```

This third example will save an image called 'Image.jpg' in JPEG format and use the maximum compression value of '10' as specified in the fourth parameter.

```
UsePNGImageEncoder()
...
SaveImage(#IMAGE_MAIN, "Image.png", #PB_ImagePlugin_PNG)
```

This fourth example will save an image called 'Image.png' in PNG format.

Introducing Screens

If you ever wanted to create your own game or write your own screensaver using PureBasic then you will always start by opening a 'Screen'. This screen is a purely graphical environment, created for the one intention of displaying graphics such as output from 2D drawing, loaded images, loaded sprites and loaded 3D models and worlds.

What Is A Sprite?

Sprites were originally special hardware accelerated images that were used to create composited 2D graphics for computer games. As processing power of computers increased through the years, the special hardware that was used to move and draw these images quickly was no longer needed. However, even today, the name still remains in use to describe 2D images that are drawn on screen to create games and the like.

Today a sprite can be described as a small graphic (usually containing a transparent background) that can be positioned and drawn independently on a screen to simulate animation or to provide static graphics.

Screens are normally opened fully occupying the entire width and height of your screen, but if you feel the need, you can also open one upon a window that has already been created. This is referred to as a Windowed Screen. Only one type of screen can be opened at any one time, either one full-screen or one windowed screen.

The reason why screens are preferred to display graphics (instead of simply drawing onto windows) to create games and the like, is that screens are fast, ...very fast! On every platform that PureBasic is available for, its screens are optimized to provide the greatest performance possible no matter what the underlying operating system.

Opening Your First Screen

To create and open a screen in PureBasic you need to follow a basic code template. Screen and sprite handling are very closely connected so you always have to initialize the sprite engine before opening a screen. This makes sure that everything is correctly initialized internally and the screen will be ready for drawing operations. Once the sprite engine has been initialized and the screen is actually open, you then need a main loop to keep the program running, just like a graphical user interface program.

The code below shows a skeleton screen program with all crucial bits of code present to initialize the sprite engine, open a screen, create a main loop and initialize the keyboard commands to provide a way of closing the program.

```
Global Quit.b = #False

;Simple error checking procedure
Procedure HandleError(Result.l, Text.s)
  If Result = 0
    MessageRequester("Error", Text, #PB_MessageRequester_Ok)
    End
  EndIf
EndProcedure

HandleError(InitSprite(), "InitSprite() command failed.")
HandleError(InitKeyboard(), "InitKeyboard() command failed.")
HandleError(OpenScreen(1024, 768, 32, "Fullscreen"), "Could not open screen.")

Repeat
  ClearScreen(RGB(0, 0, 0))

  ;Drawing operations go here

  FlipBuffers(2)
  ExamineKeyboard()
  If KeyboardReleased(#PB_Key_Escape)
    Quit = #True
  EndIf
Until Quit = #True
End
```

If you first take a look at the sprite and screen section in the PureBasic helpfile (Helpfile:Reference Manual->2D Games Libraries->Sprite & Screen) you'll find more information regarding all the new command used in this example.

This example doesn't really do anything other than open a blank screen and if you are looking at that now you can exit the program by pressing 'Esc' on your keyboard. This example is what all games and the like are born from so let me run through the important bits and explain what's happening along the way.

To start with I've created a simple error checking procedure as explained in Chapter 8 (How To Minimize And Handle Errors) and used this to make sure that the 'InitSprite()', 'InitKeyboard()' and 'OpenScreen()' commands do not return '0'. If any of them do, then that particular command is considered to have failed, so I immediately exit the program. If a failure occurs like this for whatever reason, it is always best to close the program and inform the user of the problem. Otherwise, if your program was to continue, major crashes are likely to occur.

The commands needed to initialize the sprite engine and keyboard are just simple command calls, these are 'InitSprite()' and 'InitKeyboard()', remember that we need to initialize the sprite engine before we open a screen. The 'OpenScreen()' command takes four parameters, these are the width, height and bit depth of the screen plus its text caption. This caption is what will be displayed in the taskbar if you were to minimize the screen from view.

Using The Keyboard?

In these examples I've used a few keyboard commands to initialize the keyboard and detect keypresses, etc. These can all be found in the 'Keyboard' library helpfile page (Helpfile:Reference Manual->General Libraries->Keyboard). This is a very small and easy to use library of commands, so you should be able to pick them up pretty easily.

The 'InitKeyboard()' command initializes the keyboard and should be called before any other keyboard command. The 'ExamineKeyboard()' command examines the current state of the keyboard to see if any keys are being held down, etc. The 'KeyboardReleased()' and 'KeyboardPushed()' commands return true if a given key is either released or pushed respectively. These keys can be assigned using built-in constants, of which there is a full list on the helpfile page of each command.

The width, height and bit depth parameters are very important to get right as these define what size and bit depth your screen will be. Whatever computer is going to run this program and open this screen must be capable of supporting whatever size and bit depth is used. The width and height values are collectively known as the resolution and this must be supported wholly by the graphics card and monitor connected to the target computer or else an error will be raised and the 'OpenScreen()' command will not succeed. The values I have used in this example are those that most computers are able to support and shouldn't present any problems. This is worth keeping in mind when writing a program that relies on a screen.

Fig.36 shows common screen resolutions and bit depths that should work on almost every modern computer. Just like computer games, the higher, the screen resolution, the more crisp the display looks but because there are more pixels to draw, the program may slow down. The higher, the bit depth, the more colors are able to be displayed and more lifelike graphics are able to be represented.

Common Screen Resolutions

Width	Height	Bit Depths
640	480	8, 16 & 32
800	600	8, 16 & 32
1024	768	8, 16 & 32

Fig. 36

Of course, instead of hard coding values like these into a program, it's always best to test the ability of the target computer to use these values. You can list the different resolutions and bit depths that any computer can display, by using this code:

```
InitSprite()
If ExamineScreenModes()
  While NextScreenMode()
    Width.l = ScreenModeWidth()
    Height.l = ScreenModeHeight()
    BitDepth.l = ScreenModeDepth()
    Debug Str(Width)+" x "+Str(Height)+" x "+Str(BitDepth)
  Wend
EndIf
```

Again in this snippet, we initialize the sprite engine before we use the 'ExamineScreenModes()' command, this initializes everything correctly to allow us to use these screen based commands. I then use a 'While' loop to iterate through each supported screen mode and use the 'ScreenModeWidth()', 'ScreenModeHeight()' and 'ScreenModeDepth()' commands, to construct a String describing each mode. This is then echoed to the Debug Output window for us to examine. This is a simple example and one that you should be able to understand yourself by reading the associated command helpfile pages (Helpfile:Reference Manual->2D Games Libraries->Sprite & Screen).

Double Buffered Rendering

When using a screen to display graphics you always need a main loop to keep the program running, draw graphics and test for user input, etc. and this too must follow a template when using a screen. Here is the main loop taken from the skeleton screen program on the previous page:

```
...
Repeat
  ClearScreen(0)
  ;Drawing operations go here
  FlipBuffers(2)
  ExamineKeyboard()
  If KeyboardReleased(#PB_Key_Escape)
    Quit = #True
  EndIf
Until Quit = #True
...
```

At first glace you can see it's very similar to a normal main loop of any other program but there are a few differences. There are two commands in there that are crucial to make a screen draw graphics correctly, these are 'ClearScreen()' and 'FlipBuffers()'. Before I can go into more detail about these two commands I must explain a graphical technique called double buffering.

Double buffering is a graphical technique used by PureBasic screens to avoid corrupted graphics and a flickering display. Because computer monitors constantly redraw the monitor screen usually sixty to seventy (sometimes more) times a second, it's hard to make changes to the screen, such as moving and drawing new graphics without the display showing changes before you've actually completed them. This results in torn, corrupted graphics and other strange visual artifacts. If you wanted to avoid this problem by clearing the screen every time before redrawing the whole screen again, it would cure the corrupted graphic problem but it would make the screen flicker.

Using double buffering, PureBasic solves these problems. Once a screen is opened it automatically gets assigned two video buffers in memory, exactly the same size as the opened screen. When you draw graphics onto the screen using PureBasic's graphics commands you are actually drawing onto the back buffer while the front buffer is being displayed on the screen. When the monitor has finished displaying the front buffer and the drawing operations are complete on the back buffer, both are flipped over (swapped). Now the front becomes the back and the back becomes the front, which is then displayed. When the program draws its graphics again it draws on the newly flipped back buffer. This new back buffer will probably contain old graphics because they have already been displayed, so it is standard procedure to clear the back buffer completely using a single color (usually black) before starting to draw on it again. Fig.37 shows this technique in action showing three cycles of the buffers.

Double Buffered Rendering

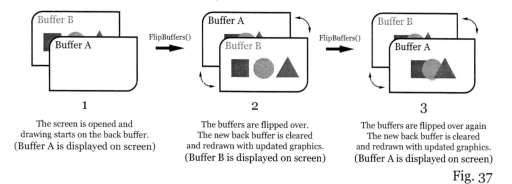

1	2	3
The screen is opened and drawing starts on the back buffer. (Buffer A is displayed on screen)	The buffers are flipped over. The new back buffer is cleared and redrawn with updated graphics. (Buffer B is displayed on screen)	The buffers are flipped over again The new back buffer is cleared and redrawn with updated graphics. (Buffer A is displayed on screen)

Fig. 37

In this diagram you can see at program start (indicated by step 1), that the front buffer ('Buffer A') has no graphics drawn on it, so nothing is displayed on screen. When we draw stuff using the PureBasic drawing commands, we draw onto the backbuffer, indicated by 'Buffer B'. Once all drawing has taken place, we can call the 'FlipBuffers()' command and the buffers are flipped. This is shown in step 2. Now, 'Buffer B' is displayed on the screen and we continue drawing onto 'Buffer A' which is now the new back buffer. Again, once all drawing operation are done, we can flip the buffers again using 'FlipBuffers()' and we arrive at step 3, where 'Buffer A' is now drawn to the screen and 'Buffer B' is once again the back buffer.

When the buffers are flipped using the 'FlipBuffer()' command, the buffer that arrives at the back will still have old graphics drawn on it. If we want to create the illusion of movement to animate graphics, we will have to clear these and redraw them in a new position before we flip the buffers again. To clear old graphics we use the 'ClearScreen()' command. 'ClearScreen()' takes one parameter which is a 24 bit color value of the color you want to clear the screen with. This can be retrieved easily using the 'RGB()' command.

The 'FlipBuffers()' command (Helpfile:Reference Manual->2D Games Libraries->Sprite & Screen->FlipBuffers) also has an optional parameter and can take these values:

'0' : Disable monitor vertical synchronization
'1' : Enable monitor vertical synchronization (default value)
'2' : Enable monitor vertical synchronization, using CPU saving mode (full screen mode only).

If '0' is used as a parameter then the 'FlipBuffers()' flips the buffer as fast as it can to achieve the highest frame rate of the drawn graphics. The only downside to this is that the monitor refresh rate might not be fast enough to draw the new graphics in realtime so some visual tearing may occur as the monitor tries to keep up with the flipped buffers.

If '1' is used as a parameter the 'FlipBuffers()' command flips the buffers in perfect synchronization with the monitors refresh rate ensuring that all graphics are drawn correctly and smoothly to the monitor. The only downside of this is that the frame rate can never exceed beyond the refresh rate of the monitor. This is the default mode if no parameter is used.

Using '2' as a parameter will have the same effect as using '1', but will switch to CPU saving mode to ensure it does not run the CPU at a hundred percent so other program don't have a chance to run.

Drawing To A Screen
Here is an example of double buffered rendering and animation created by drawing updated graphics between each 'FlipBuffers()' command: (exit this program by pressing 'Esc' on your keyboard)

```
#IMAGE_MAIN = 1
;Set the width, height and bit depth of the screen
;Abbreviated variables are used here due to page width constraints :(
Global ScrW.l = 1024
Global ScrH.l = 768
Global ScrD.l = 32
Global Quit.b = #False
XOrigin.f = (ScrW / 2) - 64 : YOrigin.f = (ScrH / 2) - 64

;Simple error checking procedure
Procedure HandleError(Result.l, Text.s)
  If Result = 0
    MessageRequester("Error", Text, #PB_MessageRequester_Ok)
```

```
      End
    EndIf
EndProcedure

;Initialize environment
HandleError(InitSprite(), "InitSprite() command failed.")
HandleError(InitKeyboard(), "InitKeyboard() command failed.")
HandleError(OpenScreen(ScrW, ScrH, ScrD, "Blobs"), "Could not open screen.")
SetFrameRate(60)

;Create an image
If CreateImage(#IMAGE_MAIN, 128, 128)
  If StartDrawing(ImageOutput(#IMAGE_MAIN))
    For x.l = 255 To 0 Step -1
      Circle(64, 64, x / 4, RGB(0, 0, 255 - x))
    Next x
    StopDrawing()
  EndIf
EndIf

;Convert Degrees to Radians
Procedure.f DegToRad(Angle.f)
  ProcedureReturn Angle.f * #PI / 180
EndProcedure

;Main loop
Repeat
  ClearScreen(RGB(0, 0, 0))
  Angle.f + 2.0
  Radius.f = ((ScrH / 2) - 100) * Sin(DegToRad(Angle))

  StartDrawing(ScreenOutput())
    For x.l = 0 To 359 Step 45
      XPos.f = XOrigin + (Radius * Cos(DegToRad(Angle + x)))
      YPos.f = YOrigin + (Radius * Sin(DegToRad(Angle + x)))
      DrawImage(ImageID(#IMAGE_MAIN), XPos, YPos)
    Next x
  StopDrawing()

  FlipBuffers()
  ExamineKeyboard()
  If KeyboardReleased(#PB_Key_Escape)
    Quit = #True
  EndIf
Until Quit = #True
End
```

In this example, I've created a new image using the 'CreateImage()' command and then later drawn this image to the screen using a 'StartDrawing()' block. Even though this code looks a little complicated, especially when calculating the 'x' and 'y' values of the drawn image, this example is purely to demonstrate the flipping of the buffers.

You can see in the main loop, that the first thing I do is clear the screen using the 'ClearScreen()' command. This is to allow me to start on a clear buffer, so no old graphics are left over from any previous drawing operations. After that I use some math to calculate new coordinates for my blob images and use a loop to draw them. After these have been drawn, they are on the back buffer so I have to use the 'FlipBuffers()' command to display them on the screen. And so it goes on, clearing, drawing and flipping, and between each flip, I change the position of the graphics.

You might of noticed another new command that I've used in this example and that is 'SetFrameRate()' (Helpfile:Reference Manual->2D Games Libraries->Sprite & Screen->SetFrameRate). This command has one parameter that sets the number of times that 'FlipBuffers()' can be executed per second. This is to provide a standard frame rate on other computers that might run this code. This should limit this example to display updated graphics sixty times a second.

This is how all animation is produced on computers, very similar to cartoons or films. Nothing actually moves on screen, it's really a slideshow of different images (buffers) in which graphics are in slightly different positions. Because it all happens very fast (sixty plus times a second) the images appear to move.

A Simple Starfield
This is one of the effects that any demo or game programmer will know how to draw. A starfield such as this has been used in hundreds of demo's and games to give the effect of traveling through space. It is an effect that draws and animates hundreds of pixels on the screen using different shades of color to give the illusion of depth and movement. There are various way of programming this effect, here is my example:

```
#APP_NAME = "Stars v1.0"
#NUMBER_OF_STARS = 10000
;Set the width, height and bit depth of the screen
;Abbreviated variables are used here due to page width constraints :(
Global ScrW.l = 1024
Global ScrH.l = 768
Global ScrD.l = 32
Global Quit.b = #False

Structure STAR
  xPos.f
  yPos.f
  xStep.f
  Color.l
EndStructure
Global Dim Stars.STAR(#NUMBER_OF_STARS)

;Simple error checking procedure
Procedure HandleError(Result.l, Text.s)
  If Result = 0
    MessageRequester("Error", Text, #PB_MessageRequester_Ok)
    End
  EndIf
EndProcedure
```

```
;init stars
Procedure InitializeStars()
  For x = 0 To #NUMBER_OF_STARS
    Stars(x)\xPos = Random(ScrW - 1)
    Stars(x)\yPos = Random(ScrH - 1)
    If x < #NUMBER_OF_STARS / 3
      Stars(x)\xStep = (Random(10) / 100) + 0.2
      Stars(x)\Color = RGB(40, 40, 40)
    ElseIf x >= #NUMBER_OF_STARS / 3 And x < (#NUMBER_OF_STARS / 3) * 2
      Stars(x)\xStep = (Random(10) / 100) + 0.6
      Stars(x)\Color = RGB(100, 100, 100)
    Else
      Stars(x)\xStep = (Random(10) / 100) + 1.2
      Stars(x)\Color = RGB(255, 255, 255)
    EndIf
  Next x
EndProcedure

;move stars on the 'x' axis
Procedure MoveStarsX()
  For x = 0 To #NUMBER_OF_STARS
    Stars(x)\xPos - .Stars(x)\xStep
    If Stars(x)\xPos < 0
      Stars(x)\xPos = ScrW - 1
      Stars(x)\yPos = Random(ScrH - 1)
    EndIf
  Next x
EndProcedure

;Initialize environment
HandleError(InitSprite(), "InitSprite() command failed.")
HandleError(InitKeyboard(), "InitKeyboard() command failed.")
HandleError(OpenScreen(ScrW, ScrH, ScrD, #APP_NAME), "Could not open screen.")
SetFrameRate(60)
InitializeStars()

Repeat
  ClearScreen(RGB(0, 0, 0))
  StartDrawing(ScreenOutput())
    For x = 0 To #NUMBER_OF_STARS
      Plot(Stars(x)\xPos, Stars(x)\yPos, Stars(x)\Color)
    Next x
    DrawingMode(#PB_2DDrawing_Transparent)
    DrawText(20, 20, #APP_NAME, #White)
    DrawText(20, 40, Str(#NUMBER_OF_STARS)+" Animated stars", #White)
    DrawText(20, 60, "Screen Resolution: "+Str(ScrW)+" x "+Str(ScrH), #White)
    DrawText(20, 80, "Screen Bit depth: "+Str(ScrD)+"bit", #White)
  StopDrawing()
  FlipBuffers()
  MoveStarsX()
```

```
  ExamineKeyboard()
  If KeyboardReleased(#PB_Key_Escape)
    Quit = 1
  EndIf

Until Quit = 1
End
```

This example uses the 2D drawing command, 'Plot()' to draw a single pixel at a time (Helpfile:Reference Manual->General Libraries->2DDrawing->Plot). This command uses three parameters, of which the third is optional. These parameters define the 'x' and 'y' position and color of the pixel to be drawn. If the last parameter is not used then this command uses the default foreground color, which is set using the 'FrontColor()' command.

In the above example, I've used a structure to keep all the information about a single pixel together, then created an array of variables using this structure. Each of the elements in the array describes the position, color and step value of all of the individual pixels. I then loop through the array, drawing each pixel on the screen using the pixel information (position, color, etc.) contained inside each structured array element. Once the drawing is complete, I then flip the buffers and update the pixel positions in the array using the associated step values. Once this is done, I clear the screen and redraw again, ...and so it goes on. Doing things this way makes the code look cleaner, it's much more easier to read and allows you to update it easily at a later stage.

Opening A Screen On A Window

Sometimes you might like to open a screen on a window, especially if you want to make a windowed game or demo, etc. You can do this using the 'OpenWindowedScreen()' command. To open a screen upon a window, you need to first create a window and then handle the events from that window in the main loop, as well as the drawing. Here is an example of using a windowed screen:

```
#WINDOW_MAIN = 1
#IMAGE_MAIN = 1

;Set the width, height and bit depth of the screen
;Abbreviated variables are used here due to page width constraints :(
Global ScrW.l = 800
Global ScrH.l = 600
Global ScrD.l = 32
Global Quit.b = #False
Global XOrigin.f = (ScrW / 2) - 64
Global YOrigin.f = (ScrH / 2) - 64

;Simple error checking procedure
Procedure HandleError(Result.l, Text.s)
  If Result = 0
    MessageRequester("Error", Text, #PB_MessageRequester_Ok)
    End
  EndIf
EndProcedure
```

```
;Convert Degrees to Radians
Procedure.f DegToRad(Angle.f)
  ProcedureReturn Angle.f * #PI / 180
EndProcedure

;Initialize environment
HandleError(InitSprite(), "InitSprite() command failed.")
HandleError(InitKeyboard(), "InitKeyboard() command failed.")

#FLAGS = #PB_Window_SystemMenu | #PB_Window_ScreenCentered
If OpenWindow(#WINDOW_MAIN, 0, 0, ScrW, ScrH, "Windowed Screen", #FLAGS)
  If OpenWindowedScreen(WindowID(#WINDOW_MAIN), 0, 0, ScrW, ScrH, 0, 0, 0)
    SetFrameRate(60)

    ;Create an image
    If CreateImage(#IMAGE_MAIN, 128, 128)
      If StartDrawing(ImageOutput(#IMAGE_MAIN))
        For x.l = 255 To 0 Step -1
          Circle(64, 64, x / 4, RGB(255 - x, 0, 0))
        Next x
       StopDrawing()
      EndIf
    EndIf

    ;Main loop
    Repeat
      Event.l = WindowEvent()
      ClearScreen(RGB(0, 0, 0))

      Angle.f + 2.0
      Radius.f = ((ScrH / 2) - 100) * Sin(DegToRad(Angle))

      StartDrawing(ScreenOutput())
        For x.l = 0 To 359 Step 45
          XPos.f = XOrigin + (Radius * Cos(DegToRad(Angle + x)))
          YPos.f = YOrigin + (Radius * Sin(DegToRad(Angle + x)))
          DrawImage(ImageID(#IMAGE_MAIN), XPos, YPos)
        Next x
      StopDrawing()

      FlipBuffers()
      ExamineKeyboard()
      If KeyboardReleased(#PB_Key_Escape)
       Quit = #True
      EndIf

    Until Event = #PB_Event_CloseWindow Or Quit = #True
  EndIf
EndIf
End
```

This example should be pretty straightforward, because most of this code you have seen before. The main difference being the 'OpenWindowedScreen()' command which takes eight parameters! The first parameter is the OS identifier of the window it is to be opened on. The second and third parameters are the 'x' and 'y' position of the new screen on the window. The fourth and fifth parameters are the width and height of the new screen. The sixth parameter is the auto-size or auto-stretch flag. If this parameter is set to '0' then no automatic resizing takes place but if it is set to '1' then the screen with automatically resize itself to the maximum size that the window will allow, disregarding parameters four and five. This means that even if you resize the parent window, the screen will automatically change its size to always fill the full parent window area. The seventh and eight parameters are margins that you can specify for when auto-stretch is enabled. These will pull the auto-sizing screen back a little from the right hand side or from the bottom respectively, to leave room for a status bar or other gadgets on the window.

It is also very important when using a screen on a window, that you always handle the events properly using the 'WindowEvent()' command. If you remember from Chapter 9, this command doesn't wait for an event to occur before returning, instead it always tries to detect and return any events that need handling. Using this command instead of 'WaitWindowEvent()' is a must because you don't want to halt the drawing and flipping of buffers for any length of time.

Sprites

Sprites in PureBasic are images that can be drawn in any position on a screen. Unlike images however, sprites have their own command set, are optimized for speed and can be drawn in several special ways to achieve many special effects. All normal sprite commands appear in the 'Sprite & Screen' section in the helpfile (Helpfile:Reference Manual->2D Games Libraries->Sprite & Screen) but there are also some other sprite commands located in the 'Sprite3D' section too (Helpfile:Reference Manual->2D Games Libraries->Sprite3D). To familiarize yourself fully with what is capable using the sprite commands, I would recommend reading both of these two sections.

The Difference Between Sprites And Sprite3D's
In PureBasic there are two different types of sprite. The first is what you would consider a normal sprite, which is created from a user drawn or loaded image and which is displayed and manipulated using the standard sprite library.

The second type is almost the same, except PureBasic uses a very small 3D engine to display the sprites. Also, the commands used for drawing and manipulating this type, allow the programmer to achieve graphical effects not possible with normal sprites. These effects include, realtime zooming, 3D transformation and sprite blending. The 3D engine that performs the transformation and displaying of the 3D sprites is not the OGRE engine as mentioned in the next chapter, but a small, self-contained 3D engine specifically created to handle this type of sprite.

Using Normal Sprites
To create a sprite for use within your program, you can either load one with the 'LoadSprite()' command (Helpfile:Reference Manual->2D Games Libraries->Sprite & Screen->LoadSprite) or create a new one using the 'CreateSprite()' command (Helpfile:Reference Manual->2D Games Libraries-

>Sprite & Screen->CreateSprite).

To load existing images to be used as sprites, the 'LoadSprite()' command is very similar to the 'LoadImage()' command and has three parameters. The first is the PB number that you wish to associate to this sprite. The second is the file name of the image you want to load as a sprite, remembering of course, to use the correct image decoder if needed. The third is the sprite mode, which determines how this sprite will be used, more on this in a moment.

To create your own sprite so you can draw on it using the 2D drawing commands, we use 'CreateSprite()'. Being very similar to 'CreateImage()', this command takes four parameters. The first parameter, is the PB number that you wish to associate to this sprite. The second and third parameters are the width and height in pixels of the new sprite, and the fourth parameter is the sprite mode.

Both of these two commands create a new sprite and both have an optional 'Mode' parameter. This mode parameter determines the internal sprite format so particular sprites can be displayed properly using other sprite commands. This format parameter is usually defined as a built-in constant, Fig.38 shows these mode constants and a description of each mode.

Depending on which sprite command you want to use to display your sprite, you have to use a correctly formatted sprite with it, and this format is set when you create or load that sprite.

Sprite Modes

Constant Used	Description Of Mode
None	The default mode. Sprite is loaded into Video RAM (if possible).
#PB_Sprite_Memory	Sprite is loaded into normal RAM instead of Video RAM for use with the 'StartSpecialFX()' command.
#PB_Sprite_Alpha	Sprite must be 8 bit grayscale and will be prepared for use with the 'DisplayAlphaSprite()' or 'DisplayShadowSprite()' commands. '#PB_Sprite_Memory' needs to be specified as well, if you are to use the 'StartSpecialFX()' command.
#PB_Sprite_Texture	Sprite is created with 3D support, so that you can create a 3D Sprite from it using the 'CreateSprite3D()' command.
#PB_Sprite_AlphaBlending	Sprite is created with alpha channel support. The image loaded must be of an image format that can contain an alpha channel. The only image formats currently supported by this mode are Png and Tiff. (If you intend on converting this sprite to a 3D sprite, the '#PB_Sprite_Texture' mode needs to be specified as well).

The modes can be combined as usual by using the Bitwise Or operator '|'.   Fig. 38

Here are examples of how to specify the mode properly for each sprite display command. Where applicable, I've given an example of how to create and load a sprite with the correct mode settings, so it will display properly when using the command before it.

'DisplaySprite()' & 'DisplayTransparentSprite()'

```
;Default format
CreateSprite(#PB_NUMBER, Width.l, Height.l)
LoadSprite(#PB_NUMBER, "Image.bmp")
```

'DisplaySprite3D()'

```
;Without an alpha channel
CreateSprite(#PB_NUMBER, Width.l, Height.l, #PB_Sprite_Texture )
LoadSprite(#PB_NUMBER, "Image.bmp", #PB_Sprite_Texture )

;With an alpha channel
;NOTE: You can't create sprites with an alpha channel in PureBasic yet.
LoadSprite(#PB_NUMBER,"Image.bmp",#PB_Sprite_Texture|#PB_Sprite_AlphaBlending)
```

'DisplayTranslucentSprite()'

```
;Load in normal RAM for processing by the 'StartSpecialFX()' command
CreateSprite(#PB_NUMBER, Width.l, Height.l, #PB_Sprite_Memory)
LoadSprite(#PB_NUMBER, "Image.bmp", #PB_Sprite_Memory)
```

'DisplayAlphaSprite()', 'DisplayShadowSprite()' & 'DisplaySolidSprite()'

```
;Load in normal RAM for processing by the 'StartSpecialFX()' command
;and specify as an alpha type sprite
CreateSprite(#PB_NUMBER, Width.l, Height.l, #PB_Sprite_Memory|#PB_Sprite_Alpha)
LoadSprite(#PB_NUMBER, "Image.bmp", #PB_Sprite_Memory | #PB_Sprite_Alpha)
```

These examples should give you a good idea of how to load and create your own sprites for every display command.

You Can Draw On Sprites Too
Once you have created or loaded a sprite, you may want to draw on it. Similar to drawing on an image, you can do this by using the standard 'StartDrawing()' command and setting the output to 'SpriteOutput()'. This allows you to use the 2D drawing commands to draw onto the sprite's surface. You can even draw a sprite onto another sprite. To do this you must switch the sprite drawing output from the back buffer to your target sprite. For this, you need use the 'UseBuffer()' command. This command takes one parameter which is the PB number of the sprite you want to direct all sprite output to. Once switched, all further sprite displaying commands draw sprites onto the target sprite. When you have finished, you can return the sprite display output back to the back buffer by using the 'UseBuffer()' command again, but this time with a parameter of '#PB_Default'.

'SpecialFX' Sprite Commands

In the mode examples I mentioned 'SpecialFX' sprites. These are still normal sprites but work a lot faster if they have the 'StartSpecialFX()' commands enclosing them. All sprites that use the special effects like this are capable of producing good looking graphics but because everything is rendered inside the computer's main RAM these sprites aren't as quick as sprites3D's. Here is a brief snippet showing the usage of these commands:

```
...
StartSpecialFX()
  DisplayAlphaSprite(#SPRITE_NUMBER, 64, 64)
  DisplayRGBFilter(100, 100, 100, 100, 0, 255, 0)
  DisplayTranslucentSprite(#SPRITE_NUMBER, 128, 128, 128)
  ;etc...
StopSpecialFX()
...
```

As you can see, the 'StartSpecialFX()' command starts the block and 'StopSpecialFX()' ends it. All special effects commands must go inside these two commands. This is done to increase the rendering speed of these special effects, otherwise without the 'StartSpecialFX()' block the display performance would be very poor.

If using these commands, it is very important to understand that these must be used before any other graphics commands. This is because of the way PureBasic handles the internals of the special effects drawing. Otherwise, if you use other graphics commands before a special effect block, they will be over written on the backbuffer once the 'StartSpecialFX()' block starts. If you are using a 'ClearScreen()' command to clear the buffer before you draw, you should include this in the 'StartSpecialFX()' block too. Another important point to make clear is that there should only ever be one 'StartSpecialFX()' block in any main loop, as this increases performance even further.

The commands that use a 'StartSpecialFX()' block are:

> 'DisplayAlphaSprite()'
> 'DisplaySolidSprite()'
> 'DisplayShadowSprite()'
> 'DisplayRGBFilter()'
> 'DisplayTranslucentSprite()'

You can read about these commands in more detail in the helpfile, in the 'Sprite & Screen' library (Helpfile:Reference Manual->2D Games Libraries->Sprite & Screen).

Displaying Normal Sprites

Normal sprites are the foundations of making a 2D game in PureBasic. This type of sprite has been used over and over again, time after time, to produce cool visuals in many top games. Here is a simple example of creating a new sprite and rendering it all over the screen using the standard 'DisplayTransparentSprite()' command:

```
#SPRITE_MAIN = 1
#NUMBER_OF_BALLS = 500

;Set the width, height and bit depth of the screen
;Abbreviated variables are used here due to page width constraints :(
Global ScrW.l = 1024
Global ScrH.l = 768
Global ScrD.l = 32
Global Quit.b = #False

Structure BALL
  x.f
  y.f
  XOrigin.l
  YOrigin.l
  Radius.l
  Angle.f
  Speed.f
EndStructure
Global Dim Balls.BALL(#NUMBER_OF_BALLS)

;Simple error checking procedure
Procedure HandleError(Result.l, Text.s)
  If Result = 0
    MessageRequester("Error", Text, #PB_MessageRequester_Ok)
    End
  EndIf
EndProcedure

;Convert Degrees to Radians
Procedure.f DegToRad(Angle.f)
  ProcedureReturn Angle.f * #PI / 180
EndProcedure

;Initialize all ball data
Procedure InitialiseBalls()
  For x.l = 0 To #NUMBER_OF_BALLS
    Balls(x)\XOrigin = Random(ScrW) - 32
    Balls(x)\YOrigin = Random(ScrH) - 32
    Balls(x)\Radius = Random(190) + 10
    Balls(x)\Angle = Random(360)
    Balls(x)\Speed = Random(2) + 1
  Next x
EndProcedure

;Initialize environment
HandleError(InitSprite(), "InitSprite() command failed.")
HandleError(InitKeyboard(), "InitKeyboard() command failed.")
HandleError(OpenScreen(ScrW, ScrH, ScrD, "Blobs"), "Could not open screen.")
SetFrameRate(60)
```

```
;Create an image
Global Offset.f = 32
If CreateSprite(#SPRITE_MAIN, 64, 64)
  If StartDrawing(SpriteOutput(#SPRITE_MAIN))
    Box(0, 0, 64, 64, RGB(255, 255, 255))
    For x.l = 220 To 1 Step -1
      Offset + 0.025
      Circle(Offset, 64 - Offset, x / 8, RGB(0, 255 - x, 0))
    Next x
  StopDrawing()
 EndIf
EndIf
TransparentSpriteColor(#SPRITE_MAIN, RGB(255, 255, 255))
InitialiseBalls()

;Main loop
Repeat
  ClearScreen(RGB(56, 76, 104))
  For x.l = 0 To #NUMBER_OF_BALLS
   Balls(x)\x=Balls(x)\XOrigin+(Balls(x)\Radius*Cos(DegToRad(Balls(x)\Angle)))
   Balls(x)\y=Balls(x)\YOrigin+(Balls(x)\Radius*Sin(DegToRad(Balls(x)\Angle)))
   Balls(x)\Angle + Balls(x)\Speed
   DisplayTransparentSprite(#SPRITE_MAIN, Balls(x)\x, Balls(x)\y)
  Next x
  FlipBuffers()

  ExamineKeyboard()
  If KeyboardReleased(#PB_Key_Escape)
   Quit = #True
  EndIf

Until Quit = #True
End
```

The 'DisplayTransparentSprite()' command allows you to display a sprite on screen very similar to 'DisplaySprite()', but when displaying a sprite using 'DisplayTransparentSprite()', it selects a single color within the image and it treats as transparent. This allows the sprite to not always appear square.

In this example, I've created a new sprite and then immediately fill it with white using a 'Box()' command. Once this is done, I then draw a shaded green sphere on it using the 'Circle()' command within a loop. This leaves me with a green sphere on a white background. After the drawing commands have finished, I set all the white pixels in the new sprite to be flagged as transparent, using the 'TransparentSpriteColor()' command. This command takes two parameters, the first is the PB number of the sprite to change and the second is the color that you would like to be flagged as transparent. Once the color has been picked, the next usage of 'DisplayTransparentSprite()' displays a sprite, minus the transparent color. Once this example is run, you should see a screen full of green spheres without any white at showing at all. This is a great way to display sprites with a transparency.

You will also notice in this example that the command to display a normal sprite doesn't have to be inside any special enclosing commands such as a 'StartSpecialFX()' or 'StartDrawing()', etc. You can use the normal sprite displaying commands by themselves. As long as the sprite engine is initialized and a screen has been opened, you can use the standard sprite commands to display a sprite. The standard sprite displaying commands are:

   'DisplaySprite()'
   'DisplayTransparentSprite()'

Using Sprites3D's
PureBasic calls it's 3D sprites by the slightly mangled name of 'sprite3D'. Each sprite3D is a 2D surface made up of two polygons. These polygons are drawn using a small 3D engine and can be transformed in 3D but each sprite3D is ultimately drawn in 2D on the screen. Confused? Good, let's continue.

A sprite3D in PureBasic is really a normal sprite that has had 3D support given to it and as such, this different type needs a small 3D engine to display them. To use any sprite3D's in your program you must initialize the sprite3D engine before using any other sprite3D related commands. This is done by using the 'InitSprite3D()' command. This command is however a child command of 'InitSprite()', which must also be called before it.

Every sprite3D starts life as a normal sprite, either loaded or created but with the '#PB_Sprite_Texture' mode defined. This normal version isn't displayed at any time, instead, this normal sprite is turned into a 3D version by using the 'CreateSprite3D()' command. This command takes two parameters, the first is the PB number that you would like to associate to the new sprite3D. The second is the sprite first created or loaded that you want to turn into a sprite3D.

This is how this conversion procedure appears in PureBasic code:

```
LoadSprite(#NORMAL_SPRITE, "Image.bmp", #PB_Sprite_Texture)
CreateSprite3D(#SPRITE_3D, #NORMAL_SPRITE)
```

Once the sprite3D has been created like this, we can then display this on the screen by using the 'DisplaySprite3D()' command. To explain things a little more clearly, here's an example of displaying and manipulating sprites3D's:

```
UsePNGImageDecoder()

Enumeration
  #SPRITE_2D
  #SPRITE_3D
EndEnumeration

#NUMBER_OF_FLOWERS = 150

;Set the width, height and bit depth of the screen
;Abbreviated variables are used here due to page width constraints :(
Global ScrW.l = 1024
Global ScrH.l = 768
```

```
Global ScrD.l = 32
;Other global variables
Global Quit.b = #False
Global XOrigin.l = ScrW / 2
Global YOrigin.l = ScrH / 2

Structure FLOWER
  XPos.f
  YPos.f
  Width.f
  Height.f
  Angle.f
  Radius.f
  RadiusStep.f
EndStructure
Global Dim Flowers.FLOWER(#NUMBER_OF_FLOWERS)

;Simple error checking procedure
Procedure HandleError(Result.l, Text.s)
  If Result = 0
    MessageRequester("Error", Text, #PB_MessageRequester_Ok)
    End
  EndIf
EndProcedure

;Convert Degrees to Radians
Procedure.f DegToRad(Angle.f)
  ProcedureReturn Angle.f * #PI / 180
EndProcedure

;Initialize all flowers
Procedure InitialiseAllFlowers()
  For x.l = 0 To #NUMBER_OF_FLOWERS
    Flowers(x)\Width = 0
    Flowers(x)\Height = 0
    Flowers(x)\Angle = Random(360)
    Flowers(x)\Radius - 1.0
    Flowers(x)\RadiusStep = (Random(30) / 10) + 1.0
  Next x
EndProcedure

;Reset a flower
Procedure ResetFlower(Index.l)
  Flowers(Index)\Width = 0
  Flowers(Index)\Height = 0
  Flowers(Index)\Angle = Random(360)
  Flowers(Index)\Radius = 1.0
  Flowers(Index)\RadiusStep = (Random(30) / 10) + 1.0
  ProcedureReturn
EndProcedure
```

```
;Initialize environment
HandleError(InitSprite(), "InitSprite() command failed.")
HandleError(InitSprite3D(), "InitSprite3D() command failed.")
HandleError(InitKeyboard(), "InitKeyboard() command failed.")
HandleError(OpenScreen(ScrW, ScrH, ScrD, "Flowers"), "Could not open screen.")
SetFrameRate(60)
Sprite3DQuality(1)

;Load sprite
LoadSprite(#SPRITE_2D,"Flower.png",#PB_Sprite_Texture|#PB_Sprite_AlphaBlending)
CreateSprite3D(#SPRITE_3D, #SPRITE_2D)

InitialiseAllFlowers()

;Main loop
Repeat

  ClearScreen(RGB(200, 100, 100))

  HandleError(Start3D(), "Start3D() command failed.")
    For x.l = 0 To #NUMBER_OF_FLOWERS
      Flowers(x)\Width + 1.5
      Flowers(x)\Height + 1.5
      Flowers(x)\Angle + 1.0
      If Flowers(x)\Width > 512.0 Or Flowers(x)\Height > 512.0
        Flowers(x)\Width = 512.0
        Flowers(x)\Height = 512.0
      EndIf
      If Flowers(x)\Radius > ScrW
        ResetFlower(x)
      EndIf
      Flowers(x)\Radius + Flowers(x)\RadiusStep
      Flowers(x)\XPos=XOrigin+(Flowers(x)\Radius*Cos(DegToRad(Flowers(x)\Angle)))
      Flowers(x)\YPos=YOrigin+(Flowers(x)\Radius*Sin(DegToRad(Flowers(x)\Angle)))
      Flowers(x)\XPos - Flowers(x)\Radius / 3.5
      Flowers(x)\YPos - Flowers(x)\Radius / 3.5
      ZoomSprite3D(#SPRITE_3D, Flowers(x)\Width, Flowers(x)\Height)
      RotateSprite3D(#SPRITE_3D, Flowers(x)\Angle, 0)
      DisplaySprite3D(#SPRITE_3D, Flowers(x)\XPos, Flowers(x)\YPos)
    Next x
  Stop3D()

  FlipBuffers()

  ExamineKeyboard()
  If KeyboardReleased(#PB_Key_Escape)
    Quit = #True
  EndIf

Until Quit = #True
End
```

To allow me to use sprite3D's in my example, I've initialized the normal sprite engine and then I've initialized the sprite3D engine, using the 'InitSprite3D()' command. This is essential to use any sprite3D related commands. After this, I've then used the 'LoadSprite()' command to load a Png format image. This image which is called 'Flower.png', uses an alpha channel to create a transparent background. Loading a Png format image with an alpha channel like this requires you to define the sprite mode correctly in the 'LoadSprite()' command. If you look at the example code, I've specified the mode as '#PB_Sprite_Texture|#PB_Sprite_AlphaBlending'. This tells the compiler I wish to use this sprite as a sprite3D and it contains an alpha channel. After this has been loaded and defined correctly I can then create a sprite3D from it using the 'CreatSprite3D()' command and it's alpha channel is preserved.

Once the sprites have been created, it's time to draw the sprites onto the screen. This is achieved using the 'DisplaySprite3D()' command inside a 'Start3D()' block. This looks something like this:

```
...
Start3D()
  DisplaySprite3D(#SPRITE_3D, x, y, Alpha)
Stop3D()
...
```

If you look at the flower example, the 'Start3D()' block is being checked using a small error checking procedure to make sure it starts properly. If it does, we can continue and draw the sprites. If it doesn't start correctly, we must not draw any sprite3D's or there may be serious program crash. A 'Stop3D()' command is used to end the sprite3D block. Inside this block you must not use any commands from the normal sprite library, this block is for sprite3D commands only.

To actually display a sprite3D you use the 'DisplaySprite3D()' command, which takes four parameters. The first is the PB number of the sprite3D you wish to display. The second and third are the 'x' and 'y' positions of the sprite on the buffer. The fourth optional parameter is the alpha value of the sprite. This alpha value defines how transparent the whole sprite is rendered on the display. This is an integer which ranges from '0', which is completely transparent, to '255', which is completely opaque.

In the flower example I've also used the 'ZoomSprite3D()' and 'RotateSprite3D()' commands to resize and rotate the sprite3D's. These commands are very easy to understand and can be read about in more detail in the PureBasic helpfile within the 'Sprite3D' section (Helpfile:Reference Manual->2D Games Libraries->Sprite3D).

Sprite3D Quality
While using sprite3D's in your program, it is possible to toggle the rendering quality of the sprites. This is done with the 'Sprite3DQuality()' command. This command takes one parameter which is the rendering mode of all sprite3D's in your program. The parameter is a numeric value which is equal to a particular mode.

Here are the definitions:

0 : No filtering (faster, but very pixelated when zooming and rotating)
1 : Bilinear filtering (slower, but blends the pixels to look better when zooming and rotating)

In my example I've used 'Sprite3DQuality(1)' which enables bilinear filtering and gives the sprites a nice smooth look when I'm resizing and rotating them. If this command is not used however, the default quality setting for that program is '0', which doesn't enable any filtering, leaving sprites3D's looking pixelated when manipulated.

11

3D Graphics

In this chapter I'm going to talk about 3D graphics and how PureBasic uses the OGRE engine to draw these to the screen. 3D graphics uses imaginary 3D models to create believable worlds that give the impression of width, height and depth, and the computer monitor is usually considered a window through which you can view these 3D worlds. This of course is a little inaccurate, while even I like to think that I'm viewing a 3D world through my monitor (especially when playing 3D games) I know for a fact that it's sophisticated math routines drawing these imaginary 3D models on my computer's monitor to give me the impression of three dimensions. Luckily, PureBasic takes care of all the mathematics that are needed to draw 3D graphics on screen by using the OGRE 3D engine. This allows you to call simple, high level commands that perform complicated 3D graphical effects. This makes programming 3D graphics in PureBasic quick, fun and very easy.

This chapter, unfortunately, will not be an exhaustive text on programming 3D graphics using PureBasic as this would be a whole book in itself, but this chapter is really a primer to using the commands and a few solutions to common problems that beginners may face.

An Overview Of The OGRE Engine

To make it possible to draw three dimensional graphics on screen, as I said before, you have to use complicated math routines to calculate the model shapes, model textures, positions and lighting, etc. and this can be very time-consuming and very hard on the brain. Thankfully for users of PureBasic, the OGRE 3D engine is used to take care of all this tedious stuff so you can concentrate on coding your program. OGRE (Open source GRaphics Engine) is an open source realtime 3D rendering engine created and developed by Torus Knot Software Limited. This engine is provided freely on the Internet and available for anybody to use, free of charge, for any purpose.

After looking at the source code of the OGRE engine, the lead developer of PureBasic, Frédéric Laboureur, decided that it was of such fantastic quality he incorporated it into PureBasic's command set. The engine itself is included with PureBasic as a dynamic linked library (DLL) and PureBasic's built-in 3D library is a wrapper to it. The only drawback with this, is that the OGRE engine has an application programming interface (API) that contains many hundreds of commands and PureBasic doesn't support all of them. This is due to some incompatibilities with the language that OGRE was programmed in and the time it takes the PureBasic team to implement and test new commands. More commands may be added in future, as the PureBasic team has expressed an interest in increasing the OGRE command set available to PureBasic users, so I guess only time will tell. You can view the current OGRE command set in the helpfile under the '3D Games Libraries' section (Helpfile:Reference Manual->3D Games Libraries).

The OGRE Mesh Format
To use OGRE to manipulate and display 3D models in your program, you will need these models to be in a particular format. This is the OGRE 'Mesh' format and these model files will have the file extension of '*.mesh'.

If you look on the OGRE website, in the downloads section, you will find many third party tools and plugins that provide extra functionality to leading 3D modeling packages. These tools enable these packages to save and export loaded and newly created models into the correct mesh format. In fact, it is probably a good idea to look here first before deciding which 3D modeling package to use for your mesh creation.

Creating Your Own OGRE Meshes

To create your own meshes you will need to use what is known as a 3D modeling program. This type of program will allow you create a model using a three dimensional display. This allows you to see a realtime updated preview of your model from any angle during the creation process. This type of program also provides tools to allow you to add image textures, to give your model a graphical skin for when it's rendered in the 3D engine. More advanced 3D modeling programs allow you precisely to align image textures to a model by un-wrapping the model into a 2D form. This two dimensional unwrapped form can then be exported as an image to provide a template from which you can draw your texture. When this texture is applied back onto the original 3D model, it will match the 3d shape perfectly. Any 3D modeling program can be used to create your 3D models as long as the finished model can be exported and saved as a '*.mesh' file, OGRE's native file format.

OGRE Texture Formats
Every model that is displayed using a 3D engine needs a texture. These textures are nothing more than images which are wrapped around models to provide a skin on which to draw detail. In fact some people do indeed refer to textures as 'skins'. Sometimes models have more than one texture to provide a greater array of textures or to provide a more detailed finish.

When using textures to provide skins for your 3D models, you must use the correct image format, otherwise the textures will not appear once your program is compiled. This is important to remember because most 3D modeling packages have the ability to load and use multiple types of image formats that aren't supported by OGRE. The OGRE engine used by PureBasic uses Png, Tga or Jpg files. If you use these image formats as textures for your models, you know everything will work as expected.

OGRE's 3D Coordinate System

When drawing and manipulating objects in 3D space you need a good coordinate system to track an object's position in that space. OGRE uses a standard right handed 'x, y, z' coordinate system, but for those of you who don't know what that is, let me explain. In a coordinate system like this, the three dimensions are assigned a different letter and this is where the 'x, y, z' comes from. Knowing which letter is assigned to what dimension is essential to use this system. Fig.39 shows the dimensions and what letter is assigned to them. This diagram also shows how three dimensional space can easily be divided and referred to using three values. If you imagine that an entire 3D scene is inside this invisible box, then any point within that scene can be described by a set of three 'x, y, z' values.

Coordinates Of OGRE's 3D Space

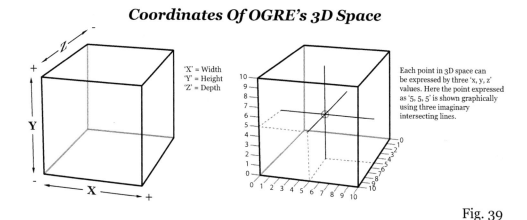

Fig. 39

The coordinates themselves are pretty simple to understand, each dimension can be referred to using a positive or negative number and the OGRE engine enumerates these in a particular way. The box on the left in Fig.39 shows this using '+' and '-' characters. If you imagine the bottom left corner of your computer monitor as existing at 3D coordinates; '0, 0, 0'. The 'x' coordinate number will increase numerically the further to the right of your monitor you travel and the 'y' coordinate will increase numerically the further up the monitor screen you go. The 'z' coordinate is a little bit different, in that it increases in value the further away from the screen, towards you, that you travel. This is again demonstrated in the right hand box if you look at the numbers along the sides.

Some people like to use the coordinates '0, 0, 0' as the center of any given 3D space, and then coordinates that refer to other objects within that world can either be positive or negative depending on which way from the center, the point that you need to describe is. Hopefully this simple diagram should give you an understanding how 'x, y, z' coordinates are handled.

OGRE API Identifiers

While using PureBasic and OGRE to produce 3D visuals, you are effectively using the OGRE API (application programming interface) to handle things behind the scenes. PureBasic doesn't expose any of this raw OGRE API to you, but instead wraps the API commands into much more friendly basic commands. On occasion however, you will still need to refer to some OGRE objects by their OGRE identifier. These identifiers are just Long type values and are very similar to OS identifiers which are also needed by an API (Win32 API). To get the OGRE identifiers of various objects you can use these PureBasic commands:

'MaterialID(#MATERIAL)'
Returns the OGRE identifier of the material specified (as a PB number) in the parameter.

'MeshID(#MESH)'
Returns the OGRE identifier of the mesh specified (as a PB number) in the parameter.

'TextureID(#TEXTURE)'
Returns the OGRE identifier of the texture specified (as a PB number) in the parameter.

A Gentle Beginning

In the following example I'm going to show you how to initialize the 3D environment, load a 3D mesh, apply a texture to it and display it onscreen. To make things a little bit more exciting, I've made the model spin around and I've included a light, so the model doesn't look too flat when being displayed.

```
Enumeration
  #MESH
  #TEX
  #MAT
  #ENTITY_INVADER
  #LIGHT
  #CAMERA_ONE
EndEnumeration

;Set the width, height and bit depth of the screen
;Abbreviated variables are used here due to page width constraints :(
Global ScrW.l = 1024
Global ScrH.l = 768
Global ScrD.l = 32
;Other global variables
Global Quit.b = #False

;Simple error checking procedure
Procedure HandleError(Result.l, Text.s)
  If Result = 0
    MessageRequester("Error", Text, #PB_MessageRequester_Ok)
    End
  EndIf
EndProcedure

;Initialize environment
HandleError(InitEngine3D(), "InitEngine3D() command failed.")
HandleError(InitSprite(), "InitSprite() command failed.")
HandleError(OpenScreen(ScrW, ScrH, ScrD, ""), "Could not open screen.")
```

```
HandleError(InitKeyboard(), "InitKeyboard() command failed.")
SetFrameRate(60)

Add3DArchive("Data\", #PB_3DArchive_FileSystem)

HandleError(LoadMesh(#MESH, "Invader.mesh"), "Can't load mesh")
HandleError(LoadTexture(#TEX, "Invader.png"), "Can't load texture")
HandleError(CreateMaterial(#MAT, TextureID(#TEX)), "Can't create Material")
CreateEntity(#ENTITY_INVADER, MeshID(#MESH), MaterialID(#MAT))

CreateLight(#LIGHT, RGB(255,255,255), 0, 5, 0)

CreateCamera(#CAMERA_ONE, 0, 0, 100, 100)
CameraLocate(#CAMERA_ONE, 0, 1, 2.5)
RotateCamera(#CAMERA_ONE, -15, 0, 0)

;Main loop
Repeat

  y.l + 2
  RotateEntity(#ENTITY_INVADER, 0, y, 0)

  RenderWorld()
  FlipBuffers()

  ExamineKeyboard()
  If KeyboardReleased(#PB_Key_Escape)
    Quit = #True
  EndIf

Until Quit = #True
End
```

This example should be quite useful to you as it shows all the necessary steps you must perform to display a 3D model on the screen. As always, the code should be pretty easy to follow but I'll go through the main points just so you don't miss anything.

Once the constants, variables and procedures have been declared, you will see I've used the 'InitEngine3D()' command to initialize the 3D environment. This command call is necessary to load the that contains the 3D engine from the compilers directory. This DLL file contains the OGRE engine in a pre-compiled form, which like this, can be used easily in your programs.

Once the 3D environment has been initialized then a screen can be created in the normal manner. First initializing the sprite engine and then opening a screen. This has to be done in this order or a compiler error will occur and the IDE will start complaining. If this happens you may have to kill the program and rearrange the initializations into the correct order before running again.

Including OGRE With Your 3D Program

When you create a 3D program using PureBasic and want to share it with other people, be it commercially or as a freeware program, you must remember to distribute the OGRE 3D engine with it.

PureBasic uses OGRE as a compiled DLL to provide all the 3D functions in a compact and portable way. When you compile your program, the OGRE commands are not embedded into your program like regular built-in PureBasic commands. Instead, all OGRE commands are called from a DLL dynamically. This means that the DLL file must always accompany your executable file in order for it to run correctly.

This is done automatically while developing, because when you hit 'F5' from within the IDE to compile and run your program, a temporary executable file in created in the '\Compilers' directory, which is exactly where the OGRE engine is installed. This ensures that testing the 3D commands is always as easy as possible. However, once you compile to an executable file elsewhere, the engine needs to be copied along with it.

The two files that you must distribute with your 3D program for it to initialize and work properly, are:

'Engine3D.dll'
'stlport_vc646.dll'

Both of these files are found in the '\Compilers' directory, within your PureBasic folder. These files must be loose (not in another folder) and must be in the same folder as your program's executable file.

Create A 3D Archive To Contain Media
After all the initializations are done we can start using the 3D commands and the very first thing we must do is specify a '3D Archive'. This is a path in which OGRE looks for external files when loading media such as models, textures, maps, etc. You must have at least one 3D archive specified in your 3D program or else the compiler will raise an error. To specify such an archive you must use the 'Add3DArchive()' command (Helpfile:Reference Manual->3D Games Libraries->Engine3D->Add3DArchive). This command takes two parameters, the first is a String specifying a file path and the second is a built-in constant that tells the compiler what sort of path it is. The built-in constants are:

'#PB_3DArchive_FileSystem'
This tells the compiler that the path specified is a normal folder.

'#PB_3DArchive_Zip'
This tells the compiler that the path specified is a compressed ZIP file.

In my Invader example I've created a 3D archive using a relative path, this tells OGRE to look inside the same directory as my program and look inside the folder called 'Data\'. Once specified like this, all required media must be in this folder. This, then allows the use of simple commands like:

```
. . .
LoadMesh(#MESH, "Invader.mesh")
. . .
```

When a command like this is encountered in our program that needs to load external media, OGRE will look inside all specified 3D archives for this file, in this case OGRE will look in the 'Data\' folder for the 'Invader.mesh' file.

If you want to order your media into a more strict filing system and include further subdirectories in the 'Data\' folder, than you can do by all means. You will then have to load this media from their new locations like this:

```
...
LoadMesh(#MESH, "Meshes\Invader.mesh")
LoadTexture(#TEX, "Textures\Invader.png")
...
```

Again this will search the original 3D archive ('Data\') for these folders ('Meshes\' and 'Textures\') and load the media from inside them. If this syntax looks a little clumsy, then instead of defining the folder names in the loading commands you could just as easily add further 3D archives for OGRE to look in when requesting media, like this:

```
...
Add3DArchive("Data\", #PB_3DArchive_FileSystem)
Add3DArchive("Data\Meshes\", #PB_3DArchive_FileSystem)
Add3DArchive("Data\Textures\", #PB_3DArchive_FileSystem)
...
```

Now we can use simpler loading commands like this:

```
...
LoadMesh(#MESH, "Invader.mesh")
LoadTexture(#TEX, "Invader.png")
...
```

OGRE will now search the folders, 'Data\', 'Data\Meshes\' and 'Data\Textures\' for these files.

You can also use ZIP files for 3D archives if you want. This can help a lot when distributing a program, because all of your media is enclosed within a single compressed file. If you wish to do this, you must specify that this 3D archive is a ZIP file when you create it. This is achieved using the '#PB_3DArchive_Zip' built-in constant as the type parameter in the 'Add3DArchive()' command. If you have subdirectories within your ZIP file, you can access these in loading commands by using the standard format:

```
...
Add3DArchive("Data.zip", #PB_3DArchive_Zip)
LoadMesh(#MESH, "Meshes\Invader.mesh")
LoadTexture(#TEX, "Textures\Invader.png")
...
```

Creating A 3D Entity

When you have created a 3D archive you are ready to create an object that's able to use your media. This object is going to be displayed on screen and can be manipulated in three dimensions using various built-in commands. OGRE calls these 3D objects, 'Entities'.

An entity is an object which is a building block of any game or demo, they are the 3D models displayed on screen that use a mesh as a structure and a texture as a skin. Entities can be anything that is modeled in 3D, they can be game maps or the characters that populate them.

Process Of Creating A 3D Entity

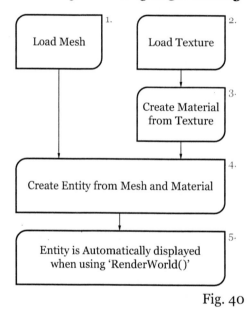

Fig. 40

Knowing how to properly create these entities is essential to display any 3D model on the screen. Fig.40 shows the process of correctly creating a 3D entity and in what order the steps must be done. I have followed this flow diagram precisely in the previous Invader example. Here is what it looks like in code:

```
. . .
HandleError(LoadMesh(#MESH, "Invader.mesh"), "Can't load mesh")
HandleError(LoadTexture(#TEX, "Invader.png"), "Can't load texture")
HandleError(CreateMaterial(#MAT, TextureID(#TEX)}, "Can't create Material")
CreateEntity(#ENTITY_INVADER, MeshID(#MESH), MaterialID(#MAT))
. . .
```

The commands used to complete this process are simple. The first one is the 'LoadMesh()' command (Helpfile:Reference Manual->3D Games Libraries->Mesh->LoadMesh) which takes two parameters.

The first is the PB number that will be associated to this mesh and the second is the actual mesh file to load from the 3D archive. The next command is 'LoadTexture()' (Helpfile:Reference Manual->3D Games Libraries->Texture->LoadTexture) which also takes two parameters. The first is the PB number associated to the newly loaded texture and the second is the name of the image to be used as this texture. When using images for textures, one thing to note is the image size in pixels. Older computer graphics cards can only support textures that are square and have an image size which is a power of '2'. For maximum compatibility with older cards, I suggest you use these sizes too. Fig.41 shows the standard texture image sizes you can use to create materials safely.

Standard Texture Image Sizes

Width In Pixels	Height In Pixels	Image Bit Depth
32	32	8, 16 & 32
64	64	8, 16 & 32
128	128	8, 16 & 32
256	256	8, 16 & 32
512	512	8, 16 & 32
1024	1024	8, 16 & 32

All standard texture sizes are powers of '2'.   Fig. 41

The next command doesn't load anything, it merely creates a material. This material is a special OGRE format texture that can have many different properties. Because we are creating one from a texture this is the simplest form of material. I will talk about the more advanced materials a little later.

To create a material you use the 'CreateMaterial()' command (Helpfile:Reference Manual->3D Games Libraries->Material->CreateMaterial) which takes two parameters. The first is the PB number that this material will be associated with, and the second is the OGRE identifier of a texture. This identifier can be returned by using the 'TextureID()' command, which uses a PB number of a texture as a parameter.

Once we have the necessary 'ingredients' we can then create our entity. This is done using the 'CreateEntity()' command (Helpfile:Reference Manual->3D Games Libraries->Entity->CreateEntity), like this:

```
...
CreateEntity(#ENTITY_INVADER, MeshID(#MESH), MaterialID(#MAT))
...
```

As you can see from this line this command takes three parameters. The first is the PB number that this entity will be associated with. The second is the OS identifier of the mesh we want to make this entity out of, and the third is the OGRE identifier of the material that we want to cover the mesh with.

These last two OGRE identifiers can be returned by using the 'MeshID()' and 'MaterialID()' command respectively. These two commands take a PB number as a parameter and return an OGRE identifier.

Once a 3D entity has been created it then is queued, ready to be drawn onto the screen at the coordinates '0, 0, 0' in three dimensional space. Until then we'll carry on with our breakdown of the Invader example.

Lighting The Way
After the entity has been created, I've created a light to illuminate the scene better. This light provides a bright illumination source, that can be any color, to make this entity stand out better. When you create a 3D environment it already contains a default amount of ambient light but this light is not actually emitted from any one point, but instead as the name suggests it's ambient. This can make the entity look flat because it can't calculate which sides should shine and which sides should have shadow. When you add a light to a scene, you allow the entity to change it's facial lighting to simulate shine and shade depending on where the light is located in relation to the mesh used. To create a light I've used the 'CreateLight()' command. (Helpfile:Reference Manual->3D Games Libraries->Light->CreateLight)

```
...
CreateLight(#LIGHT, RGB(255,255,255), 0, 5, 0)
...
```

This command takes five parameters, the first of which is the PB number that will be associated to this light. The second is the color of light that should be emitted which should be entered as a 24 bit color value (the 'RGB()' command can be used for this). The third, forth and fifth parameters are optional and specify the position of the light in 3D space using the 'x, y, z' coordinate system. If these parameters are not used, then the light is created at a position of '0, 0, 0', which is the center of the 3D space. In the Invader example I've used the position of '0, 5, 0', which elevates the light off the floor by '5' units. See Fig.39 for a graphical representation of 3D space using the 'x, y, z' coordinate system.

The Camera Is Rolling
Now that the 3D elements are in place, we need to create a viewport through which to look at our 3D scene. OGRE calls these viewports, Cameras, but really we need to distinguish between the two to avoid confusion. A viewport is a 2D viewport that exists on the currently opened screen and displays what the 3D camera is looking at. Once a camera viewport is created it automatically creates a 3D camera positioned at coordinates '0, 0, 0' and the newly created viewport displays what the 3D camera is looking at. The 3D camera can be positioned and rotated at will but the viewport is always locked in the same position on-screen.

To create a camera viewport and automatically create a 3D camera in the current 3D world, you use the 'CreateCamera()' command. (Helpfile:Reference Manual->3D Games Libraries->Camera->CreateCamera) This command takes five parameters and as usual the first is the PB number that will be associated to this camera object. The second and third parameters are the 'x' and 'y' positions of the top left hand corner of the viewport on the 2D screen. The forth and fifth parameters are the width and height of the viewport through which the 3D scene is viewed. When using this command it is very important to understand the values it uses because they are very different to most PureBasic commands. The parameter values that the 'CreateCamera()' command uses are not in pixels, but in percentages of the currently opened screen. In the Invader example I create a camera like this:

```
...
CreateCamera(#CAMERA_ONE, 0, 0, 100, 100)
...
```

To understand this fully, let's break down this command call on an individual parameter basis. The first parameter is the PB number which is easy enough to understand so we'll skip quickly past this one. The second parameter has been defined as a '0'. This means that this will be calculated as zero percent of the screen width ('1024') which is '0'. The third parameter is defined as '0' too. This is also a percentage but a percentage of the screen height ('768') so this also equates to '0'. The forth parameter has been defined as '100'. This equates to one hundred percent of the screen width, which in this case is '1024'. The fifth parameter is also defined as '100', and this will equate to one hundred percent of the screen height, which is '768'. This gives us overall screen coordinates for this camera viewport as being 'x=0, y=0, width=1024, height=768', this completely covers the screen to give us a full screen camera viewport into the 3D world.

Percentages are used for this command instead of pixels, so that camera viewport positions are completely independent of the screen size. This is an easy way to support camera positions across different screen resolutions. For example, if I create a camera viewport half of the screen width and height, this viewport will always be half of the screen width and height regardless of what screen resolution used.

Multiple Camera Viewports
Using percentages is also a good way of supporting multiple camera viewports. Imagine if you need to code a game in split or quad screen, you will need a good way to calculate the viewport size for each given screen resolution (if it's user selectable). This is all done for you in PureBasic using percentages by always ensuring that each camera viewport always takes up the same screen space regardless of the screen resolution used. Also, when creating multiple cameras, the creation order is very important. All viewports created later in your code will always appear over the top of viewports created earlier. For example, look at this code:

```
...
CreateCamera(#CAMERA_ONE, 0, 0, 100, 100)
CreateCamera(#CAMERA_ONE, 75, 0, 25, 25)
...
```

Here, I create one camera viewport taking up the full screen and another camera viewport over the top of it, in the top right hand corner. This smaller viewport would be positioned three quarters of the width of the screen across and it's width and height would be a quarter of the current screen. If the smaller viewport was created first then it would be hidden by the bigger camera viewport.

Each multiple camera created can also be independently moved and rotated in the 3D world to give users more views of your world on-screen. For example, you might use a second camera as a rear view mirror in a 3D first person driving game. This camera viewport could be positioned at the top of the 2D screen and have it's 3D camera pointing towards the rear of the car.

Moving And Rotating Cameras

Once you have created a viewport you also automatically create a 3D camera which can rotate and move around at will in the 3D scene. You can move and position this 3D camera wherever, and whenever you want by using positional commands in the main loop. In my Invader example I've used two commands to fine tune the position of the camera, like this:

```
. . .
CameraLocate(#CAMERA_ONE, 0, 1, 2.5)
RotateCamera(#CAMERA_ONE, -15, 0, 0)
. . .
```

The first command, 'CameraLocate()' moves the camera to an absolute position within the 3D scene and takes four parameters. The first parameter is the PB number of the camera you want to move, while the second, third and forth parameters are 'x, y, z' coordinates of where you would like to move it to. The second command used is 'RotateCamera()', this rotates the camera around a specified axis. This command also takes four parameters, with the first being the PB number of the camera you wish to rotate. The second, third and forth parameters are relative rotation angles along each of the 'x, y, z' axis.

Rotations In 3D Space

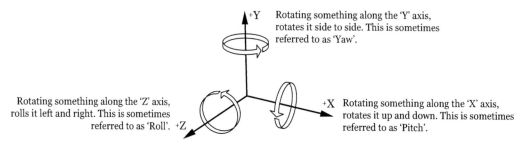

+Y   Rotating something along the 'Y' axis, rotates it side to side. This is sometimes referred to as 'Yaw'.

Rotating something along the 'Z' axis, rolls it left and right. This is sometimes referred to as 'Roll'. +Z

+X   Rotating something along the 'X' axis, rotates it up and down. This is sometimes referred to as 'Pitch'.

The arrows show positive number rotations

Fig. 42

If you look at Fig.42 you will see what axis refer to what type of rotation. For example, if I wanted my camera to twist from side to side then I would use rotation on the 'y' axis. When specifying numbers for the 'x, y, z' coordinates in any 3D rotation command, number can be negative as well as positive, this allow for the rotation to be reversed. If you look at the rotation arrows in Fig.42 these show the direction that the rotation will occur if positive numbers are used. If negative numbers are used then this rotation will be reversed. As a small example, if I wanted to twist my camera forty five degrees to the left I would enter '45' for the 'y' rotation parameter. If I wanted to twist my camera forty five degrees to the right, I would use '-45' for the 'y' rotation.

All move and rotation commands can be used either inside or outside the main loop to rotate and move cameras or other entities. Using these commands outside the main loop is good for when you need to set up the position of static objects. Using these commands inside your main loop provides a way of moving and rotating your entities in realtime, often reacting to user input.

All commands in PureBasic that use 3D rotations will use the same 'x, y, z' system. If you look inside the main loop of the Invader example, I have used the 'RotateEntity()' command (Helpfile:Reference Manual->3D Games Libraries->Entity->RotateEntity) to rotate the invader entity during runtime. Again, this command uses the same set of rotation axis as described in Fig.42. When using any command that uses 3D rotation, Fig.42 can provide a reference for what rotation might be needed.

You can learn more about the commands available to use with OGRE cameras in the PureBasic helpfile. (Helpfile:Reference Manual->3D Games Libraries->Camera)

Rendering The 3D World To The Screen
When using the 3D commands to create a 3D world, unlike the 2D commands, your meshes, lights and particles, etc. aren't drawn to the screen immediately. Instead they exist in memory, ready to be captured and drawn. Once everything is in place in your 3D scene, you must use the 'RenderWorld()' command (Helpfile:Reference Manual->3D Games Libraries->Engine3D->RenderWorld) to tell all currently existing 3D cameras to each take a snapshot of what they are pointing at. These snapshots are then drawn onto the backbuffer, scaled and positioned to the size and position of the related camera's viewport. Then, once the 'FlipBuffers()' command is called, the backbuffer is flipped to the front and the 3D scene is drawn to the computer screen. You can see this in action in the Invader example. If you do not use the 'RenderWorld()' command, no 3D graphics will be drawn onto the back buffer. Hopefully this is the Invader example fully explained now, so you should be able to load and display models of your own using this example as a reference.

A Simple First Person Camera

After running the Invader example you are probably eager to write your own 3D program or even have a go at writing a game. The first thing I thought of when seeing the 3D capabilities of PureBasic is, I wonder if I could make a first person shooter game? I came up with this next piece of code as an example of how to code a first person camera within a 3D world. Granted, it's not a full game, far from it, but it can be used as a learning example for beginners. This code will show you how to create a terrain and move the camera around using the cursor keys and mouse:

```
Enumeration
  #TEXTURE_GLOBAL
  #TEXTURE_DETAIL
  #MATERIAL_TERRAIN
  #CAMERA_ONE
EndEnumeration

#MOVEMENT_SPEED = 1

;Set the width, height and bit depth of the screen
;Abbreviated variables are used here due to page width constraints :(
Global ScrW.l = 1024
```

```
Global ScrH.l = 768
Global ScrD.l = 32

;Other global variables
Global Quit.b = #False
Global MouseXRotation.f,MouseYRotation.f,KeyX.f,KeyZ.f,DesiredCameraHeight.f
Global CurrentCamXPos.f = 545
Global CurrentCamZPos.f = 280

;Simple error checking procedure
Procedure HandleError(Result.l, Text.s)
  If Result = 0
    MessageRequester("Error", Text, #PB_MessageRequester_Ok)
    End
  EndIf
EndProcedure

;Initialize environment
HandleError(InitEngine3D(), "InitEngine3D() command failed.")
HandleError(InitSprite(), "InitSprite() command failed.")
HandleError(OpenScreen(ScrW, ScrH, ScrD, ""), "Could not open screen.")
HandleError(InitMouse(), "InitMouse() command failed.")
HandleError(InitKeyboard(), "InitKeyboard() command failed.")
SetFrameRate(60)

;Set 3D Archive
Add3DArchive("Data\", #PB_3DArchive_FileSystem)

;Create Terrain
HandleError(LoadTexture(#TEXTURE_GLOBAL, "Global.png"), "Can't load texture")
HandleError(LoadTexture(#TEXTURE_DETAIL, "Detail.png"), "Can't load texture")
CreateMaterial(#MATERIAL_TERRAIN, TextureID(#TEXTURE_GLOBAL))
AddMaterialLayer(#MATERIAL_TERRAIN,TextureID(#TEXTURE_DETAIL),#PB_Material_Add)
CreateTerrain("Terrain.png", MaterialID(#MATERIAL_TERRAIN), 1, 2, 1)

;Create Viewport and 3D Camera
CreateCamera(#CAMERA_ONE, 0, 0, 100, 100)
DesiredCameraHeight.f = TerrainHeight(CurrentCamXPos, CurrentCamZPos) + 10
CameraLocate(#CAMERA_ONE,CurrentCamXPos,DesiredCameraHeight,CurrentCamZPos)

;Main loop
Repeat

  ;Update Mouse
  If ExamineMouse()
    MouseYRotation = -MouseDeltaX() / 10
    MouseXRotation = MouseDeltaY() / 10
  EndIf
  RotateCamera(#CAMERA_ONE, MouseXRotation, MouseYRotation, 0)
  ;Update Key Presses and position the Camera accordingly
  If ExamineKeyboard()
```

```
    If KeyboardPushed(#PB_Key_Left)  : KeyX = -#MOVEMENT_SPEED : EndIf
    If KeyboardPushed(#PB_Key_Right) : KeyX = #MOVEMENT_SPEED : EndIf
    If KeyboardPushed(#PB_Key_Up)    : KeyZ = -#MOVEMENT_SPEED : EndIf
    If KeyboardPushed(#PB_Key_Down)  : KeyZ = #MOVEMENT_SPEED : EndIf
    MoveCamera(#CAMERA_ONE, KeyX, 0, KeyZ)
    KeyX = 0
    KeyZ = 0
    CurrentCamXPos.f = CameraX(#CAMERA_ONE)
    CurrentCamZPos.f = CameraZ(#CAMERA_ONE)
    DesiredCameraHeight.f = TerrainHeight(CurrentCamXPos, CurrentCamZPos) + 10
    CameraLocate(#CAMERA_ONE,CurrentCamXPos,DesiredCameraHeight,CurrentCamZPos)
  EndIf

  RenderWorld()
  FlipBuffers()

  If KeyboardReleased(#PB_Key_Escape)
    Quit = #True
  EndIf

Until Quit = #True
End
```

This example is similar to the Invader example in that it sets up the 3D environment in the same way, so you should be familiar with this now. The main difference here in this example is that I've created a terrain to provide a floor on which to walk about on.

Terrains
To create a terrain you have to create a multi-layered material first, to be used as the terrain's surface. To create a multi-layered material you need to create a normal material then apply another material layer to it. If you look at the FPS example you will see the following lines in the code:

```
...
HandleError(LoadTexture(#TEXTURE_GLOBAL,  "Global.png"), "Can't load texture")
HandleError(LoadTexture(#TEXTURE_DETAIL,  "Detail.png"), "Can't load texture")
...
```

These two commands load in two Png format images as standard textures using the 'LoadTexture()' command. The first image, 'Global.png', is going to be the main material which is applied as a huge blanket that covers the new terrain's surface. The second image, 'Detail.png', is a secondary texture that is blended with the first and is tiled across the terrain to provide more detail across it. To actually create the multi-layered material I've used these two commands:

```
...
CreateMaterial(#MATERIAL_TERRAIN, TextureID(#TEXTURE_GLOBAL))
AddMaterialLayer(#MATERIAL_TERRAIN,TextureID(#TEXTURE_DETAIL),#PB_Material_Add)
...
```

The first line creates a standard, one layer material as explained in the Invader example. The second command loads another texture to add as a second layer to the previously created material. The 'AddMaterialLayer()' command (Helpfile:Reference Manual->3D Games Libraries->Material->AddMaterialLayer) takes three parameters. The first is the PB number of the material that you wish to add a layer to. The second is the OGRE identifier of the texture you wish to add as another layer. The third parameter is the blending mode of the new texture with the existing material. This blending mode can be defined as one of four built-in constants:

'#PB_Material_Add'
Blends the new material layer with the existing one using an 'Add' operation.

'#PB_Material_Replace'
Blends the new material layer with the existing one using a 'Replace' operation.

'#PB_Material_AlphaBlend'
Blends the new material layer with the existing one using an 'Add' operation. This mode will also use any alpha channel information found in the texture. Only Png and Tga image format textures are supported.

'#PB_Material_Modulate'
Blends the new material layer with the existing one using a 'Modulate' operation.

Once you have created a multi-layered material then you are ready to create a terrain using the 'CreateTerrain()' command (Helpfile:Reference Manual->3D Games Libraries->Terrain->CreateTerrain). In the FPS example, I've created one like this:

```
...
CreateTerrain("Terrain.png", MaterialID(#MATERIAL_TERRAIN), 1, 2, 1)
...
```

The 'CreateTerrain()' command takes six parameters. The first parameter is the name of an image that will be used as a height map for the terrain. The second is an OGRE identifier of a multi-layered material to be used as the terrain surface. The third, forth and fifth are optional and can be used to scale the terrain on the 'x', 'y' or 'z' axis. These values are multiplication values, meaning that if a value of '1' is used then the terrain will remain the same size on that axis. If a value of '2' is used then that axis will be doubled, etc. The sixth and final parameter is an optional terrain quality value which ranges from '1' to '20'. The lower, the value passed, the higher, the terrain render quality and higher the CPU usage to draw it. Higher values have the opposite effect.

Terrain Height Map Details
When using a height map image to create a terrain there are a few rules you must follow when creating the height map image. First this image must be square, as OGRE in PureBasic can only create square terrains (although you can scale them during creation). Secondly, the image must be saved in an 8 bit grayscale format to provide '256' levels of gray. Pure black will be treated as a height of '0' while full white will be treated as a height of '255'. Thirdly this image must be of a certain size because it will also define the number of triangles (polygons) used in the terrain's mesh. The size of a height map image should be that of a normal texture size but plus one pixel on each dimension. This is to ensure that the

terrain height is calculated correctly from the image. Fig.43 shows recommended sizes of height map images and how many triangles (polygons) will be used to generate that terrain's mesh.

Terrain Height Map Image Sizes

Width	Height	Terrain Polygons
65	65	8192
129	129	32768
257	257	131072
513	513	524288
1025	1025	2097152

All height map texture sizes are powers of '2' + '1'.   Fig. 43

Looking at Fig.43 you can see how the triangle count goes up when a higher resolution height map image is used. A higher resolution height map can improve the rendering accuracy of the terrain to the height map but at the cost of slowing performance. Large height map resolutions, such as '1025 x 1025' are not normally used because of the high polygon count of the newly created terrain.

Terrains And Automatic 'Level Of Detail'
All terrains created in PureBasic using OGRE have automatic and dynamic levels of detail. This means that when a terrain is not shown through a camera or some terrain features hide others (such as hills) the hidden portions of the terrain are not drawn. Also when the camera has traveled a certain distance from a terrain feature, that feature will automatically lower its complexity, lowering the polygon count on screen to ease drawing a larger scene. This is easily demonstrated in the FPS example by focusing on any particular hill and moving backwards away from it and watching its structure. You will see the hill lower its complexity when being far away from the camera.

First Person Perspective
Once the terrain is created and the FPS example is running, I've used different commands to gather information from the mouse and keyboard and then positioned the camera accordingly. The mouse commands are:

'MouseDeltaX()'
(Helpfile:Reference Manual->2D Games Libraries->Mouse-> MouseDeltaX)
This command returns the number of pixels the mouse has moved on the 'X' screen axis (left to right) since the last iteration of the main loop.

'MouseDeltaY()'
(Helpfile:Reference Manual->2D Games Libraries->Mouse-> MouseDeltaY)
This command returns the number of pixels the mouse has moved on the 'Y' screen axis (up and down) since the last iteration of the main loop.

These two returned values are then placed in the 'x' and 'y' parameters of the 'RotateCamera()' command to rotate the 3D camera by whatever value the mouse moves. Here is the actual code:

```
...
If ExamineMouse()
  MouseYRotation = -MouseDeltaX() / 10
  MouseXRotation = MouseDeltaY() / 10
EndIf
RotateCamera(#CAMERA_ONE, MouseXRotation, MouseYRotation, 0)
...
```

This creates our mouse controlled camera. Notice the minus sign in front of the 'MouseDeltaX()' command. This is there to invert the value returned by this command, because if you remember from earlier, you need positive values to turn left and negative values to turn right. The 'MouseDeltaX()' command returns these inverted due to it returning 2D screen coordinates instead of rotation angles.

To move the camera around in the 3D world and to make it appear as if we are traveling over the terrain, I have used code like this:

```
...
If ExamineKeyboard()
    If KeyboardPushed(#PB_Key_Left) : KeyX = -#MOVEMENT_SPEED : EndIf
    If KeyboardPushed(#PB_Key_Right) : KeyX = #MOVEMENT_SPEED : EndIf
    If KeyboardPushed(#PB_Key_Up) : KeyZ = -#MOVEMENT_SPEED : EndIf
    If KeyboardPushed(#PB_Key_Down) : KeyZ = #MOVEMENT_SPEED : EndIf
    MoveCamera(#CAMERA_ONE, KeyX, 0, KeyZ)
    KeyX = 0
    KeyZ = 0
    CurrentCamXPos.f = CameraX(#CAMERA_ONE)
    CurrentCamZPos.f = CameraZ(#CAMERA_ONE)
    DesiredCameraHeight.f = TerrainHeight(CurrentCamXPos, CurrentCamZPos) + 10
    CameraLocate(#CAMERA_ONE,CurrentCamXPos,DesiredCameraHeight,CurrentCamZPos)
  EndIf
...
```

Here, I use the 'KeyboardPushed()' command to test wether or not a key is being held down. If it is I assign a value to the relevant variables, then use these as parameters in the 'MoveCamera()' command. This will move the camera throughout the 3D world but doesn't take into consideration the height of the terrain.

To move the camera up and down so it is always a set distance away from the terrain, I use the 'CameraLocate()' command. Because this command uses absolute values, I need to retrieve the current 'x' and 'z' coordinates of the camera so I can set these again when altering the 'y' value. To get the current camera coordinates I use the 'CameraX()' and 'CameraZ()' commands (Helpfile:Reference Manual->3D Games Libraries->Camera). These two command have only one parameter which is the PB number of a camera to get the values from. Once I have these values I need to find out what the terrain height is at these coordinates. To retrieve this I use the 'TerrainHeight()' command (Helpfile:Reference Manual->3D Games Libraries->Terrain->TerrainHeight). This command takes two parameters. These are the 'x' and 'z' coordinates of the point of the terrain we wish to know the height of. Once I have this value, I add '10' to raise the camera off the ground slightly and now I have my three 3D coordinates needed for the 'CameraLocate()' command. During every main loop iteration a new 'y' coordinate is calculated to adjust the camera height when moving over the terrain.

A Little More Advanced

In this next section, I'll talk about slightly more advanced features of OGRE and PureBasic. These features include particles and a material scripts. Particles are used in 3D engines for a variety of different things, mainly to produce visuals for random effects such as snow, rain, fire and smoke. I've used them in the following example to simulate fire. Material scripts are a way to encapsulate all material properties into one material script file, to make your PureBasic source code a lot cleaner and easier to read. Material scripts allow you to load a mesh containing a reference to a material and if that material appears in a script file, then the mesh uses that material negating the need to do anything further in your source code. This allows for ease of use and further customizability, because certain advanced material properties are only available by using scripts. In the following example, I've used a material script to specify that the loaded mesh uses sphere texture mapping, something that is otherwise unavailable. Here is the code:

```
Enumeration
  #MESH
  #TEXTURE
  #MATERIAL
  #ENTITY
  #CAMERA_ONE
  #LIGHT_ONE
  #LIGHT_TWO
  #PARTICLE_ONE
EndEnumeration

;Set the width, height and bit depth of the screen
;Abbreviated variables are used here due to page width constraints :(
Global ScrW.l = 1024
Global ScrH.l = 768
Global ScrD.l = 32
;Other global variables
Global Quit.b = #False

;Simple error checking procedure
Procedure HandleError(Result.l, Text.s)
  If Result = 0
    MessageRequester("Error", Text, #PB_MessageRequester_Ok)
    End
  EndIf
EndProcedure

;Convert Degrees to Radians
Procedure.f DegToRad(Angle.f)
```

```
  ProcedureReturn Angle.f * #PI / 180
EndProcedure

;Initialize environment
HandleError(InitEngine3D(), "InitEngine3D() command failed.")
HandleError(InitSprite(), "InitSprite() command failed.")
HandleError(OpenScreen(ScrW, ScrH, ScrD, ""), "Could not open screen.")
HandleError(InitKeyboard(), "InitKeyboard() command failed.")
SetFrameRate(60)

Add3DArchive("Data\", #PB_3DArchive_FileSystem)
Parse3DScripts()
CreateEntity(#ENTITY, LoadMesh(#MESH, "Statue.mesh"), #PB_Material_None)

LoadTexture(#TEXTURE, "Flame.png")
  CreateMaterial(#MATERIAL, TextureID(#TEXTURE))
  DisableMaterialLighting(#MATERIAL, 1)
  MaterialBlendingMode(#MATERIAL, #PB_Material_Add)

CreateParticleEmitter(#PARTICLE_ONE, 2, 2, 0,#PB_Particle_Point,12.9, 69, 15.7)
  ParticleSize(#PARTICLE_ONE, 5, 5)
  ParticleMaterial(#PARTICLE_ONE, MaterialID(#MATERIAL))
  ParticleEmissionRate(#PARTICLE_ONE, 50)
  ParticleTimeToLive(#PARTICLE_ONE, 0.25, 0.25)
  ParticleColorRange(#PARTICLE_ONE, RGB(255, 0, 0), RGB(255, 200, 0))
  ParticleVelocity(#PARTICLE_ONE, 1, 10)

CreateLight(#LIGHT_ONE, RGB(255,255,255))
CreateLight(#LIGHT_TWO, RGB(255, 200, 0), 12.9, 72, 15.7)
CreateCamera(#CAMERA_ONE, 0, 0, 100, 100)

;Main loop
Repeat

  Angle.f + 0.5
  PosX.f = 75 * Sin(DegToRad(Angle))
  PosY.f = (50 * Sin(DegToRad(Angle / 2))) + 65
  PosZ.f = 75 * Cos(DegToRad(Angle))
  LightLocate(#LIGHT_ONE, PosX, PosY + 100, PosZ)
  LightColor(#LIGHT_TWO, RGB(255, Random(200), 0))
  CameraLocate(#CAMERA_ONE, PosX, PosY, PosZ)
  CameraLookAt(#CAMERA_ONE, 0, 60, 0)
  RenderWorld()
  FlipBuffers()

  ExamineKeyboard()
  If KeyboardReleased(#PB_Key_Escape)
    Quit = #True
  EndIf
Until Quit = #True
End
```

This example should be straightforward as it follows the style of the last few 3D examples. First we initialize the environment, open a screen and specify a 3D archive. Once this is done, I use a new command, 'Parse3DScripts()'. This command, when called, will look inside all specified 3D archives and read all script files that it finds in them. There are many types of OGRE script files, but at this moment in time, PureBasic only supports material scripts.

Material Scripts

Once the 'Parse3DScripts()' command is called, all material scripts are read and parsed from all specified 3D archives. This means that each script is read to see what material definitions it contains and then each material's properties are read into memory. If a mesh is loaded later on which uses a material that has the same name as one specified in a material script, it will use the textures and properties as defined in the script. Used material names can be saved with the mesh when saving from a 3D modeling program. This allows you to specify the material when you are creating your mesh and then easily load it into a PureBasic 3D program, retaining all material properties.

Material scripts can be written by hand using a simple text editor or they can be exported from some 3D modeling programs along with the mesh. The syntax of material scripts is described on the OGRE website which can be found in Appendix A (Useful Internet Links). Here is the material script that I used for the statue model in the Statue example, this script file is called 'Statue.material':

```
material Statue
{
  technique
  {
    pass
    {
      texture_unit
      {
        texture SphereMap.png
        env_map spherical
        filtering trilinear
      }
    }
  }
}
```

This simple file describes the 'Statue' material, more precisely, it tells OGRE to use the image, 'SphereMap.png' as a texture, use spherical texture mapping and use trilinear filtering. To enable the Statue mesh to use this material, I specified it's name in my 3D modeling program.

If you look at the Statue example you can see I create an entity, fully textured using one line of code as opposed to the Invader example where I had to use multiple lines to load textures and create materials etc. This line is:

```
...
CreateEntity(#ENTITY, LoadMesh(#MESH, "Statue.mesh"), #PB_Material_None)
...
```

This loads the 'Statue.mesh' file and uses the material defined in the material script. Because we are using a material script to define the material, when using the 'CreateEntity()' command, the material ID parameter must be '#PB_Material_None'. This built-in constant ensures that this entity is not assigned a material, other than the one defined in the script.

Particle Effects

Creating particles can be quite a complicated affair, especially when so many effects can be produced by using them. Currently, PureBasic supports eighteen commands to customize particles in nearly every way imaginable.

Particle Scripts?

Like material scripts, particle scripts are a way of encapsulating complicated properties under a simple name. Then, when you next create a particle emitter you can specify the particle property name and all the properties defined under that name are applied to the emitter. This makes testing and creating particle effects quicker and easier.

At the moment, PureBasic does not support particle scripts but the OGRE engine does. When asked, the PureBasic team said that particle script support will be added to PureBasic in the near future. So maybe when you are reading this, PureBasic already has this support. For more information refer to the OGRE website and the online PureBasic forums, both addresses can be found in Appendix A (Useful Internet Links).

Particles, like meshs need a material assigned to them to display properly and I've created one in the Statue example using the 'Flame.png' image as a texture. This image will be used for every single particle that leaves the emitter. A particle emitter is a coordinate in 3D space that will be the point that all particles are emitted from. I've defined this in my example like this:

```
...
CreateParticleEmitter(#PARTICLE_ONE, 2, 2, 0,#PB_Particle_Point,12.9, 69, 15.7)
...
```

The 'CreateParticleEmitter' command (Helpfile:Reference Manual->3D Games Libraries->Particle->CreateParticleEmitter) takes eight parameters. The first, as usual is the PB number that will be associated to this particle emitter. The second, third and forth parameters are how far from the center point the particles are emitted along the 'x', 'y' and 'z' axis. The fifth is the particle mode. This can either be '#PB_Particle_Point' or '#PB_Particle_Box'. Emitter points are usually used for fire and smoke, etc. when the particles emanate from a particular point, while emitter boxes are usually used for area effects such as rain or snow. The last three parameters are coordinates in the 3D world that define where this emitter will be placed. These last three are also optional and if not used the emitter will be placed at '0, 0, 0'. You can later move the emitter by using the 'ParticleEmitterLocate()' command.

The other particle commands used in the Statue example are all to do with configuring the particle emitter to produce the desired effect. These other commands are:

```
...
ParticleSize(#PARTICLE_ONE, 5, 5)
ParticleMaterial(#PARTICLE_ONE, MaterialID(#MATERIAL))
ParticleEmissionRate(#PARTICLE_ONE, 50)
ParticleTimeToLive(#PARTICLE_ONE, 0.25, 0.25)
ParticleColorRange(#PARTICLE_ONE, RGB(255, 0, 0), RGB(255, 200, 0))
ParticleVelocity(#PARTICLE_ONE, 1, 10)
...
```

All these commands are self explanatory and are capable of producing thousands of different effects. They can all be read about in more detail in the PureBasic helpfile (Helpfile:Reference Manual->3D Games Libraries->Particle).

Looking At A Particular Point

In the Statue example I've used another new camera command which can very useful. This is the 'CameraLookAt()' command. (Helpfile:Reference Manual->3D Games Libraries->Camera) Using this, it is possible to angle the camera to look at any point in 3D space with one command. In my example I've used it like this:

```
...
CameraLookAt(#CAMERA_ONE, 0, 60, 0)
...
```

The first parameter is the PB number of the camera that you want to rotate. The second, third and forth are the 'x, y, z' coordinates that you want this camera to look at. In my example this makes the camera look directly at the center of the statue while the camera rotates around it.

Dynamic Lighting

In the Statue example I've also used a couple of lighting tricks to help enhance the scene. The first one is to have a white light always following the camera. This makes sure the statue mesh is always fully lit. The second lighting trick I've used is to have a flickering light positioned just above the particle emitter and have it change color on every iteration of the main loop. I do this by placing this command in the main loop:

```
...
LightColor(#LIGHT_TWO, RGB(255, Random(200), 0))
...
```

This command changes the specified light's color whenever it is used. In the main loop of the Statue example, I randomize the green component of this light's color between the values of '0' to '200'. Because the light already has the red component set to '255' and the blue component set to '0' this means that this light will flicker from red to yellow. Once this program is running you can set the color flickering on the statue's face.

Using a few tricks like material scripts to build more complex materials and using particles to create cool effects will help lift your game or demo above the rest in terms of quality and style. I've only given you a brief demonstration of what is possible with these commands the rest is up to you. To learn more about these commands try coding your own 3D programs and experiment with a few settings, especially with the particle commands.

What's Next?

Hopefully this has been a helpful, albeit brief chapter on programming 3D graphics using PureBasic. I hope that you have been inspired to learn more about what PureBasic can achieve using the OGRE engine. I would recommend reading through the entire '3D Games Libraries' section in the PureBasic helpfile to understand fully what PureBasic has to offer. This chapter has not covered every command that is contained there because of space and time constraints, but hopefully I've given you a good primer on how to start, the rest now is up to you.

Learning how to program 3D graphics can be quite tricky as sometimes it relies on complicated math routines and 3D modeling skills. The mathematics used in the examples in this chapter is quite elementary and is something which I think every college student will probably know. Saying that though, the one piece of advice I would give to all beginners of 3D programming is to learn your maths. There will be times when programming 3D graphics that you will be stopped dead in your tracks because your math ability has fallen behind your programming ability, so it's best to be prepared.

Take a look on the Internet, as there are hundreds of 3D math tutorials you can work through and a myriad of books you can read that cover this very topic in detail.

12

Sound

At some point while programming, you may need sounds to be played by a program. It might be an audible chime that lets the user know that a task has finished or it might be a sound effect in a game. However you use sound, you will need to know how to load and playback particular sound files. This chapter explains how to load various different sound files and gives examples on how to play those sound files from within a program.

Wave Files

Wave files are one of the most common sound formats on personal computers, due to their creation by a join effort between Microsoft and IBM. Wave files, which usually have the file extension of '*.wav', are the native sound format used by all PCs. Although this format has no native compression for the sound data, it's still used for every day purposes.

The following example loads a wave file called 'Intro.wav' and plays it:

```
#SOUND_FILE = 1
If InitSound()

  LoadSound(#SOUND_FILE, "Intro.wav")
  PlaySound(#SOUND_FILE)

  StartTime.l = ElapsedMilliseconds()
  Repeat
    Delay(1)
  Until ElapsedMilliseconds() > StartTime + 8000
  End
EndIf
```

This example would probably not be used in a real program but it shows you the correct steps needed to play a wave file. First, we have to initialize the sound environment using the 'InitSound()' command.

This correctly initializes all the hardware and software needed to play your file. If this returns true, we know that it has initialized properly and we can continue. There's no point continuing with sound if the sound initialization fails, the computer probably doesn't have a sound card installed.

Once the initialization is done and checked we load the sound file using the 'LoadSound()' command (Helpfile:Reference Manual->2D Games Libraries->Sound->LoadSound). This loads the sound into memory ready for us to play it. The 'LoadSound()' command takes two parameters, the first is the PB number that you wish to be associated to this sound file and the second is a String containing the filename of the sound you wish to load.

Once the wave file has been loaded you can play it at any time in your program by using the 'PlaySound()' command (Helpfile:Reference Manual->2D Games Libraries->Sound->PlaySound). This command takes one parameter, which is the PB number of the sound file you wish to play.

If you take a closer look at the wave file example you will see I've used quite an elaborate loop on the end of the program. This is to stop this example program exiting too soon. When this program exits, all sound currently being played by it will stop and be unloaded from memory. I don't want this to happen straight away, so I've coded this loop to give the program eight seconds to play the file and then exit. You will probably never see this on a real program because it will probably have a main loop to keep the program 'alive' while the sound is playing.

Embedding Wave Files

Sometimes in your programs you may not want to load external wave files, but have the files actually contained within your program so the whole thing can be distributed as one file. This can be done by embedding your wave file inside a 'DataSection', similar to embedding an image, as explained in Chapter 9 (Including Graphics In Your Program). There is one difference however, instead of using the 'CatchImage()' command to load the file from the 'DataSection' we use the 'CatchSound()' command instead, here is an example:

```
#SOUND_FILE = 1
If InitSound()

  CatchSound(#SOUND_FILE, ?SoundFile)
  PlaySound(#SOUND_FILE)

  StartTime.l = ElapsedMilliseconds()
  Repeat
    Delay(1)
  Until ElapsedMilliseconds() > StartTime + 8000
  End
EndIf

DataSection
  SoundFile:
    IncludeBinary "Intro.wav"
EndDataSection
```

The sound file is embedded in the 'DataSection' by using the 'IncludeBinary' command in exactly the same way as an image, and the label, 'SoundFile:' marks the start of the file in memory. To load this sound from the 'DataSection' when the program is running, we use the 'CatchSound()' command (Helpfile:Reference Manual->2D Games Libraries->Sound->CatchSound). This command takes two parameters, the first is the PB number that will be associated to this sound and the second is the address in memory where this sound file should be loaded from. This address will be the label's address because this marks where the sound file is in memory. To retrieve the address of any label we use a question mark in front of its name, like this: '?SoundFile'. Notice we don't need the colon after the label name though. Once a wave file is 'caught' in this way, you can use it like you would any other wave file, in this case, I play the sound by using the 'PlaySound()' command again.

Many wave files can be embedded like this in the same program, you just need to give all of them unique labels ready for 'catching'.

Altering Sounds In Realtime
Using the sound commands in the PureBasic sound library, it's possible to do some cool volume changes, sound pans and frequency shifts. Volume increases or decreases the loudness of the sound, panning means moving the sound from one speaker to another, usually to the left or right and changing the frequency will in effect speed up, or slow down the playback of a wave file while it is playing. To demonstrate these effects, I've created a small sound player program that uses realtime volume, panning and frequency controls. Try it for yourself, open it up, load a wave file, press play and slide the trackbars about.

```
Enumeration
  #WINDOW_ROOT
  #SOUND_FILE
  #TEXT_FILE
  #BUTTON_CHOOSE_FILE
  #TEXT_VOLUME
  #TRACKBAR_VOLUME
  #TEXT_PAN
  #TRACKBAR_PAN
  #TEXT_FREQUENCY
  #TRACKBAR_FREQUENCY
  #BUTTON_PLAY_FILE
  #BUTTON_STOP_FILE
EndEnumeration

Global FileName.s = ""

#FLAGS = #PB_Window_SystemMenu | #PB_Window_ScreenCentered
If OpenWindow(#WINDOW_ROOT, 0, 0, 500, 250, "Sound Player", #FLAGS)
  If CreateGadgetList(WindowID(#WINDOW_ROOT))
    TextGadget(#TEXT_FILE, 10, 10, 480, 20, "", #PB_Text_Border)
    ButtonGadget(#BUTTON_CHOOSE_FILE, 10, 40, 150, 20, "Choose Wave File...")

    TextGadget(#TEXT_VOLUME, 10, 70, 480, 20, "Volume")
    TrackBarGadget(#TRACKBAR_VOLUME, 10, 90, 480, 20, 0, 100)
    SetGadgetState(#TRACKBAR_VOLUME, 100)
```

```
TextGadget(#TEXT_PAN, 10, 120, 480, 20, "Pan")
TrackBarGadget(#TRACKBAR_PAN, 10, 140, 480, 20, 0, 200)
SetGadgetState(#TRACKBAR_PAN, 100)

TextGadget(#TEXT_FREQUENCY, 10, 170, 480, 20, "Frequency")
TrackBarGadget(#TRACKBAR_FREQUENCY, 10, 190, 480, 20, 100, 10000)
SetGadgetState(#TRACKBAR_FREQUENCY, 4400)

ButtonGadget(#BUTTON_PLAY_FILE, 10, 220, 100, 20, "Play File")
ButtonGadget(#BUTTON_STOP_FILE, 130, 220, 100, 20, "Stop Sound")

If InitSound()
 Repeat
   Event.l = WaitWindowEvent()
   Select Event
    Case #PB_Event_Gadget

     Select EventGadget()
      Case #BUTTON_CHOOSE_FILE
        FileName=OpenFileRequester("Choose","","Wave File (*.wav)|*.wav",0)
        If filename <> ""
          SetGadgetText(#TEXT_FILE, GetFilePart(FileName))
          LoadSound(#SOUND_FILE, filename)
        EndIf

      Case #TRACKBAR_VOLUME
        If filename <> ""
          SoundVolume(#SOUND_FILE, GetGadgetState(#TRACKBAR_VOLUME))
        EndIf

      Case #TRACKBAR_PAN
        If filename <> ""
          SoundPan(#SOUND_FILE, GetGadgetState(#TRACKBAR_PAN) - 100)
        EndIf

      Case #TRACKBAR_FREQUENCY
        If filename <> ""
          SoundFrequency(#SOUND_FILE,GetGadgetState(#TRACKBAR_FREQUENCY) * 10)
        EndIf

      Case #BUTTON_PLAY_FILE
        If filename <> ""
          PlaySound(#SOUND_FILE)
        EndIf

      Case #BUTTON_STOP_FILE
        If filename <> ""
          StopSound(#SOUND_FILE)
        EndIf
     EndSelect
```

```
        EndSelect
      Until Event = #PB_Event_CloseWindow
    EndIf
  EndIf
 EndIf
End
```

This example introduces three new sound commands:

'SoundVolume()'
This command is used to control the 'loudness' of the loaded sound. It doesn't change the original sound file in any way, it merely changes the volume of the sound when it's played back. To use this command you must pass it two parameters, the first is the PB number of the sound you wish to change and the second is the volume level you wish to change it to. The volume level is a number between '0' and '100'. With '0' being silent and '100' being the loudest setting.

'SoundPan()'
This command pans the sound to and from the left and right channel. To use this command you need to pass two parameters. The first is the PB number of the sound you wish to pan and the second parameter is the pan value. This pan value is a number which ranges from '-100' to '100'. If you use a value of '-100', then the sound is fully panned to the left. If you use a value of '100', then the sound is fully panned to the right.

'SoundFrequency()'
This command changes the frequency of the sound to be played. The frequency of a sound file is measured in Hertz and is explained as the number of times a particular waveform is read per second. For example, all music stored on a compact disc is sampled at a rate of 44.1kHz (kilohertz). This means that the waveform containing the sound information on a CD is read forty four thousand, one hundred times a second. This makes sure that there is necessary resolution within the waveform to encode even the slightest variation of sound. If a sound is encoded at 44.1kHz and you use this command to change its frequency to 22,050Hz, then once this sound is played back, it will play back at half the speed of the original. To use this command in PureBasic to change the frequency of a loaded sound, you pass it two parameters. The first is the PB number of the sound you want to alter and the second is a number that expresses the new frequency in Hertz. This second parameter must be between '1000' to '100000'.

To learn more about the commands that manipulate wave files, see the sound library in the PureBasic helpfile (Helpfile:Reference Manual->2D Games Libraries->Sound).

Module Files

These types of files use formats that represents music using digital patterns. Internally, they store several patterned pages of music data in a form similar to that of a spreadsheet. These patterns contain note numbers, instrument numbers, and controller messages which tell the program reading the file when to play notes, using what samples and for how long. Module files also hold a list which defines the order in which to play the patterns. The number of notes that can be played simultaneously depends on how many tracks there are per pattern. Early programs which were available allowed users to create their own modules using four tracks. The biggest advantage of modules over standard sound files is that modules include their own audio samples and should sound the same from one player to another.

Module files are often called tracker modules, and the art of composing modules is known as tracking, simply because the first ever program that allowed users to create modules was called 'Soundtracker'. This program, although originally poorly received, was eventually released into the public domain and was cloned many times, sporting better features and different names such as 'Noisetracker' or 'Protracker', these became extremely popular especially with Commodore Amiga game and demo creators. Programs that can create module files are today collectively known as trackers.

Module files can have many different file extensions because they come in many different formats, these extensions usually reveal the file's creator program. Module file types which are supported by PureBasic are:

FastTracker ('*.xm')
Scream Tracker ('*.s3m')
Protracker ('*.mod')
Impulse Tracker ('*.it')

These different types of modules are treated in the same way when loading and playing in your PureBasic program. Here is an example showing how to load and play any of the above types of module:

```
#MODULE_FILE = 1

If InitSound().
  If InitModule()

    LoadModule(#MODULE_FILE, "Eighth.mod")
    PlayModule(#MODULE_FILE)

    StartTime.l = ElapsedMilliseconds()
    Repeat
      Delay(1)
    Until ElapsedMilliseconds() > StartTime + 15000

    StopModule(#MODULE_FILE)

  End
  EndIf
EndIf
```

First, we need to initialize the sound environment just like the wave file example by using the 'InitSound()' command. Next, we need to initialize the module playing capabilities of PureBasic by using the 'InitModule()' command. Both of these commands should be tested to ensure that both are initialized correctly.

Once the environment is set up we can load a module by using the 'LoadModule()' command (Helpfile:Reference Manual->2D Games Libraries->Module->LoadModule). This command takes two parameters, the first is the PB number that you wish to be associated with this module and the second is the filename of the module to be loaded.

Once it's loaded we can play this module at any time using the 'PlayModule()' command (Helpfile:Reference Manual->2D Games Libraries->Module->PlayModule). Just like the 'PlaySound()' command, this one takes one parameter, which is the PB number of the module you want to play. To stop the module from playing you can use the 'StopModule()' command.

The Downsides Of Using Modules
There are two big downsides of using modules in your PureBasic programs. The first is that there is no easy way to embed and load from memory any modules that need to be played. This means that you have to distribute all the used module files along with your executable. There are however, ways of storing the module in your executable, and then writing it to disk before loading and playing it, but this is a little bit cumbersome. The second downside is that you have to distribute the 'Midas11.dll' file along with your program. This dynamic linked library is loaded by the command; 'InitModule()' and will error if it doesn't find it. You may think that this isn't too bad but the license connected to using this 'Midas' library forbids the use of it for any commercial purposes. This license also prevents the 'Midas11.dll' file being included within the PureBasic package, so you have to download it for yourself from the 'Housemarque Audio System' website, which can be found in Appendix A (Useful Internet Links).

To learn about other commands that can be used to manipulate module files, see the module library in the PureBasic helpfile (Helpfile:Reference Manual->2D Games Libraries->Module).

Mp3's

MP3 files are quickly becoming the most popular sound file format of all time, largely due to the fact that the MP3 file format is the de-facto standard for nearly all downloadable music on the Internet. MP3 is an anacronym that stands for 'MPEG-1 Audio Layer 3' which is quite a mouthful, so you will probably understand why it was shortened.

MP3 files are handled a little bit differently in PureBasic and in order to play them we must use the commands from the 'Movie' library (Helpfile:Reference Manual->General Libraries->Movie). It may seem a little odd using the movie commands to play mp3 files but the movie commands are capable of much more than just playing movies. The 'Movie' library provides a convenient way to load and play nearly all media that has a codec installed on the host computer. Not only can you play movie formats using these commands, but you can also play audio file formats.

Here is a list of the more popular file formats that the 'Movie' library is able to play as long as the required plugins and/or codecs are installed first. You may even be able to play more formats than what is shown on this list:

Movie Files:
Audio Video Interleave ('*.avi')
MPEG Video ('*.mpg')

Audio Files:
Midi Files ('*.mid')
MP3 Files ('*.mp3')
Ogg Vorbis ('*.ogg')
Wave Files ('*.wav')

The 'Movie' library may seem like a 'one stop shop' for all your media playing needs and some people have even asked for it to be renamed to the 'Media' library, but the one thing to remember is that if something loads and plays on your computer, it might not load and play on another person's computer. This is because there might be different plugins and/or codecs installed, (or not) on other machines. However, saying this, the list above seems to be pretty standard on most machines, but don't quote me on that.

In this next example I've used the movie commands to create a simple MP3 player and provide simple volume and pan controls. It may not rival WinAmp but it gives you an idea of how easy media players are to create in PureBasic.

```
Enumeration
  #WINDOW_ROOT
  #SOUND_FILE
  #TEXT_FILE
  #BUTTON_CHOOSE_FILE
  #TEXT_VOLUME
  #TRACKBAR_VOLUME
  #TEXT_PAN
  #TRACKBAR_PAN
  #BUTTON_PLAY_FILE
  #BUTTON_PAUSE_FILE
  #BUTTON_STOP_FILE
EndEnumeration

Global FileName.s = ""
Global FilePaused.b = #False

#FLAGS = #PB_Window_SystemMenu | #PB_Window_ScreenCentered
If OpenWindow(#WINDOW_ROOT, 0, 0, 500, 215, "MP3 Player", #FLAGS)
  If CreateGadgetList(WindowID(#WINDOW_ROOT))
    TextGadget(#TEXT_FILE, 10, 10, 480, 20, "", #PB_Text_Border)
    ButtonGadget(#BUTTON_CHOOSE_FILE, 10, 40, 150, 20, "Choose MP3 File...")
    TextGadget(#TEXT_VOLUME, 10, 70, 480, 20, "Volume")
    TrackBarGadget(#TRACKBAR_VOLUME, 10, 90, 480, 20, 0, 100)
    SetGadgetState(#TRACKBAR_VOLUME, 100)
    TextGadget(#TEXT_PAN, 10, 120, 480, 20, "Pan")
    TrackBarGadget(#TRACKBAR_PAN, 10, 140, 480, 20, 0, 200)
    SetGadgetState(#TRACKBAR_PAN, 100)
```

```
ButtonGadget(#BUTTON_PLAY_FILE, 10, 180, 100, 20, "Play")
ButtonGadget(#BUTTON_PAUSE_FILE, 130, 180, 100, 20, "Pause")
ButtonGadget(#BUTTON_STOP_FILE, 250, 180, 100, 20, "Stop")

If InitMovie()
 Repeat
   Event.l = WaitWindowEvent()
   Select Event
     Case #PB_Event_Gadget

       Select EventGadget()
         Case #BUTTON_CHOOSE_FILE
           FileName=OpenFileRequester("Choose","","MP3 File (*.mp3)|*.mp3",0)
           If filename <> ""
             SetGadgetText(#TEXT_FILE, GetFilePart(FileName))
             LoadMovie(#SOUND_FILE, filename)
           EndIf

         Case #TRACKBAR_VOLUME, #TRACKBAR_PAN
           If filename <> ""
             Volume.l = GetGadgetState(#TRACKBAR_VOLUME)
             Balance.l = GetGadgetState(#TRACKBAR_PAN) - 100
             MovieAudio(#SOUND_FILE, Volume, Balance)
           EndIf

         Case #BUTTON_PLAY_FILE
           If filename <> ""
             PlayMovie(#SOUND_FILE, #Null)
             FilePaused = #False
             SetGadgetText(#BUTTON_PAUSE_FILE, "Pause")
           EndIf

         Case #BUTTON_PAUSE_FILE
           If filename <> ""
             If FilePaused = #False
               PauseMovie(#SOUND_FILE)
               FilePaused = #True
               SetGadgetText(#BUTTON_PAUSE_FILE, "Resume")
             Else
               ResumeMovie(#SOUND_FILE)
               FilePaused = #False
               SetGadgetText(#BUTTON_PAUSE_FILE, "Pause")
             EndIf
           EndIf

         Case #BUTTON_STOP_FILE
           If filename <> ""
             StopMovie(#SOUND_FILE)
             FilePaused = #False
             SetGadgetText(#BUTTON_PAUSE_FILE, "Pause")
           EndIf
```

```
        EndSelect

      EndSelect
    Until Event = #PB_Event_CloseWindow
   EndIf
  EndIf
 EndIf
End
```

Looking at this small example, you can see that to use the movie commands, you must initialize the environment properly just like wave files and modules. To initialize the movie commands you use the 'InitMovie()' command. After this has been called you are free to use the other 'Movie' library commands. As with other initialization commands it must be tested and if it fails, you won't be able to continue using the movie commands.

To load a movie (or in this case a MP3 file) we use the 'LoadMovie()' command (Helpfile:Reference Manual->General Libraries->Movie->LoadMovie). This command takes two parameters. The first one is the PB number that you want associated to the media about to be loaded and the second parameter is a String containing the filename of the actual media to load.

Once the media has been loaded we can play it back using the 'PlayMovie()' command (Helpfile:Reference Manual->General Libraries->Movie->PlayMovie). This command takes two parameters to be able to support movies as well as audio media. The first parameter is the PB number of the media you want to play, while the second parameter is an OS identifier of a window. This OS identifier is required if you are playing back a movie because this window is where the movie display will be rendered. If you are playing back a file that only consists of audio data (such as a MP3) then you can use the built-in constant '#Null' as an OS identifier, this doesn't then associate any window to the playback of the file:

```
...
PlayMovie(#SOUND_FILE, #Null)
...
```

Also in the example I've used the 'PauseMovie()' and 'ResumeMovie()' commands, these are simple to use, they both take one parameter which is the PB number of the media you want to pause or resume.

To enable you to stop the playback of your files, I've also used the 'StopMovie()' command in this example. Again, this is a simple one to use, as you only need to pass it one parameter. This is the PB number of the media you wish to stop playing.

Even though this is a skeleton of a media player and it only supports MP3's, it would be a trivial task to convert this code to make your own media player capable of handling all of the formats listed above. Why don't you try?

CD Audio

Playing an audio CD is a good way to provide high quality music for any game or application that would need music. There are many free tools available on the Internet, for composing and burning your music onto a CD. Using CD's to provide music is a great idea because playing them requires very little system resources and the quality is fantastic. Here is an example which uses the PureBasic 'AudioCD' library, to create a very simple CD player:

```
Enumeration
  #WINDOW_ROOT
  #BUTTON_PREVIOUS
  #BUTTON_PLAY
  #BUTTON_STOP
  #BUTTON_NEXT
  #BUTTON_EJECT
  #TEXT_STATUS
  #PROGRESS_SONG
  #LIST_TRACKS
EndEnumeration

;Global variables, etc.
Global NumberOfTracks.l
Global CurrentTrack.l

;Convert seconds into a String containing minutes
Procedure.s ConvertToMin(Seconds.l)
  ProcedureReturn Str(Seconds / 60) + ":" + Str(Seconds % 60)
EndProcedure

;Set the current track
Procedure UpdateStatusText(Track.l)
  If NumberOfTracks > 0
    TrackLength.l = AudioCDTrackLength(Track)
    TrackLengthString.s = ConvertToMin(TrackLength)
    TrackTimings.s = " (" + TrackLengthString + ")"
    SetGadgetText(#TEXT_STATUS, "Track: " + Str(Track) + TrackTimings)
    SetGadgetState(#PROGRESS_SONG, 0)
    If AudioCDStatus() > 0
      TimeElapsed.l = AudioCDTrackSeconds()
      TrackTimings.s=" ("+ConvertToMin(TimeElapsed)+" / "+TrackLengthString+")"
      SetGadgetText(#TEXT_STATUS, "Track: " + Str(Track) + TrackTimings)
      Progress.f = (100 / TrackLength) * TimeElapsed
      SetGadgetState(#PROGRESS_SONG, Progress)
    EndIf
    SetGadgetState(#LIST_TRACKS, Track - 1)
  Else
    SetGadgetText(#TEXT_STATUS, "Please insert an Audio CD")
  EndIf
EndProcedure
```

```
;Move to next track
Procedure NextTrack()
  If CurrentTrack < NumberOfTracks
    CurrentTrack + 1
    UpdateStatusText(CurrentTrack)
    If AudioCDStatus() > 0
      PlayAudioCD(CurrentTrack, NumberOfTracks)
    EndIf
  EndIf
EndProcedure

;Move to previous track
Procedure PreviousTrack()
  If CurrentTrack > 1
    CurrentTrack - 1
    UpdateStatusText(CurrentTrack)
    If AudioCDStatus() > 0
      PlayAudioCD(CurrentTrack, NumberOfTracks)
    EndIf
  EndIf
EndProcedure

;Populate the list to show all tracks on a disc
Procedure PopulateTrackListing()
  ClearGadgetItemList(#LIST_TRACKS)
  NumberOfTracks = AudioCDTracks()
  If NumberOfTracks > 0
    For x.l = 1 To NumberOfTracks
      TrackLength.s = ConvertToMin(AudioCDTrackLength(x))
      AddGadgetItem(#LIST_TRACKS, -1, "Track "+Str(x)+" ("+TrackLength+")")
    Next x
    If CurrentTrack = 0
      CurrentTrack = 1
    EndIf
  Else
    CurrentTrack = 0
  EndIf
EndProcedure

#FLAGS = #PB_Window_SystemMenu | #PB_Window_ScreenCentered
If OpenWindow(#WINDOW_ROOT, 0, 0, 320, 250, "CD Player", #FLAGS)
  If CreateGadgetList(WindowID(#WINDOW_ROOT))
    ButtonGadget(#BUTTON_PREVIOUS, 10, 10, 60, 20, "Previous")
    ButtonGadget(#BUTTON_PLAY, 70, 10, 60, 20, "Play")
    ButtonGadget(#BUTTON_STOP, 130, 10, 60, 20, "Stop")
    ButtonGadget(#BUTTON_NEXT, 190, 10, 60, 20, "Next")
    ButtonGadget(#BUTTON_EJECT, 250, 10, 60, 20, "Eject")
    TextGadget(#TEXT_STATUS, 10, 40, 300, 20, "", #PB_Text_Center)
    ProgressBarGadget(#PROGRESS_SONG,10,65,300,10,0,100,#PB_ProgressBar_Smooth)
    ListViewGadget(#LIST_TRACKS, 10, 90, 300, 150)
```

```
    If InitAudioCD()
      PopulateTrackListing()

      StartTime.l = ElapsedMilliseconds()

      Repeat
        Event.l = WindowEvent()
        Select Event
          Case #PB_Event_Gadget
            Select EventGadget()
              Case #BUTTON_PREVIOUS
                PreviousTrack()
              Case #BUTTON_PLAY
                If NumberOfTracks > 0
                  PlayAudioCD(CurrentTrack, NumberOfTracks)
                EndIf
              Case #BUTTON_STOP
                StopAudioCD()
              Case #BUTTON_NEXT
                NextTrack()
              Case #BUTTON_EJECT
                EjectAudioCD(#True)
                PopulateTrackListing()
              Case #LIST_TRACKS
                If EventType() = #PB_EventType_LeftDoubleClick
                  CurrentTrack = GetGadgetState(#LIST_TRACKS) + 1
                  UpdateStatusText(CurrentTrack)
                  PlayAudioCD(CurrentTrack, NumberOfTracks)
                EndIf
            EndSelect
        EndSelect

        CurrentTime.l = ElapsedMilliseconds()
        If CurrentTime > StartTime + 1000
          PopulateTrackListing()
          UpdateStatusText(CurrentTrack)
          StartTime.l = ElapsedMilliseconds()
        EndIf
        Delay(1)

      Until Event = #PB_Event_CloseWindow
      StopAudioCD()
    EndIf
  EndIf
 EndIf
End
```

This example is an extremely simple CD player which provides the bare minimum of functionality to control and play CD's. All the 'AudioCD' library commands that have been used can be read about in more detail in the PureBasic helpfile (Helpfile:Reference Manual->General Libraries->AudioCD).

To use the 'AudioCD' commands you first have to initialize the resources needed to be able to play CD's. To do this we use the 'InitAudioCD()' command. This command must be tested to determine if it was successful or not. As a byproduct, the return value of this command is the number of CD drives connected to the computer and of which are available for use to play music. If the return value is '0' then the computer either doesn't have a CD drive installed or another problem has been encountered which prevents the CD drive from playing music. As long as the return value is above '0' then all should be well.

Once the CD audio has been initialized, you are then free to use all of the other commands available in the 'AudioCD' library.

Here is a list of the ones I've used in my CD player example:

'PlayAudioCD()'
This command is used to play a track on the current CD which is inserted into your drive. This command takes two parameters. The first is the track to start playing from and the second is the track to stop playing once the end has been reached. So for example, If I called the command like this:

```
PlayAudioCD(1, 3)
```

Track '1' would start playing, then continue afterwards to the next track. The play back would then stop after track '3' had finished.

'StopAudioCD()'
This command can be used at any time to stop the playback of any track currently playing on the CD.

'EjectAudioCD()'
This command will either open or close the tray on the CD drive depending on what parameter is passed to it. This command only takes one parameter and if that parameter is '1' the drive tray will be opened, effectively stopping playback and ejecting the CD. If the parameter is '0' the drive tray is closed, effectively loading any CD that is placed in it.

'AudioCDStatus()'
This command doesn't have any parameters but returns a result that gives us a realtime status of the CD in the drive. If you call this command and it returns '-1' then the drive is not ready, meaning that the drive either contains no CD or that the drive tray is currently open. If this command returns the value '0' then a CD has been detected correctly and is in the drive but the CD is not playing. If this command returns a value which is above '0' then the CD drive is playing a CD track. The number which was actually returned, is the track number which is being played back.

'AudioCDTracks()'
This command doesn't take any parameters and when called, returns the number of tracks on a loaded CD that are available to be played back.

'AudioCDTrackLength()'
This command requires one parameter and that is a track number from a loaded CD. With this information, this command will return that track's length in seconds.

'AudioCDTrackSeconds()'
This command doesn't take any parameters. When called, it will return the amount of time elapsed in seconds that the current track has been playing for.

If you look closer at my CD player example, I've also used the command; 'WindowEvent()' instead of 'WaitWindowEvent()'. This means that the main loop will always be running regardless of if an event is detected or not. I needed this particular program to do this because I use a timed procedure call in the main loop to update the status text in the CD player's graphical user interface. If I didn't use this command, the status text would only be updated if an event was detected, which could be sometime.

'WindowEvent()' and 'WaitWindowEvent()' are covered in more detail in Chapter 9 (Understanding Events).

IV

Advanced Topics

In this section, I explain things that are a little more advanced than what the rest of this book deals with. This section is for those who have further questions on a particular facet of PureBasic or want to learn a little more about what goes on 'under the hood'.

You don't need to know any of what is contained in this section to write good, solid and feature-rich programs, but I have included it here for those who want to delve a little deeper.

13

Beyond The Basics

This chapter contains a mish-mash of topics because I felt all these subjects needed to be explained but each one really didn't warrant a full chapter. These things are not essential to know if you want to write PureBasic programs but are for programmers who want to increase their knowledge of the more advanced features of the PureBasic language.

Topics covered in this chapter include; Compiler Directives and how to control the compiler using code, Advanced Compiler Options to get more from the PureBasic compiler, How to pass Command Line Arguments to you program for writing command line tools, How PureBasic stores numeric data types, What Pointers are and how to use them, What Threads are and how to use them, What Dynamically Linked Libraries are and how to create them and How to use the Window Application Programming Interface natively in PureBasic.

Compiler Directives And Functions

Compiler directives are commands that control the PureBasic compiler during compile time. As such, these directives allow you to have total control over what parts of your source code are compiled and allow you to retrieve information from the compiler. Compiler directives only have an effect during compile time, where they are parsed and acted on. They cannot be utilized while your program is actually running.

Compiler functions are different from directives as these are commands which enable you to gather information about something that has already been compiled (usually a data type). Unlike directives, compiler functions can be utilized while the program is running.

Earlier on in this book you have already seen examples of compiler directives and compiler functions but you might not have noticed, for example, I demonstrated the 'EnableExplicit' command in Chapter 8 (How To Minimize And Handle Errors). This compiler directive switches the compiler to explicit mode and makes sure all variables are explicitly declared, making sure the scope and type of each new variable is defined. You have also seen the 'SizeOf()' and 'OffsetOf()' commands in Chapter 5. These compiler functions gather information from compiled structures and interfaces, such as the size in Bytes of a particular structure in memory or the offset of where a particular field is within a structure or interface.

There are a few more directives and functions to add to this list, but before I can continue to explain these any further, I'll need to explain the built-in reserved compiler constants that they nearly all use.

Reserved Compiler Constants

These built-in reserved constants are just like any other constant, but what is different is that their values largely depend on the current state of the compiler. All these constants can be tested at compile time to make decisions on how to proceed with the compilation and some constants even provide information about the compiling process itself. Here is a full list of the reserved compiler constants and what information you may get from them.

'#PB_Compiler_OS'
This is a special constant that is assigned a value depending on what platform the compiler is running on. It also has some associated constants to help you determine what it's value may mean. For example, if the '#PB_Compiler_OS' constant has a value equal to any one of either '#PB_OS_Windows', '#PB_OS_Linux', '#PB_OS_AmigaOS' or '#PB_OS_MacOS' then the compiler is running on that particular platform.

'#PB_Compiler_Date'
This constant's value contains a date in numeric form, which is the date of when your program was compiled. This value is encoded in the PureBasic date format to integrate nicely with the commands in the 'Date' library (Helpfile:Reference Manual->General Libraries->Date).

'#PB_Compiler_File'
This constant's value is a String that contains the full path and name of the file (*.pb) being compiled.

'#PB_Compiler_Line'
This constant's value is the line number of the current file which is being compiled.

'#PB_Compiler_Version'
This constant's value contains a floating point number which is the version of the compiler being used to compile the program.

'#PB_Compiler_Home'
This constant's value is a String containing the full path of PureBasic's installation folder on your computer.

'#PB_Compiler_Debugger'
This constant can have one of two values. If its value is equal to '#True' then the debugger was enabled before the program was compiled. If its value is equal to '#False' then the debugger was disabled before compilation.

'#PB_Compiler_Thread'
This constant can have one of two values. If its value is equal to '#True' then the compiler was switched to thread-safe mode before compilation. If its value is equal to '#False' then the thread-safe compiler mode wasn't used.

'#PB_Compiler_Unicode'
This constant can have one of two values. If its value is equal to '#True' then the compiler was switched to unicode mode before compilation. If its value is equal to '#False' then the unicode compiler mode wasn't used.

All these reserved compiler constants can be used as normal in statements and expressions, in fact you can use them anywhere where you would use a normal constant. However, most of these compiler constants are only really useful when they are used with the following directives.

The 'CompilerIf' Directive
If you understand how to use 'If' statements in PureBasic you will understand how to use 'CompilerIf's. A 'CompilerIf' is a statement that acts exactly like any other 'If' statement but which is never actually compiled. It's basically a compiler version of an 'If' statement.

Unlike a normal 'If', a 'CompilerIf' decides which piece of code to compile based on the result of a constant expression (no variables allowed). In contrast, a normal 'If' decides which piece of (already compiled) code to run based on a variable expression.

Let me show you an example of one of the most common uses of a 'CompilerIf':

```
CompilerIf #PB_Compiler_OS = #PB_OS_Windows
  MessageRequester("Info", "This compiler is running on Microsoft Windows")
CompilerElse
  MessageRequester("Info", "This compiler is NOT running on Microsoft Windows")
CompilerEndIf
```

Here the 'CompilerIf' tests this constant expression; '#PB_Compiler_OS = #PB_OS_Windows'. If this expression equals true then we know that this piece of code is being compiled on a computer running Microsoft Windows. If it equals false then it isn't, it's as simple as that. This seems pretty straightforward but what's clever about using 'CompilerIf's is that whichever branch the 'CompilerIf' statement takes, it will only compile that piece of code. With that in mind, if we compiled this example on a Microsoft Windows computer, then the line:

```
MessageRequester("Info", "This compiler is NOT running on Microsoft Windows")
```

Will never get compiled and therefore never be included in the program's executable file.

A 'CompilerIf' statement consists of three commands, all of which are demonstrated in the above example. The 'CompilerElse' component, which is similar to a standard 'Else', is entirely optional but the whole statement must end with 'CompilerEndIf'.

Some programmers use 'CompilerIf's to limit the functionality of a program especially if it's compiled as a trial version. For example, if I write a useful program and want to give my users a demo to try before they buy, and I'm afraid that some might attempt to crack it to remove any limitations. I could code my program like this:

```
#DEMO = #True

CompilerIf #DEMO

  ;Demo code
  MessageRequester("Info", "This is a demo, You must buy the full version.")

CompilerElse

  ;Full version code
  Procedure.d MyPI()
    ProcedureReturn ACos(-1)
  EndProcedure

  Test.s = "This is the full version." + #LF$ + #LF$
  Test.s + "The value of Pi is: " + StrD(MyPI(), 16)
  MessageRequester("Info", Test)

CompilerEndIf
```

Just simply changing the value of the constant '#DEMO' will now force the compiler to compile different versions of the source code. This is useful as it can prevent cracking of your demo programs because they simply will not contain the code contained inside the full version. Try changing the value of the '#DEMO' constant to '#False' to compile the full version of this program.

The 'CompilerSelect' Directive
The 'CompilerSelect' statement is a compiler version of the popular 'Select' statement. This means that multiple sections of source code can be compiled depending on the different values of a selected constant. Similar to a 'CompilerIf', 'CompilerSelect's can only test constant values, this is again because the test is done at compile time instead of runtime. Here's another operating system test done using a 'CompilerSelect':

```
CompilerSelect #PB_Compiler_OS

  CompilerCase #PB_OS_Windows
    ;Windows specific code
    MessageRequester("Info", "This is being compiled on Microsoft Windows.")

  CompilerCase #PB_OS_Linux
    ;Linux specific code
    MessageRequester("Info", "This is being compiled on Linux.")
```

```
  CompilerCase #PB_OS_MacOS
   ;MacOS specific code
   MessageRequester("Info", "This is being compiled on MacOS X")

  CompilerCase #PB_OS_AmigaOS
   ;AmigaOS specific code
   MessageRequester("Info", "This is being compiled on Amiga OS.")

 CompilerEndSelect
```

Using something like this, it's possible to customize your program to exhibit different behavior based on what operating system it's compiled for. Your program might also use commands from a particular operating systems API, and because commands like that are not cross-platform, you might use a 'CompilerSelect' to use other operating system's APIs to produce the same result on all platforms.

PureBasic provides support for several keywords to give a 'CompilerSelect' the same functionality as a normal 'Select' statement. These keywords are, 'CompilerSelect', 'CompilerCase', 'CompilerDefault' and 'CompilerEndSelect'. You have seen three of these commands in the 'CompilerSelect' example above. The forth one, 'CompilerDefault' is used as a fallback case keyword to handle a default state just incase the 'CompilerCase' commands don't return true, like this:

```
 CompilerSelect #PB_Compiler_OS

  CompilerCase #PB_OS_AmigaOS
   ;AmigaOS specific code
   MessageRequester("Error", "This source code does not support Amiga OS.")

  CompilerDefault
   ;This code will compile on all other operating systems.
   MessageRequester("Info", "This is code will compile fine on this OS.")

 CompilerEndSelect
```

In this example I've thrown up an error if someone tries to compile this code on AmigaOS but for all other operating systems (handled by the 'CompilerDefault' keyword) it runs fine.

Although my examples for the 'CompilerIf' and 'CompilerSelect' mainly use the '#PB_Compiler_OS' constants, you must remember that any constants, compiler reserved or not, can be tested by them. This is so you can customize the compiling process using PureBasic code as much as you see fit.

The 'CompilerError' Directive
This directive can be used by itself or within other compiler directives, such as 'CompilerIf' or 'CompilerSelect' to raise a compiler error, complete with helpful text. This is handy when you want to stop the compilation process and give the user a graceful compiler error message. Here is the above 'CompilerSelect' example translated to use a real compiler error message:

```
CompilerSelect #PB_Compiler_OS

  CompilerCase #PB_OS_MacOS
    CompilerError "This source code does not support MacOS."

  CompilerDefault
    MessageRequester("Info", "This is code will compile fine on this OS.")

CompilerEndSelect
```

Looking at this example, you can see that the 'CompilerError' directive does not use brackets to enclose any parameters like a normal command. Instead we simply use the 'CompilerError' directive with a literal String following it. This String will be the error text that is displayed when the compiler error is thrown. When the compiler encounters an 'CompilerError' directive, the compilation is stopped and the error text is presented.

The 'Subsystem()' Compiler Function

To explain this compiler function I must first explain subsystems in general, and how they relate to PureBasic. Subsystems are an easy concept to grasp, basically, if you are not happy with the functionality of any of PureBasic 's built-in commands you can override them with your own versions, these new versions are contained within a subsystem.

If you take a look inside the PureBasic installation folder, you will see a folder called 'PureLibraries', this folder contains library files which contain PureBasic's built-in commands. These library files are the ones that are replaced when a subsystem is used. When I say replaced, I don't mean actually deleted or copied over. A subsystem library merely takes priority over standard libraries.

To create a subsystem you must first rewrite and compile a PureBasic library (there is more information regarding this in the PureBasic 'Library SDK' folder). This new library must contain all commands of the original library and all these commands must be named in exactly the same way as the originals. You must then make sure that the name of the newly compiled library matches the name of the library you want it to replace.

Once you have done this, it should be an almost identical copy of the original library, apart from the functionality of the commands it contains (you can write these to have any functionality you wish). To install this library as a subsystem, so you can use it during compilation, you need to create a new folder within the 'SubSystems' folder in your PureBasic installation directory. The name you give this new folder will be the name of your new subsystem. Inside this new subsystem folder you now must have a folder called 'PureLibraries', and this is where you put your replacement libraries. So the directory structure of these folders will looking something like this:

'..\PureBasic\SubSystems\YourSubSystem\PureLibraries\YourNewLibrary'

To make PureBasic use your new subsystem, you must add a subsystem flag to the compiler so it uses the libraries from your subsystem and not those from the standard 'PureLibraries' folder. To do this open the 'Compiler Options' window (Menu:Compiler->Compiler Options...) and type the subsystem folder name (the one that you created in the 'SubSystems' folder) into the 'Library Subsystem:' field, then click 'OK'. When your program is next compiled, the compiler will scan the 'SubSystems' and 'PureLibraries' folders looking for libraries, if it finds that these two folders contain identically named libraries, the compiler will always choose the specified subsystem over the standard one, therefore replacing the original.

There is already an example of a subsystem in the 'SubSystems' directory. If you look in there, you will find a folder called 'OpenGL', inside which is a 'PureLibraries' folder, and inside that, there are replacement libraries for 'Screen', 'Sprite' and 'Sprite3D'. These are the libraries this subsystem will replace if this subsystem is used. Once activated via a compiler flag, this subsystem will use OpenGL for 2D graphics instead of DirectX.

Now, as mentioned earlier I will explain the 'Subsystem()' compiler function.

During compilation, the 'Subsystem()' compiler function lets you know if a particular subsystem has been activated using a compiler flag. The syntax is easy enough to understand, For example, if I had enabled the 'OpenGL' subsystem the following debug message would be displayed:

```
If Subsystem("OpenGL")
  Debug "The OpenGL subsystem is being used."
EndIf
```

The 'Subsystem()' compiler function takes one parameter, this is a literal String of the subsystem you want to test for, (variables cannot be used here). If this subsystem has been activated and is being used to compile this program, then the 'Subsystem()' compiler function will return true.

The 'Defined()' Compiler Function
Sometimes when coding software you need to test wether a particular data object has been defined. This is achieved by using the 'Defined()' compiler function. This function takes two parameters, the first is a data object to test for, and the second is the data type of that object. If this particular object has been defined, then the 'Defined()' compiler function will return true. The value of the object being tested doesn't matter, only that it has been defined. The data objects that can be tested are constants, variables, arrays, linked lists, structures and interfaces.

When using the 'Defined()' compiler function, the first parameter must only be the name of the data object to test and must not contain any of the usual prefixes or suffixes that are usually used for that object. For example, constant names must not contain the '#' character and array and linked list names must not contain brackets. For the second parameter, where you pass the type of the object you are testing, you can use built-in constants, here is the full list of what is available:

'#PB_Constant'
'#PB_Variable'
'#PB_Array'
'#PB_LinkedList'
'#PB_Structure'
'#PB_Interface'

I've made this command sound like it's quite complicated to use, so I better dismiss that with a simple example of how easy it really is. This example tests if the variable; 'Name.s' has been defined, if not, it defines it:

```
Global Name.s = "Name 1"

If Not Defined(Name, #PB_Variable)
  ;This will only define this variable if it hasn't been defined before
  Global Name.s = "Name 2"
EndIf

Debug Name
```

You can test this piece of code by commenting out the first line. If you do this, the variable definition now takes place inside the 'If' statement and the String variable's value will now be 'Name 2'. Code like this is invaluable for large projects, where you may be including a lot of source code files into a main one and you need to test if something important has been defined before. If not, then define it.

Advanced Compiler Options

When using PureBasic you may need to change modes on the compiler for a particular program or you may need to have the compiler output specific information. To be able to do this, PureBasic offers several compiler options for you to use. You can enable or disable most of these options visually in the IDE from within the 'Compiler Options' window (Menu:Compiler->Compiler Options...). To gain access to all supported compiler options, you have to call the compiler using a shell command and pass the options as parameters.

So what is a command line interface anyway? Well, it's a small program that usually comes with your operating system (sometimes called a Shell Interface), that allows you to navigate your computer's hard drive or start programs and control computer functions by typing in recognized text commands. It does not have any other user interface other than text input. There are numerous command line interface programs available, and these seem to be some of the most popular:

    'CLI' on AmigaOS
    'Command Prompt' on Microsoft Window XP
    'BASH' on Linux
    'Terminal' on MacOS X

For these command line interfaces to work correctly with PureBasic, you may need to add the full directory path to the compiler to your 'PATH' environment variable. This is so the command line interface always knows where the compiler is located. Using an environment variable like this will negate the need to type in the full path of the compiler when using it in a shell command. Using a command line interface, in my opinion, is not very user friendly, but it's the only way to use some of the more advanced features of the PureBasic compiler. Saying that though, sometimes having a compiler that you can use on the command line is useful, especially if you want to use your own code editor, then you can set it up as an external tool.

Using The Compiler On The Command Line

Using the compiler on the command line is simple enough, you just have to make sure you pass the optional parameters correctly. The actual compiler command itself must always start with the name of the PureBasic compiler followed by any parameters that are required. The only mandatory parameter is a file to pass to the compiler for processing.

Using the command line compiler in its simplest form to produce an executable file from a PureBasic file, doesn't need any optional parameters to be passed to it, but it does need the name of a '*.pb' file. Open a command line interface window, type this in it and hit return:

```
PBCompiler MyProgram.pb
```

If your 'PATH' environment variable is configured correctly, this command will start the PureBasic compiler and pass the 'MyProgram.pb' file to it. The compiler will create a temporary executable file in the same directory as the compiler and launch that program, in the same way as if you had hit the 'Compile/Run' button in the IDE. This is probably the simplest way of compiling a program using the command line.

If you want to compile a program to an executable file which has a user defined name, and want that file to appear in the same directory as the source code file, then you can use this shell command:

```
PBCompiler MyProgram.pb /exe "MyProgram.exe"
```

This would compile the 'MyProgram.pb' file and create an executable file from it. This compiled executable file will be called 'MyProgram.exe' and will be placed in the same directory as the specified '*.pb' file. Notice in this command we are using a new compiler option; '/exe'. This tells the compiler that we want a properly named executable file. The String after this compiler option is what that file should be called. All command line compiler options start with a forward slash '/' like this. These two examples are fairly easy to understand, but these actual commands are seldom used in practice. People prefer instead to use the PureBasic IDE to perform simple compilations. These two are useful to know though, especially if you want to set up another code editor.

When using compiler options on the command line, it's also important to understand that many options can be used at the same time. For example, if I wanted to compile a '*.pb' file to an executable and assign an icon to it, I would use a shell command like this:

```
PBCompiler MyProgram.pb /exe "MyProgram.exe" /icon ".\icons\MyIcon.ico"
```

The compiler recognizes that the String after the '/exe' option is what the executable file should be called and the String after the '/icon' option is the icon file that should be applied to this executable. All command line compiler options must always be separated by spaces.

PureBasic Command Line Compiler Options

What follows now is a complete list of all PureBasic's command line compiler options, including an explanation of each one and a small example of its usage. Remember, most of these options can be enabled visually in the IDE, using a checkbox or a drop-down menu in the 'Compiler Options' window.

This enables you to control the compiler's behavior more easily. All these command line options are also completely case insensitive, so you can enter them in upper or lowercase, it's entirely up to you.

/?
This is a command line only option which displays a helpful page detailing all available PureBasic command line compiler options. The help page is printed to the shell interface window. This compiler option also overrides any others used in the same shell command.

```
PBCompiler /?
```

/Commented
This is another command line only option which creates a commented Assembly file in the 'PureBasic\Compilers' folder called 'PureBasic.asm' along with any executable file output. This file is the raw output of the PureBasic compiler and contains the raw compiler generated assembly source code of the '*.pb' file. This file can be re-compiled into an executable file, using the '/reasm' compiler option, even if modifications are made to it.

```
PBCompiler MyProgram.pb /commented
```

/Console
This compiler option enables you to compile a true console application. Here's a simple example:

```
PBCompiler MyProgram.pb /exe "MyProgram.exe" /console
```

For more information regarding console applications, please refer to Chapter 9 (Console Programs).

/Constant (Name=Value)
This is another command line only option which enables you to define a constant dynamically on the command line. This can be useful if, for example, you code a program that changes its functionality depending on the value of that constant. For example: 'DEMO=1' or 'DEMO=0'.

```
PBCompiler MyProgram.pb /exe "MyProgram.exe" /constant MY_STRING="Hello World"
```

As you can see from this example, when defining a constant on the command line you must not use the '#' character to prefix the constant name and there must be no space around the equals sign ('='). Also, if you are defining a String constant, I would advise enclosing it within double quotation marks as in my example. This is not one hundred percent necessary because the compiler tries to automatically convert it into a String if they are missing, but it may get confused and error if that String contains spaces. For safety sake, use double quotes for Strings.

/Debugger
If this compiler option is used by itself, the standalone (GUI) debugger is enabled to debug the resulting temporary executable file. If this option is used with the '/exe' option, the console debugger is embedded into the resulting executable file. The console debugger will then display a console window along with the launched executable file to allow command line based debugging of that program. Here's these two examples:

```
PBCompiler MyProgram.pb /debugger
PBCompiler MyProgram.pb /exe "MyProgram.exe" /debugger
```

/DLL
This compiler option allows you to create a DLL (dynamically linked library) file from your PureBasic source code. If this option is used during compilation, the resulting DLL file is created within the 'PureBasic\Compilers' folder called 'PureBasic.dll'. This file can then be renamed as you see fit. As a byproduct of creating a DLL like this, a static library file called 'PureBasic.lib' and an export file called 'PureBasic.exp' is also created in the same folder.

```
PBCompiler MyProgram.pb /dll
```

PureBasic source code files that are used to create DLL's are usually composed of procedures only. Some of these procedure are specially named to give you extra functionality within your compiled library. Read further on in this chapter for more information on DLL's.

/DynamicCpu
This command line option is almost equivalent to specifying all the options; '/mmx', '/3dnow', '/sse' and '/sse2' in one go. If your program's source code contains ASM routines that support all these processor extensions and you use the '/dynamiccpu' compiler option then the resulting executable file will contain all of the processor specific code. What's happens when this executable is run, is it looks at the processor type of the system it's being run on and chooses between the compiled routines to select the one that matches that particular processor's architecture. Meaning that it dynamically uses different code contained within it for different processors. This could make the executable file larger than usual because it may contain many versions of the same routine, but it can make the program run faster because those different routines can contain specific processor optimized code.

```
PBCompiler MyProgram.pb /exe "MyProgram.exe" /dynamiccpu
```

/Exe "FileName"
This compiler option is pretty straightforward, the String after the '/exe' part is the name that the executable file will be compiled as. A String specifying the executable name must always follow the '/exe' part and must always be contained within double quotation marks, otherwise you may get unexpected results. Also when compiling a program like this, the generated executable file will be placed in the same directory as the source code used to compile it.

```
PBCompiler MyProgram.pb /exe "MyProgram.exe"
```

/Icon "IconName"
This compiler option lets you specify an icon on your hard drive that you would like your executable to use. The String after the '/icon' part must be defined and must be enclosed in double quotation marks, as this is the location on your hard drive of where the desired icon file is located. The String containing the location of the icon file can be a relative String if needed, as in this example:

```
PBCompiler MyProgram.pb /exe "MyProgram.exe" /icon ".\icons\MyIcon.ico"
```

/IgnoreResident "FileName"

This is a command line only option which enables you to stop an installed resident file from loading during compilation. This is handy if you want to re-compile a resident file that is already installed in the 'PureBasic\Residents' folder. If the installed resident file is not ignored and you are re-compiling that file again, you may get 'Already defined' errors.

```
PBCompiler MyProg.pb /resident "MyResid.res" /ignoreresident "MyResid.res"
PBCompiler MyProgram.pb /exe "MyProgram.exe" /ignoreresident "MyResid.res"
```

The first line shows an example of compiling a resident file while ignoring the previously installed version. The second line is an example of what you may need to do if you are re-defining constants or structures in your program that are already present in an installed resident file.

/InlineAsm

This compiler option enables inline assembly programming within your '*.pb' file. In other words if you have used any assembly language commands within your PureBasic source code, you should enable this feature so the assembly commands are passed correctly to the PureBasic compiler.

```
PBCompiler MyProgram.pb /exe "MyProgram.exe" /inlineasm
```

/LineNumbering

This compiler option adds support for internal line numbering of commands within your executable file. This is useful for third party debugging tools or if you are using the built-in 'OnError' library.

```
PBCompiler MyProgram.pb /exe "MyProgram.exe" /linenumbering
```

Be aware that if you are using line numbering for your executable, it could slow down the speed with which it runs, because you are adding slightly more 'overhead' to the executable than usual.

/Linker "FileName"

This is a command line only option which enables you to pass a file straight to the linker which can contain linker commands.

```
PBCompiler MyProgram.pb /exe "MyProgram.exe" /linker "MyLinkerCommands.txt"
```

/MMX, /3DNow, /SSE And /SSE2

These four compiler options create very processor specific executables depending on which option is used. Only one of these options can be used at a time, as they tailor the executable file to only include routines that specifically run on processors that support such extensions. If you have created many routines using ASM that support all processor extensions, only the ones which match the compiler option will be used in the final executable. For example, if you create an executable that uses the '/mmx' compiler option, only the MMX routines used in the source code will be used for the final executable and that executable will only run on processor that support the MMX extensions.

```
PBCompiler MyProgram.pb /exe "MyProgram.exe" /mmx
PBCompiler MyProgram.pb /exe "MyProgram.exe" /3dnow
PBCompiler MyProgram.pb /exe "MyProgram.exe" /sse
```

```
PBCompiler MyProgram.pb /exe "MyProgram.exe" /sse2
```

/Quiet
This is a command line only option which suppresses all unnecessary text output from the command line compiler. This is handy when you want to use the compiler as an external tool from another code editor, etc.

```
PBCompiler MyProgram.pb /exe "MyProgram.exe" /quiet
```

/ReAsm
This is a command line only option which enables you to re-assemble and compile a previously exported, commented '*.asm' file. These commented '*.asm' files are created using the '/commented' compiler option.

```
PBCompiler PureBasic.asm /reasm
```

When using this command, the '*.asm' file to be re-assembled must be in the 'PureBasic\Compilers' folder, otherwise a compiler error will occur.

/Resident "FileName"
This is a command line only option which enables you to create a resident file from a standard '*.pb' file. Resident files are usually composed of constant and structure definitions only.

```
PBCompiler MyProgram.pb /resident "MyResident.res"
```

A String enclosed in double quotation marks must be defined after the '/resident' part of this compiler option, as this defines the name of the new resident file. If this String is missing or not enclosed in double quotes, then a compiler error will occur. Using this compiler option will create a resident file inside the same directory as the source code file.

/Resource "FileName"
This compiler option is for Microsoft Windows only as it appends a Windows resource file to the compiled DLL or executable file. A String enclosed in double quotation marks must follow the '/resource' part of this compiler option which specifies the resource file to add. Only one resource file may be added but this file can contain references to other resource files if needed. The resource file must not be a compiled resource either, but be an ASCII file containing directives.

```
PBCompiler MyProgram.pb /exe "MyProgram.exe" /resource "MyResource.rc"
```

/Standby
This command line option is used by the IDE to load the compiler into memory to wait for commands to be passed to it. This is not a command that normal users would usually use because documentation is very scarce regarding how to interface with the compiler once it's loaded into memory.

/Subsystem "SubsystemName"

This compiler option enables you to specify a subsystem to use for the compilation of your program. I've given subsystems a full description a little earlier in this chapter, so I'll not repeat myself here. By default there are a few built-in subsystems which you can choose from when compiling your program, these are:

Windows:
```
PBCompiler MyProgram.pb /exe "MyProgram.exe" /subsystem "NT4"
PBCompiler MyProgram.pb /exe "MyProgram.exe" /subsystem "OpenGL"
```

Linux:
```
PBCompiler MyProgram.pb /exe "MyProgram.exe" /subsystem "GTK2"
```

MacOS X:
```
PBCompiler MyProgram.pb /exe "MyProgram.exe" /subsystem "GTK"
PBCompiler MyProgram.pb /exe "MyProgram.exe" /subsystem "GTK2"
```

As you can see from these examples, after the '/subsystem' part of this compiler option you must specify a subsystem name, enclosed within double quotation marks.

/Thread

This compiler option will enable thread-safety for the compiled executable file. This option should be used if you are compiling a program that makes use of threads. One thing to remember when using this command is that the resulting executable file may run slightly slower than a non-threadsafe one. This is because of the extra 'overhead' needed to make the executable thread safe.

```
PBCompiler MyProgram.pb /exe "MyProgram.exe" /thread
```

More information about threads can be found later in this chapter.

/Unicode

This compiler option will enable unicode support for your compiled executable. Unicode is a character encoding scheme using 16 bits (2 Bytes) per character to allow all characters of all major world languages, living and dead, to be encoded in a single character set. Using this compiler option means that all PureBasic commands used and the internal String management will be fully unicode compatible.

```
PBCompiler MyProgram.pb /exe "MyProgram.exe" /unicode
```

/Version

This is a command line only option, and its only function is to print the version of the PureBasic compiler used in the command line interface window. This compiler option overrides any others used in the same shell command.

```
PBCompiler /version
```

/XP

This compiler option is for Microsoft Windows XP only. It adds Windows XP skin support to your executables, to make them show themed gadgets and windows correctly when a theme is used for the Windows GUI.

```
PBCompiler MyProgram.pb /exe "MyProgram.exe" /xp
```

Parsing Command Line Parameters

Sometimes when developing programs using PureBasic you may want to create command line tools that accept certain parameters when being launched using a shell command. This is a similar way to how the PureBasic compiler works. The program is started and parameters are passed to it, the values of these parameters determine what function the program performs. In this section I will show you how to parse these types of parameters that are passed to your program.

Explaining Parameters?

When passing parameters (sometimes called arguments) to command line programs, you need to keep in mind how they are passed and what actually constitutes a parameter. For example, if we take this compiler example from earlier on in this chapter:

```
PBCompiler MyProgram.pb /exe "MyProgram.exe"
```

This shell command instructs the operating system to launch the 'PBCompiler' program and pass three parameters, ('MyProgram.pb', '/exe' and '"MyProgram.exe"'). Even though we are only using one compiler option after the '*.pb' file name (which is the first parameter), that option consists of two further parameters.

When passing parameters to programs like this, the program makes a decision about how many parameters are passed based on how many spaces it sees after the program name. If you need to have spaces within a single parameter, then you must enclose that parameter in double quotation marks. For example, all these shell commands would pass two parameters to the program called 'MyProgram'.

```
MyProgram /a 105
MyProgram /play /now
MyProgram /play "Me And My Shadow"
MyProgram "Put It In The" "Back"
```

As you can see from these examples, parameters can be either numbers or Strings, but when they are passed into your program they are all automatically converted into Strings. If you are enclosing parameters in double quotation marks when passing them (especially for parameters with spaces) you should keep in mind that these quotation marks are stripped out before the String is actually passed, so you are only passing the String inside them, not the quotes.

Reading Passed Parameters From Inside Your Program

When parameters are passed to your program from a shell command, they are stored internally for you to read in your program when you see fit. By calling the 'ProgramParameter()' command you can return one parameter at a time from this internal list. When all parameters have been returned by the 'ProgramParameter()' command, it then returns an empty String. Here is an example program showing how to list all parameters that are passed to a program:

```
NumberOfParameters.l = CountProgramParameters()
Text.s = "List of parameters passed:" + #LF$ + #LF$

If NumberOfParameters > 0
  For x.l = 1 To NumberOfParameters
    Text.s + ProgramParameter() + #LF$
  Next x
Else
  Text.s + "None"
EndIf

MessageRequester("Info", Text)
```

The first line of this example uses the 'CountProgramParameters()' command, this returns the exact number of valid parameters that was passed to your program. After this command has been called, I then use a 'For' loop to call the 'ProgramParameter()' command over and over again to return all parameters. If I compile this piece of code to an executable file and called it 'ListParameters.exe', I could then pass some parameters to it using a shell command, like this:

```
ListParameters /one /two /three
```

These parameters are just made up for this example so you can use any you like, I've used a forward slash to prefix my parameters as this seems to be the norm for console programs I use. Once this command has been entered and the program has been launched. The value stored in the 'NumberOfParameters' variable would be '3' and each time the program calls the 'ProgramParameter()' command, each one of these parameters will be returned in sequence. The first time it's used, the 'ProgramParameter()' command will return '/one', the second time it's used it will return '/two' and the third time '/three' is returned. If I called the 'ProgramParameter()' command a forth time, it would return an empty String.

Testing Command Line Parameters Using The IDE

When developing an application in the IDE that will accept command line parameters, you don't really want to be compiling to a final executable and calling that through a command line interface every time you want to test it. Instead of this long process, the PureBasic IDE helps you out by providing a field where you can enter command line parameters that you want to pass to your program when you compile it. This field can be found in the 'Compiler Options' window, which is accessible from the 'Compiler' menu. If you look three quarters of the way down you will see the field marked 'Executable Commandline'. This is where you enter parameters that you would like passing to your program when you hit the 'Compile/Run' button. Try entering some parameters in there to test the examples in this section.

Making Decisions Based On Parameters

If you are using command line parameters to control the functionality or output of your program, you will need it to perform different actions depending on the values of those passed parameters. Sometimes you will need your program to do something completely different if a particular parameter is passed. Making decisions based on what parameters have been passed is not as hard as you may think, you just use regular 'If' and 'Select' statements to test the values of the parameters.

This next example demonstrates this approach, testing to see if one or more of the parameters passed is either, 'Mouse', 'Cat' or 'Dog'. Try passing one or two of these parameters to this program to see the output:

```
;Count parameters
NumberOfParameters.l = CountProgramParameters()

;Add all command line parameters to a linked list
Global NewList Parameters.s()
If NumberOfParameters > 0
  For x.l = 1 To NumberOfParameters
    AddElement(Parameters())
    Parameters() = UCase(ProgramParameter())
  Next x
EndIf

;Check to see if a particular parameter was passed
Procedure ParameterPassed(Parameter.s)
  ForEach Parameters()
    If Parameter = Parameters()
      ProcedureReturn #True
    EndIf
  Next
  ProcedureReturn #False
EndProcedure

;Check to see if the parameter 'Mouse' was passed
If ParameterPassed("MOUSE")
  MessageRequester("Info", "'Mouse' was specified as a parameter.")
EndIf
;Check to see if the parameter 'Cat' was passed
If ParameterPassed("CAT")
  MessageRequester("Info", "'Cat' was specified as a parameter.")
EndIf
;Check to see if the parameter 'Dog' was passed
If ParameterPassed("DOG")
  MessageRequester("Info", "'Dog' was specified as a parameter.")
EndIf
```

If you look closely at this example I'm using the 'UCase()' command (Helpfile:Reference Manual->General Libraries->String->UCase) to convert all passed parameters to uppercase lettering. This so I can perform String comparisons on the parameters without worrying about its case. If you do this in your programs, then you can just use uppercase String comparisons, as shown in the 'If' statements. This is good practice because it doesn't matter how the user enters parameters (uppercase, lowercase, mixed case) they will always be converted to uppercase before the 'If' comparison.

Giving your programs command line support by utilizing parameters in this way may seem an old fashioned way of doing things, and to be honest, it is. However, giving your users the potential to use your application or tool from the command line will get more people using it and will give the program more versatility. It's definitely something to think about when creating a piece of software.

A Closer Look At Numeric Data Types

Numeric data types allow you to store numbers in several different formats and each type allows you to use slightly different amounts of memory to store those numbers. This doesn't sound like such a big deal but the amount of memory a numeric type uses strictly defines its numerical limit. If you look back in Chapter 2 at Fig.2, you will see a diagram detailing all PureBasic's numerical type limits. These limits are imposed by the finite number of bits contained within the memory that these data types allocate. For example, if you look at the Byte data type (.b) you will see that it uses one Byte of memory, which consists of eight binary digits or 'bits'. These bits can only be manipulated in a finite amount of ways to express numbers. In fact, eight bits can only be ordered into two hundred and fifty six (256) unique patterns, with each bit being either '1' or '0'. This means only two hundred and fifty six unique numbers are capable of being expressed by an eight bit binary number (Byte).

In this section I will explain to you, how numbers are stored in memory and how binary numbers are actually calculated. Hopefully this will give you a little more insight into the inner workings of not only PureBasic but of computers in general.

When dealing with numbers in computer languages there needs to be made a clear distinction between integers and floating point numbers. Integers are numbers which can be positive or negative but do not contain a decimal point. Floating point numbers on the other hand can be positive or negative but always contain a decimal point. This has been explained earlier in this book but I thought I would refresh your memory here.

What Is Binary?
Binary Notation, or base-two as it's sometimes called, is a numerical system where the digits of a binary number can only have one of two values, '0' or '1'. Similar to the Decimal system (which is sometimes called base-ten) each position of a binary digit represents another quantity.

Let me explain this concept a little more clearly, here is an example of a decimal number:

```
542
```

In this example, the '2' digit is in the position associated with the quantity one, the '4' digit is in the position associated with the quantity ten and the '5' digit is in the position associated with the quantity hundred. Each associated quantity is ten times the quantity to its right. To find out what number this represents you simply multiply the value of each digit by the quantity associated with that digit's position and then add those results together i.e. ('5' x hundred) + ('4' x ten) + ('2' x one) = '542' (five hundred and forty two).

This is also how binary (base-two) numbers work when dealing with integers. The position of each digit in a binary number is also associated with a quantity, except that the quantity associated with each position is twice that of the position to it's right, this is base-two after all. While that might sound like a mouthful, its surprisingly easy to understand using a diagram. Look at Fig.44.

Unsigned Byte

Binary Digits (bits)	0	1	0	0	1	1	0	1	= 77
Associated Quantity	128	64	32	16	8	4	2	1	

———— 8 bit number ————
(1 byte)

Numerical range: '0' to '255'   Fig. 44

To extract the value represented by this binary number, we follow the same procedure as in decimal (base-ten). We multiply the value of each digit by the quantity associated with its position then add the results. For example, the value represented by '01001101' as shown in Fig.44 is '77'. Since binary notation only uses the digits 0 and 1, this 'multiply-and-add' process demonstrated earlier with base-ten numbers, reduces to just addition of the quantities associated with the positions occupied by a binary value of '1'. So, if you look at Fig.44 and add up the quantities of where a binary value of '1' appears, you get: '64 + 8 + 4 + 1 = 77'.

You can probably see now from Fig.44 that only a finite amount of numbers can be represented in binary using only this number of bits. This is why certain types have certain limits, they simply run out of bits to use. Bigger types work in exactly the same way, they just have more bits to calculate.

Signed And Unsigned Integers
Earlier on in Fig.2, you can see many of PureBasic's integer types range from negative to positive numbers. These are known as Signed number types, because their values can potentially contain a negative sign. Unsigned types, on the other hand, refer to integer types which have a numerical limit that ranges from zero to a larger positive number. The PureBasic Character type is an example of an unsigned integer type and which is also shown in Fig.2. Because there is only a finite number of bits allocated by these data types, there are two methods needed to interpret these binary numbers depending on wether they should be read as signed or unsigned.

If you take a look at Fig.45 every integer data type has two ways of being read. The Byte for example, can be both signed and unsigned, and both flavors can contain a value taken from a range of two hundred and fifty six (256) possible numbers, including zero...yes, zero is a number too!

Data Type	Numerical Range
Signed Byte	`-128 to 127`
Unsigned Byte*	`0 to 255`
Signed Word	`-32768 to 32767`
Unsigned Word*	`0 to 65535`
Signed Long	`-2147483648 to 2147483647`
Unsigned Long*	`0 to 4294967295`

* Not available in PureBasic v4 (maybe in future versions?) Fig. 45

Reading Unsigned Integers Using Binary

An unsigned number is easy to represent in binary as we have seen from Fig.44. You just keep turning the bits to 1 and add together the associated values where a '1' appears. For example, the maximum value of an unsigned Byte expressed using binary is '11111111' ('255') where all the bits are set to '1'. Nice and simple.

Reading Signed Integers Using Binary

A signed integer follows slightly different rules to express using binary. PureBasic uses a system called Two's Complement to express signed integers. In two's complement form, the left most bit of a signed binary number (sometimes called the most significant bit) indicates if the actual sign (-) is present in the integer. If the left most bit is '0' the integer being expressed by the bits is a positive integer and can be read by using the unsigned binary method explained earlier. If the left most bit is '1' the integer being expressed is negative and must be read using two's complement form, as explained below.

Because the left most sign bit is reserved to indicate wether a sign is present or not you are only left with the remainder of bits to express the rest of the integer. Let's take a Byte as an example again, if we left the sign bit as '0' to express a positive number that only leaves us with seven remaining bits to make a number out of, so we'll turn all these to '1', like this: '01111111'. This is now expressing the maximum positive integer that a signed Byte can hold, which in this case is '127'.

If we want to express a negative integer using binary we have to do it in a slightly different manner. Let's first look at the unsigned binary representation of the number '9', which is '00001001'. The left most bit is zero so we know for definite this is a positive integer. To convert this to two's complement form and express it as a negative integer, we first need to invert the bits and then we add one ('1') to the inverted binary number. So the number '-9' looks like this: '11110111'. When I talk about inverting the bits, what I mean is that if a bit is '0' then change it to '1', and if a bit is '1' then change it to '0' and do this for all bits contained in the type. As you can see the left most bit is now '1' indicating this binary number represents a negative (signed) integer. Inverting the bits and adding '1' to a positive integer is the two's complement method of expressing that integer's negative form.

To convert this negative integer back to its positive form, you follow exactly the same procedure. After inverting '-9' ('11110111') the binary number now looks like this: '00001000', we then add one ('1') to this number and it becomes: '00001001', which gives us a positive '9' when read using the normal unsigned binary method. Fig.46 shows a signed Byte visually holding the value of '-9'.

Signed Byte

Sign (-) Bit

Binary Digits (bits)	1	1	1	1	0	1	1	1	= -9
Associated Quantity		64	32	16	8	4	2	1	

———— 8 bit number ————
(1 byte)

Numerical range: '-128' to '127'   Fig. 46

Even though I've used the Byte type in these last few sections to describe how to read binary, these methods are universal for any numerical integer type no matter what its size. In all integer types the associated quantities of each bit position grows by a power of '2' as you move to the left within the binary number. In signed binary numbers, the left most bit is always the sign bit.

Floating Point Numbers And Binary
A floating point number is a number which contains a decimal point and which can be either negative or positive. Numbers like these are stored in a way that makes the point 'float' around the number, so that it is possible to store very large or very small numbers. Using a storage method like this makes it possible to have a huge range of numbers that can be stored but at the cost of numeric accuracy. Even though floating point numbers are extremely versatile, you have to account for the fact that some precision may be lost if you are storing a lot of decimal places.

PureBasic currently supports two data types to handle floating point numbers, these are the normal Float type and the Double type. The difference between these two types is the amount of bits they use to store the floating point number. A Float uses 32 bits (4 Bytes) and a Double uses 64 bits (8 Bytes), so obviously Doubles are a lot more accurate for holding large numbers. So why not use Doubles all the time, instead of Floats? Well, speed for one. Floats can be a lot faster at reading from memory especially when using large Float arrays. This is because of the fact that you are only retrieving half the number of Bytes from memory than you would be with Doubles. Usually programs such as games tend to use Floats while programs that need more accuracy tend to use Doubles.

Storing Floating Point Numbers Using Binary
Because of the special nature of floating point numbers, which need to store a decimal point along with a large number to the right, left or both sides of that point, a different method of storing numbers in binary is used. This method is quite complicated and is described in the 'IEEE 754' standard for binary

encoding of floating point numbers. I'll see if I can describe it as simply as possible.

First, all floating point numbers are stored in three binary parts. These parts are the Sign, the Exponent and the Significand. These three parts all fall inside the bit limit as defined by using either a Float or a Double. See Fig.47.

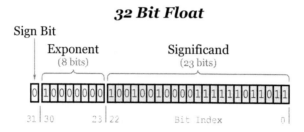

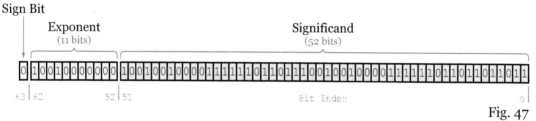

Fig. 47

Here, you can see how the type is divided internally to support each of the three sections. Now all we need to understand is how a floating point number is encoded to fit into these sections. The sign bit is probably the easiest of the sections to explain. If the number to be encoded is positive then the sign bit will be '0' and if the number is negative the sign bit will be '1'. Let's start with an example number and I'll demonstrate how it is encoded into a 32 bit Float. Let's take the number: '10.625'.

Step One, Encode The Number To Binary
To encode this number to fit within the binary sections of a Float we have to follow several steps. The first, is we have to convert both sides of the decimal point into binary, like this:

'10.625' = '1010.101'

This might look a little odd because you will probably not have seen a decimal point (or radix point as it's more accurately called here) within a binary number. This is only to visualize the number at this stage so don't be alarmed. Encoding a number into binary like this is a little different from what was explained before, because you are dealing with a whole number on one side of the radix point and a fraction on the other side. The whole number part is the easy one to encode because it follows standard unsigned binary encoding as explained in Fig.44, i.e. decimal '10' = binary '1010'. The fractional part on the other hand uses a similar method but in the binary representation of a fraction the associated quantities are fractions themselves instead of whole numbers. Also, for these binary numbers, we don't pad them with unnecessary zeros.

In standard unsigned binary, associated quantities start at '1' and increase by a factor of '2' the further left you go along the binary number, while in fractional binary the associated quantities start at '0.5' and decrease by a factor of '2' the more right you go along the binary number. Take a look at Fig.48.

Encoding A Fractional Decimal Into Binary

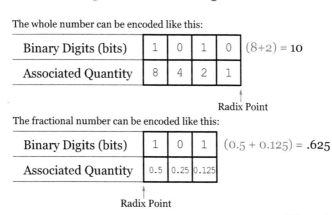

Original Number: **10.625**

The whole number can be encoded like this:

Binary Digits (bits)	1	0	1	0	(8+2) = 10
Associated Quantity	8	4	2	1	

Radix Point

The fractional number can be encoded like this:

Binary Digits (bits)	1	0	1	(0.5 + 0.125) = .625
Associated Quantity	0.5	0.25	0.125	

Radix Point

Fig. 48

Here, you can see the associated quantities of the fractional binary number starting at '0.5' and decreasing by a factor of '2' in each place moving to the right, so they are calculated as, '0.5', '0.25', '0.125', etc. The more places you go to the right the more precision a fractional number can contain. Because our number has a fractional part of '.625' it is easily represented by '0.5' + '0.125' so that's where the binary '1's appear.

Knowing how a fractional number is represented in binary does not necessarily help you to encode it though, especially when dealing with huge decimal fractions. Luckily though there is an easy way to encode these numbers using the 'doubling' trick.

First, we take our starting fraction '.625' and double it and see if it is above or equal to '1.0'. If it is then we mark down a binary '1'. We then take the fractional part of the last sum and double and test it again. If at any stage the doubling does not produce a number which is equal to or above '1.0' then we mark down a binary '0'. Here's how this works in practice:

.625 * 2 = 1.25 - This is above or equal to '1.0' so we mark a binary '1'.
.25 * 2 = 0.5 - This is not above or equal to '1.0' so we mark a binary '0'.
.5 * 2 = 1.0 - This is above or equal to '1.0' so we mark a binary '1'.

When no more fractional parts are available to test or you have run out of bits to fill you stop calculating. If you now look at the resulting binary digits from these calculations reading from top to bottom you can see it's '101', exactly as expected for '.625'.

Now we know how to encode a fractional decimal number into binary, I can continue to explain how these numbers are encoded in 32 bit Floats. So, step one was first to encode our number into a binary form, like this:

'10.625' = '1010.101'

Step Two, Move The Radix Point And Calculate The Exponent

In this step we need to move the radix point, as this will not be encoded in the final binary number. Because the radix point defines where the decimal point is in the decimal version of this number we do actually need to remember where it was, so we can put it back to its original position when it's decoded. To do this we shift the radix point along the binary number until there only remains a '1' to it's left. Any extra zeros on the left can be ignored but their positions must be counted if the radix point moves past them. Look at this example:

'1010.101' (original)
'1.010101' (Radix point moved 3 places to the left)

When moving the radix point we need to note of how many places we move it. Here, I've moved it '3' places to the left to leave a leading '1' to the left of it, so the number of places the radix point has moved will be a positive number. If the original binary number was something like '0.0001101' then I would have to move the radix point to the right to leave a single leading '1' to the left of it (disregarding the zeros) which would give me a negative radix point movement value of '-4'. (I'll explain about this '1' always being to the left in a minute).

The number of places you need to move the radix point to leave only a leading '1' to its left, is noted as the Exponent. This exponent is then added to a preset number (depending on what size of floating point type you are using), to make sure it is encoded as an unsigned number. For example, when using a 32 bit Float the number you have to add '127' this is called the Exponent Bias.

In our original example, we moved the radix point '3' places to the left (which is a positive 3), so we add '127' to '3' and get '130'. This number is then encoded to binary using the standard unsigned method as described in Fig.44, which would be '10000010'. This is then saved in the exponent section within the 32 bit Float as shown in Fig.47. Because we save the number of places the radix point has moved, this means that the bit count of the exponent section actually imposes a limit on how far we can record the radix point moving. This limit is '127' places to the left and '(-)126' places to the right. Anything above '127' and the number is considered to be 'infinite' and anything below '-126' the number is considered to be a denormalized number of which is a special case where the exponent is kept at '-126' and the leading '1.' is changed to a leading '0.'.

Step Three, Calculate The Significand

The significand is the part of the floating point number which contains the significant part of the number. In fact this is where the actual number is stored, the exponent merely tells you where the radix point should sit relative to the significand. After moving the radix point in step two, our binary number should now look like this: '1.010101'

To calculate the significand from this, we first completely disregard the '1' at the beginning of this binary number. This '1' never has to be encoded because it is always there, any number we want to encode using a floating point type will always have a '1' there, so it's completely safe to disregard as long as we remember to put it back when we decode this binary number. Disregarding this number allows us to gain one more bit within the significand to help us represent the original decimal number. Remember the more bits we have, the more precisely we can be to represent the original.

After disregarding the '1' in front of the binary number the radix point is then meaningless too, so we can get rid of that as well. So now the binary number looks like this: '010101'. This is our significand. If the significant is smaller than 23 bits as in this example we need to pad this number with zeros to make it up to the 23 bit length it should be. These zeros must be on the right hand side, like this: '01010100000000000000000'. This is now the full significand which is saved in the significand section within the 32 bit Float as shown in Fig.47.

So in total the binary representation of the number '10.625' would be:
'0 10000010 01010100000000000000000'

Limitations Of Floating Point Numbers
Even though floating point numbers are very versatile, they are also inherently inaccurate because of the way the number is stored using binary. Do not be shocked to see a number being read from a Float that was different to what was originally assigned to it. Only about 7 decimal digits are represented correctly in single precision Floats, and about 16 in Doubles. Precision of decimal numbers can also be lost when performing arithmetic with floating point numbers too, chipping away at the overall precision again. This is always something to keep in mind when using Floats and Doubles.

Using Binary Numbers Directly In PureBasic
Binary numbers can be assigned to variables directly by using the '%' prefix. Using the percent sign like this should not be confused with the modulo operator from Chapter 3 (An Introduction To Operators) even though they use the same symbol. PureBasic recognizes this as a binary assignment because there isn't an expression to the left of it and there is no space to the right of it. Here's an example:

```
BinaryVariable.b = %01101101
Debug BinaryVariable
```

All PureBasic's numerical types can be assigned using binary like this.

Pointers

I think its fair to say that pointers in computer programming scare a lot of people. I have no idea why, because pointers can give you immense power when dealing with certain programming problems. Maybe it's the fear of the unknown that makes people avoid them? I don't know, but what I do know is that, when pointers are explained to people properly, they always wonder why they avoided them for so long. This next section is about pointers and how PureBasic creates and uses them and what advantages they give you as a programmer.

So what is a pointer? Well, put simply, a pointer in PureBasic is a variable that holds a numeric address of a location in memory. It's that simple! So what are memory addresses? Well, just think of all the Bytes in memory each being associated with a unique number, as if they are all inside a huge array. Every Byte in memory can be looked up via it's number (address). Because there are thousands of Bytes present in modern computer systems these numbered addresses are usually quite large numbers.

Getting A Memory Address

Now we know that a pointer is just a variable that holds a memory address, we now need to know how to get the memory address of something useful. For this we use special one character functions that return the memory address of the data objects they prefix.

Memory Address Functions

Data Object	Function	Usage Example
Variables	@	@VariableName
Arrays	@	@ArrayName()
Procedures	@	@ProcedureName()
Labels	?	?LabelName

Fig. 49

In Fig.49 you can see the two special memory address functions and which data objects they work with. The '@' function is the most versatile as it works with variables, arrays and procedures. The '?' function is reserved for labels. Here's a simple example showing how to retrieve the memory address of a Byte variable:

```
MyByteVar.b = 100
Debug MyByteVar
Debug @MyByteVar
```

In this example, I've defined a Byte variable called 'MyByteVar' which is given the value of '100', which is all pretty straightforward. In the last line of code, I retrieve that variable's memory address by using '@' in front of its name. Using '@' like this will return the memory address of 'MyByteVar' which I've then echoed to the Debug Output window. If you run the above example and look in the Debug Output window you will see that the original value of '100' is displayed along with the address of the Byte variable beneath it. The address is typically a huge number, usually about seven or eight digits long and this address may change depending on what computer you run it on. This is because some machines may allocate memory for the storage of that Byte in slightly different ways.

When I run the this example on my PC, I get this displayed in the Debug Output window:

```
100
4298004
```

This tells me that the Byte variable which is used to store the value of '100' is located at memory address '4298004'.

Using these special memory address functions, it's possible to get the memory address of all variable types, arrays, procedures and labels, which can be very useful. Here is an example which would be pretty useless in the real world, but demonstrates getting the addresses of all these different data objects and echoing these memory addresses to the Debug Output window:

```
MyByteVar.b = 1
MyWordVar.w = 2
MyLongVar.l = 3
MyQuadVar.q = 4
MyFloatVar.f = 5
MyDoubleVar.d = 6
MyStringVar.s = "Seven"
Dim MyLongArray.l(8)

Procedure MyProcedure(Test.l)
  Debug "Testing my procedure."
EndProcedure

Debug "Byte variable address: " + Str(@MyByteVar)
Debug "Word variable address: " + Str(@MyWordVar)
Debug "Long variable address: " + Str(@MyLongVar)
Debug "Quad variable address: " + Str(@MyQuadVar)
Debug "Float variable address: " + Str(@MyFloatVar)
Debug "Double variable address: " + Str(@MyDoubleVar)
Debug "String variable address: " + Str(@MyStringVar)
Debug "Array address: " + Str(@MyLongArray())
Debug "Procedure address: " + Str(@MyProcedure())
Debug "Label address: " + Str(?Label)

DataSection
  Label:
    Data.s "Testing"
EndDataSection
```

Notice when getting the address of arrays, procedures or labels you do not need to specify any decoration such as type identifiers, array dimensions, or parameters, etc. And even though the array in the above example was defined like this:

```
...
Dim MyLongArray.l(8)
...
```

To get its memory address you just need to use its name with brackets on the end, like this:

```
@MyLongArray()
```

Similarly, when getting the address of a procedure, you only need its name with brackets:

```
@MyProcedure()
```

No types or parameters are needed. The same is also true for labels. Even though they are defined using a colon on the end of their name, the colon is completely omitted when using them with a memory address function, like this:

```
?Label
```

Getting the memory address of all these different data objects is easy because of the simple way that the memory address functions work. To begin with, and for clarity's sake, I would recommend that all retrieved memory addresses are kept within variables, to keep code neat and readable, always remembering to give them good meaningful names.

Creating And Naming Pointers
As I said in the beginning, a pointer is a variable that holds a numeric address of a memory location, but what I didn't say is that a pointer is a special kind of variable that follows a few rules. For a start, pointers in PureBasic are created by using an asterisk '*' as the first character in its name. Like this:

```
*Pointer
```

Secondly, pointers are a numeric type that can change size depending on what computer architecture is compiling the program. For example, on a 32 bit system, a pointer will use 4 Bytes of memory to store a number, while on a 64 bit system, a pointer will use 8 Bytes to store a number.

Also a pointer in PureBasic is not associated with any particular type. Meaning that if you define a pointer using an asterisk along with any of the built-in numeric types, the built-in type is discarded to make sure the pointer is the correct size for your particular computer architecture. So if you defined a pointer like this, using a Byte type:

```
*Pointer.b = @Variable
```

The Byte type is discarded and the pointer will still use 4 Bytes on a 32 bit system and 8 Bytes on a 64 bit system.

This asterisk used as part of the pointer name, is also a permanent character, meaning that once you have defined your pointer then you have to keep it as part of its name when using it. For example, these two are completely different and have no relationship towards each other:

```
MyVariable.l
*MyVariable.l
```

Even though the only difference between these variables is the asterisk, the first variable is a Long type variable, while the second one is a pointer (defined by the asterisk). In other languages, an asterisk prefixes variables to return its value or memory address interchangeably, so it's important to understand that PureBasic doesn't have this extended functionality. They are treated as two entirely different variables.

Using asterisks to create pointer variables is an effective way to differentiate them from other types in PureBasic, and giving you a good visual indication of what data they may hold. In the helpfile, all the syntax examples that deal with memory also use this convention to help programmers know where pointers are needed. Just take a look at some of the syntax examples of the memory commands (Helpfile:Reference Manual->General Libraries->Memory), there are asterisks everywhere.

Using this convention, the first example can be re-coded like this:

```
MyByteVar.b = 100
*MemoryAddress = @MyByteVar
Debug MyByteVar
Debug *MemoryAddress
```

Notice the asterisk prefixing the pointer name? Using this method it's easy to spot which variables are pointers and which are not.

Accessing Memory In A Structured Way, Via A Pointer

In this next example I'll show you how you can use a pointer to act as a structured variable. This pointer is the same size as any other but we can access the memory that it points to in a more structured way.

```
Structure DETAILS
  Age.l
  Height.l
EndStructure

My.DETAILS
My\Age = 32
My\Height = 168

*Pointer.DETAILS = @My

Debug *Pointer\Age
Debug *Pointer\Height
```

Here, you can see I've defined a structure called 'DETAILS' which contains two Long fields. Immediately after that, I define a variable called 'My' using this structure and assign some data to the String fields within it. Now this is where the special function of the asterisk can be helpful when creating a pointer. If we create a structured variable pointer using an asterisk, we are able to set its value by assigning to it a memory address, like this:

```
*Pointer.DETAILS = @My
```

This creates a pointer called '*Pointer' and sets its value to be the memory address of the 'My' structured variable. Because we used a structure as a type when defining this '*Pointer' variable, we can access the memory it points to in a structured way.

So these two lines that are echoing data to the Debug Output window:

```
Debug *Pointer\Age
Debug *Pointer\Height
```

are actually echoing the data contained within the 'My' structured variable, we are just retrieving this data using our newly created pointer. Again, the pointer created here is just a variable which contains a numeric memory address, it's not making a duplicate of any data. Fig.50 shows visually how this works in memory.

The 'My.DETAILS' Structured Variable In Memory

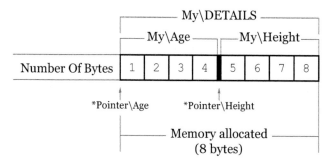

Fig. 50

So what is this useful for? Well, it could be used to return more than one value from a procedure. For example, you could create a 'Static' structured variable within a procedure and assign it values. Then return it's memory address from the procedure. This memory address can then be used to create a structured variable pointer giving you access to that data which was assigned in the procedure. Kind of like this:

```
Structure MEALS
  Breakfast.s
  Dinner.s
  Tea.s
EndStructure

Procedure.l GetMeals()
  Static Gary.MEALS
  Gary\Breakfast = "Cornflakes"
  Gary\Dinner = "Cheese sandwiches"
  Gary\Tea = "Spaghetti bolognese"
  ProcedureReturn @Gary
EndProcedure
```

```
*Gary.MEALS = GetMeals()

Debug *Gary\Breakfast
Debug *Gary\Dinner
Debug *Gary\Tea
```

We use the 'Static' keyword here to preserve the data in the 'Gary' structured variable when the procedure returns, otherwise it will be destroyed. The memory address returned by this procedure is then assigned to the structured variable pointer called '*Gary' (notice the asterisk). We can then access that memory using the 'MEALS' structure. As you can see, very handy indeed.

For added flexibility memory addresses from any variable type can be assigned to a newly created structured variable pointer, even PureBasic's built-in types can be used. Here's a demonstration:

```
Structure SCREENCOORDS
  x.w
  y.w
EndStructure

Coordinates.l = %00000011000000000000010000000000
*Screen.SCREENCOORDS = @Coordinates

Debug *Screen\x
Debug *Screen\y
```

Here, I define a Long type 32 bit variable using binary and call it 'Coordinates'. Then I assign its memory address to a newly created structured variable pointer called '*Screen'. Because the structure I used for the pointer contains two 16 bit Words, the 32 bit value pointed to won't fit into just one of the fields but will overlap across both of them, split in the middle. This allows me to return two values from this one variable, giving you the two 'x' and 'y' values.

Passing A Structured Variable Into A Procedure Via A Pointer

Any structured variable can be passed into a procedure as a pointer to allow that procedure to manipulate it. This is the only way in PureBasic that you can actually pass a structured variable into a procedure. When passing structured variables like this, you are actually passing them 'By Reference', very similar to arrays and linked lists. What this means is that values aren't actually 'copied' into any parameters. Instead a pointer is passed to the procedure and this is used to manipulate the original structured variable. One of the main things you need to consider when using this method, is that when you pass a structured variable into a procedure, the parameter name of that procedure might not have the same name as the structured variable you are passing, but whatever name you give to the parameter, you are still manipulating the original passed structured variable. Here's an example:

```
Structure COORDINATES
  x.l
  y.l
EndStructure
Point.COORDINATES
```

```
Procedure IncreaseValues(*Var.COORDINATES)
  *Var\x + 10
  *Var\y + 10
EndProcedure

Point\x = 100
Point\y = 100

IncreaseValues(@Point)
Debug Point\x
Debug Point\y
```

Here, I've defined a structure called 'COORDINATES' and created a structured variable from it called 'Point'. When all field values have been assigned to this variable, I then pass its memory address to the 'IncreaseValues()' procedure.

In the definition of the 'IncreaseValues()' procedure, I've defined one parameter in the form of '*Var.COORDINATES'. A parameter defined like this tells the procedure to expect a pointer from a structured variable which has been created from the 'COORDINATES' structure. The name '*Var' can be anything you like (as long as it's prefixed by an asterisk), it's merely used as a friendly way to manipulate the passed pointer. So, when I do this in the above procedure:

```
  . . .
  *Var\x + 10
  *Var\y + 10
  . . .
```

What I am really doing is this:

```
  Point\x + 10
  Point\y + 10
```

because the procedure is manipulating the data stored at the passed memory address.

Using this method of passing structured variables to procedures can be very handy for situations where you want to pass lots of information nicely grouped together. For example, Address details, configuration details or any specifically grouped settings or values. Also using this method you can have less parameters being passed to procedures, as you can pass them all in one structured variable. As an example of real world use, I wrote an email procedure a few years ago, to which I could pass a structured variable containing the mail account details along with the recipient, subject and message, etc... It just makes things a little more readable and manageable.

Reading And Writing Values Using Pointers

When you retrieve a memory address, you are able to use it in a variety of different ways. Arguably the most common way is reading values from that memory location or storing new data there. This is called peeking and poking. You use a 'Peek' command to retrieve data from a memory location and use a 'Poke' command to store new data there.

In PureBasic there are eight 'Peek' commands and eight 'Poke' commands to accommodate fully all of the built-in data types. Each one of these commands are named in pretty much the same way, except the last letter of the command name is the same as the type it works with. For example, if you want to peek a Byte from a particular memory address, you would use the command called 'PeekB()' which (as the 'B' in its name suggests) would return a Byte from that location in memory. Similarly, if you wanted to poke a String into a particular memory address, then you would use 'PokeS()'. All these sixteen commands can be read about in more detail in the 'Memory' section within the PureBasic helpfile (Helpfile:Reference Manual->General Libraries->Memory).

Peeking Values Held In Memory Locations

Using a peek command is quite straightforward, you pass it a memory location (maybe being held inside a pointer) and the peek command will return the data that resides there. To return a particular data type you have to use the associated peek command. Here is an example of peeking a Byte from a memory location using the 'PeekB()' command:

```
Weight.b = 30
*Weight = @Weight
ReadValue.b = PeekB(*Weight)
Debug ReadValue
```

Here, I assign the value '30' to a Byte variable named 'Weight'. In the next line I assign its memory address to a pointer called '*Weight' (Notice the asterisk). The next line contains the 'PeekB()' command which actually reads a Byte value from the passed pointer and returns it. You are not forced to use pointers for the address parameter (although it is advisable for the sake of clarity), we could of written this example like this:

```
Weight.b = 30
ReadValue.b = PeekB(@Weight)
Debug ReadValue
```

Here, I use the Byte variable with the memory address function directly, completely doing away with the pointer altogether. I guess it depends what you are most comfortable with. At the end of the day, all the 'Peek' commands need a memory location as a parameter, which ultimately can be supplied by a defined pointer or (more directly) by the return value of a memory address function.

Poking Values Into Memory Locations

Poking values into memory locations is just as easy as using a 'Peek' command. For poking however, you need to supply a new value along with the memory address of where to put it. Here's an example of poking a new Long value into an existing Long variable's memory location:

```
Weight.l = 1024
*Weight = @Weight
PokeL(*Weight, 333)
Debug Weight
```

Here we start with the original value of '1024' being assigned to the 'Weight' variable. Then I've created a pointer called '*Weight' which contains the memory address of 'Weight'. The 'PokeL()' command is then used to poke the value of '333' into the memory location specified in the first parameter. The new value of 'Weight' is then echoed to the Debug Output window.

A Word Of Warning When Poking New Values

Be very careful about where you are poking new values. Using PureBasic's memory commands can be quite dangerous of you don't know what you are doing. For example, the 'Poke' commands have no internal checking to tell you wether or not you can safely poke a value into a particular memory address. You could pass a random number to any 'Poke' command as a memory address and it will quite happily poke a value into it. This is a double edged sword, because you sometimes need this power to re-arrange values in memory but it can lead to problems. If you get it wrong, you could mess up a memory location that some essential program might need to read. Leading to a program crash or something more damaging, like an operating system crash.

To safely poke values into memory you should poke into an existing variable or array's memory location or poke into memory allocated using the 'AllocateMemory()' command (Helpfile:Reference Manual->General Libraries->Memory->AllocateMemory). Ensuring that any values poked into these memory areas do not exceed the allocated space. For example, it would be bad practice to poke a Long value into a Byte variable's memory location, because you are poking 3 more Bytes of data than you should be. This would actually work though, because there is no error checking, but you would overwrite 3 Bytes of potentially essential data, corrupting whatever was there.

Using A Memory Address As A Start Index

When using contiguous blocks of memory to peek values from or to poke values into, it's possible to use the starting Byte's memory address as a starting index for the rest of the block. This is especially useful when using pointers to arrays. Take a look at this example:

```
Dim Numbers.l(2)

Numbers(0) = 100
Numbers(1) = 200
Numbers(2) = 300

*ArrayPointer = @Numbers()

Debug PeekL(*ArrayPointer)
Debug PeekL(*ArrayPointer + 4)
Debug PeekL(*ArrayPointer + 8)
```

After creating an array of Long type variables called 'Numbers' I assign each of it's indices a numerical value, ranging from '100' to '300'. Once this is done I create a pointer called '*ArrayPointer' which holds the array's memory address.

When you create any array like this, all its indices are created in a continuous block of memory, so all data that the array holds is stored next to one another. The memory address returned by a memory address function prefixing an array, is the address of the first index. In effect, the pointer called '*ArrayPointer' holds the memory address of the array index 'Numbers(0)'.

When we use a line of code like this:

```
...
Debug PeekL(*ArrayPointer)
...
```

We are peeking the value from the first index's memory location. You can see this is true by the first value echoed to the Debug Output window. To peek other values from the array, we must use this pointer as a starting location and add to it the number of Bytes we wish to move through memory by. We know that Long types use four Bytes so we can increase the pointer by '4' to retrieve the next Long value held inside the memory that's allocated to this array. The following lines of code, from the above example does just that, they peek values from further into the array's memory by using the array's pointer as a starting location.

```
...
Debug PeekL(*ArrayPointer + 4)  ;This echoes the second Long value: '200'
Debug PeekL(*ArrayPointer + 8)  ;This echoes the third Long value: '300'
```

I've shown this visually in Fig.51. If I was using an array of Bytes then of course I would have to increase the array's pointer by '1' to peek the second Byte and by '2' to peek the third, etc.. Similarly, if I was using Word types, then the pointer would have to be increased by '2' Bytes each time.

The 'Numbers' Array In Memory

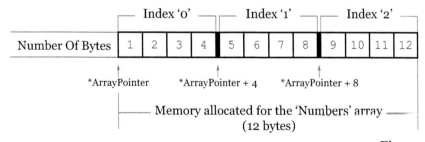

Fig. 51

Threads

A thread is a single sequence of instructions executed as a separate task but still remaining part of the originating program. Any program can have several threads running concurrently, each performing a different task, such as waiting for events or performing a time-consuming job. Threads are an offshoot of the main program, that can execute instructions independently of it. If the originating program is closed, then the thread will automatically be stopped and destroyed too. So, what kind of programs would use threads? Well, any program can potentially use them, but mainly they are coded into programs that need to do more than one thing at once. For example, if you wrote a search tool to search for files on your hard drive, you would probably write the search code to be executed from within a thread. This would then not interfere with the redrawing of the GUI or the event handling in the main loop. The searching could be done independently, without impairing the responsiveness of the main interface. For another example, you may have a program that manipulates large files. Because these files take quite a while to manipulate in whatever way, you may want to deal with them in a thread, so that the main program can be doing other things. These are just two of the many ways threads could defeat a particular programming problem.

Using Threads

Before I continue showing you how to use threads, let me show you a simple program that isn't threaded to base a comparison upon. This example calls a procedure twice, each time to insert values into two different list view gadgets. Notice that when you press the 'Start Test' button, you can't move the window or see any text actually being entered into the gadgets until both procedure calls have finished.

```
Enumeration
  #WINDOW_ROOT
  #LIST_ONE
  #LIST_TWO
  #BUTTON_TEST
EndEnumeration

Procedure InsertText(Gadget.l)
  For x.l = 1 To 25
    AddGadgetItem(Gadget, -1, Str(x))
    Delay(100)
  Next x
EndProcedure

#FLAGS = #PB_Window_SystemMenu | #PB_Window_ScreenCentered
If OpenWindow(#WINDOW_ROOT, 0, 0, 290, 200, "Thread Test", #FLAGS)
  If CreateGadgetList(WindowID(#WINDOW_ROOT))
    ListViewGadget(#LIST_ONE, 10, 10, 130, 150)
    ListViewGadget(#LIST_TWO, 150, 10, 130, 150)
    ButtonGadget(#BUTTON_TEST, 95, 170, 100, 20, "Start Test")
    Repeat
      EventID.l = WaitWindowEvent()
      Select EventID
        Case #PB_Event_Gadget
          Select EventGadget()
            Case #BUTTON_TEST
              InsertText(#LIST_ONE)
              InsertText(#LIST_TWO)
          EndSelect
      EndSelect
    Until EventID = #PB_Event_CloseWindow
  EndIf
EndIf
End
```

You will also notice that when you run this example, the two procedure calls to 'InsertText()' in the main loop are run one after another. Meaning, the first procedure will have to finish before the second one can begin, this is after all, how procedural programs work. In this case, that doesn't really matter to us, because we can't see any updates happening in the list view gadgets because of the 'Delay()' command used in the 'InsertText()' procedure.

Compiling Thread Safe Programs

PureBasic has a compiler setting to create thread safe executables, which is a must for trouble free programming using threads. If you are using the compiler on the command line you can use the '/Thread' compiler option or you can switch on thread safe compilation in the IDE from the 'Compiler Options' dialog box (Menu:Compiler->Compiler Options...->Compiler Options->Create Threadsafe Executable).

If this mode is not enabled and you are compiling and running your program, your finished executable might not be one hundred percent thread safe. This means, that because the threads contained in your program all use shared resources from within your executable, those resources can sometimes get corrupted. This is especially true regarding String usage. Without the thread safety compiler option being used, you may find that Strings used in your program may get corrupted and may return unexpected results.

Using the thread safe compilation mode comes at a small price though. Because of the extra code automatically included in your executable file to handle thread safety, you may find that your program will run slightly slower than one compiled without the thread safety mode. This is why the decision to use threads must be well thought out.

For all beginners using threads in PureBasic, I would recommend that the 'Create Threadsafe Executable' compiler option is always enabled when compiling programs that use threads.

This delay is even delaying the program from processing internal messages to re-draw the user interface or handle the movement of the window within the operating system. We just click the button and have to wait for the procedures to finish before we can interact with the program again. Now imagine if this was an image processing program, and these two procedures take thirty minutes to finish whatever they do. That's a lot of time to wait until you can move that program's window or see any update in the user interface. We wouldn't even be able to draw a progress bar!

If we want both of these procedure calls to run at the same time and be completely independent of the main user interface, we could create two threads to run at the same time as the main program. This is how you could do it:

```
Enumeration
  #WINDOW_ROOT
  #LIST_ONE
  #LIST_TWO
  #BUTTON_TEST
EndEnumeration
```

```
;Insert text into the specified list gadget
Procedure InsertText(Gadget.1)
  For x.1 = 1 To 25
    AddGadgetItem(Gadget, -1, Str(x))
    Delay(100)
  Next x
EndProcedure

#FLAGS = #PB_Window_SystemMenu | #PB_Window_ScreenCentered
If OpenWindow(#WINDOW_ROOT, 0, 0, 290, 200, "Thread Test", #FLAGS)
  If CreateGadgetList(WindowID(#WINDOW_ROOT))
    ListViewGadget(#LIST_ONE, 10, 10, 130, 150)
    ListViewGadget(#LIST_TWO, 150, 10, 130, 150)
    ButtonGadget(#BUTTON_TEST, 95, 170, 100, 20, "Start Test")
    Repeat
      EventID.1 = WaitWindowEvent()
      Select EventID
        Case #PB_Event_Gadget
          Select EventGadget()
            Case #BUTTON_TEST
              Thread1.1 = CreateThread(@InsertText(), #LIST_ONE)
              Thread2.1 = CreateThread(@InsertText(), #LIST_TWO)
          EndSelect
      EndSelect
    Until EventID = #PB_Event_CloseWindow
  EndIf
EndIf
End
```

If you look closely, the only difference between these two examples is how the procedures have been called. Every newly created thread in PureBasic starts life as a standard procedure, defined as usual in the source code and always defined with one parameter. To create a thread from it, you use the 'CreateThread()' command (Helpfile:Reference Manual->General Libraries->Thread->CreateThread) which itself takes two parameters. The first is the memory address of the procedure you want to launch as a thread. The second is a mandatory parameter which can be of any type. You always have to pass this parameter to the procedure even if you use it or not, here I've used it to specify which gadget to insert the text to.

When creating a thread like this, if the 'CreateThread()' command returns a value that is greater than zero the thread has been successfully created and has been immediately launched. Also, this value (if successful) is a Long type thread identifier that can be used with other commands from the 'Thread' library (Helpfile:Reference Manual->General Libraries->Thread).

So let's recap on what rules we must follow to create a thread from a procedure.

1). The thread procedure must have one, and only one parameter.
2). No value can be returned by the thread procedure. If it does return a value, it will be lost.

When this threaded example is run, you will see values being inserted to both of the list view gadgets in realtime. While these value are being inserted, you can also move the program's window around the screen and you will notice that it is now being redrawn and updated as normal. The two newly created threads have become independent parts of the same program, which run at the same time as it. If the main program should close at any time, these two threads will be terminated and closed too.

If you notice any garbled text being inserted into any of the gadgets, you must ensure that the 'Create Threadsafe Executable' compiler option is enabled, as described in the 'Compiling Thread Safe Programs' box.

Waiting For Threads To Finish
Using threads can be a bit tricky sometimes, and can sometimes introduce new problems while solving others. If you use threads in your main program, they are always at the mercy of that program's life span. Meaning, that when the main program finishes or is closed by a user, the associated threads are terminated too.

In PureBasic you can get around this problem by using the 'WaitThread()' command (Helpfile:Reference Manual->General Libraries->Thread->WaitThread). This command will make sure a thread has completed its task before continuing with the main program. Here's an example:

```
Procedure DrawNumbers(Unused.l)
  For x.l = 1 To 20
    PrintN(Str(x))
    Delay(75)
  Next x
EndProcedure

If OpenConsole()
  ThreadID.l = CreateThread(@DrawNumbers(), 0)
  WaitThread(ThreadID)
  Print("Press Return to quit") : Input()
  CloseConsole()
EndIf
End
```

After the thread creation line you can see I've used the 'WaitThread()' command. This takes one parameter which is a thread identifier of a previously created thread. This command will halt normal program execution until the thread specified in the thread identifier has finished running, or in other words, until the procedure used to create the thread has completed its task. The 'WaitThread()' command can take an optional second parameter if needed, which specifies a time-out value in milliseconds. Once this time-out value has elapsed, the program execution is resumed regardless of the specified thread's state. I've not used this optional second parameter in my example because I want to make sure the threaded procedure has finished before you are able to 'End' the program. If you comment out the 'WaitThread' line of code, you will notice that you can press the Return key at any time while the program is running and close it, effectively cutting short the thread's task. With the 'WaitThread()' command in place however, you have to wait for the thread to finish before the keypress is acted on.

Using Shared Resources Safely

When using many threads in the same program, you have to code their actions very carefully, especially if your allowing these threads to use shared resources. Having many threads attempting to read and write to the same file or memory location at exactly the same time is always going to end in corrupted files and a lot of tears. To avoid this, PureBasic provides a simple mechanism for only allowing one thread at a time to gain access to any shared resource. This mechanism is in the form of a Mutex.

A Mutex is a data object that can be used as a lock to stop threads using a resource if it's being used by another thread. Once used in your code to protect a shared resource, a mutex will prevent threads from proceeding unless they have locked it. Once a thread has locked the mutex object, they are then free to use that protected resource. If another thread tries to lock the same mutex in the meantime, that second thread will be effectively paused until the mutex is unlocked by the first one, thus stopping it from reading or writing to the shared resource. Here is an example where I use a mutex to control printing access to the console.

```
Global ConsoleAccess.l = CreateMutex()

Procedure DrawNumbers(ThreadNumber.l)
  LockMutex(ConsoleAccess)
    ConsoleLocate(ThreadNumber * 20, 0)
    ConsoleColor((ThreadNumber + 1) * 3, 0)
    Print("Thread " + Str(ThreadNumber) + " locked.")
    For x.l = 1 To 20
      ConsoleLocate(ThreadNumber * 20, x + 1)
      Print(Str(x))
      Delay(75)
    Next x
  UnlockMutex(ConsoleAccess)
EndProcedure

If OpenConsole()
  EnableGraphicalConsole(#True)
  Thread0.l = CreateThread(@DrawNumbers(), 0)
  Thread1.l = CreateThread(@DrawNumbers(), 1)
  Thread2.l = CreateThread(@DrawNumbers(), 2)
  WaitThread(Thread0)
  WaitThread(Thread1)
  WaitThread(Thread2)
  ConsoleLocate(0, 23)
  Print("Press Return to quit") : Input()
  CloseConsole()
EndIf
End
```

When this code is run, numbers will be printed to the console by each thread, but because I've used a mutex in the 'DrawNumbers()' procedure only one thread at a time can lock the mutex and continue to print to the console.

The first line of code creates a new mutex object, this is done with the 'CreateMutex()' command (Helpfile:Reference Manual->General Libraries->Thread->CreateMutex). This command doesn't require any parameters but when used will return a handle to a newly created mutex object. The returned handle is a 32 bit numeric value, so I've stored it in a Long type variable called 'ConsoleAccess'.

Once the mutex object is created, I then need to make my thread procedures obey its status if it becomes locked or unlocked. To do this I need to add the lock and unlock commands to all thread procedures that are going to use this shared resource. In my example I have only one thread procedure, so I need to add this functionality there. If I were to add more thread procedures that printed to the console, I would have to code them to obey this mutex status too.

In order for a thread to be able to acquire a lock on a mutex object we use the 'LockMutex()' command (Helpfile:Reference Manual->General Libraries->Thread->LockMutex). This command takes one parameter which is the mutex handle of the mutex object we want to lock. If the mutex is currently unlocked, the 'LockMutex()' command will lock it and continue as normal. If, however, the mutex has already been locked by another thread, the 'LockMutex()' command will pause the thread until it is able to lock it itself, which would be after the other thread has unlocked it.

You can see this in action in my mutex example, I lock the mutex before I print to the console and then unlock it when I have finished, allowing other threads to lock it and continue printing. Unlocking the mutex object is as simple as calling the 'UnlockMutex()' command (Helpfile:Reference Manual->General Libraries->Thread->UnlockMutex) while passing a mutex handle as a parameter of the mutex object you want to unlock.

Continuing Your Thread If A Mutex Is Locked

Sometimes when your thread uses a shared resource protected by a mutex, it may be useful for it to not halt entirely when it cant lock an already locked mutex object. You may need your thread to continue doing something else, or provide feedback on the mutex status itself. If this is the case you can use the 'TryLockMutex()' command (Helpfile:Reference Manual->General Libraries->Thread->TryLockMutex). The 'TryLockMutex()' command does what it says on the tin, it tries to lock the mutex specified in the first parameter. If it fails because another thread has already locked the specified mutex, this command will return 'o' (zero). If, however, it is able to lock it, then this command will return a non zero value (meaning a numeric value other than zero).

Here's an example that shows three threads, all trying to lock the 'Lock' mutex object using the 'TryLockMutex()' command. If any of them fail to do so then instead of just sitting idle and waiting until it's unlocked, they display the amount of time they have been waiting in the relevant String gadget.

```
Enumeration
  #WINDOW_ROOT
  #TEXT_ONE
  #TEXT_TWO
  #TEXT_THREE
  #BUTTON_START
EndEnumeration
```

```
Global Lock.l = CreateMutex()

Procedure Update(Gadget.l)
  StartTime.l = ElapsedMilliseconds()
  Repeat
    If TryLockMutex(Lock)
      For x.l = 1 To 20
        SetGadgetText(Gadget, Str(Gadget) + " has locked the mutex. " + Str(x))
        Delay(250)
      Next x
      UnlockMutex(Lock)
      Break
    Else
      Time.s = "(" + Str((ElapsedMilliseconds() - StartTime) / 1000) + " Secs)"
      SetGadgetText(Gadget, Str(Gadget) + " is waiting for mutex. " + Time)
      Delay(1)
    EndIf
  ForEver
  SetGadgetText(Gadget, Str(Gadget) + " has finished.")
EndProcedure

#FLAGS = #PB_Window_SystemMenu | #PB_Window_ScreenCentered
If OpenWindow(#WINDOW_ROOT, 0, 0, 290, 130, "'TryLockMutex()' Test", #FLAGS)
  If CreateGadgetList(WindowID(#WINDOW_ROOT))
    StringGadget(#TEXT_ONE, 10, 10, 270, 20, "")
    StringGadget(#TEXT_TWO, 10, 40, 270, 20, "")
    StringGadget(#TEXT_THREE, 10, 70, 270, 20, "")
    ButtonGadget(#BUTTON_START, 95, 100, 100, 20, "Start")
    Repeat
      EventID.l = WaitWindowEvent()
      Select EventID
        Case #PB_Event_Gadget
          Select EventGadget()
            Case #BUTTON_START
              Thread1.l = CreateThread(@Update(), #TEXT_ONE)
              Thread2.l = CreateThread(@Update(), #TEXT_TWO)
              Thread2.l = CreateThread(@Update(), #TEXT_THREE)
          EndSelect
      EndSelect
    Until EventID = #PB_Event_CloseWindow
  EndIf
EndIf
End
```

Here you can see inside the thread procedure I've used a 'Repeat' loop to keep the thread active even if it can't lock the mutex object. Once the mutex is locked, the thread counts to twenty, updating the String gadget as it goes. Once the count is finished the mutex is unlocked and the 'Break' keyword is used to exit the loop and ultimately end the thread. An 'If' statement is used to test the 'TryLockMutex()' command to decide which course of action is required depending on the status of the mutex.

In Summary
Threads are another useful tool in a programmer's toolbox and like any tool need to be used correctly. When compiling any program that uses threads I would recommend that you always use the thread-safe compiler option and try to use as few threads as possible.

Also I would recommend that you thoroughly read through the entire 'Thread' section in the PureBasic helpfile (Helpfile:Reference Manual->General Libraries->Thread), as it lists many more useful thread commands than I have demonstrated in these pages. Before using threads you need to be completely aware of their uses and limitations.

Dynamic Link Libraries

Dynamic link libraries, also known as dynamically linked libraries and usually abbreviated to just 'DLLs', are Microsoft's implementation of a shared code library for the Microsoft Windows operating system, and as such are only available for use on Microsoft operating systems. DLLs enable programmers to compile code into a shared library to enable many computer programs to use the code contained within. Programs can dynamically connect to the DLL during runtime and use the library's commands. When finished, the program can unload the library, freeing any memory associated with its use.

The DLL concept was one that was thought to decrease program filesize and memory requirements by storing libraries on the hard disk, then loading and using when needed. The reality however, especially prevalent in Microsoft Windows operating systems, is that many different versions of the same DLL are needed by different programs for compatibility reasons, meaning that sometimes many copies of the same DLL (albeit different versions) are required. This particular problem has been given the moniker 'DLL Hell', to imply the problems it can create.

Operating system problems aside, DLLs can be very useful to break a program into a modular approach. If you consider any code that you write to be useful for future programs, you can compile it into a DLL and then it will be available to any program that wants to use it.

PureBasic makes using DLLs simple by providing a built-in library of commands (Helpfile:Reference Manual->General Libraries->Library) to load and use DLLs, while the PureBasic compiler has an option to compile your code to a DLL, making PureBasic the perfect choice for using and creating DLLs.

Creating A DLL
When creating your own DLLs there are a few things you must do as a matter of course, but don't worry they are quite painless. The first thing to remember when writing code to be used as a DLL is that nearly all your code must be written inside procedures. This is because, when a program loads your DLL, it runs the code contained within it by calling the compiled procedure names. Opening a library doesn't automatically run the DLL like a program, instead, you have to call procedures from it. So what do I mean by nearly all code must be written like this? Well, variable and structure definitions don't have to be written inside procedure definitions inside a DLL, but they are the only thing that don't.

When writing code for DLLs there are four special reserved procedure names that are automatically called by Windows once the DLL is loaded. These four procedures are defined like any other DLL procedure but if they are named correctly, Windows will call each one when a particular condition arises surrounding the DLL. I personally define these in all DLLs I write, even if I don't use them. This is so, if ever I need to go back to development of that particular DLL, they are always there ready to use if needed. Here is a list of the four reserved procedure names and what conditions automatically trigger their execution:

'AttachProcess(Instance.l)'
This procedure is called once, when a program loads this DLL. This procedure is the only place in your code that you can define arrays and linked lists. I also use it to define variables and structures too, keeping everything in one place and not having anything outside procedures. The only limitation of this procedure is that DirectX initialization routines must not be written in here.

'DetachProcess(Instance.l)'
This is called when the program closes this DLL. All clean-up code should be in here, such as freeing any resources used by this DLL.

'AttachThread(Instance.l)'
This procedure is called each time a thread is created in the program that loads this DLL.

'DetachThread(Instance.l)'
This procedure is called each time a thread exits in the program that loads this DLL.

As you can see from this list, they are not very complicated to understand and use simple names. If you want to use these automatically called procedures in your DLL, you just need to define the procedure names as shown. The 'Instance' parameter that all of these procedures create, is an instance handle (sometimes called a module handle). This can be handy for more advanced programming. This parameter always needs to be defined if you are using these procedures, even if you don't intend on using the parameter in your code.

So now you know how a DLL should be coded (everything must be inside procedures) and you now know the names of the special reserved procedures, let me show you an example of a simple DLL.

```
ProcedureDLL AttachProcess(Instance.l)
  Global Message.s = "This is my DLL."
EndProcedure

ProcedureDLL ShowAlert()
  MessageRequester("Alert", Message)
EndProcedure
```

Here, I've not used all the special reserved procedures for the sake of brevity, the only one I've shown in this example is the 'AttachProcess()' procedure, within which I define a global String variable called 'Message'. The second procedure in this example is called 'ShowAlert()'. This will be the procedure I call when I open this DLL in another program. As you can see the message requester defined in the 'ShowAlert()' procedure uses the String that's defined in the 'AttachProcess()' procedure.

You will also notice in this example that I've used a different keyword for defining these procedures, instead of 'Procedure' I've used 'ProcedureDLL'. This is essential for defining the special reserved procedures and for any procedure you want to be available for other programs to use. You can still use the standard 'Procedure' keyword to define procedures, but these wont be accessible externally by other programs that load your DLL. These are mainly used for internal calculations, etc.

Once we have coded our DLL in the style above we need to test it. So first things first, let's compile this example into a DLL. Because dynamic link libraries are a little bit different to standard programs, we need to tell the compiler to compile a DLL instead of a regular program. If your using the command line you can do this by using the '/DLL' compiler option or if your using the IDE you can set it visually in the 'Compiler Options' dialog box (Menu:Compiler->Compiler Options...->Compiler Options->Executable Format->Shared DLL). Fig.52 shows where you need to select 'Shared DLL' within the 'Compiler Options' dialog box. Once this has been set you can select 'Create Executable...' in the 'Compiler' menu to actually produce the DLL. This allows you to specify a name and location for your DLL.

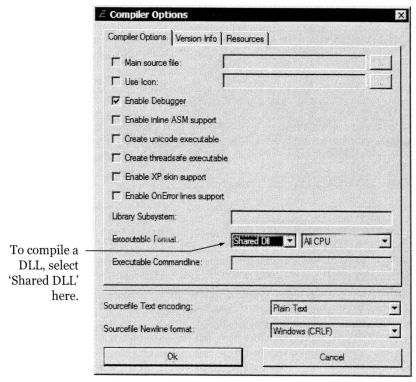

To compile a DLL, select 'Shared DLL' here.

The 'Compiler Options' dialog box
as it appears on Microsoft Windows.

Fig. 52

Once you have compiled your DLL, you will notice that the compiler creates three files. Say for example, we called our DLL, 'Demo.dll', you will end up with these three files:

'Demo.dll'   'Demo.exp'   'Demo.lib'

The first one is of course the compiled DLL, the second is an export file and the third is a static library file. PureBasic only needs the DLL file to use the commands within, but the other files can be useful to people who use this DLL with other languages. If you are going to distribute your DLL file, I would recommend distributing all these files together, but if you are only using your DLL for use with PureBasic, you only need the DLL file and the other two can be discarded.

Using A DLL In Your Code

Using a DLL in a program is easy, you simply open the library and call the procedure you want to run. This is handled in PureBasic by using the commands from the 'Library' section (Helpfile:Reference Manual->General Libraries->Library). Here is an example of how we would call the 'ShowAlert()' procedure from the 'Demo.dll'. Make sure you put the 'Demo.dll' in the same folder as the source code file that contains this code:

```
#LIBRARY_DEMO = 0
If OpenLibrary(#LIBRARY_DEMO, "Demo.dll")
  CallFunction(#LIBRARY_DEMO, "ShowAlert")
  CloseLibrary(#LIBRARY_DEMO)
EndIf
```

First, you open the library using the 'OpenLibrary()' command. This takes two parameters, the first is the PB number you want to associate to this newly opened library and the second is the name of the DLL you want to open. To call a function from within the opened DLL you use the 'CallFunction()' command, which takes two mandatory parameters. The first of which is the PB number of the library that you want to call a procedure from and the second is the name of the procedure you want to call. Notice that when you specify the name of the procedure to call, you don't need to include the brackets on the end. After these two mandatory parameters, the 'CallFunction()' command can take up to twenty (20) optional parameters to pass values as parameters to the called DLL procedure. This is useful if the DLL procedure you are calling needs parameters to be passed. The last command I've used in this example is the 'CloseLibrary()' command, which closes the DLL associated with the PB number passed within its single parameter.

Creating and using DLLs can get a little more complicated than this, but the examples used here show the outline of the whole process. All DLLs consist of procedures and to use them, you just need to open the library and call them (using whatever method), it's that simple.

When using a DLL like this you may be tempted to open the DLL, use a procedure and then immediately close the library. While this is fine for the odd one or two procedures to be called, you may run into performance issues if your program uses the DLL a lot. A better way to do things is that when your program initially starts up, open the DLL ready for use. Then in your program use the DLL procedures when needed. Then, when your program shuts down, close the DLL library along with it. This ensures that the DLL is only opened once and closed only once, removing any performance issues associated with these file operations.

Returning Values From DLL Procedures

When using procedures contained within DLLs, it may sometimes be necessary to return a value from one of them. You can do this by using the 'ProcedureReturn' keyword as you would in any ordinary procedure. Here is a simple example of a DLL procedure coded to return a result.

```
ProcedureDLL.l MultiplyValues(x.l, y.l)
  ProcedureReturn x * y
EndProcedure
```

As you can see it's pretty straightforward and apart from the 'ProcedureDLL' keyword, it looks like any other normal procedure. Compile this piece of code into a DLL and then call it using this code:

```
#LIBRARY = 0
If OpenLibrary(#LIBRARY, "Demo.dll")
  ReturnValue.l = CallFunction(#LIBRARY, "MultiplyValues", 22, 33)
  Debug ReturnValue
  CloseLibrary(#LIBRARY)
EndIf
```

Here, I'm using the 'CallFunction()' command again but this time I'm using two of the optional parameters to pass values to the 'MultiplyValues' DLL procedure. The values I'm passing are '22' and '33'. When these two are passed to the 'MultiplyValues' DLL procedure, it uses them as parameters and processes them accordingly. In this case, it multiplies them together and returns the result. The returned value is then passed back to the 'CallFunction()' command which returns it into our program. I've used a Long type variable called 'ReturnValue' to hold the returned value from the DLL procedure, which I then echo to the Debug Output window.

While this way of returning values is fine for most built-in integer types (see Limitations When Working With DLLs overleaf), for Strings it's a little bit different. For a start, any Strings that you need to return from a DLL must be defined as global. This is to preserve the String after the DLL procedure has returned. Also, when a String is supposed to be returned from a DLL procedure, a memory address for the String is actually returned instead, even if the return type was defined as a String in the procedure definition.

Here's an example to demonstrate this:

```
ProcedureDLL AttachProcess(Instance.l)
  Global MyString.s = "Lorem ipsum dolor sit amet."
EndProcedure

ProcedureDLL.s GetString()
  ProcedureReturn MyString
EndProcedure
```

In this example, I've defined the 'GetString()' procedure to return a String and made sure the 'MyString' variable is global. Try compiling this to a DLL and call it using this code:

```
#LIBRARY = 0
If OpenLibrary(#LIBRARY, "Demo.dll")
 *ReturnValue = CallFunction(#LIBRARY, "GetString")
 Debug PeekS(*ReturnValue)
 CloseLibrary(#LIBRARY)
EndIf
```

You'll see that the 'CallFunction()' command returns a Long type number, so we have to use a numerical variable to hold it. So, I've created a pointer called '*ReturnValue' to hold the returned memory address, from which, I read the String pointed to using the 'PeekS()' command.

Limitations When Working With DLLs
The only real limitations that exist when using DLLs is the passing and returning of values to and from the DLL. Bytes, Words and Longs are relatively painless to use and all DLL commands support them but for the other types there can be a bit of a headache. You've already seen the peculiarity of Strings returned as a memory address instead of the actual String itself. While Floats seem to get completely mangled when being returned from the DLL. Quads and Doubles are completely unsupported using the standard 'Library' commands but can be handled by using PureBasic prototypes which are a little beyond the scope of this book.

To handle returning a Float from a DLL procedure your best bet is to return its memory address instead and then read the returned value using 'PeekF()'. Here is a little example of how to successfully return a Float from a DLL procedure. First, here is the example DLL:

```
ProcedureDLL AttachProcess(Instance.l)
 Global MyFloat.f = 3.1415927
EndProcedure

ProcedureDLL.l GetPi()
 ProcedureReturn @MyFloat
EndProcedure
```

Instead of returning the actual Float value, the DLL procedure 'GetPi()' is defined to return a Long. This allows me to return the Float's memory address. Once this is compiled into a DLL I can call it using this code:

```
#LIBRARY = 0
If OpenLibrary(#LIBRARY, "Demo.dll")
 *ReturnValue = CallFunction(#LIBRARY, "GetPi")
 Debug PeekF(*ReturnValue)
 CloseLibrary(#LIBRARY)
EndIf
```

The memory address, once returned, gets assigned to the '*ReturnValue' pointer, then I use the 'PeekF()' command to read the Float value pointed to in memory. In fact this trick of returning memory addresses can be used in a similar fashion to return memory address to Quads and Doubles, so in effect you can say PureBasic supports returning them.

There is just no way at the minute of passing Quads or Doubles to DLL procedures as parameters using the 'Library' commands.

Using DLLs is quite simple once you've got your head around passing variables to the DLL and how you return and use the returned values. They can make code re-usable by coding it into a neatly packaged library. There are a few issues regarding some built-in types but these can be overcome by using more advanced methods, usually by just returning a pointer to what data you need returned. The more complicated approaches, such as prototypes are unfortunately a little too advanced to be going into at this stage, but you can always look them up in the PureBasic helpfile (Helpfile:Reference Manual->Prototype) to familiarize yourself with them just incase. Just don't be shocked if you can't understand them in your first go. It's also worth reading the whole 'Library' section (Helpfile:Reference Manual->General Libraries->Library) in the PureBasic helpfile to learn about all the commands that can be used with DLLs. This should give you a good understanding of what's available when you decide to develop your first real DLL.

DLL Calling Conventions

When using PureBasic there are two calling conventions that may be used with DLLs. As standard PureBasic assumes that any given DLL uses the 'stdcall' calling convention and that any DLLs created using PureBasic via the 'ProcedureDLL' keyword are also considered to be using the 'stdcall' calling convention. This convention is used as standard in PureBasic because it is the standard calling convention of Microsoft Windows.

If needed though, the 'cdecl' calling convention can be used by using the complementary 'C' functions from the PureBasic 'Library' group of commands. For example, instead of using the 'ProcedureDLL' keyword to create a 'stdcall' DLL procedure you can make that procedure use the 'cdecl' calling convention by using the 'ProcedureCDLL' keyword instead. The same goes for calling procedures from DLLs. Instead of calling a 'stdcall' procedure using the 'CallFunction()' command, you can call a 'cdecl' procedure using the 'CallCFunction()' command.

There are more of these complementary 'C' functions available to be used in PureBasic, look at the helpfile in the 'Library' section for a complete list.

The Windows Application Programming Interface

You are probably wondering why I'm including a section on Windows programming in a book describing a computer language which is cross-platform. Well, I'm including it here because the Windows version of PureBasic has a rather cool and useful ability to be able to use the Windows Application Programming Interface natively. Let me explain a little more fully.

The Windows Application Programming Interface (Usually shortened to just the Win32 API) is found in all new versions of the Microsoft Windows operating system and is a common interface available for all computer programs to use. The Win32 API is basically a command library, contained within many different DLLs installed by default during a normal Windows installation. The API itself is part of the operating system and available to be used by any computer program to carry out almost anything that the operating system is capable of, e.g. opening windows, manipulating Strings, drawing shapes, etc.

Using Win32 API Commands

To use a Win32 API command, a user can simply load the DLL that contains the needed command and then call it, passing any relevant parameters that are needed. This can be done easily in PureBasic using the 'Library' commands but because PureBasic for Windows supports the Win32 API natively, you can use the API as easily as you would any other PureBasic command. For example, other more cumbersome programming languages would have to do things this way to display a simple message requester using the Win32 API:

```
#LIBRARY = 0
If OpenLibrary(#LIBRARY, "User32.dll")
 MB_OK = 0
 Caption.s = "Test"
 TextString.s = "This is a Win32 API Test"
 CallFunction(#LIBRARY, "MessageBoxA", #Null, @TextString, @Caption, MB_OK)
 CloseLibrary(#LIBRARY)
EndIf
```

As you can see, you would have to open the DLL where the required command resides, Here, it's a command called 'MessageBoxA' located in 'User32.dll'. Once this is open, you can call the necessary command passing any parameters needed. This is all well and good, but it's a bit complicated and long winded. In PureBasic you can use that same command like this:

```
MessageBox_(#Null, "This is a Win32 API Test", "Test", #MB_OK)
```

Notice the underscore ('_') after the command name? That denotes that this is an API command and calls it from the necessary DLL automatically. I think you'll agree, this way is a lot simpler and quicker to use. We are using the Win32 API command as if it were another native command in the standard PureBasic package.

The underscore can be used to automatically include any command from the Win32 API. For example, there is a command called 'CharUpper' in the Win32 API for converting Strings to uppercase, we can use this command as if it's a native PureBasic command by using an underscore after it's name and before the brackets, like this:

```
TextString.s = "this is all lowercase text."
CharUpper_(@TextString)
Debug TextString
```

This command needs a memory address of a String as a parameter according to the Win32 API documentation, so that's what I've passed. When you run this example and look in the Debug Output window, you will see the text String has now been converted to uppercase.

Using the Win32 API like this alleviates all the hassle of opening the required DLLs yourself and allows you to use an API command whenever you need to in your code. In fact if your using the Windows version of PureBasic you can mix regular and API commands as much as you like in your source code.

Using Win32 API Constants And Structures
To complement the ease of use of Win32 API commands in the Windows version of PureBasic, all the associated constants and structures have also been predefined. This means that if you ever need a constant or a structure to use with a Win32 API command, they have already been defined internally ready for immediate use.

You can see this in the PureBasic version of the 'MessageBox' command example on the other page, where I've used the constant '#MB_OK' without defining it. This is because the Win32 API constant 'MB_OK' has already been defined internally. To use any Win32 API constant in PureBasic, you just need to add the hash symbol ('#') to the beginning of the Win32 API constant name and it should then be useable as if it was defined natively in your source code.

Win32 API Constant: 'MB_OK'
PureBasic's version: '#MB_OK' (This doesn't need defining, because it already has been internally.)

The same goes for Win32 API structures, whenever you need to use one, you just use it. There is no need to define it. Take a look at this example:

```
DesktopInfo.RECT
DesktopHandle.l = GetDesktopWindow_()
GetClientRect_(DesktopHandle, @DesktopInfo)

DesktopSize.s = "Your current desktop size is: "
DesktopSize + Str(DesktopInfo\right) + " x "
DesktopSize + Str(DesktopInfo\bottom)
Debug DesktopSize
```

Here, I'm using the Win32 API structure called 'RECT' without defining it and then I go on to use the Win32 API commands, 'GetDesktopWindow' and 'GetClientRect' as if they were native commands (notice the underscores?). As you can see from the 'RECT' structure, all Win32 API structures have been defined using uppercase names. This is the standard form when programming using the Win32 API and my naming preference for structures, as described in Chapter 8 (My Coding Format).

This naming convention matches exactly the way in which structures are defined in the Win32 API reference manuals and to avoid confusion when it comes to use them.

For example, if the Win32 API documentation says that a particular command needs a variable defined with the structure 'RECT', then you can just use 'RECT' in your PureBasic source code as a structure.

Take this example text from the Win32 API documentation, detailing the 'BeginPaint' API command:

```
The BeginPaint function prepares the specified window for painting and fills a
PAINTSTRUCT structure with information about the painting.

HDC BeginPaint(
    HWND hwnd, // handle to window
    PAINTSTRUCT lpPaint // pointer to structure for paint information);

Parameters

 hwnd
  Identifies the window to be repainted.

 lpPaint
  Pointer to the PAINTSTRUCT structure that will receive painting information.

Return Values
 If the function succeeds, the return value is the handle to a display device
 context (HDC) for the specified window. If the function fails, the return
 value is NULL, indicating that no display device context is available.
```

You can see that this command needs a pointer (or memory address) to a structured variable as the second parameter, and this structured variable must be created from the 'PAINTSTRUCT' structure. To create such a variable in PureBasic we can do this:

```
PaintVariable.PAINTSTRUCT
```

And that's it. The 'PAINTSTRUCT' structure has already been defined internally, so we can just use it without a definition. A full usage example of this command might look like this inside your main code:

```
...
PaintVariable.PAINTSTRUCT
WindowHandle.l = WindowID(#MY_WINDOW)
HDC.l = BeginPaint_(WindowHandle, @PaintVariable)
...
```

Viewing Internally Defined Constants And Structures

So now you know that a lot of handy data has been defined internally but you don't necessarily know what exactly has been defined. To clear up any confusion and let you see what exactly has been defined the PureBasic IDE has a handy viewer for looking up all such data. This tool is called the 'Structure Viewer' and can be found in the 'Tools' menu in the IDE (Menu:Tools->Structure Viewer). Fig.53 shows the Structure Viewer as it appears on the Window operating system and notes many of the features that make this such an useful tool.

Once the Structure Viewer is open, you are greeted with a list of all structures that have been defined internally. This list can be searched and filtered alphabetically by using the appropriate control detailed in the diagram. Although this list initially shows defined structures, this can be changed by selecting a different tab to display defined interfaces or constants. Although interfaces haven't been discussed in this book, the constants list will be helpful to you as this shows all internally defined constants and their values. All built-in PureBasic constants are shown here too.

To view the actual definitions of internally defined structures you just double-click their names in the data list. When you do this the 'Insert Copy' and 'Insert' buttons become active. The 'Insert Copy' button inserts a copy of the structure definition into your PureBasic source, while the 'Insert' button inserts code to actually use and define the fields within the structure. Open a new PureBasic source file and have a play to get used to how it works.

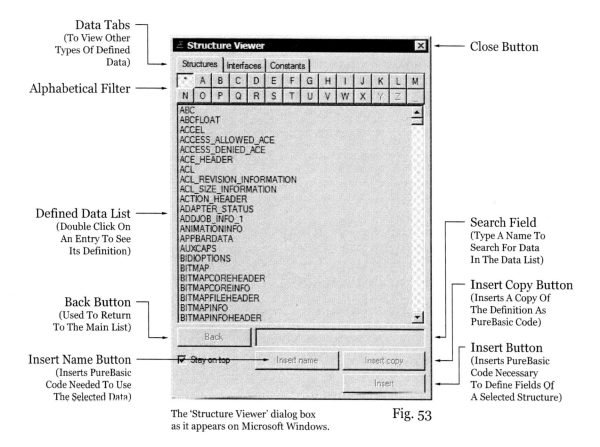

Data Tabs
(To View Other
Types Of Defined
Data)

Alphabetical Filter

Defined Data List
(Double Click On
An Entry To See
Its Definition)

Back Button
(Used To Return
To The Main List)

Insert Name Button
(Inserts PureBasic
Code Needed To Use
The Selected Data)

Close Button

Search Field
(Type A Name To
Search For Data
In The Data List)

Insert Copy Button
(Inserts A Copy Of
The Definition As
PureBasic Code)

Insert Button
(Inserts PureBasic
Code Necessary
To Define Fields Of
A Selected Structure)

The 'Structure Viewer' dialog box   Fig. 53
as it appears on Microsoft Windows.

Documentation On The Win32 API

When using the Win32 API you are going to need a good reference documentation to understand what commands are available for use and to understand how to use them. The first port of call would probably be Microsoft's Developers Network on the Internet (www.msdn.com) but this can be confusing for new users as the site is massive and contains information on every conceivable aspect of Windows programming, so it can be a pain to navigate. I've found the best solution (for me personally), is to consult a smaller more focused reference and then search the MSDN if more information is needed about a particular command or syntax.

The smaller reference I use is the 'Win32.hlp' file, a Windows helpfile that contains a reference for the Win32 API commands. This helpfile is not part of the normal PureBasic package so you will have to hunt it down and install it yourself, to be helpful I've provided an Internet link in Appendix A (Useful Internet Links). Once you have the 'Win32.hlp' file you should install it manually into the 'Help' folder which is inside your PureBasic folder. If a 'Help' folder doesn't appear inside your PureBasic folder then just create one and place the 'Win32.hlp' file(s) inside that newly created folder. Sometimes the helpfile is accompanied with other files such as 'Win32.cnt' and 'Win32.kwf', if this is the case all must be installed together. Once this has been done, you can then take advantage of the integration between this file and the IDE.

Once this file is correctly installed, you can select any Win32 API command within the IDE by placing your cursor within it and then hitting 'F1'. Now, instead of the usual PureBasic helpfile appearing, the 'Win32.hlp' file is opened on the correct page for the highlighted Win32 API command. This behavior doesn't stop the standard PureBasic helpfile from functioning, it just opens a different helpfile depending on what command is highlighted within the IDE.

Try it for yourself, type this code in from a previous example, place the flashing text cursor within the 'GetClientRect' command and hit 'F1'.

```
DesktopInfo.RECT
DesktopHandle.l = GetDesktopWindow_()
GetClientRect_(DesktopHandle, @DesktopInfo)

DesktopSize.s = "Your current desktop size is: "
DesktopSize + Str(DesktopInfo\right) + " x "
DesktopSize + Str(DesktopInfo\bottom)
Debug DesktopSize
```

You should now see the 'Win32.hlp' file opened and displaying the page on the 'GetClientRect' command. Don't forget, the 'Win32.hlp' file is a standard Windows helpfile and as such is easily navigated and fully searchable, so it's maybe worth a read at some point if you plan on doing a lot of Win32 API programming.

Disadvantages Of Using The Win32 API In PureBasic
One of the biggest disadvantages of using the Win32 API in a PureBasic program is that you can only use these commands on a Microsoft Windows operating system. This means that any program you write using these commands will only be able to be compiled using PureBasic for Windows.

Another big disadvantage is that the Win32 API was originally designed to be used by the C and C++ programming languages and as such contains references to many advanced data types that simply don't exist in PureBasic. For the most part however, you can substitute a PureBasic type in place of a C/C++ type. Fig.54 shows a diagram of what PureBasic types can be used instead of the C/C++ types listed. For example, if you read in a Win32 API command description that a particular command needs a variable of type 'DWORD32', looking at Fig.54 you can see that you can use a PureBasic Long type instead.

PureBasic Substitute Types For Win32 API Types

Byte	**Character**	**Word**	**Quad**	***Pointer**
BOOLEAN BYTE CHAR UCHAR †	TBYTE † TCHAR	SHORT USHORT † WCHAR WORD	DWORD64 INT64 LONG64 LONGLONG POINTER_64	DWORD_PTR INT_PTR LONG_PTR UINT_PTR ULONG_PTR

Long

BOOL	HKL	LPCVOID	PLONG
COLORREF	HLOCAL	LPCWSTR	PLUID
DWORD	HMENU	LPDWORD	POINTER_32
DWORD32	HMETAFILE	LPHANDLE	PSHORT
HACCEL	HMODULE	LPINT	PSTR
HANDLE	HMONITOR	LPLONG	PTBYTE
HBITMAP	HPALETTE	LPSTR	PTCHAR
HBRUSH	HPEN	LPTSTR	PTSTR
HCONV	HRGN	LPVOID	PUCHAR
HCONVLIST	HRSRC	LPWORD	PUINT
HCURSOR	HSZ	LPWSTR	PULONG
HDC	HWINSTA	LRESULT	PUSHORT
HDDEDATA	HWND	PBOOL	PVOID
HDESK	INT	PBOOLEAN	PWCHAR
HDROP	INT32	PBYTE	PWORD
HDWP	LANGID	PCHAR	PWSTR
HENHMETAFILE	LCID	PCRITICAL_SECTION	SC_HANDLE
HFILE	LCTYPE	PCSTR	SC_LOCK
HFONT	LONG	PCTSTR	SERVICE_STATUS_HANDLE
HGDIOBJ	LONG32	PCWCH	UINT †
HGLOBAL	LPARAM	PCWSTR	UINT32 †
HHOOK	LPBOOL	PDWORD	ULONG †
HICON	LPBYTE	PFLOAT	ULONG32 †
HIMAGELIST	LPCOLORREF	PHANDLE	WPARAM
HIMC	LPCRITICAL_SECTION	PHKEY	
HINSTANCE	LPCSTR	PINT	
HKEY	LPCTSTR	PLCID	

Float
FLOAT

Double
DOUBLE

Types marked with '†' need to be read correctly after a command call. This is because these
types may be unsigned or signed opposite to the PureBasic type they are using.   Fig. 54

You will notice that some types listed in Fig.54 are marked with a '†' symbol. This is to show that these
types do not exactly match their PureBasic counterparts. The reason for this mismatch is that all the
marked Win32 API types are unsigned (except for 'TBYTE') while the substitute PureBasic types are
all signed. Because of this, some types might suffer from numerical wrapping issues. The odd one out
is the API type: 'TBYTE', which is signed while the PureBasic Character type which substitutes it, is
unsigned. This ultimately shouldn't raise massive problems in your program, because with a little bit
of coding you can easily convert signed values to unsigned values and vice versa. Here are a few
procedures that you could use to convert all these problem types:

```
;Returns the correct unsigned value from a UCHAR.
Procedure.w UCHAR(UCHAR.b)
  ProcedureReturn UCHAR & $FF
EndProcedure
```

```
;Returns the correct signed value from a TBYTE.
CompilerIf #PB_Compiler_Unicode
  Procedure.w TBYTE(TBYTE.c)
CompilerElse
  Procedure.b TBYTE(TBYTE.c)
CompilerEndIf
  ProcedureReturn TBYTE
EndProcedure

;Returns the correct unsigned value from a USHORT.
Procedure.l USHORT(USHORT.w)
  ProcedureReturn USHORT & $FFFF
EndProcedure

;Returns the correct unsigned value from a UINT.
Procedure.q UINT(UINT.l)
  ProcedureReturn UINT & $FFFFFFFF
EndProcedure

;Returns the correct unsigned value from a UINT32.
Procedure.q UINT32(UINT32.l)
  ProcedureReturn UINT32 & $FFFFFFFF
EndProcedure

;Returns the correct unsigned value from a ULONG.
Procedure.q ULONG(ULONG.l)
  ProcedureReturn ULONG & $FFFFFFFF
EndProcedure

;Returns the correct unsigned value from a ULONG32.
Procedure.q ULONG32(ULONG32.l)
  ProcedureReturn ULONG32 & $FFFFFFFF
EndProcedure
```

For example, if you used a PureBasic Byte (which is signed) to store a 'UCHAR' unsigned value, then you can only read that unsigned value correctly by using the 'UCHAR()' procedure like this:

```
MyUCHAR.b = 255 ; This represents '-1' signed and '255' unsigned.
Debug MyUCHAR ; This echoes the signed value of '-1'.
UnsignedValue.w = UCHAR(MyUCHAR)
Debug UnsignedValue ; This echoes the unsigned value of '255'.
```

The only drawback in using these procedures is that the value they return, (although totally correct) uses twice the amount of memory of the type you passed as a parameter. Just look at the 'UCHAR()' procedure in the last example. This accepts a Byte as a parameter of the 'UCHAR' you want to read, and then returns a Word containing the correct unsigned value. That's double the size of the original Byte. This is done because nearly all PureBasic's types are signed, so we have to use a big enough type to correctly express an unsigned value, avoiding any wrapping issues.

Assigning unsigned values to signed types on the other hand is easy. As shown in the last example, you can assign an unsigned value to a signed type, but that value is always stored as a signed value. So, this line of code:

```
MyUCHAR.b = 255
Debug MyUCHAR
```

Would actually store '-1' as its value. This is implemented in PureBasic to ease such Win32 API conversion issues.

A Quick Note Regarding Win32 API String Pointer Types
When using Win32 API String pointer types, it's useful to know how to read and write to memory correctly for each of the different types of String they point to. For example, a pointer of type 'LPCSTR' would be used by the Win32 API to point to a one Byte per character ASCII String, while a pointer of type 'LPCWSTR' would point to a two Bytes per character unicode String. Even though all String pointers use a PureBasic Long type to represent the actual pointer and hold a memory location, you have to peek and poke each one from memory using a different mode of the 'PeekS()' and 'PokeS()' commands to properly observe each String type's character encoding.

Here are the Win32 API String pointer types, and more importantly, how to correctly read and write each type of String from the memory location they point to:

'LPCSTR'
One Byte per character (ASCII) String, even if the program is compiled in unicode mode.

```
PeekS(StringPointer.l, StringLength, #PB_Ascii)
PokeS(StringPointer.l, Text.s, StringLength, #PB_Ascii)
```

'LPCWSTR' 'PCWSTR' 'PWSTR' 'LPOLESTR'
Two Bytes per character (Unicode) String, even if the program isn't compiled in unicode mode.

```
PeekS(StringPointer.l, StringLength, #PB_Unicode)
PokeS(StringPointer.l, Text.s, StringLength, #PB_Unicode)
```

'LPCTSTR' 'LPTSTR' 'LPSTR' 'PCTSTR' 'PTSTR'
Exactly the same as a standard PureBasic String, which is one Byte per character if the program is not compiled in unicode mode and two Bytes per character if the program is compiled in unicode mode.

```
PeekS(StringPointer.l, StringLength)
PokeS(StringPointer.l, Text.s, StringLength)
```

A Doorway To A Larger World
Hopefully this brief introduction to the Win32 API will spur you on to read more about it and perhaps use it in your Windows programming. Sometimes when using PureBasic and writing software for Microsoft Windows, you may need the occasional API command to provide extra functionality that is not currently available natively in PureBasic.

Appendices

This next section contains the appendices to this book. This supplementary material contains a variety of useful information including useful Internet links, a few pages of helpful charts and a complete computer science glossary.

These final pages provide you with a quick reference to some of the more useful information that you will want to look at time and time again.

Useful Internet Links

The following pages contain many useful web address from the Internet that you will want to take a look at when starting out with PureBasic. These websites contain lots of useful information, such as code snippets, tool and utilities, where to get technical support and where to ask questions.

PureBasic Beginners
http://www.pb-beginners.co.uk
The website associated to this book. Most of the code, images and sounds used in the examples contained in this book can be downloaded from this website along with other useful tools and utilities, including the elusive 'Win32.hlp' help file.

Official PureBasic Website
http://www.purebasic.com
The official website of PureBasic. This is where you buy and download the full PureBasic package. You can also find the latest development news on PureBasic and access support via the website's menu.

Official PureBasic Forums
http://forums.purebasic.com
Hopefully this will be one of your first stops when using PureBasic. All you need to do is register with the forum and you can ask as many questions as you like. This online forum is monitored closely by the PureBasic team who regularly contribute to discussions and answer questions relating to PureBasic. The wealth of information regarding PureBasic stored on this site should not be underestimated. Not only do you have access to the shared knowledge of hundreds of PureBasic programmers willing to help you, but every post is archived and fully searchable, meaning you literally have years worth of PureBasic knowledge at your fingertips detailing almost any programming task you may encounter.

PureArea
http://www.purearea.net
This site contains lots of PureBasic related material including, thousands of PureBasic code examples contained in the downloadable Code Archive, downloadable third party user libraries and links to hundreds of freeware and shareware utilities written in PureBasic. There is also an online PureBasic reference manual.

The PureBasic Visual Designer
http://www.purebasic.be
This site contains news and updated builds of the new official PureBasic visual designer. Everything to do with the development of the visual designer is contained on this site.

PureProject
http://pureproject.reelmedia.org
More PureBasic code snippets including games and applications and more downloadable third party user libraries. There's also a Windows API section too.

PureVision
http://purevision.reelmedia.org
A third party commercial replacement for the standard PureBasic visual designer. This professional visual designer also has full support for GUI skinning.

Microsoft Windows API Documentation
http://msdn.microsoft.com/library
Microsoft's Windows API website detailing all the Windows Application Programming Interface. Use the search box on the webpage to quickly find information.

API-Guide
http://www.allapi.net/agnet/apiguide.shtml
A program called 'API-Guide' that allows you to explore the commands available in the Win32 API. Details of all commands and parameters are given with examples for nearly all commands. Note: The examples are coded for VisualBasic but can easily be converted to PureBasic.

The OGRE Engine
http://www.ogre3d.org/
The website of the OGRE 3D engine, this is the one that PureBasic uses to provide 3D graphics.

Housemarque Audio System
http://www.s2.org/hmqaudio/
This is the sound system that PureBasic uses to play modules. You will need to download the 'midas11.dll' file to provide module playback capabilities in your programs. This file is part of the Housemarque 'Standard distribution package'. For more information see Chapter 12 (Module Files).

B

Helpful Charts

This appendix contains many useful charts, some of which have already appeared earlier on in this book. Some are reprinted here for your convenience to make finding them easier when needed.

Operator Precedence

Priority*	Operators					
1	(	)				
2	~					
3	<<	>>	%	!		
4	|	&				
5	*	/				
6	+	-				
7	>	>=	<	<=	=	<>
8	And	Or	Not	XOr		

* The operators at the top of this list are evaluated first.   Fig. 13

Operator Quick Reference

Operator	Description
=	Equals. This can be used in two ways. The first is to assign the value of the expression on the RHS to the variable on the LHS. The second way is when the result of the operator is used in an expression to test whether the values of the expression on the LHS and the RHS are the same (if they are the same the equals operator will return true, otherwise it will return false).
+	Plus. Gives a result of the value of the expression on the RHS added to the value of the expression on the LHS. If the result of this operator is not used and there is a variable on the LHS, then the value of the expression on the RHS will be added directly to the variable on the LHS.
-	Minus. Subtracts the value of the expression on the RHS from the value of the expression on the LHS. When there is no expression on the LHS this operator gives the negative value of the value of the expression on the RHS. If the result of this operator is not used and there is a variable on the LHS, then the value of the expression on the RHS will be subtracted directly from the variable on the LHS. (This operator cannot be used with strings).
*	Multiplication. Multiplies the value of the expression on the LHS by the value of the expression on the RHS. If the result of this operator is not used and there is a variable on the LHS, then the value of the variable is directly multiplied by the value of the expression on the RHS. (This operator cannot be used with strings).
/	Division. Divides the value of the expression on the LHS by the value of the expression on the RHS. If the result of this operator is not used and there is a variable on the LHS, then the value of the variable is directly divided by the value of the expression on the RHS. (This operator cannot be used with strings).
&	Bitwise AND. You should be familiar with binary numbers when using this operator. The result of this operator will be the value of the expression on the LHS AND'ed with the value of the expression on the RHS, bit for bit. Additionally, if the result of the operator is not used and there is a variable on the LHS, then the result will be stored directly in that variable. (This operator cannot be used with strings).
|	Bitwise OR. You should be familiar with binary numbers when using this operator. The result of this operator will be the value of the expression on the LHS OR'ed with the value of the expression on the RHS, bit for bit. Additionally, if the result of the operator is not used and there is a variable on the LHS, then the result will be stored directly in that variable. (This operator cannot be used with strings).
!	Bitwise XOR. You should be familiar with binary numbers when using this operator. The result of this operator will be the value of the expression on the LHS XOR'ed with the value of the expression on the RHS, bit for bit. Additionally, if the result of the operator is not used and there is a variable on the LHS, then the result will be stored directly in that variable. (This operator cannot be used with strings).
~	Bitwise NOT. You should be familiar with binary numbers when using this operator. The result of this operator will be the NOT'ed value of the expression on the RHS. i.e. the result will have it's bits inverted compared to the value of the expression. (This operator cannot be used with strings).
<	Less than. This is used to compare the values of the expressions on the LHS and RHS. If the value of the expression on the LHS is less than the value of the expression on the RHS this operator will give a result of true, otherwise the result is false.
>	More than. This is used to compare the values of the expressions on the LHS and RHS. If the value of the expression on the LHS is more than the value of the expression on the RHS this operator will give a result of true, otherwise the result is false.
<=	Less than or equal to. This is used to compare the values of the expressions on the LHS and RHS. If the value of the expression on the LHS is less than or equal to the value of the expression on the RHS this operator will give a result of true, otherwise the result is false.
>=	More than or equal to. This is used to compare the values of the expressions on the LHS and RHS. If the value of the expression on the LHS is more than or equal to the value of the expression on the RHS this operator will give a result of true, otherwise the result is false.
<>	Not equal to. This is used to compare the values of the expressions on the LHS and RHS. If the value of the expression on the LHS is equal to the value of the expression on the RHS this operator will give a result of false, otherwise the result is true.
And	Logical AND. This is used to compare the values of the expressions on the LHS and RHS. If the value of the expressions on the LHS and the RHS are both true then the result is true, otherwise the result is false.
Or	Logical OR. This is used to compare the values of the expressions on the LHS and RHS. If the value of the expression on the LHS or the RHS is true then the result is true, otherwise the result is false.
Not	Logical NOT. This is used to perform logical negation of a boolean value. In other words if an expression returns a true value, using the Not operator can invert this value to a false. Conversely if the expression on the RHS of this operator returns false then Not will return true.
XOr	Logical XOR. This is used to compare the values of the expressions on the LHS and RHS. If only one of the expressions on the LHS or the RHS is evaluated as true then the result is true. If both expressions are either true or both false then the XOr operator returns false.
<<	Arithmetic shift left. Shifts each bit in the value of the expression on the LHS left by the number of places given by the value of the expression on the RHS. Additionally, when the result of this operator is not used and the LHS contains a variable, that variable will have its value shifted by the amount on the RHS. It probably helps if you understand binary numbers when you use this operator, although you can use it as if each position you shift by is multiplying by an extra factor of 2.
>>	Arithmetic shift right. Shifts each bit in the value of the expression on the LHS right by the number of places given by the value of the expression on the RHS. Additionally, when the result of this operator is not used and the LHS contains a variable, that variable will have its value shifted by the amount on the RHS. It probably helps if you understand binary numbers when you use this operator, although you can use it as if each position you shift by is dividing by an extra factor of 2.
%	Modulo. Returns the remainder of the LHS divided by RHS using integer division.
( )	Brackets. You can use sets of brackets to force part of an expression to be evaluated first, or in a certain order. Expressions in brackets are evaluated first before any other part of the current expression. In nested brackets the inner-most set are evaluated first and then each evaluated outwards.

RHS = Right hand side   LHS = Left hand side

Fig. 15

PureBasic's Numeric Types

Type	Suffix	Memory Usage (RAM)	Numerical Limit
Byte	.b	1 byte (8 bits)	-128 to 127
Char (Ascii)	.c	1 byte (8 bits)	0 to 255
Char (Unicode)	.c	2 bytes (16 bits)	0 to 65535
Word	.w	2 bytes (16 bits)	-32768 to 32767
Long	.l	4 bytes (32 bits)	-2147483648 to 2147483647
Quad	.q	8 bytes (64 bits)	-9223372036854775808 to 9223372036854775807
Float	.f	4 bytes (32 bits)	Unlimited*
Double	.d	8 bytes (64 bits)	Unlimited*

* This will be explained fully in Chapter 13 (*A Closer Look At Numeric Data Types*).   Fig. 2

PureBasic's String Types

Type	Suffix	Memory Usage (RAM)	Character Limit
String	.s	4 bytes (32 bits)	Unlimited
String	$	4 bytes (32 bits)	Unlimited
Fixed Length String	.s{length}	4 bytes (32 bits)	User Defined*
Fixed Length String	${length}	4 bytes (32 bits)	User Defined*

* The 'length' parameter defines the string's maximum length.   Fig. 3

PureBasic Substitute Types For Win32 API Types

Byte

BOOLEAN
BYTE
CHAR
UCHAR †

Character

TBYTE †
TCHAR

Word

SHORT
USHORT †
WCHAR
WORD

Quad

DWORD64
INT64
LONG64
LONGLONG
POINTER_64

*Pointer

DWORD_PTR
INT_PTR
LONG_PTR
UINT_PTR
ULONG_PTR

Long

BOOL	HKL	LPCVOID	PLONG
COLORREF	HLOCAL	LPCWSTR	PLUID
DWORD	HMENU	LPDWORD	POINTER_32
DWORD32	HMETAFILE	LPHANDLE	PSHORT
HACCEL	HMODULE	LPINT	PSTR
HANDLE	HMONITOR	LPLONG	PTBYTE
HBITMAP	HPALETTE	LPSTR	PTCHAR
HBRUSH	HPEN	LPTSTR	PTSTR
HCONV	HRGN	LPVOID	PUCHAR
HCONVLIST	HRSRC	LPWORD	PUINT
HCURSOR	HSZ	LPWSTR	PULONG
HDC	HWINSTA	LRESULT	PUSHORT
HDDEDATA	HWND	PBOOL	PVOID
HDESK	INT	PBOOLEAN	PWCHAR
HDROP	INT32	PBYTE	PWORD
HDWP	LANGID	PCHAR	PWSTR
HENHMETAFILE	LCID	PCRITICAL_SECTION	SC_HANDLE
HFILE	LCTYPE	PCSTR	SC_LOCK
HFONT	LONG	PCTSTR	SERVICE_STATUS_HANDLE
HGDIOBJ	LONG32	PCWCH	UINT †
HGLOBAL	LPARAM	PCWSTR	UINT32 †
HHOOK	LPBOOL	PDWORD	ULONG †
HICON	LPBYTE	PFLOAT	ULONG32 †
HIMAGELIST	LPCOLORREF	PHANDLE	WPARAM
HIMC	LPCRITICAL_SECTION	PHKEY	
HINSTANCE	LPCSTR	PINT	
HKEY	LPCTSTR	PLCID	

Float

FLOAT

Double

DOUBLE

Types marked with '†' need to be read correctly after a command call. This is because these types may be unsigned or signed opposite to the PureBasic type they are using.

Fig. 54

Built-in PureBasic Gadgets

Gadget Name	Sample Image	Description
Button Gadget	Button	Creates a clickable button with user defined text.
Button Image Gadget		Creates a clickable button with a user defined image.
Text Gadget	Lorem ipsum dolor sit amet.	Creates an editable text label which can not accept any typed text.
String Gadget	Lorem ipsum dolor sit amet.	Creates an editable text field which can accept typed text.
Check Box Gadget	☑ Check Box	Creates a box that can be checked on and off via a small tick, alongside user defined text.
Option Gadget	⦿ Option 1 ○ Option 2	Creates radio buttons that can be toggled on and off, alongside user defined text.
Spin Gadget	254 ⬍	Creates a number gadget who's value can be increased and decreased by the arrow buttons.
IP Address Gadget	192.168. 0 . 1	Creates a four field gadget for displaying IP numbers.
Track Bar Gadget		Creates a slidable bar to increment and decrement values in realtime.
Progress Bar Gadget	▮▮▮▮▮▮	Creates a user controllable progress bar to show progress of a user defined action.
Scroll Bar Gadget	◀ ▶	Creates a scroll bar that can be configured to scroll a partly seen object such as an image.
Hyperlink Gadget	www.google.co.uk	Creates a clickable, editable text label, similar to a webpage hyperlink.
Combo Box Gadget	String 1 ▼ String 1 String 2 String 3	Creates a fully editable drop-down menu style list. Clicking the button on the right opens the list fully for making another selection.
Date Gadget	Date: 03/13/2006 Time: 17:32 ▼	Creates a combo box that displays and returns any user defined date. Clicking the button on the right allows another date to be chosen.

(Sample images from Microsoft Windows)   Fig. 55

Built-in PureBasic Gadgets continued.

Gadget Name	Sample Image	Description
Panel Gadget	Panel 1 · Panel 2 · Panel 3	Creates a gadget with a user defined number of panels. Each panel has a user defined label and each one can hold a separate interface.
Frame 3D Gadget	Frame	Creates a 3D frame along with a user defined label. This frame is purely for aesthetic reasons only and provides a nice graphical way of grouping associated interface items.
Web Gadget	Blog.htm Lorem ipsum dolor sit amet, consectetuer adipiscing elit. Nam rhoncus tempus ipsum. Donec mollis. Proin	Creates a gadget that can display a webpage, either from the Internet or from a local source such as your hard drive.
Tree Gadget	String 1 String 2 String 3 String 4	Creates a gadget that displays user defined strings in a tree-like structure.
List View Gadget	String 1 String 2 String 3	Creates a gadget that displays user defined strings in a list.
List Icon Gadget	Column 1 · Column 2 String 1 · String 2 String 3 · String 4 String 5 · String 6	Creates a gadget that contains rows and columns which can be populated by user defined strings and icons.

(Sample images from Microsoft Windows)

Fig. 55 continued.

Built-in PureBasic Gadgets continued.

Gadget Name	Sample Image	Description
Image Gadget		Creates a gadget, within which you can display an image.
Editor Gadget		Creates a gadget that can hold a huge amount of user defined text, ideal for using as a text editor.
Container Gadget		Creates a container gadget that can hold many other gadgets within. These gadgets when contained can be manipulated as a unit, i.e. moving and hiding.
Scroll Area Gadget		Creates a scrollable area complete with scroll bars. This area can contain lots of other gadgets and have the ability to scroll them around as necessary.
Explorer List Gadget		Creates a gadget that displays hard drive and directory information in rows and columns very similar to a List Icon Gadget.
Explorer Tree Gadget		Creates a gadget that displays hard drive and directory information in a tree-like structure.

(Sample images from Microsoft Windows)   Fig. 55 continued.

Built-in PureBasic Gadgets continued.

Gadget Name	Sample Image	Description
Explorer Combo Gadget		Creates a gadget that displays hard drive and directory information within a Combo Gadget.
Splitter Gadget		Creates a splitter between two other gadgets which when moved will resize both dynamically.
MDI Gadget		Creates a Multiple Document Interface gadget that can contain multiple child windows. Each child window can contain it's own interface.
Calendar Gadget		Creates a gadget that displays a configurable calendar. Any date can be displayed or retrieved from this gadget.

(Sample images from Microsoft Windows)

Fig. 55 continued.

Associated Character, Ascii, Hexadecimal and Binary Table

Character	Ascii	Hex	Binary		Character	Ascii	Hex	Binary
NULL	0	00	00000000		@	64	40	01000000
SOH	1	01	00000001		A	65	41	01000001
STX	2	02	00000010		B	66	42	01000010
ETX	3	03	00000011		C	67	43	01000011
EOT	4	04	00000100		D	68	44	01000100
ENQ	5	05	00000101		E	69	45	01000101
ACK	6	06	00000110		F	70	46	01000110
BEL	7	07	00000111		G	71	47	01000111
BS	8	08	00001000		H	72	48	01001000
TAB	9	09	00001001		I	73	49	01001001
LF	10	0A	00001010		J	74	4A	01001010
VT	11	0B	00001011		K	75	4B	01001011
FF	12	0C	00001100		L	76	4C	01001100
CR	13	0D	00001101		M	77	4D	01001101
SO	14	0E	00001110		N	78	4E	01001110
SI	15	0F	00001111		O	79	4F	01001111
DLE	16	10	00010000		P	80	50	01010000
DC1	17	11	00010001		Q	81	51	01010001
DC2	18	12	00010010		R	82	52	01010010
DC3	19	13	00010011		S	83	53	01010011
DC4	20	14	00010100		T	84	54	01010100
NAK	21	15	00010101		U	85	55	01010101
SYN	22	16	00010110		V	86	56	01010110
ETB	23	17	00010111		W	87	57	01010111
CAN	24	18	00011000		X	88	58	01011000
EM	25	19	00011001		Y	89	59	01011001
SUB	26	1A	00011010		Z	90	5A	01011010
ESC	27	1B	00011011		[	91	5B	01011011
FS	28	1C	00011100		\	92	5C	01011100
GS	29	1D	00011101		]	93	5D	01011101
RS	30	1E	00011110		^	94	5E	01011110
US	31	1F	00011111		_	95	5F	01011111
Space	32	20	00100000		`	96	60	01100000
!	33	21	00100001		a	97	61	01100001
"	34	22	00100010		b	98	62	01100010
#	35	23	00100011		c	99	63	01100011
$	36	24	00100100		d	100	64	01100100
%	37	25	00100101		e	101	65	01100101
&	38	26	00100110		f	102	66	01100110
'	39	27	00100111		g	103	67	01100111
(	40	28	00101000		h	104	68	01101000
)	41	29	00101001		i	105	69	01101001
*	42	2A	00101010		j	106	6A	01101010
+	43	2B	00101011		k	107	6B	01101011
,	44	2C	00101100		l	108	6C	01101100
-	45	2D	00101101		m	109	6D	01101101
.	46	2E	00101110		n	110	6E	01101110
/	47	2F	00101111		o	111	6F	01101111
0	48	30	00110000		p	112	70	01110000
1	49	31	00110001		q	113	71	01110001
2	50	32	00110010		r	114	72	01110010
3	51	33	00110011		s	115	73	01110011
4	52	34	00110100		t	116	74	01110100
5	53	35	00110101		u	117	75	01110101
6	54	36	00110110		v	118	76	01110110
7	55	37	00110111		w	119	77	01110111
8	56	38	00111000		x	120	78	01111000
9	57	39	00111001		y	121	79	01111001
:	58	3A	00111010		z	122	7A	01111010
;	59	3B	00111011		{	123	7B	01111011
<	60	3C	00111100				124	7C	01111100
=	61	3D	00111101		}	125	7D	01111101
>	62	3E	00111110		~	126	7E	01111110
?	63	3F	00111111		?	127	7F	01111111

Fig. 56

Associated Character, Ascii, Hexadecimal and Binary Table continued.

Character	Ascii	Hex	Binary	Character	Ascii	Hex	Binary
€	128	80	10000000	À	192	C0	11000000
?	129	81	10000001	Á	193	C1	11000001
,	130	82	10000010	Â	194	C2	11000010
ƒ	131	83	10000011	Ã	195	C3	11000011
„	132	84	10000100	Ä	196	C4	11000100
…	133	85	10000101	Å	197	C5	11000101
†	134	86	10000110	Æ	198	C6	11000110
‡	135	87	10000111	Ç	199	C7	11000111
ˆ	136	88	10001000	È	200	C8	11001000
‰	137	89	10001001	É	201	C9	11001001
Š	138	8A	10001010	Ê	202	CA	11001010
‹	139	8B	10001011	Ë	203	CB	11001011
Œ	140	8C	10001100	Ì	204	CC	11001100
?	141	8D	10001101	Í	205	CD	11001101
Ž	142	8E	10001110	Î	206	CE	11001110
?	143	8F	10001111	Ï	207	CF	11001111
?	144	90	10010000	Ð	208	D0	11010000
'	145	91	10010001	Ñ	209	D1	11010001
'	146	92	10010010	Ò	210	D2	11010010
"	147	93	10010011	Ó	211	D3	11010011
"	148	94	10010100	Ô	212	D4	11010100
•	149	95	10010101	Õ	213	D5	11010101
–	150	96	10010110	Ö	214	D6	11010110
—	151	97	10010111	×	215	D7	11010111
~	152	98	10011000	Ø	216	D8	11011000
™	153	99	10011001	Ù	217	D9	11011001
š	154	9A	10011010	Ú	218	DA	11011010
›	155	9B	10011011	Û	219	DB	11011011
œ	156	9C	10011100	Ü	220	DC	11011100
?	157	9D	10011101	Ý	221	DD	11011101
ž	158	9E	10011110	Þ	222	DE	11011110
Ÿ	159	9F	10011111	ß	223	DF	11011111
NB Space	160	A0	10100000	à	224	E0	11100000
¡	161	A1	10100001	á	225	E1	11100001
¢	162	A2	10100010	â	226	E2	11100010
£	163	A3	10100011	ã	227	E3	11100011
¤	164	A4	10100100	ä	228	E4	11100100
¥	165	A5	10100101	å	229	E5	11100101
¦	166	A6	10100110	æ	230	E6	11100110
§	167	A7	10100111	ç	231	E7	11100111
¨	168	A8	10101000	è	232	E8	11101000
©	169	A9	10101001	é	233	E9	11101001
ª	170	AA	10101010	ê	234	EA	11101010
«	171	AB	10101011	ë	235	EB	11101011
¬	172	AC	10101100	ì	236	EC	11101100
	173	AD	10101101	í	237	ED	11101101
®	174	AE	10101110	î	238	EE	11101110
¯	175	AF	10101111	ï	239	EF	11101111
°	176	B0	10110000	ð	240	F0	11110000
±	177	B1	10110001	ñ	241	F1	11110001
²	178	B2	10110010	ò	242	F2	11110010
³	179	B3	10110011	ó	243	F3	11110011
´	180	B4	10110100	ô	244	F4	11110100
µ	181	B5	10110101	õ	245	F5	11110101
¶	182	B6	10110110	ö	246	F6	11110110
·	183	B7	10110111	÷	247	F7	11110111
¸	184	B8	10111000	ø	248	F8	11111000
¹	185	B9	10111001	ù	249	F9	11111001
º	186	BA	10111010	ú	250	FA	11111010
»	187	BB	10111011	û	251	FB	11111011
¼	188	BC	10111100	ü	252	FC	11111100
½	189	BD	10111101	ý	253	FD	11111101
¾	190	BE	10111110	þ	254	FE	11111110
¿	191	BF	10111111	ÿ	255	FF	11111111

Fig. 56

C

Glossary

This glossary is a list of words and terms that you might come into contact with while programming. In this appendix I've attempted to be as comprehensive and concise as possible in describing the meaning of these words and terms to make your life a little easier when you come across something your not familiar with.

3D Engine
A 3D engine is an environment explicitly programmed to provide a construct in which to realize 3D graphics. A 3D engine can be explained as a layer of abstraction to allow artists or developers quickly put together 3D graphics using simplified methods rather than programming all the low level stuff themselves. For example, a 3D engine might provide a 'LoadModel()' command to load a 3D model and display it, making things easier for the user. 3D engines are sometimes provided with other helpful features such as collision detection and physics modeling.

Absolute
Can relate to a value or a path. An absolute value is a value that stands on it's own and is not relative to another. An absolute path is one that specifies a path in it's entirety. For example, all Internet addresses are absolute paths, as shown in the address bar of an Internet browser. Absolute paths are used so there is no ambiguity as to where a particular file or folder exists.

ActiveX
A Microsoft specification for reusable software components. ActiveX is based on COM which specifies how components interact and interoperate. ActiveX controls can add further functionality to an application by incorporating further pre-made modules within its interface. Modules can be interchanged but still appear as parts of the original software. On the Internet, ActiveX controls can be included in webpages and downloaded by an ActiveX-compliant browser. ActiveX controls can provide functionality for webpages making them perform task like any other program launched from a server. ActiveX controls can have full system access! In most instances this access is entirely legitimate, but history has shown that this access has been exploited by malicious ActiveX applications.

Algorithm
An explicit step by step procedure for producing a solution to a given problem.

Alpha Channel
In an image, a portion of each pixel's data that is reserved for transparency information. Some 32-bit image formats contain four channels, three eight bit channels for red, green, and blue and one eight bit alpha channel. The alpha channel is a mask. It specifies how much of the pixel's color should be merged with another pixel when the two are overlaid, one on top of the other.

Anti-virus Software
Software that scans a computer's memory and disk drives for viruses. If it finds a virus, the application informs the user and may clean, delete or quarantine any files, directories or disks affected by the malicious code.

API (Application Programming Interface)
A set of functions that an application uses to request and carry out lower level services performed by a computer's operating system or third party program command library. Simply, an API is any interface that enables one program to use facilities provided by another. The Microsoft Win32 API is probably the most famous of all the different API's.

Applet
Any miniature application transported over the Internet, especially as an enhancement to a webpage.

Array
A simple data structure for holding equally sized data elements, generally of the same data type. Individual elements are accessed via an index using a consecutive range of integers. Some arrays are multi-dimensional, meaning they are indexed by a fixed number of integers. Generally speaking, one and two dimensional arrays are the most common.

ASCII (American Standard Code For Information Interchange)
A character encoding scheme that assigns numerical values to characters such as letters, numbers, punctuation, and other symbols. ASCII allows only 7 bits per character (for a total of 128 characters). The first 32 characters are unprintable control characters (line feed, form feed, etc.) used for controlling hardware devices. Extended ASCII adds an additional 128 characters that vary between computers, programs and fonts. Computers use these extended characters for accented letters, graphical characters or other special symbols.

ASCII Art
Drawings created using the characters from a standard ASCII character set. Mono-spaced fonts are usually used to make sure each character uses the same space as any other within the drawing.

ASM (Assembly Language)
A human readable notation for machine code that a specific computer architecture uses. This Machine code is made readable by replacing the raw numeric values with symbols called mnemonics.

Assembler
A computer program for translating assembly language into object code.

Attributes
Characteristics assigned to all files and directories. Attributes include: Read Only, Archive, Hidden or System.

Back Door
A feature programmers often build into programs to allow special privileges normally denied to regular users of the program. Often programmers build back doors so they can fix bugs. If hackers or others learn about a back door, the feature may pose a security risk.

Background Task
A program executed by the system that generally remains invisible to the user. The system usually assigns background tasks a lower priority on CPU usage than foreground tasks. Often malicious software is executed by a system as a background task so the user does not realize unwanted actions are occurring, e.g. viruses, spyware, etc.

Backup
A duplicate copy of data made for archiving purposes or for protecting against damage or loss of the original.

Batch files
Text files containing one MS-DOS command on each line of the file. When run, each line executes in sequential order. One example of this is the Microsoft Windows file 'AUTOEXEC.BAT' which is executed when the computer is booted up.These files have the extension '*.bat'.

Binary
Refers to the base-two number system. This system contains only two numbers, 0 and 1.

BIOS (Basic Input/Output System)
A basic operating system that identifies a set of programs needed to initialize and start the computer before locating the operating system boot disk. The BIOS is located in the ROM area of a motherboard and is usually configurable.

BIT (Binary Digit)
The smallest unit of information a computer can use. A bit is represented as a '0' or '1'.

Bit Depth
The number of bits used to describe the color of a single pixel in any given digital image or computer display is called it's bit depth. Common bit depths are 1 bit, 8 bit, 16 bit, 24 bit, and 32 bit.

Boot
To start (cold boot) or reset (warm boot) the computer so it is ready to run programs for the user. Booting the computer executes various programs to check and prepare the computer for use.

Bug
An unintentional fault in a program that causes actions neither the user nor the program author intended.

Byte
A group of eight bits (binary digits). Also the name of an integer that can be expressed using these eight bits.

Cache
A memory area where frequently accessed data can be temporarily stored for rapid access.

CGI (Common Gateway Interface)
A standard for the exchange of information between a Web server and computer programs that are external to it. The external programs can be written in any programming language that is supported by the operating system on which the Web server is running. CGI is not a programming language in itself.

Checksum
An identifying number calculated from file characteristics. The slightest change in a file changes its checksum.

Child
A window (or object) that is based on or enclosed within another window (or object).

Class
An OOP template that can be instantiated to create objects with common definitions, properties, methods, operations, and behavior.

Client
A computer system or piece of software that accesses a remote service provided by another computer using some kind of network. A web browser is a client of a web server.

Code
A slang term for Source Code.

Coding
A slang term for computer programming.

Compile Time
The time when a compiler compiles code written in a programming language into an executable form.

Compiler
A software development tool that translates high level language program source codes into machine code instructions (object code) that a particular computer architecture can understand and execute.

Constant
A named item that retains a constant value throughout the execution of a program. Constants can be used anywhere in your code in place of actual values. A constant can be a String or numeric value.

Cookies
Blocks of text placed in a file on your computer's hard disk. Web sites use cookies to identify users who revisit a site. Cookies might contain login names and passwords or user preferences. When a webpage is viewed that has previously written a cookie, the server can use the information stored in the cookie to customize the Web site for the user.

CPU (Central Processing Unit)
The main processor responsible for the overall processing of a computer.

Data Member
In OOP a data member is a variable defined and encapsulated within a class or object. Each instance of an object retains a unique value for each data member in the class, as opposed to the class having one variable that every instantiation shares. This is just another name for a Property.

Data Type
The characteristics of a variable that describes whether it is numeric, alphabetic, or alphanumeric. It also specifies the range of values that a variable can hold, and how that information is stored in the computer memory.

DirectX
A set of low level application programming interfaces (API's) provided by Microsoft for creating high performance multimedia applications. DirectX allows programs to interface with, and use built-in high speed 3D graphic routines on graphic cards for faster processing. The DirectX API also allows easy access to computers hardware such as sound cards, joysticks and even network adapters.

DLL (Dynamic Linked Library)
A file that contains compiled code that can be loaded and executed by programs dynamically. Because several different programs can reuse the same DLL instead of having that code in their own file, this dramatically reduces required storage space for the executable.

DOS (Disk Operating System)
Generally any computer operating system, though often used as shorthand for 'MS-DOS' the operating system used by Microsoft before Windows was developed.

Double (Double Precision Floating Point Number)
A floating point number that uses double the memory of a normal floating point number to more accurately calculate and store the information of the numbers beyond the decimal point. Doubles typically use eight Bytes in memory.

Encapsulation
An OOP scheme used for defining objects. Encapsulation hides detailed internal specifications of an object and publishes only its external interfaces. Thus, users of an object only need to use these

interfaces. By encapsulation, the internal data and methods of an object can be changed or updated without changing the way users use the object.

Encryption
The scrambling of data so it becomes difficult to unscramble and interpret.

EXE (Executable) file
A file that can be executed, such as a computer program, usually by double-clicking its icon or a shortcut on the desktop, or by entering it's name in a command prompt. Executable files can also be executed from other programs, batch files or various script files. The vast majority of known viruses infect executable files.

Expression
A combination of values, Strings, operators, commands or procedures, interpreted according to the rules of precedence, which computes and returns a value.

File Extension
A tag of three or four letters, preceded by a period, which identifies a data file's format or the application used to create the file.

Firewall
These typically prevent computers on a network from communicating directly with external computer systems. The firewall software analyzes information passing between the two and stops it, if it does not conform it's pre-configured rules.

Floating Point Number (or a Real Number)
A number which has a decimal portion, even if that decimal portion is zero. A floating point number is also sometimes called a 'real number' which is often shortened to just 'real'. Floating point numbers typically use four Bytes in memory.

Function
Same as a procedure.

Hexadecimal
A numbering system which uses a base of 16. The first ten digits are '0' to '9' and the next six are 'A' to 'F'. This enables very large numbers to be expressed using very few characters. 'FF' in hexadecimal equals '255' in decimal. Webpages use hexadecimal numbers to express a 24 bit color value.

High Level Programming Language
A programming language where each instruction corresponds to many machine code instructions. Commands in this language must be translated by a compiler or interpreter before they can be executed by a particular computer architecture. A high level programming language is also more user friendly, more easily readable by humans, often cross-platform, and abstract from low level computer processor operations. PureBasic is a high level language.

HTML (Hypertext Markup Language)

The authoring software language used on the Internet's world wide web. HTML is used for creating World Wide Webpages.

HTTP (Hypertext Transfer Protocol)

The underlying protocol used by the world wide web. HTTP defines how messages are formatted and transmitted, and what actions Web servers and browsers should take in response to various commands. For example, when you enter a URL in your browser, this actually sends a HTTP command to the Web server directing it to fetch and transmit the requested webpage.

Hyperlink

A link in a document that links to information within the same document or a different document. These links are usually represented by highlighted words or images. When a reader selects a hyperlink, the computer display switches to the linked document or portion of the document referenced by the hyperlink.

Inheritance

The process in OOP, in which objects inherit functionality and data from a deriving class.

Integer

A number without a decimal point. Integer values can be less than, equal to, or greater than zero.

Internet

An electronic network of computers that today includes nearly every university, government, and research facility in the world. Initially created in 1969 to provide a backbone of communication in the event of nuclear war, the Internet has seen an explosion in public and commercial use since the development of easy to use software for accessing the information contained within it.

Interpreter

A program that executes programs written in high level programming languages line by line directly from the source code. This is in contrast to a compiler which does not execute its input (source code) but translates it into executable machine code (object code) which is for later linking and execution.

IP (Internet Protocol) Address

A number that identifies each sender or receiver of information that is sent across a TCP/IP network. The IP address takes the form of four numbers separated by dots, for example: 127.0.0.1

IRC (Internet Relay Chat)

A form of instant communication over the Internet. It is mainly designed for group communication in discussion forums called channels, but also allows one to one communication.

JavaScript

A scripting language that can run wherever there is a suitable script interpreter such as in web browsers.

LAN (Local Area Network)
A local area network is a computer network covering a local area, like a home, an office or small group of buildings such as a school.

Link Time
The time during executable compilation when object code is linked with the final executable file.

Linked List
A data structure that mimics the behavior of what would be a dynamic array. Allowing elements to be inserted and deleted dynamically during runtime. Linked lists can be created using any of the available language's data types. However, unlike an array, each element also holds pointers to the previous and next element in the list, not allowing the list to occupy a sequential area in RAM and thus perform slower than an array while retrieving data.

Linker
A program that links compiled object code files and other data files to create an executable program. A linker can also have other functions, such as creation of libraries.

Linking
The process of combining object code files into the final executable file.

Linux
A free open source operating system based on Unix. Linux was originally created by Linus Torvalds with the assistance of developers from around the globe.

Localhost
The computer system the user is working on, often assigned the IP address: 127.0.0.1

Long
An integer that uses four Bytes in memory.

Low Level Programming Language
A programming language that provides little or no abstraction from a computer's microprocessor. The word 'low' does not imply that the language is inferior to high level programming languages but refers to the reduced amount of abstraction between the language and the hardware it's controlling. Assembly is an example of a low level language.

Mac OS X
The latest version of the Mac OS, the operating system used for Apple Macintosh computers. Mac OS X, unlike it's predecessors, is based upon a Unix core with an updated user interface.

Malicious Code
A piece of code designed to damage a system or the data it contains, or to prevent the system from being used in its normal manner.

Malware

A generic term used to describe malicious software such as: viruses, trojan horses, spyware, adware, etc.

MBR (Master Boot Record)

The program located in the master boot sector. This program reads the partition table, determines what partition to boot and transfers control to the program stored in the first sector of that partition. There is only one master boot record on each physical hard disk.

MBS (Master Boot Sector)

The first sector of a hard disk. This sector is located at sector '1', head '0', track '0'. The sector contains the master boot record.

Member Function

A function or procedure that is a component of an OOP class, that performs some computation, usually related to the data members of the class. This is another name for a Method.

Method

A function or procedure that is a component of an OOP class, that performs some computation, usually related to the properties of the class.

MS-DOS (Microsoft Disk Operating System)

The operating system Microsoft developed for the IBM platform before Windows. Windows 3.x, 95 and 98 rely heavily on MS-DOS and can execute most MS-DOS commands.

Newsgroup

An electronic forum where readers post articles and follow-up messages on a specified topic. An Internet newsgroup allows people from around the globe to discuss common interests. Each newsgroup name indicates the newsgroup's subject.

NTFS (New Technology File System)

A file system used to organize and keep track of files which is the standard file system of Windows NT and its descendants: Windows 2000, Windows XP and Windows Server 2003.

Object

An instance of an OOP class. This object inherits all the functionality and data programmed into the originating class.

Object Code

The output of compilers and assemblers and the input and output of a linker are files containing object code. There are a variety of standardized and proprietary object file formats, meaning that development tools from one vendor can rarely read the object code produced by those of another.

OCX (OLE Control Extension)

An independent program module that can be accessed by other programs in a Windows environment. OCX controls have now been superseded by ActiveX controls. OCX controls end with a '*.ocx' extension and even though superceded are still compatible with ActiveX, meaning some ActiveX compatible programs can still use these modules.

OLE (Object Linking And Embedding)
This has been renamed as, and superceded by ActiveX.

OOP (Object Oriented Programming)
A style of programming that supports encapsulation, inheritance, and polymorphism. Some programming languages are inherently object oriented such as C++, java and Python, and as such allow real or imaginary objects to be modeled effectively using programming language constructs.

Open Source Software
Refers to any program whose source code is made available for use or modification as users or other developers see fit. Open source software is usually developed as a public collaboration and made freely available.

OpenGL (Open Graphics Library)
A specification defining a language independent API for writing applications that render 2d and 3d graphics. OpenGL is open source and cross platform, unlike DirectX which is it's closest rival.

Operating System
The operating system is the underlying software that enables you to interact with the computer. The operating system controls things such as computer storage, communications and task management. Examples of common operating systems include: Mac OS X, Linux and Windows XP.

Parent
A primary or enclosing window (or object) that creates, and sometimes handles, its child windows (or objects).

Polymorphism
An OOP term that means allowing a single definition to be used with different types of data. For example, a polymorphic procedure definition can replace several type specific ones, and a single polymorphic operator can act in expressions of various types.

POP (Post Office Protocol)
An email protocol to allow email clients to retrieve e-mail from a remote server over a TCP/IP connection. Nearly all subscribers to individual Internet service provider email accounts can access their email using client software that uses POP3 (Post Office Protocol version 3).

Port
(1) An interface through which data is sent and received. (2) To 'Port' can mean the act of re-coding a program's source code (sometimes using another language) to allow it to be compiled or run on another computer platform.

Procedure
A named sequence of statements executed as a unit by calling it's name. Procedures can also accept

parameters to allow user data to be passed into the sequence. Unlike subroutines, procedures can return a calculated value. Procedures can be 'called' several times allowing programs to access the code repeatedly without the procedure's code having been written more than once.

Process
A running instance of a program. A multitasking operating system switches between processes to give the appearance of simultaneous execution, though in reality only one process at any given time can use the CPU.

Property
In OOP a Property is a variable defined and encapsulated within a class or object. Each instance of an object retains a unique value for each property in the class, as opposed to the class having one variable that every instantiation shares.

Protocol
A formal description of message formats and the rules that two computers must follow in order to exchange those messages.

Quad
An integer that uses eight Bytes in memory.

Radix Point
In mathematics, the radix point refers to the symbol used in numerical representations to separate the integral part of the number (to the left of the radix) from its fractional part (to the right of the radix). The radix point is usually a small dot, either placed on the baseline or halfway between the baseline and the top of the numerals. In base 10, the radix point is called the decimal point.

Refresh Rate
The number of times a monitor's image is repainted per second to the screen. The refresh rate is expressed in hertz (Hz) so a refresh rate of 75 means the image is refreshed 75 times a second. The refresh rate for any particular monitor depends on specifications of said monitor and graphics card used.

Registry
An internal database that Microsoft Windows uses to store hardware and software configuration information, user preferences and setup information.

Relative
Can relate to a value or a path. A relative value is one that relates to or builds upon another. A relative path is one which is in relation to another. Relative paths are usually used when specifying the location of resources for a program in the source code, which are relative to the executable file. For example, if an image is to be loaded by a program from an 'Images' folder, then the relative path is defined as '\Images' because this folder is in the same directory as the executable, and is therefore relative to the program.

Reset
To restart a computer without turning it off.

RGB (Red, Green And Blue)
These are the primary colors of light, which computers use to display images on a computer screen. RGB colors are usually composed of Red, Green And Blue values ranging from '0' to '255'. These colors are then mixed using an additive color model. For example, when all color values are at maximum (255) the color produced is white.

Runtime
The time when a program is running, or executing.

SDL (Simple DirectMedia Layer)
An open source, application programming interface (API) for creating high performance multimedia applications. SDL is very simple, it acts as a thin, cross platform wrapper, providing support for 2D pixel operations, sound, file access, event handling, timing, threading, and more. OpenGL is often used with SDL to provide fast 3D rendering. SDL is often thought of as a cross platform version of DirectX, although it lacks some if it's more advanced functionality.

Server
Any application or computer that serves another, for example, the computers that hold webpages are called servers since they serve web resources to client applications such as web browsers.

Service
A program that can be automatically started as part of the operating system startup process and that runs continuously as a background task.

Shareware
Software distributed for evaluation without cost, but that requires payment to the author for full rights of usage. If, after trying the software, you do not intend to use it, you simply delete it. Using unregistered shareware beyond the evaluation period is considered software piracy.

SMTP (Simple Mail Transport Protocol)
A simple email delivery format for transmitting email messages between servers which is the current standard for e-mail transmission across the Internet.

Software Pirate
An individual who breaks the law regarding copyright of software. Laws are subject to the country in which the individual lives.

Source Code
The code that a program consists of before being compiled, i.e. the original building instructions of a program that defines to a compiler what actions a program should perform once compiled to a binary executable file.

Statement
A programming command that rarely returns any value and can contain other components such as a constant or expression. One or more statements are needed to create a program.

Static Library
A library whose code is included into an executable at link time and thus becomes static within the program. Once a program is compiled it no longer needs the library, as all code is now inside the executable file.

String
A consecutive series of letters, numbers, and other characters contained within (double or single) quotation marks.

Subroutine
A labeled sequence of statements executed as a unit by jumping to the start of the sequence, usually using a 'Goto' or 'GoSub' command. Once the sequence has executed then program flow returns to the origin of the jump, usually using a 'Return' command. Unlike procedures, subroutines cannot return a calculated value. Subroutines can be jumped to several times allowing programs to access the code repeatedly without the subroutine's code having been written more than once.

Syntax
The rules by which words in a program's source code are combined to form commands that are valid to an interpreter or compiler.

TCP/IP
This Internet protocol suite is a set of communication protocols that implement a protocol stack on which the Internet and most commercial networks run. It is called the TCP/IP protocol suite, after the two most important protocols in it: the Transmission Control Protocol (TCP) and the Internet Protocol (IP), which were also the first two defined.

Thread (Thread Of Execution)
A thread is a single sequence of instructions executed as a separate task but still part of the originating process. A process can have several threads running concurrently, each performing a different task, such as waiting for events or performing a time-consuming job that the program doesn't need to complete before moving on to do something else. When a thread has finished its job, the thread is suspended or destroyed. Multi-threaded programs can finish tasks quicker than non-threaded programs if programmed right, because some processors support running two or more threads simultaneously, such as the Intel Hyperthreading family of CPUs.

Trojan Horse
A malicious program that pretends to be useful and non-harmful but when executed, purposefully does something the user does not expect and sometimes doesn't realize. Trojans are not viruses since they do not replicate, but Trojan horse programs can be just as destructive.

UNC (Universal Naming Convention)
A standard for identifying servers, printers and other resources on a network, which originated from

the Unix community. A UNC path uses double forward-slashes or double back-slashes to precede the name of the computer. The path (disk and directories) within that computer are then separated with single forward-slashes or single back-slashes. Microsoft Windows generally uses back-slashes and Unix (Linux) uses forward-slashes.

Unicode
A character encoding scheme using 16 bits (2 Bytes) per character to allow all characters of all major world languages, living and dead, to be encoded in a single character set and like ASCII be assigned a unique number. Unicode character sets can contain over 65,000 characters.

Unix
An operating system co-created by researchers at AT&T. Unix is well known for its hardware independence and portable application interfaces. UNIX is designed to be used by many people at the same time and has TCP/IP networking built-in. It, and it's derivatives (Linux) are the most common operating systems for servers on the Internet.

URL (Uniform Resource Locator)
A HTTP address used by the world wide web to specify a certain place and file. This is the unique identifier, or address, of a webpage on the Internet.

Usenet
An informal system of electronic bulletin boards or discussion groups commonly distributed over the Internet. Usenet predates the Internet, although today most Usenet material is distributed over the Internet.

VBS (Visual Basic Script)
A programming language that can invoke any system function, including starting, using and shutting down other applications even without the users knowledge. VBS programs can be embedded in HTML files and provide active content via the Internet. Visual Basic Script files have the extension '*.vbs'.

Virus
A computer program file capable of attaching to disks or other files and replicating itself repeatedly, typically without user knowledge or permission. Some viruses attach to files so when the infected file executes, the virus also executes. Other viruses sit in a computer's memory and infect files as the computer opens, modifies or creates the files. Some viruses display symptoms, and some viruses damage files and computer systems, but neither symptoms nor damage is essential in the definition of a virus, a non-damaging virus is still a virus.

VM (Virtual Machine)
Software that mimics the performance of a hardware device. A virtual machine is a self-contained operating environment that behaves as if it was a separate computer. For example, Java applets run in a Java virtual machine that has no access to the host operating system.

VSync (Vertical Synchronization)
Vertical Synchronization is an option found in many games that allows the frame rate of the game to be matched to the refresh rate of the monitor. Generally, enabling VSync provides the greatest

stability, but turning it off can allow for much higher frame rates. The downside of the greater speed is the potential for visual artifacts like graphics tearing to develop.

W3C (Wide Web Consortium)
The governing body for world wide web standards.

WAN (Wide Area Network)
A group of computer networks connected together over long distances. The Internet is a WAN.

Word
An integer that uses two Bytes in memory.

World Wide Web
A system for browsing Internet sites. It is named the web because it is made of many sites linked together. Users can travel from one site to another by clicking on hyperlinks.

Worm
Parasitic computer programs that replicate, but unlike viruses, do not infect other computer program files. Worms can create copies on the same computer, or can send copies to other computers via a network.

Wrapper
A programming interface between a program and a separate wrapped piece of code. This may be done for compatibility reasons, for example, if the wrapped code is compiled as a DLL or uses different calling conventions. The implication is that the wrapped code can only be accessed via a wrapper.

WSH (Windows Scripting Host)
A Microsoft integrated module that lets programmers automate operations throughout the Windows desktop.

XML (Extensible Markup Language)
A standard for creating markup languages which describe the structure of data. It is not a fixed set of elements like HTML but a language for describing languages. XML enables authors to define their own tags.

ZIP File
An archive that contains compressed collections of other files. ZIP files are popular on the Internet because users can deliver multiple files in a single container which also save disk space and download time.

Index

About The Author

Gary Willoughby is a professional graphic artist, Internet web developer and software engineer. Having first cut his teeth programming using interpreted languages such as PHP, Python and Javascript during the late nineties, Gary decided to spend his free time moving into application development using compiled languages.

After using C++ for a while and noticing the massive marathon of programming needed for even a simple piece of software, a search began for a simpler, more intuitive and elegant programming language to realize well designed software within a shorter time frame. All of these wishes were fulfilled by a little known French company called Fantaisie Software. The programming language they developed and marketed was PureBasic.

Since the summer of 2002, Gary has been an active community member of the official online PureBasic forum (under the pseudonym of 'Kale') and has written several pieces of successful commercial software using PureBasic.